D1467021

AGRICULTURAL ECONOMICS AND AGRIBUSINESS:
AN INTRODUCTION

AGRICULTURAL ECONOMICS AND AGRIBUSINESS:
AN INTRODUCTION

Gail L. Cramer
Montana State University
Clarence W. Jensen
Montana State University

John Wiley & Sons

New York
Chichester
Brisbane
Toronto

Library of Congress Cataloging in Publication Data

Cramer, Gail L
  Agricultural economics and agribusiness.

  Includes index.
    1. Agriculture—Economic aspects. 2. Agricultural
industries—United States. I. Jensen, Clarence W.,
joint author. II. Title.

HD1411.C84   338.1'0973   78-11713
ISBN 0-471-04429-6

Printed in the United States of America

10 9 8 7 6 5 4 3 2

To Our
Families

Marilyn, Karilee,
and Bruce Cramer

Elaine, Marcia,
and Daryll Jensen

PREFACE

Agriculture is front page news. On any given day we read of large grain or fiber sales, food shortages, or surpluses, farm strikes, meat boycotts, embargoes, or subsidies. These events have a significant impact on human beings, both domestically and internationally, and can be understood and predicted with a good background in technical agriculture and sound training in agricultural economics or agribusiness.

This book explores the structure and organization of agriculture and then discusses economics principles as they apply to agriculture. Principles of economics are used to demonstrate to the student that theory makes reality more understandable. Theory allows us to abstract from the workaday world in order to simplify real world problems so they can be examined and explained.

The text material is designed for a one-quarter or one-semester class in an introductory agricultural economics or agribusiness course. However, if all the applied chapters are covered with some outside reference work, it could be used for a two-quarter sequence.

There can be two different routes through the material; for a freshman-level course, we recommend Chapters 1, 2, 3 (excluding indifference curve analysis), 4, 6, 7, 8, and then selecting applied chapters. In a sophomore-level course, we recommend that all theory chapters be covered before dealing with the applied chapters.

We are interested in presenting the basic economic concepts applied to agriculture in a clear and understandable manner. Many general economics textbooks have been able to accomplish this goal with respect to other industries. Agriculture, however, is a unique area of study, with its own characteristics and opportunities. Moreover, we feel that students interested in agriculture should have a textbook directly relating to their profession. This book provides the necessary background for more advanced agricultural economics, agribusiness, and economics courses.

It is impossible to write a book without the help and contributions of many other people. We owe a large debt to our instructors, and to the authors of other textbooks. We cannot thank everyone who has been of help to us, but we would like to single out a few people who have been of direct assistance to us in the preparation of this book. Dr. John M. Marsh reviewed many of the original chapters, and

Marilyn Cramer both reviewed and typed rough drafts of many other chapters. Our colleagues at Montana State University have given us continued encouragement. Dr. Richard J. McConnen, Head of Agricultural Economics and Economics at Montana State University, has supported this project in many ways.

We are indebted for many valuable suggestions made by John Adrian of Auburn University; Kenneth Boggs of the University of Missouri—Columbia; James Garrett of the University of Nevada—Reno; Dean Linsenmeyer of the University of Nebraska—Lincoln; Lester Mandersheid of Michigan State University; and Carl Pherson of the University of California—Fresno.

A special note of appreciation also is due Mrs. June Freswick and Mrs. Dana Morgan for their skill and resourcefulness in typing the final manuscript. Finally, while we appreciate all the excellent advice and counsel of others, errors and omissions that remain are the sole responsibility of the authors.

GAIL L. CRAMER
CLARENCE W. JENSEN

CONTENTS

A LIST OF REFERENCE BOOKS FOR THE BEGINNING STUDENT

BASIC SOURCES OF AGRICULTURAL STATISTICS

GLOSSARY

INDEX

Courtesy of Montana State University Photographic Services Department, Bozeman.

INTRODUCTION

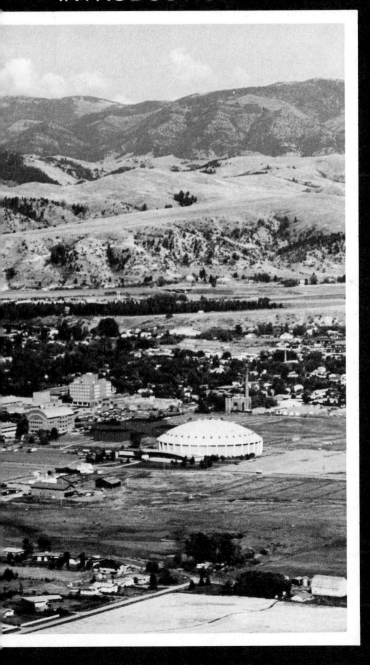

INTRODUCTION

There are at least two important characteristics of the agricultural industry that make it distinct from all others. One is the cyclical nature of production caused primarily by physical and biological factors. The other is price instability resulting from the effects of changes both physically-caused and from within the market for agricultural products.

The cyclical nature of production can be seen in the cattle market for instance, where there is a long lag between the time when increasing beef prices motivate producers to increase production and when the results of their decisions show up at the meat counter of the local grocery store.

It takes almost one and a half years from breeding a cow to weaning her heifer calf. Another year is normally required before that heifer can be bred. Yet another year is required before the heifer's calf can be started along the way toward the market for slaughter. An additional year and a half is needed to fatten and market the first offspring from the enlarged beef herd. Herd reduction can be a much more rapid process, but it still adds up to present cattle production cycles of about 10 years duration.

Climatic conditions and diseases also affect production, causing price and income fluctuations. The corn blight in the United States in 1970 is an example. Only about 20 percent of the corn crop was affected, yet the price of corn increased from $1.07 to $1.43 per bushel as news of the disease spread. There also was concern that the blight would infect the next year's crop because of the manner in which hybrid seed is developed. To combat the problem, scientists worked on blight resistant varieties, and government policy was changed to encourage increased planting. Greater corn acreage and favorable growing conditions in 1971 resulted in a record crop and a more than 30 percent decline in the farm price of corn.

Producer decisions, shifting emphasis between their major crop and livestock enterprises, also contribute to changing the prices of their products. Following the large sale of grains to Russia in 1972–73, and given no reason to expect higher livestock prices in the near future, many acres of forage and range land were converted from livestock to crop production.

Substantial cost outlays are required in preparing land for

cropping, but returns can begin in a year, or less. Switching from crops to livestock takes a considerably longer time, however. Some production from hayland is possible within the first year of replanting. But earnings from land reseeded to grass are postponed over the several years it may take to get a productive stand of grass reestablished. Thus a sizeable increase in the relative price of beef is needed before it becomes possible to increase livestock output from such land.

Certain market characteristics also have an impact on prices. Agriculture in general is relatively competitive. This is especially so in the production of beef, hogs, and food and feed grains because there are many producers that, individually, do not produce a large enough volume to have any influence on market prices. And the products of these firms are very like the same commodity produced by other firms, either because of the characteristics of the product itself, or through the grades and standards established by the market.

These conditions cause the total supply and demand for each product to influence its price (as discussed in more detail in Chapter 6). The high proportion of fixed costs in agriculture frequently inhibits output reduction even though prices signal that such a change is desired. Consumers of agricultural products also change their buying habits as prices change. These factors cause wide fluctuations in agricultural prices, resulting in the boom or bust nature of agricultural incomes.

In 1972, United States agriculture broke out of isolation from the world market. Until that time, it was protected from the "free market" through production controls and an inventory policy that built up large "surplus stocks." Then, in 1972–73, world grain production fell three percent. This drop in world output caused a 250 percent increase in many American commodity prices[1] and a sharp reduction in stocks of agricultural products. With stocks low, producers began operating when special government output restrictions were removed. Surpluses have appeared again.

Choice and Its Economic Meaning

Nature and man combine to cause the need to economize in deciding what things we will buy with our spendable incomes, and require decisions on how and for what purposes our resources will be used. Few people, if any, have enough money, nor do they have sufficient

---

[1]Ray A. Goldberg, "U.S. Agribusiness Breaks Out of Isolation," *Harvard Business Review*, Boston, Mass.: Harvard Business School, May–June 1975, pp. 81–95.

resources to produce the goods and services it would take to satisfy completely all of their wants.

This basic fact is a problem, not just for individuals, but for nations as well. Whether the nation utilizes a free market or total government control, the problem remains. The relationship between the amounts of things available and the amounts desired causes a universal condition for any good or service that we call "scarcity."

A good or service is scarce when we must give up some amount of one thing to get some of another good or service. And the moment we realize that something is being sacrificed so as to gain something else, we become aware of the economic meaning of the word "cost." As we make our choices in the face of scarcity, costs are generated. These costs we call "opportunity costs" because they constitute the value of alternative opportunities foregone, or sacrificed.

As we choose between desired alternatives, with the value of forfeited opportunities being the true cost of any chosen alternatives, we can consider ourselves better off only if that choice is worth more to us than the one sacrificed. But what determines worth? It can't be the physical amount of something we give up, but how we value that something. To get a couple of fresh eggs to eat you would probably give up rotten eggs by the hundreds of dozens, yet be unwilling to sacrifice a T-bone steak dinner for those two eggs. We value goods and services because of the satisfactions we can get for them. You're probably a jump ahead of us here: "Surely the amounts of a good we now have must influence how strongly we want another unit of that good," and you are right!

Let's discard the rotten eggs as useless, and look at the fresh eggs and T-bone steak, for example. If you have a great many eggs and very little steak you would place a high value on steak (willing to give quite a few eggs in exchange for one steak), but if you have no eggs at all, and a freezer full of T-bone, you'd likely give quite a few of those steaks in exchange for only a few eggs.

The principle involved here, called the "law of diminishing marginal utility," is quite clear. The more of any good we have, the less we value another unit of it because the satisfaction derived from each additional unit declines as we consume more and more of that good. Because of this phenomenon, anything available in the market will be purchased by some people (it's "worth" more than the sacrificed goods), yet others pass it up as not worth the cost.

This is fundamental in making rational choices. We buy (first) those things that will generate the greatest amount of satisfaction per dollar spent until we have reached the limit of our spendable incomes.

The same principle holds true in the area of resource use. Our gains have been maximized when we have so allocated our resources that no greater value of output can be derived from them in alternative uses.

As an example, suppose a rancher has 100 cows in the brood herd, and only one (tired) bull. If the market prices of bulls and cows were such that one bull were equal in value to five cows, our rancher (with limited funds to invest in brood stock) might be willing to give as many as ten cows to get just one more bull. On the other hand, if he had 25 bulls and 100 cows, their values would be sharply different: A one-for-one exchange might now seem like a bargain. Diminishing returns limits what one more cow could add to total output in the first instance, or in the latter, what an additional bull could add to production. Their values to the owner are affected accordingly.

Economics in Brief

Economics is a social science because it deals with people in their daily activities where choices are required. The science of economics has developed over a long period of time in response to the need for appropriate criteria by which choices can properly be made. Essentially, economics is a reasoning method that compares the benefits resulting from an action with the costs of that action.

In the overall, economics is concerned with overcoming the effects of scarcity by improving the efficiency with which scarce resources are allocated among their many competing uses, so as to best satisfy human wants. Economics is thus concerned with the future rather than the past, by attempting to predict what will happen if some action is taken.

The field of economics spans two major areas of economic activity. When the subject studied is a single decision-making entity—a consumer or producer—we call this "microeconomics." The problem may be one of the type a family faces in deciding how best to stretch its limited budget funds among all the possible ways that money could be spent. Or the problem may be that of a producing firm deciding which of the many possible different uses of its scarce resources will be the most profitable. The point of emphasis in such cases is the individual decision unit.

On the other hand, the economic system as a whole may be the point of interest and we call it "macroeconomics." We may be studying changes in the money supply, its causes and effects in flows of goods and services, employment and unemployment, or national income, and the important analytical tool is macroeconomics.

Model Building.   In the complexity of the real world we are forced to simplify a situation by making a number of assumptions that will permit a clear identification of cause-effect relationships. An economic model may be a simple "if, then" statement of the relationships between two variables. The model may be a word description, a diagram or graph relating two variables, or more complex mathematical equations describing the relationships within a system.[2] Whatever the situation, we are forced to consider only those facts relevant to the situation, varying some, holding other influential factors constant, while also ignoring an infinite number of unrelated real world facts.

We may or may not recognize it, but we do essentially the same thing in many of our everyday activities. Step on the gas while driving down the highway and we expect our speed of travel to increase, assuming, however, that we're not already driving at full speed, that the wheels won't fall off or the motor blow apart, or the tank run dry just at the time of pushing the throttle down, etc. Other possible happenings, if totaly unrelated to the vehicle's increased speed, will be ignored: an accident on a Los Angeles freeway, a traffic jam in New York City, etc., are unrelated (not caused by this decision) phenomena.

The farmer who is deciding whether to install a sprinkler irrigation system, to irrigate a 160-acre field, will ignore many facts about the farm and be concerned only with estimating the additional revenue generated by the greater crop output to compare with additional costs caused by installing and operating the system, exactly as we do later in this text. With other farm costs and returns unchanged, "What happens to total costs and returns as this irrigation system is added?" is the only question in need of an answer for a proper decision to be made.

Agricultural Economics.   Agricultural economics may be defined as an applied social science dealing with how mankind chooses to use technical knowledge and scarce productive resources such as land, labor, capital, and management to produce food and fiber and to distribute it for consumption to various members of society over time. Like economics, its parent discipline, agricultural economics seeks to discover cause-effect relationships. It uses the scientific method of economic theory to find answers to problems in agriculture and agribusiness.

---

[2]Students frequently voice a fear of economics "because it is so mathematical," or "because it is graphs," yet there is little factual basis for this attitude. Neither mathematics nor graphics is economics: They are simply shorthand methods by which the analysis of economic problems is facilitated, and nothing more.

The application of economic theory to agricultural problems has gone through a process of slow acceptance. Like a tree's roots, the origins of the field now known as agricultural economics reach back in many directions and over a long period of time. We may briefly outline the growth of this field as coming from two separate sources: first in time, from the physical sciences, and later, from economic theorists.

The severity and length of the agricultural depression beginning in the 1880s caused increasing attention to be devoted to its causes and possible solutions. The most notable early efforts were made primarily by agronomists and horticulturists. They recognized that the ability to grow plants and animals was not sufficient to make farmers succeed. The scientific interests of some of these people shifted to the problems of managing the farm, with special emphasis on the selection and handling of crop and livestock enterprises within the farm firm.

The study of enterprise costs and returns was begun in 1902 by W. M. Hays and Andrew Boss at Minnesota. These men, both agronomists, established a route system in which a number of farmers were contacted on a regular basis to collect detailed information on the costs of various enterprises maintained by those farms. Variations between farms were analyzed in terms of the types of enterprises, their labor and other input requirements, and the apparent differences in management capabilities of the participating farmers.

G. F. Warren, a horticulturist at Cornell University, took over and redirected a survey of farms in Tompkins County, New York, that had been initiated the year before by T. F. Hunt. Under Warren's direction this and later studies became the primary source of costs and returns information for New York agriculture over the following 40 or more years. Furthermore, that method was the prototype of many such studies conducted by a large number of state Experiment Stations throughout the country.

The Cornell method was founded on the idea that the factors affecting a farmer's success or failure could be identified only by studying a large number of farms with similar enterprise organizations. With the conviction that averages tell the story, elements of cost were identified and tallied for each farm enterprise. Over the years, the survey method evolved into a set of performance standards which sought to determine the most profitable size and type of farm for each area studied.[3]

[3]Selecting only the Minnesota and Cornell approaches should not be taken to imply that they were the only important methods, or that their contributions were better than those of the many other respected workers in this period of time. The Minnesota and Cornell methods are only representative of two distinctly different approaches to the same problem; and they gained the widest acceptance throughout the country over the next two decades.

Ignored early by economic "purists" and suffering outright rejection by other agricultural sciences at first, the "economics of agriculture" gained grudging acceptance before finally winning its present stature.

Early proponents of the usefulness of economic theory in solving agricultural problems drew on the principles developed and handed down through Adam Smith, Thomas R. Malthus, David Ricardo, Alfred Marshall and many other well-known economic theorists.

Foremost among the early theorists were H. C. Taylor and T. N. Carver. While at the University of Wisconsin, Taylor taught a course in agricultural economics during the 1902–03 school year. In that course, emphasis was put on the law of diminishing returns and its use in identifying the proper intensity of applying labor and capital to land. Taylor published a book in 1903, *Introduction to the Study of Agricultural Economics,* whose title alone suggests the broader use of economic concepts than the more restricted use of economics in the farm management books of his contemporaries.[4]

Professor Carver taught his first agricultural economics course at Harvard, in 1904, under the title of "The Economics of Agriculture With Special Reference to American Conditions." He, too, treated the problem of resource use-intensity as an economic problem subject to the law of diminishing returns (or, as he preferred, variable proportions). This and other topics in agricultural economics were contained in Carver's book, *The Distribution of Wealth,* published in 1904.[5]

A third theoretical treatment of problems in agriculture warrants special recognition. John D. Black's book, *Production Economics,*[6] published in 1926, demonstrated the applicability of economic theory to a broad array of problems of the farm firm and the agricultural industry.

The following rapid growth in the ranks of professional agricultural economists, and the ever-increasing public use of their special talents, bear testimony to the foresight of those early pioneering theorists.

Most beginning students probably have only a vague concept of agricultural economics. For the student, it is a blend of many subject areas. An agricultural economics curriculum ordinarily includes classes in technical agriculture, science, statistics, mathematics, business, general economics, and other social sciences.

[4]Henry C. Taylor, and Anne Dewees Taylor, *The Story of Agricultural Economics in the United States, 1840–1932,* Ames, Iowa: The Iowa State College Press, pp. 81, 127–29.
[5]Ibid.
[6]John D. Black, *Production Economics,* London: George G. Harrap and Co., Ltd, 1926.

Students taking a curriculum in agricultural economics may major in such areas as farm management, production economics, agricultural marketing, agricultural policy, finance, economic development, natural resources, and community development or public affairs.

Many agricultural economics undergraduate degrees may be called agribusiness programs. This trend began in the early 1960s to more adequately describe the job opportunities for certain majors in agricultural economics. While there were fewer possibilities for students to return to production agriculture, the employment horizons were broadening in the total food and fiber sector that services agriculture.

Agricultural economists are involved throughout our economic system in financial institutions, on farms and ranches, with oil companies, grain elevators, railroads, fertilizer companies, universities, feedlots, etc.

Some interpret the word "agribusiness" narrowly, meaning only very large or conglomerate businesses within the agricultural industry. We favor the original meaning given by Davis and Goldberg, when they defined agribusiness to include "the sum total of all operations involved in the manufacture and distribution of farm supplies; production operations on the farm; and the storage, processing, and distribution of farm commodities and items made from them."[7] For Bachelor of Science graduates, agribusiness probably describes much better the type of positions in which most students will be employed. At this level of training, there is not much difference between traditional agricultural economics degrees and degrees in agribusiness at the land grant colleges and universities.

Agricultural economics is an important subject area because it is concerned with society's basic needs. Getting food and fiber to all people in the world in the right form at the right time is an extremely complex process. About 60 percent of the world's population is involved in the basic industry of providing food. Many think of the United States as a highly industrialized country with agriculture being a relatively small part, but over 60 percent of the total assets of all U.S. corporations and farms combined is in agribusiness.[8] Also, around 20 percent of our labor force is employed in agribusiness operations and roughly 25 percent of our consumer expenditures are for food and clothing made from U.S. farm products.

Because of the rapid increase in world population, increasing

[7]John H. Davis, and Ray A. Goldberg, *A Concept of Agribusiness,* Boston, Mass.: Research Division, Harvard Business School, 1957.
[8]Ray A. Goldberg, Unpublished paper, Harvard Business School, May 23, 1975.

food output will receive greater attention in future years. To date, three major world food conferences have been held. The first convened in Washington, D.C. in 1963, the second in The Hague in 1970, and the third in Rome in 1974. The main theme of these conferences was to attempt to get the world to make an effort to wipe out poverty and hunger. This, of course, will not be done overnight because of the complex nature of the problem. Progress is being made and this book should assist in giving the reader a better understanding of the economic realities of this nagging problem of mankind. The dilemma involves the entire food sector, from farm supply firms to farming and ranching to food processing and distribution.

Agriculture is an integral part of the world food system. Crop and animal production are the foundation of that system. Agricultural economists must have a thorough understanding of that foundation because of the impact it has in the purchasing of inputs and in meeting the needs of consumers.

In order to understand the economic interrelationships which form the conceptual focus, the student must recognize the physical basis of all agricultural products. Each type of product has its own characteristics. The student should have an understanding of the influence of climatic environments in determining how and which commodities can be produced and distributed. In addition, the student should be aware of government policies of all types and their impact on production and distribution patterns.

Choice and the Functions of Management. In its broadest sense, management is the process used to control or direct a situation. Each of us makes choices every day that affect our lives, thus we are managers. Whenever a choice of one action over another is made, there is an implication that the chosen alternative was (rationally) preferred over the one discarded. This decision process, a prerogative of management, is discussed more fully in Chapter 4, but it bears more than passing mention here.

Ordinarily, the information for decisions is available to the individual only after conscious effort to obtain it. How does one know what kinds of, how much, and when data are needed, or would be of use? Bradford and Johnson have identified and outlined five basic steps as the foundation for managerial decisions:[9]

1. Observing a problem and thinking about its solution.

2. Analyzing with further observations.

[9]Lawrence A. Bradford, and Glenn L. Johnson, *Farm Management Analysis,* New York: John Wiley and Sons, 1953, pp. 3–12.

3. Making the decision.

4. Taking action.

5. Accepting responsibility.

Let us note each of these steps in a little more detail. Management must first have a set of objectives or goals. We often think of the goal of businesses in general as the maximization of profits. But personal and family satisfactions, participating in community activities or services, and increased leisure time might also be basic goals. Problems and opportunities will then be identified within this framework of objectives.

A problem exists when conditions are such that one would prefer them to be improved. The present situation thus deviates from one's ideal of that situation, giving rise to the need for information to help in its solution.

The assembling of facts may take many forms depending on the seriousness and complexity of the problem. Observation may simply be in reading about the problem in a trade magazine, station bulletin, or other source of information, or noting the experiences of others in handling the same problem.

The type and intensity of analysis also depends upon the particular problem. Careful analysis and consideration of several alternatives may be necessary before major decisions are attempted.

It is then time to make the decision and to take action, based upon the analysis and within the framework of goals. Some managers find themselves unable to carry out this fourth step, a not uncommon failing. They may have good, well thought out ideas for improving a situation, yet never seem able to carry them out.

After a decision has been made and a project launched, the final step is to accept the responsibility for action taken. One must be able to accept blame for the unwanted results of a wrong decision as well as credit for successes. Because of uncertainties over weather, disease, prices, etc., expectations often do not materialize. Failure may cause serious financial consequences which management must be in position to withstand.

The detail and attention given each of these steps will vary with different problems. In practice it might be difficult to clearly separate each step from the others. However, if the process leading through carrying a decision to its conclusion is analyzed, you will find that all five of these points have been followed.

Value Judgments.   The type of economics referred to as *positive economics* deals with what is, or what can be. If a farmer were to ask "what can I do to increase my net income?" a careful appraisal might result in the following conclusion: "You could buy a nearby acreage and your net income will increase by y dollars; rent that land and your net income will increase by z dollars." Were these the only alternatives available the farmer could decide on the basis of positive economic information. Those conclusions can be tested and proved correct or incorrect.

Suppose, on the other hand, that you were to note another's financial situation and tell that person they should do thus and so to increase their net income. This is *normative economics*. You would have based your recommendation on the belief that the other individual *should* try to increase his income. And this is a value judgment. It may even rank low on the scale of things that other person holds to be important in life, and be rejected because it conflicts with that individual's values.

As social scientists economists find it difficult to remain impartially objective concerning economic matters of importance to people. We all have been exposed to economic incidents throughout our lives, and have formed opinions of their causes and meanings. But our individual interpretations are formed within (and biased by) the framework of religious, ethical, moral, family and social attitudes, and beliefs that we have accepted during our lives. These attitudes and beliefs form the basis for ideas or convictions we hold about the way things *ought to be,* or what we *should* do. Such normative statements can neither be proved right or wrong because they stem from basic values that we hold. They constitute value judgments.

Holding different value systems, economists frequently disagree over fundamental economic policies and what should be done to improve particular situations. They too have values and biases that influence their attitudes about where emphasis should be placed. Where value judgments cannot be avoided, the agricultural economist as a public policy advisor, finds it necessary to state the judgments involved so that people may understand that person's position.

Using Graphs. A fundamental purpose of economic analysis is to explain people's responses to changes in their economic environment. If the causal relationships in this sphere can be correctly identified and specified, future behavior can be predicted with some degree of certainty.

As with any science, relationships between two or more variables can be stated in words alone. But words alone often lead to dry and tedious explanations. Whatever can be put in words can also be described in a graph. Simple graphs frequently make things much

clearer because they can visualize abstract economic ideas and relationships. We can see the situation so much better than with just
words alone.

A graph can visually demonstrate relationships between variables. Because of the extensive use we make of graphs in economics,
a well-grounded understanding of their methods and meaning is
especially helpful both in learning economics and in comprehending
economic solutions.

In Figure 1-1, we draw two intersecting lines, one horizontal
and the other vertical. These lines divide the graph space into four
quadrants which can be used to show how two variables are related.
The vertical line we label Y, and the horizontal X, each showing
positive and negative quantities in directions opposite from the zero
point.

Four quadrants can be noted, which we label as Quadrant I in
the northeast part of the diagram, counterclockwise to Quadrant II,
etc. Positive values are measured along the X-axis to the right of zero
(negative to the left), and upward from zero along the Y-axis (negative downward from zero). Only in Quadrant I do both X and Y
have positive values. In Quadrant II, values of X are negative and Y
values are positive; Quadrant III has negative values of both X and

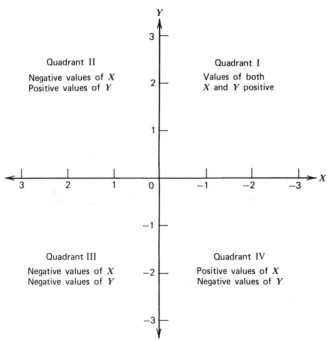

Figure 1-1.   The four quadrants of a graph.

Y; and in Quadrant IV, *X* values are positive while *Y* values are negative. In this book we make almost exclusive use of Quadrant I to demonstrate relationships, so we can now direct our attention to that quadrant.

The four different graphs (charts A, B, C, and D) in Figure 1-2 generalize the major types of relationships between the two variables *X* and *Y* that you can expect to use in this course of study.

We use charts such as these to show how the quantity of one variable (*Y*) varies with quantities of the other variable (*X*). More specifically, we chart how *Y*, the *dependent variable,* is changed because of changes in the *independent variable X,* that is, that *Y* is a function of (or depends on) the quantity of *X*.[10]

In chart A, the line of relation has a negative (or downward) slope. When the quantity of *X* is increased the amount of *Y* declines, similar to the typical demand curve (discussed in Chapter 3) and a number of other economic relationships discussed elsewhere in the text.

Chart B exhibits a positive relationship between *X* and *Y*; as the quantity of *X* is increased the number of units of *Y* also increases as a consequence. This chart demonstrates, in a general way, a topic such as market supply in which price of the product and quantities produced are positively related (as in Chapters 6 and 7).

Charts C and D demonstrate changing relationships between *X* and *Y*. In chart C the effect of *X* on *Y* diminishes as larger quantities of *X* are involved, similar to the functional relationships discussed in Chapter 4. The changing relationship shown in chart D is of a type similar to the cost curves discussed in Chapter 6. With increasing quantities on the *X*-axis, the *Y*-axis values first decline, then the relationship changes and the *Y*-axis values increase with further increases in *X*.

There are special requirements in the use we make of graphs, *implicit assumptions* if you will, that we wish to make especially evident here.

We make frequent use of the Latin phrase *ceteris paribus* (*cet. par.*), which means "all other things remaining equal," or "constant." This means that all things not measured along the two axes (that could affect the relationship shown in the graph) are held constant.

---

[10]We will use the *Y*-axis quantity as the dependent (or resulting) variable and the *X*-axis for the independent (or causative) variable, *except* when discussing demand or supply separately. A demand curve question that asks "How much of this good will consumers buy at a number of different prices?" and a supply curve question that asks "How much of this good will firms produce at a number of different prices?" have reversed the causal sequence. Stated in this way the question has made the *Y*-axis variable (price) the independent or causal variable and the quantities measured along the *X*-axis dependent on those different prices.

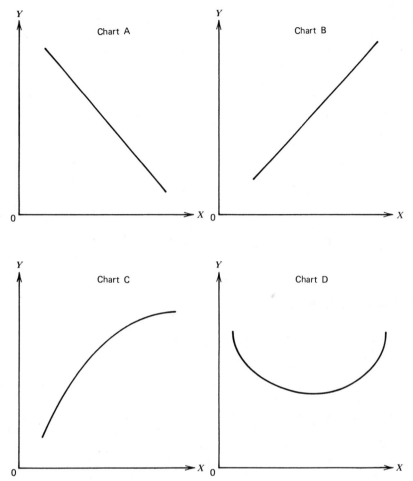

Figure 1-2. Some typical graphs used in economics.

For instance, time is an important variable, and must therefore be held constant as a single time period over which a relationship is specified or tested.

When you mark off a scale of units with a ruler along the two axes, you use a constant measure to indicate a given number of units. Each unit away from the zero point is exactly the same length as all other similar units along that scale. We must adhere rigidly to the same requirements when measuring physical units of resources or products along the axes. We make this clear with the requirement of *homogeneous units* of X and Y: Each unit along the X-axis is an exact duplicate of every other unit, and similarly for Y-axis units.

Another assumption, *divisibility,* means that we assume we can divide units into small fractions of the units measured along the axes. This permits a smooth curve to be drawn through identified points in the quadrant space, as in the charts above.

In a number of graphs throughout this book, we have used straight lines (such as those in charts A and B) to help explain a principle. In some instances, there is no need to raise questions of degree of curvature and possibly divert our attention from the basic principle of the relationship between the two variables.

A caveat to you, the student: *don't try to memorize* any of the graphic demonstrations sprinkled throughout this book. You will make economics far more difficult than it need be. Instead, we urge you to *learn the economic principles* displayed by the graphs. In doing this you will find it much easier to apply these principles to a wide variety of real world problems. And this will help you better to reason your way to problem solutions, which is the name of the game.

Looking Ahead

The food and fiber system is very large and complex. A basic understanding of its structure and participants is needed to come to grips with the economic relationships within the industry.

Next, and more importantly, this book deals with the principles of consumer behavior as people make their choices; of producer behavior in choosing rates of resource use and resource combinations, and which goods to produce; and supply and price determination in the market, within the context of a free enterprise system. Considerable effort is made to move slowly through the theoretical concepts. Applications of the theory are used to enhance meaning and help familiarize you with the economic way of thinking and analyzing problems.

The final chapters present the use of the theoretical concepts in problems of agricultural marketing, policy, finance, natural resources, agricultural trade, and world food supplies. Students will find these applied areas relevant to fitting the agricultural industry into a connected whole. Any economic change has direct and indirect effects on the entire agricultural sector. The impact on some subsectors is more pronounced than on others. You should be able to analyze these interrelationships as they bear on decision making.

The "Chapter Highlights" section at the end of each chapter summarizes briefly the major topics of that chapter, and serves as special reminders to the student. If the meaning and use of these ideas is not quite clear, it should prompt a rereading of the text.

Chapter Highlights

1. The cyclical nature of production and price instability are two important characteristics of agriculture.
2. Agriculture is a relatively competitive industry.
3. It is because of scarcity that we must economize in choosing between desired alternatives.
4. Sacrificing one thing for another gives rise to the true costs of making choices.
5. The economic method abstracts from the complex real world in order to discover causal relationships within the economy.
6. Graphs are used because they help in visualizing economic relationships.
7. Agriculture economics is a social science applied to agricultural problems.
8. Management is the decision-maker, coordinating the uses of all the resources in a farm or business firm.
9. Positive economics results from a scientific analysis of facts relevant to a situation; normative economics also involves our personal values.
10. Agribusiness includes the functioning of the entire food and fiber system from the input supply industry, to the farm or ranch, and the ultimate consumer.

Review Questions

1. What is the meaning of scarcity?
2. Is scarcity a problem that cannot be solved?
3. How is scarcity involved in improving your grades this term? What sacrifices would be required? Would you consider those sacrifices as "costs?"
4. The facts about most any situation surely are around somewhere. So why construct an economic "model" of that situation? Won't facts speak for themselves?
5. What is economics? Agricultural economics? What makes either of them a "social science?"
6. Suppose you are a farmer with a swampy area in one of your fields.
   a. Apply the five steps in management to draining that wet area.
   b. How would your decision be biased if you were opposed to land drainage of any kind?
   c. would the economic appraisal in your decision be affected if you couldn't tolerate an untillable area in one of your fields?
7. In a play on words, some wag once said that "if you fill this room with economists they would all point in different directions." How is it possible that in a field which claims a "science" status its professionals can arrive at such widely different solutions to the same problem?

Suggested Readings

1. Barkely, Paul W. *Economics, The Way We Choose.* New York: Harcourt, Brace Jovanovich, Inc., 1977, pp. 1–33.

2. Bradford, Lawrence A., and Glenn L. Johnson. *Farm Management Analysis.* New York: John Wiley and Sons, Inc., 1953, pp. 1–37.
3. Castle, Emergy N., and Manning H. Becker. *Farm Business Management.* New York: The Macmillan Co., 1962, pp. 1–61.
4. Efferson, J. Norman. *Principles of Farm Management.* New York: McGraw-Hill Book Co., 1953, pp. 1–67.
5. Forster, G. W. *Farm Organization and Management,* Rev. ed. New York: Prentice-Hall, Inc., 1946, pp. 19–47.
6. Taylor, Henry C., and Anne Dewees Taylor. *The Story of Agricultural Economics in the United States, 1840–1932.* Ames, Iowa: The Iowa State College Press, 1952.

Courtesy of Doug Warren, Editor, Montana Agricultural Experiment Station, Bozeman.

DIMENSIONS OF
AMERICAN AGRICULTURE

DIMENSIONS OF AMERICAN AGRICULTURE

It is impossible to understand the economics of American agriculture without a knowledge of the dimensions of the industry, the interrelationships within the industry, and how it is interconnected with the total economic system. This chapter will describe U.S. agriculture. How many farmers and ranchers are there in the United States? What is their financial structure? What is the role of corporations and cooperatives? Where do producers market their products? Are international markets important?

Agriculture is an integral part of the general economic system. We subdivide our national economy so that the fundamental structure can be seen. Producing firms and consumers are the central economic units in the system.

Agriculture's Role in the U.S. Economy

Agriculture is by no means a homogeneous industry. It is made up of small "family farms;"[1] large corporate organizations; credit and other input supply firms; marketing and processing firms; transportation networks; wholesalers; restaurants; and food and fiber retailers. The agriculture or agribusiness industry is composed of a complex series of firms. These firms supply inputs to farms, produce farm products, process agricultural products, and market these commodities to the final consumers. No longer do we think of agriculture as solely the physical and biological production of agricultural commodities.

The United States is one of the most productive countries in the world. The efficiency of American agriculture is second to none. If the U.S. has a relative advantage in the production of any product at this time, it is in agricultural commodities.

By providing quality food and fiber at reasonable prices to all consumers, agriculture is vital to the U.S. economy. Two measures of the national importance of an industry are the number of people

---

[1]A family farm is usually defined as one in which the farm family constitutes the basic labor force.

Table 2-1 Industry Distribution of National Output and
Employed Labor Force, United States, 1975

Type of Industry	National Output (%)	Employed Labor Force (%)
Agriculture	3	5
Mining and construction	6	5
Manufacturing	23	23
Transportation, communication, and utilities	9	6
Wholesale and retail trade	18	21
Finance, insurance, real estate	15	5
Services	12	17
Government (state, local, and federal)	14	18

Source: "Economic Report of the President," United States Government Printing Office, Washington, D.C.: 1977.

it employs and the value of its production. These measures are shown in Table 2-1.

The most important economic activities in the United States are manufacturing, government, and other services. Manufacturing is currently the major economic activity, as it has been since about 1890. It accounts for approximately one-fourth of the national output and employs some 19 million people. Manufactured items include two broad categories of goods termed durable and nondurable. Durable goods or "hard goods" are products like metals, machinery, automobiles, and household appliances. Nondurable goods are "soft goods," which include food products, textiles, and apparel.

In terms of employment government is the third major industry because of large expenditures on education, military, and social programs. Next in importance are other services. The service sector accounts for more than one-half of all final goods and services produced (gross national product), while basic goods industries (agriculture, mining and manufacturing) account for less than one-third of the gross national product.

These measures indicate that agriculture is one of the smaller industries, producing three percent of national output and directly employing five percent of the employed labor force. However, agriculture indirectly accounts for much employment in other industries such as manufacturing and processing, wholesaling, and retail trade. In total, agriculture employs 4.4 million in farm production, 10 million in marketing farm products, and 2 million in the production of farm equipment and supplies. Agriculture is thus responsible for employing approximately 19 percent of the labor force in the United States.

The Business Structure of Farms

Most of the farms in the United States are classified as family farms. In 1974, individual or family farms accounted for 89 percent of all farms, partnerships accounted for nine percent, corporations two percent and others (estates and trusts) less than one percent. Since many of the partnerships and corporations are family organizations, about 98 percent of our farms are really family farms. Of the 1.7 million commercial farms, 28,700 were operated under a corporate management. The number of corporate farms in agriculture has increased 33 percent since 1969. Of the corporations, a very large percentage had 10 or fewer shareholders. This also tends to indicate a family-type of structure. These corporate units accounted for 11 percent of the farm land and 18 percent of product sales.

In 1974 there were over 8100 corporations in the livestock industry, 3500 in horticultural specialty farms and 2900 in fruit and tree nut farms. These corporate farms sold 32 percent of all cattle and calves, 60 percent of the nursery and greenhouse products and 31 percent of all fruits, nuts, and berries sold in the United States.

In terms of their number, the corporation is not an important type of business organization in agriculture. However, many people are concerned about corporate activity in agriculture because of the economic consequences that could occur with concentrated resource control. As a result, some states have attempted to limit the growth of corporation farming. Laws passed in three states (North Dakota, Kansas, and Minnesota) prohibit corporate farming. Some restrictions are also placed on Texas corporations that are in the cattle business.

Most producers are concerned about farming corporations because they think corporations are more efficient, and that their size gives them market advantages that may put the family farm operators at a competitive disadvantage. Farmers believe the tax laws, capital markets, volume buying of production inputs, and volume selling of output afford advantages to corporate farms which are not available to them. However, most studies show that moderate sized family farms are as efficient as most corporate farms. With this situation plus the generally low returns to agricultural investments, one would expect very little growth in corporate agriculture. This does not mean, however, that corporations will not buy agricultural land for speculative purposes and farm it for a while if the rate of return on a given piece of land is expected to be high. A large shift to corporate farming is unlikely to occur unless agricultural profits become more consistent and predictable and superior to investment alternatives.

The Three Sectors of Agriculture

Farms in the United States may also be grouped according to economic classes, or sectors. Because of changes in their numbers through time, we may refer to them as the expanding, declining, and noncommercial sectors.

By classifying farms according to the value of farm products sold, three classifications can be established: (1) those with sales over $20,000, (2) those with sales between $2500 and $20,000, and (3) those with sales under $2500. The number of farms falling into the first class is increasing, thus the "expanding" sector; the number falling into the second group is decreasing, thus the "declining" sector. The noncommercial sector includes farms with annual farm product sales of less than $2500. This latter classification was the largest group in number of farms in 1960 and 1976 even with a large increase in the farm price level over this time period.

The expanding sector of agriculture numbered 350,000 farms in 1960, increasing to 782,000 by 1976 (Table 2-2). These farms accounted for 28 percent of all farms, produced over 90 percent of the value of agricultural output, and received 76 percent of the government support payments. Off-farm income averaged $7708 per farm. Average total income per farm including off-farm income, nonmonetary income and government payments amounted to about $29,000.

The declining sector of agriculture includes those farms that sold between $2500 and $20,000 worth of products in 1976 (Table 2-3). These farms decreased in number from 1.8 million in 1960 to 913,000 by 1976. Farms of this size-class produced nine percent of the agricultural output, 14 percent of the net income in agriculture,

Table 2-2 Expanding Sector of Agriculture—Farms with Sales Greater Than $20,000 Annually, Number and Percentage of Total, 1960 and 1976

	1960	*Percentage*	*1976*	*Percentage*
Number of farms	350,000	8.6	782,000	28.1
Cash receipts (millions)[a]	$17,969	51.6	$86,791	90.1
Realized net farm income (millions)	$ 4,110	35.0	$16,798	76.7
Off-farm income per farm	$ 1,844		$ 7,708	
Total all income per farm	$13,932		$29,188	
Direct government payments per farm	$ 218	31.0	$ 717	76.4

Source: Economic Research Service, USDA, "Farm Income Statistics," July 1977.

[a] Includes other income.

Table 2-3 Declining Sector of Agriculture—Farms with Sales Between $2,500 and $19,999 Annually, Number and Percentage of Total, 1960 and 1976

	1960	*Percentage*	*1976*	*Percentage*
Number of farms	1,774,000	44.8	913,000	32.9
Cash receipts (millions)[a]	$14,897	42.7	$ 8,296	8.6
Realized net income (millions)	$ 6,047	51.5	$ 3,028	13.8
Off-farm income per farm	$ 1,580		$ 8,859	
Total all income per farm	$ 4,990		$12,175	
Direct government payments per farm	$ 384	54.7	$ 150	18.7

Source: Economic Research Service, USDA, "Farm Income Statistics," July 1977.

[a] Includes other income.

and received 19 percent of the government payments. Total income for these farm operators averaged $12,175 per farm.

The noncommercial farms in the United States totaled 1.1 million farms in 1976 (Table 2-4). They produce very little agricultural output and receive very little income from agriculture or from direct government payments. Off-farm income is relatively large. Out of a total income per farm of $17,551, almost 90 percent ($15,630) is derived from nonfarm sources. It is apparent from these data that most of the noncommercial farms are only part-time or retirement operations that should not be included in commercial agriculture.

Table 2-4 Noncommercial Sector of Agriculture—Farms with Sales Less Than $2,500 Annually, Number and Percentage of Total, 1960 and 1976

	1960	*Percentage*	*1976*	*Percentage*
Number of farms	1,849,000	46.6	1,083,000	39.0
Cash receipts (millions)[a]	$2,042	5.8	$ 1,335	1.4
Realized net income (millions)	$1,491	13.4	$ 2,082	9.5
Off-farm income per farm	$2,732		$15,630	
Total all income per farm	$3,538		$17,551	
Direct government payments per farm	$ 54	14.3	$ 33	4.9

Source: Economic Research Service, USDA, "Farm Income Statistics," July 1977.

[a] Includes all other income.

Vertical Coordination in Agriculture

Many people are concerned with the amount of vertical coordination in agriculture, since it affects the decision-making ability of producers and also affects the control of resources. The terms "vertical coordination," "contract production," and "vertical integration" are often used interchangeably.

Vertical coordination is the term most generally used and it includes the linkage of successive stages in the marketing and production of a commodity in one decision entity. Vertical integration means that successive production stages and/or marketing stages are coordinated within one firm. An example of this type of integration might be a wheat farmer buying a flour mill or vice versa.

Contract production involves the use of production agreements between farmers or ranchers and processors, dealers, or others who are at the first stage before or after the farm. These agreements specify the type of crop to produce, how the crop is to be grown and harvested and perhaps the price to be paid the producer.

The proportion of total farm production under various forms of contracting and vertical integration increased from about 19 percent in 1960 to 22 percent in 1970. Contract production increased from 15 to 17 percent and vertical integration from four to five percent over the same span of years. Both contracting and vertical integration are more concentrated in livestock, poultry, and fruits and vegetables than in crops (Table 2-5). These total numbers reflect considerable stability in vertical coordination, and there is probably little reason to expect a rapid increase into these forms of closer coordination.

Table 2-5 Volume of Farm Marketings Under Vertical
Coordination for Selected Commodities, 1960 and 1970
(Percentage of Total)

	Production Contracts		Vertical Integration	
Commodity	*1960*	*1970*	*1960*	*1970*
Fresh vegetables	20	21	25	30
Processed vegetables	67	85	8	10
Dry beans and peas	35	1	1	1
Citrus fruits	60	55	20	30
Sugar beets	98	98	2	2
Sugar cane	40	40	60	60
Seed crops	80	80	1	1
Fed cattle	10	18	3	4
Fluid milk	95	95	3	3
Broilers	93	90	5	7
Turkeys	30	42	4	12
All Commodities	15	17	4	5

Source: Economic Research Service, USDA.

Farmer Cooperatives

Farmer cooperatives are an integral part of agriculture and the free enterprise economy. As an organizational form they are an alternative or addition to an individual proprietorship, partnership, or corporation. A cooperative is defined as a business that is organized, capitalized, and managed for its member-patrons, furnishing and/or marketing goods and services to the patrons at cost.[2] Farmer members sell their products through marketing cooperatives or buy their inputs through supply cooperatives. In doing business with these cooperatives they derive a profit called "net savings." These savings or patronage dividends are returned to the member-patrons in proportion to their business transactions with the cooperative. Therefore, in a cooperative the primary purpose is to make a "profit" for the patron-owners and not for investors as in a corporation.

The latest available data show that in 1972–73 there were 4897 farmer marketing cooperatives, down from 1960s total of 5727. Farm supply cooperatives declined to 2801 by 1972–73 from the 3222 that were in business in 1960. Estimated total membership of farmer cooperatives is around 6.1 million. Farmer cooperatives are important to agricultural producers, marketing about 30 percent of the agricultural products produced and providing about 20 percent of the agricultural inputs used by American farmers.

Farm Output

Farm output increased by 58 percent between 1950 and 1976. This was essentially accomplished with larger amounts of purchased inputs embodying a significant amount of technical change, improved management and less labor. The total number of farms has been declining while the average size of farms has been increasing (Table 2-6). In 1977, there were 2.8 million farmers farming an average of 393 acres per farm, compared to 1920 when 6.5 million producers farmed an average of 147 acres per farm.

Between 1950 and 1976, the number of farm workers in agriculture dropped from 9.3 million to 4.4 million. Most of these laborers migrating out of agriculture were family workers. Of those remaining, family workers totaled 3.0 million and hired workers totaled 1.4 million.

[2]Ewell P. Roy, *Cooperatives Today and Tomorrow,* Danville, Ill.: The Interstate Printers and Publishers, Inc., 1964, p. 1.

Table 2-6 The Number, Population, and Size of Farms
in the United States

Year	Number of Farms[a]	Farm Population (000)	Average Farm Size in Acres	U.S. Population on Farms (%)
1920	6,518,000	31,974	147	30.1
1930	6,546,000	30,529	151	24.9
1940	6,350,000	30,547	167	23.2
1950	5,648,000	23,048	213	15.3
1960	3,962,000	15,635	297	8.7
1970	2,924,000	9,712	383	4.8
1971	2,876,110	9,425	389	4.6
1972	2,869,710	9,610	381	4.6
1973	2,843,890	9,472	383	4.5
1974	2,820,570	9,264	384	4.4
1975	2,808,480	8,864	387	4.2
1976	2,778,380	8,253	390	3.9
1977	2,752,080	7,800	393	3.6

Source: Statistical Reporting Service, USDA.

[a] Over time the Bureau of the Census has used varying definitions of a farm. In 1959, 1964, and 1969, places of less than 10 acres were counted as farms if estimated sales of agricultural products for the year amounted to at least $250, and places of 10 acres or more if sales amounted to at least $50. The Census definition of a farm in 1974 was any establishment which had or normally would have had sales of agricultural products of $1,000 or more.

Much of the off-farm migration has been caused by advances in agricultural science and technology. These improvements have increased output and lowered agricultural prices. As a result, some producers have been forced to find other employment where the probability of higher wages exists. On the other hand, some producers engage in agricultural pursuits at lower wage rates than could be earned in the nonfarm economy. They do so because of the added amenities of living in a rural area, the social impediments to mobility such as family and friends, or for other reasons that may be strictly personal in nature. These reasons may stem back to what some refer to as "agricultural fundamentalism."

Agricultural fundamentalism is a philosophy that draws deeply on the French Physiocratic school that dates from the mid 1700s. This school of thought held the basic belief that industry, trade, and the professions were useful, but unproductive. Only agriculture, forestry, fisheries, and mining were productive since they appeared to produce a "surplus." The Physiocrat's concept of production held that productive effort in these industries caused useful physical material to appear that previously did not exist. Agricultural fundamentalism holds that there is something special and unique about the farm way of life. Today, however, we realize that all industry is productive and agriculture is a business like any other economic activity.

Commercial farms are many and heterogenous. Table 2-7 indicates the relative importance of various classifications of farms, as shown graphically in Figure 2-1.

Cash grain farms totaled 580,000 and represented 34 percent of the commercial farms in 1974. This type is comprised primarily of farms producing wheat, corn, and soybeans. These grain farms accounted for 31 percent of the total cropland from which crops were harvested. Cash grain crops are important all across the United States, however, the greatest concentration of cash grain farms was in the North Central Region. Wheat was the principal cash-grain crop in twelve states. Cash grain farms had an average size of 485 acres including an average of 356 acres of cropland.

Tobacco farms use relatively few acres of land and much labor. They made up 5.6 percent of all commercial farms while containing only 1.6 percent of total cropland. These farms are located predominantly in the South where nearly 90 percent of them are concentrated in five states. The average size of a tobacco farm was 129 acres, and the average amount of land cropped was 67.2 acres. There are 83 percent of the tobacco farms which are less than 50 acres in size.

Table 2-7 Types of Farms in the United States, 1964, 1969, and 1974

	Number in 1974	*Number in 1969*	*Number in 1964*
Total U.S.	1,695,047	1,733,683	1,817,440
Cash grain	580,254	369,312	368,518
Tobacco	95,493	89,903	125,593
Cotton	30,725	40,534	117,241
Other field crops	81,415	31,190	31,299
Vegetable	19,548	19,660	17,345
Fruit and nut	51,270	53,754	50,108
Poultry	42,690	57,545	76,322
Dairy	196,057	260,956	349,244
Livestock	493,816	647,884	470,715
General	59,654	126,527	175,103
Miscellaneous[a]	44,125	36,418	35,952

Source: U.S. Department of Commerce, Census of Agriculture 1969 and 1974.

[a] Includes nursery, greenhouse products, and such things as mink production.

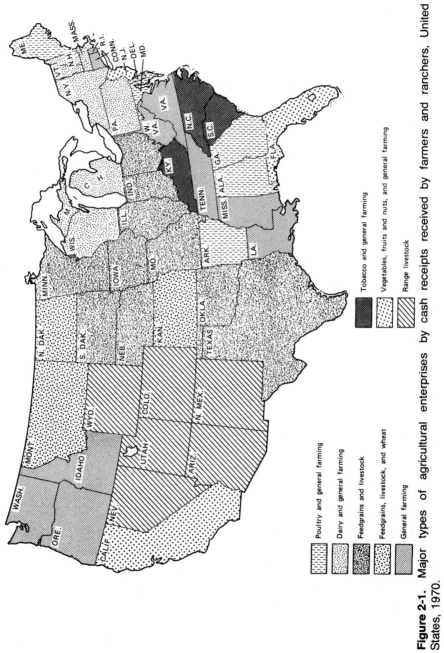

Figure 2-1. Major types of agricultural enterprises by cash receipts received by farmers and ranchers, United States, 1970.

Poultry and general farming

Dairy and general farming

Feedgrains and livestock

Feedgrains, livestock, and wheat

General farming

Tobacco and general farming

Vegetables, fruits and nuts, and general farming

Range livestock

The total number of cotton farms declined by 65 percent between 1964 and 1969 and another 24 percent between 1969 and 1974. The steady decline in numbers of cotton farms has been associated with an increase in the size of the remaining farms, averaging about 580 acres. Cotton farms comprised 3.2 percent of total cropland. The leading states in cotton production are Texas, Mississippi, Arkansas, California, Louisiana, and Alabama.

Approximately 4.8 percent of the commercial farms are "other field crop" farms. They cultivate 5.4 percent of the total cropland, with an average size of 478 acres. Irish potatoes and peanuts are the principal crops in this classification.

Vegetable farms are widely scattered, but seven states are important in producing fresh and processed vegetables. Production of vegetables is concentrated on a small number of highly specialized farms. Much of the cropland used for vegetable production is irrigated. The average size of vegetable farms is 240 acres, accounting for 1.2 percent of all commercial farms and one percent of the total cropland.

Fruit and nut farms are also highly specialized. A wide variety of fruits and nuts are grown in California, Florida, Washington, and Michigan. These states had 72 percent of all fruit and nut farms. Due to climate, different fruits are predominant in each of these states. Grapes, oranges, peaches, prunes, and pears are important in California while oranges and grapefruits are the major fruits in Florida. In Washington the principal crops are apples, pears, cherries, grapes, and peaches, and in Michigan the main fruit crops are apples, cherries, peaches, grapes, pears, and strawberries. These farms comprise 3.0 percent of all farms and 1.1 percent of the total cropland averaging 149 acres per farm.

Most of the poultry operations are located east of the Mississippi. These farms account for 2.5 percent of the commercial farms.

The greatest concentration in dairying is in the Northeast, California, and the six states bordering the Great Lakes. Dairy farms numbered 196,000 in 1974, with an average size of 276 acres.

Livestock farms constitute the second largest group of farms, comprising 29 percent of all farms, and contain 47 percent of all land in farms. In 1974, livestock farms sold 81 percent of all cattle and calves, 75 percent of all hogs and pigs, and 83 percent of all sheep and lambs. These farms are rather large and average 896 acres per farm. Livestock ranches, a classification used primarily in the western states, are very large specialized cow-calf or sheep operations.

General farms are those with 50 percent or more of the total value of all farm products sold from seed crops, hay, and silage and are farms on which no one product provided 50 percent or more of the total value of all farm products sold. These farms comprised 3.5 percent of all farms. The average size of these farms was 494 acres.

Even though many farms are still rather small, specialized agriculture continues to grow. Whether or not farms will continue to become larger, more specialized organizations depends on factors such as capital limitations, management ability, technological developments, and the risk and uncertainty facing farm producers.

The Agribusiness Complex

The farming industry is closely related to the marketing industries that are essential to transform, transport, and transfer food and fiber to the consumer. In addition, farming is served by a large number of industries which manufacture and distribute durable goods and other farm supplies used in agriculture (Figure 2-2).

Farmers are buying more of their inputs rather than using farm produced inputs. These inputs include feed, fertilizer, petroleum products, farm machinery, chemicals, and other farm supplies and services.

Food processors are the link between farmers and food wholesalers and retailers. There are about 22,000 processing firms that add form utility to the raw farm product, for example, the transformation of sugar beets into sugar and wheat into bread.

Processors may sell to wholesalers and retailers through food brokers. The broker is an independent sales agent for the processor who neither takes possession nor title to grocery products.

Food wholesalers link food processors with retailers who sell directly to consumers, and institutional outlets. There are about 40,000 of these wholesalers.

A retail food chain is a group of 11 or more stores owned and operated by the same firm. Chain stores began in 1859 with the Great Atlantic and Pacific Tea Company. Between 1910 and 1930 Atlantic and Pacific expanded, and by 1930 they had over 15,000 stores.

The major impact of the retail chain store movement was on wholesale operations. Chain stores combined wholesaling with retailing, and to a lesser extent, processing and were able to lower costs. They were able to cut prices, forcing higher priced independents out of business. Then after World War II, the chains began adopting the supermarket type of operation.

Because the independent grocery retailers and wholesalers lost business to the chains, they responded with their own vertically inte-

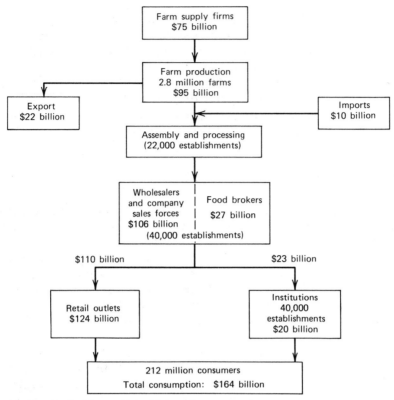

(*Source:* Ray A. Goldberg, Unpublished Paper, 1975.)

Figure 2-2. Functional organization of U.S. food agribusiness, 1974.

grated organizations. In some cases, groups of independent retailers created cooperative wholesale systems to supply them with merchandise. In other cases, wholesalers assembled "voluntary groups" of retailers into chain-type organizations, adopting most of the methods used by the chains. The number of grocery stores in the United States declined from about 280,000 in 1954 to less than 195,000 in 1972. Grocery store chains with 11 or more stores sell about 60 percent of all grocery items. Sales per store have increased fourfold since 1954.

Consumers spent $172.3 billion for farm foods at the retail level in 1976. The farm value of that food was $56.3 billion, and the total marketing bill was $116.0 billion. One must remember that the marketing job is extremely important since the farm products are raw materials, and the marketing system adds time, form, place, and ownership utility or satisfaction costing more than twice as much as the farm value of the original output.

The major factors increasing the marketing bill over time have been rising labor costs, the demand for services such as special packaging and convenience foods, plus increased volume of food products handled by the system. Affluence has permitted the replacement of domestic workers in the kitchen with mechanical devices and prepared foods.

The American consumer has a wide selection of food products from which to choose at a relatively low proportion of disposable personal income. United States consumers spend about 17 percent of their disposable personal income for food, one of the lowest in any country in the world and this percentage has been declining for 25 years, except for 1974–76.

Consumer demand for food, however, changes over time. In general, per capita consumption of red meat, poultry, fish, sugar, fruit, and vegetables has been increasing while consumption of coffee, tea, cocoa, fresh potatoes, dairy products, and eggs has been declining.

International Trade

Since the "Russian wheat deal of 1972," international trade in agricultural commodities has received much national attention from consumers and producers. Crop shortages, rising incomes and population growth have increased the value of exports of agricultural commodities by 217 percent to $23 billion in the calendar year 1976 (Table 2-8). The rapid rise in U.S. exports of farm commodities boosted the U.S. agricultural trade balance (exports minus imports) by $10.5 billion to a record $12 billion. Imports in 1976 increased 91 percent to $11 billion, also a record (Table 2-9). The increase in grain exports, particularly wheat and feed grains, accounted for 53 percent of the total increase in agricultural exports.

Although international trade is relatively unimportant to the total U.S. economy, it is very important to agriculture and to our level of living. The U.S. exports and imports only five to six percent of its gross national product. Agriculture exports one half of its wheat production and one fourth of its feed grain production, or the production from one out of every three and one-half acres harvested in the United States. Trade is also vital to our consumers. Through trade it is possible to obtain coffee, tea, bananas, and other products that cannot be produced in the United States except at very high costs.

Table 2-8 U.S. Agricultural Exports: Value by Commodity, Calendar Years, 1970 and 1976

	1970	1976
Commodity Exports	*(Millions of Dollars)*	
Animals and animal products		
Dairy products	127	142
Fats, oils and greases	247	443
Hides and skins	187	518
Meat and meat products	132	617
Poultry and poultry products	56	262
Other	101	916
Total animals and animal products	850	2,380
Grains and preparations		
Feedgrains	1,064	6,028
Rice	314	629
Wheat	1,111	4,087
Other	107	131
Total grains and preparations	2,596	10,875
Oilseeds and products		
Cottonseed and soybean oil	244	586
Soybeans	1,228	3,315
Protein meal	358	899
Other	91	270
Total oilseeds and products	1,921	5,070
Other products and preparations		
Cotton	372	1,049
Tobacco	517	940
Fruits and preparations	334	770
Vegetables and preparations	206	674
Other	463	1,238
Total other products and preparations	1,892	4,671
All Commodities	7,259	22,996

Source: Economic Research Service, USDA, "Foreign Agricultural Trade of the United States."

Table 2-9 U.S. Agricultural Imports: Value by Commodity,
Calendar Years, 1970 and 1976

	1970	*1976*
Commodity Imports	*(Millions of Dollars)*	
Animals and animal products		
Cattle	111	157
Dairy products	125	269
Hides and skins	110	88
Meat and meat products	1,011	1,423
Other	204	381
Total animals and animal products	1,561	2,318
Grains and preparations	70	164
Oilseeds and products		
Coconut oil	77	182
Copra	38	0
Olive oil	20	38
Other	67	301
Total oilseeds and products	202	521
Other products and preparations		
Sugar cane	725	1,148
Tobacco	139	294
Fruits and preparations	146	279
Inedible molasses	43	111
Nuts and preparations	100	177
Vegetables and preparations	298	455
Wine	145	315
Malted beverages	32	139
Bananas	188	282
Cocoa beans	201	358
Coffee	1,160	2,633
Crude rubber	231	512
Spices	55	96
Tea	53	95
Carpet wool	31	21
Other	390	1,074
Total other products and preparations	3,937	7,989
All Commodities	5,770	10,992

Source: Economic Research Service, USDA, "Foreign Agricultural Trade
of the United States."

Overview of our Economic System

Two major economic entities are involved in our free enterprise economic system. These are households and business firms (including farms and ranches).

Households are our dwelling places made up of families or individuals. They are consuming units that purchase the nation's goods and services. In addition they own our economic resources.

Business firms, on the other hand, are the economic actors that produce the nation's output of goods and services. In order to accomplish this process they must purchase or hire economic resources. Business firms in the United States are organized as either single proprietorships, partnerships, corporations, or cooperatives.

A circular flow diagram in Figure 2-3 is used to illustrate how households and business firms interact in our economy. The right-hand side of the model shows the flow of finished goods and services from business firms to consumers. This movement of products represents all markets for consumer goods and services such as food, clothing, furniture, television sets, and so on. The reverse money flow shown in the figure is the payments made by householders for those goods and services. The product market for goods and services establishes prices that regulate the quantity and quality of goods produced and consumed.

The left side of the circular flow diagram shows the movement of economic resources (land, labor, capital, and management) from households to business firms. The return money flow is from business firms paying for these resources in the form of wages and

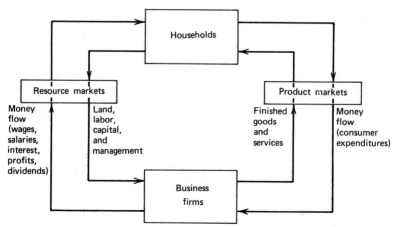

Figure 2-3. Circular flow diagram—households exchanging resources for money income to spend on goods and services.

salaries for labor and management, dividends and interest for capital and rents on land. These flows make up the resource market. This market determines resource prices that regulate the flow of resources from consumers to producers.

Now if we visualize the entire diagram, you can see that households are selling their resources to firms in order to purchase finished goods and services. Also business firms are selling goods and services to consumers in order to purchase factors of production to continue the production process.

Households are the selling side of the resource market and the buying side of the product market. Business firms are on the buying side of the resource market and the selling side of the product market. The money flowing through the product market is determined by the "dollar votes" of consumers in the market and the prices at which goods and services sell. The amount of money flowing through the resource market depends upon the amounts of resources put on the market by households and the price of resources that is determined in the resource market.

The transactions between households and business firms are limited by scarcity. Consumers have limited incomes, but unlimited wants. Business firms are also constrained in production by limited resources to produce final goods and services.

A farm or ranch is both a household and a business firm. The farm family provides some of the economic resources to produce food and fiber which it sells to other households. With that money flow it can purchase final goods and services from other producers and purchase other economic resources from other households. Thus, this simplified circular flow model applies to the individual farm or ranch as it does to the entire economic system.

Summary

Agriculture is a very large, heterogeneous industry. It involves many types of businesses in producing and distributing food and fiber to consumers. Agriculture includes: farms; credit and supply firms; marketing, processing, and distribution firms; restaurants and retailers.

American agriculture has about 2.8 million farms and ranches. These farms vary widely in size, but the average size of farm is only about 400 acres. Most farms are cash grain and livestock operations, scattered throughout the country.

The American consumer has a wide selection of nutritious food available at "reasonable" prices. American consumers spend about

17 percent of their disposable income for food, one of the lowest in the world. International consumers are purchasing more American farm products. Corn, wheat, and soybeans are the major export commodities. At present the United States is exporting the products from one out of every three and one-half acres harvested. Coffee, meat, and sugar are our major imported items.

Households and business firms are the two economic actors in our free enterprise economic system. Households sell resources to business firms for money and in turn spend this money on final goods and services produced by business firms.

Chapter Highlights

1. Agriculture is composed of the complete food and fiber system. It does not consist solely of the physical and biological production of agricultural commodities.
2. Agriculture produces three percent of the U.S. gross national product (GNP), and directly employs five percent of the labor force. The total agribusiness system, however, employs 19 percent of the U.S. labor force.
3. Contrary to popular opinion, most farms and ranches are family enterprises. Corporations account for only two percent of U.S. farms, eleven percent of the farm land, and 18 percent of agricultural sales.
4. Most family farms are as efficient as corporation farms.
5. Farms that sold over $20,000 worth of products in 1976 make up about thirty percent of all farms, produce about 90 percent of U.S. farm output, and have a per family income of $29,000 per year.
6. The average noncommercial farmer has an off-farm income of $16,000 per year or 90 percent of total income.
7. About one fourth of U.S. agricultural production is contracted or produced under vertically integrated arrangements.
8. Farmer cooperatives market 30 percent of U.S. agricultural products and handle 20 percent of all agricultural inputs.
9. Most American farms are small, on the average. In 1977 the mean farm size was 393 acres.
10. Agriculture includes 22,000 food processors, 40,000 wholesalers, and 700,000 retail and institutional (schools, hotels, hospitals, etc.) outlets.
11. Consumers spend about $170 billion on farm foods or about 17 percent of their disposable incomes.
12. International trade is very important to agriculture and to U.S. consumers.
13. Households and business firms are the two major economic entities in our economic system.
14. Households buy products and sell resources.
15. Business firms buy resources and sell products.

Review Questions

1. What is a farm? Why has the definition of a farm been changed in the past few years?
2. The number of American farms has been declining. What are some factors influencing this trend?
3. How does a cooperative differ from a "for profit" corporation?
4. Corporate farms have been increasing in number. What impact could this development have on family farms?
5. Agricultural producers are responsible for producing the final product that the consumer purchases. Thus, the agricultural marketing system is unproductive. Discuss.
6. Farmers and ranchers should adjust their production to the food and fiber needs of consumers. Discuss.
7. The U.S. government should restrict imports of agricultural commodities, since we can produce all commodities more efficiently than any other country. Discuss.

Suggested Readings

1. Abrahamsen, Martin A. *Cooperative Business Enterprise.* New York: McGraw-Hill Book Company, 1976, Chapters 1, 2, and 3.
2. *1974 Census of Agriculture,* December 1977, Volume 1, Part 51, United States Summary and State Data. Washington D.C.: U.S. Government Printing Office, Bureau of the Census, U.S. Department of Commerce.
3. *Agricultural Outlook,* a monthly magazine. Washington, D.C.: Economics, Statistics, and Cooperatives Service, U.S. Department of Agriculture.
4. *Handbook of Agricultural Charts.* Washington, D.C.: Economics, Statistics, and Cooperatives Service, U.S. Department of Agriculture.
5. Goldberg, Ray A. *Agribusiness Coordination,* Boston, Mass.: Division of Research, Harvard Business School, Soldiers Field, 1968, Chapter 1.
6. McConnell, Campbell R. *Economics,* 7th ed. New York: McGraw-Hill Book Company, 1978, Chapter 3.

3

Courtesy of the Chicago Mercantile Exchange.

CONSUMER BEHAVIOR
AND DEMAND

CONSUMER BEHAVIOR AND DEMAND

In the last chapter, it was noted that households and business firms were the major economic actors in our economic system. This chapter will concentrate only on households or consumers and the behavior of people in meeting their desire for goods and services. It is in the observed market behavior of people that the concept of demand rests. While demand will be specifically discussed later in the chapter, let it suffice at this point to say that demand means the quantities of a product bought at alternative prices holding everything else constant.

When consumer behavior is studied, certain characteristics can be noted. One feature is that consumers spend everything they earn on goods and services. Another is that consumers never seem to get enough of most things. We can infer from this characteristic of consumer behavior that human wants are insatiable and that more is preferred to less.

One of the reasons consumers do not buy infinite quantities of everything is that they have a limited amount of money income. In economics, we assume that consumers, with a given money income, will purchase clothing, housing, food, haircuts, and all the other things that they want in amounts that will maximize utility or satisfaction for them. The utility of a product or service means the inherent characteristics or qualities that cause them to be desired. These may be objective or subjective qualities. But it is unlikely that two individuals would attain the same utility or satisfaction from the consumption of the same amount of a product.

The Utility Basis of Demand

Another noticeable feature of consumer behavior is that income is not spent on a single item; a variety of goods and services is purchased. The reason for this behavior is contained in what is called the law of diminishing marginal utility. This law means that when an individual consumes additional units of a specific commodity, consumption of other goods and services unchanged, the amount of satisfaction derived from each additional unit of that good decreases. (Remember that marginal means additional.)

An Example of Diminishing Marginal Utility. Assume a traveler has been in Death Valley without water for three days. Under these conditions that person may be dead, but let us assume our traveler is alive (and still rational). Let's also assume that this individual has some money and encounters an entrepreneur who has water to sell. For the first glass of water, our traveler may be willing to pay a great deal of money because the utility derived from that first glass of water is very high. A second glass of water will also add utility, but a lesser amount than the first, so the traveler would be willing to pay less for this second glass of water since it adds less utility than the first. If you carry this example to its logical conclusion, the traveler would not be willing to pay anything for, say, the thirtieth glass because that person would be full, with no desire for more.

Note that the concept of utility requires a specified time period. If, for instance, the supplier of water were to leave in one hour, the amount of water our thirsty traveler would be willing to buy and drink would be quite different than if the supplier were to travel along with him for a day, a week, or more. And if our buyer could purchase canteens full to carry along with him, the amount purchased would also be quite different.

Were even these few conditions to change, we would be unable to determine what effect a glass of water has on utility, or satisfaction. The same problem would exist for all other goods, and economists might as well use a roulette wheel to determine the answers to economic questions. But *ceteris paribus* (all other things remaining unchanged) saves it for us. With all other things held constant, the effect of one variable on another is determinable.

The concept of utility, fundamental as it is to understanding demand, is just that—a theoretical concept. It gives us no more measurable a basis by which to determine the demand for a good. Neither can a physicist specify the comfort one would feel when the thermometer registers 70 degrees Fahrenheit.

If we could assign values to the traveler's units of utility, the problem would be much simpler. That person would buy more water until the value of the last glass of water bought was worth just what it cost. The next glassful would not be purchased because it would not be worth its cost.[1]

Another Example of Diminishing Marginal Utility. The law of diminishing utility can be made more explicit by assuming the following utility schedule for doughtnuts consumed by Tom.

---

[1] How much water to buy for the utility it can produce is identical to the producer's problem of using quantities of a valuable resource to produce something else of value, as will be discussed in the next chapter.

The first column in Table 3-1 shows Tom's consumption of doughnuts per day. The second column indicates the total amount of satisfaction measured in terms of some unit such as "utils" from consuming various amounts of doughnuts per day. For instance if Tom consumes two doughnuts per day his total utility is 11 utils. If he eats seven doughnuts in a day his total utility is 21 utils. Thus Tom's total utility curve for doughnuts rises and then levels off, as more doughnuts are consumed.

Column 3 shows added or *marginal* utility. Notice that Tom's added utility from consuming additional doughnuts decreases which is consistent with the law of diminishing marginal utility. Tom's marginal utility from consuming the first doughnut is six utils; from the fourth, three utils, and from the seventh, zero utils. In comparing Tom's total and marginal utility schedules for doughnuts, be aware of the fact that when marginal utility is positive, total utility is rising. When marginal utility is zero, total utility is constant. Also it is possible for Tom's marginal utility to be negative at higher levels of doughnut consumption. If that was the case, total utility would decrease. A negative marginal utility suggests that additional doughnuts are a "surplus" problem. He has eaten all his stomach can hold, and consuming more doughnuts would actually create disutility.

Table 3-1 Tom's Utility Schedule for Doughnuts

(1) Number per day	(2) Total utility	(3) Marginal utility
0	0	
		6
1	6	
		5
2	11	
		4
3	15	
		3
4	18	
		2
5	20	
		1
6	21	
		0
7	21	

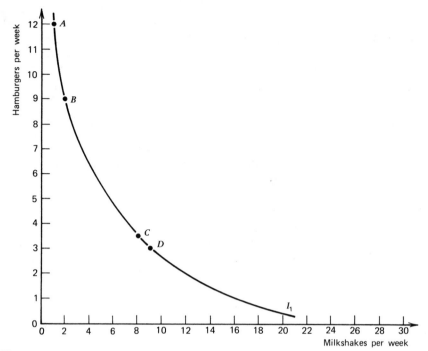

Figure 3-1. Susan's indifference curve.

Consumer Choice

The fact that people buy a certain combination of goods with their spendable money, and not some other combination, implies that the choice made was more satisfying to the consumer than some other allocation of those funds might have been.[2]

The theoretical basis of such choices can be demonstrated graphically as in Figure 3-1, where the problem is limited to choosing between two goods only. We measure units of one good along the horizontal axis and units of the other good along the vertical axis. Some generalizations about the amounts of utility derived from consuming different quantities and proportions of those goods can be made.

Indifference Curves. Consider a student—Susan—choosing between different combinations of hamburgers and milkshakes. Her food

[2]We assume that the consumer is rational and that the person maximizes the satisfaction to be obtained from his or her spendable income.

preferences are shown by the *indifference curve,* labeled I_1. That curving line is called an indifference curve because it shows all the combinations of those two goods that will give her the same amount of satisfaction or utility. All points *along* the indifference curve are equally satisfying; utility is constant at all points on that curve.

With many different combinations of hamburgers and milkshakes being able to produce identical amounts of utility, as indicated by the curve I_1, there can be no reason for preferring one combination over another. Thus we can say that Susan is indifferent regarding the combinations shown (12:1, 9:2, 3.5:8, and 3:9 hamburgers and milkshakes). Connecting those four identified points traces out the curve of constant utility. The indifference curve shows that 12 hamburgers and one milkshake (point *A*) give Susan the same satisfaction as three hamburgers and nine milkshakes (point *D*); the proportions indicated by points *B* and *C* also produce the same utility.

The shape of the indifference curve shows the willingness to substitute one good for another. At point *A*, our student has, relatively speaking, many hamburgers and few milkshakes. Because of diminishing marginal utility, the twelfth hamburger adds only a little utility; the second milkshake adds quite a bit. Consequently, Susan would be willing to exchange three hamburgers for another milkshake. But as we move downward on the indifference curve, the marginal utility of another milkshake is falling, while the marginal utility of another hamburger is rising. By the time we get to point *D*, we can see that Susan would be willing to give up the ninth milkshake in exchange for only one-half of a hamburger. Their values to her depend upon how much more utility she would get from consuming one more unit of either good, rather than on their prices. Between points *A* and *B* a milkshake is worth three hamburgers, or six times more valuable than between points *C* and *D* where a milkshake is worth only one-half of a hamburger.

As we move from point *A* to point *B*, compared with moving from point *C* to point *D*, we can see a change in the *rate* at which milkshakes will substitute for hamburgers, a characteristic called the *diminishing marginal rate of substitution.* We use the symbolism MRS_{mh} to mean the "marginal rate of substitution of milkshakes for hamburgers," and Δh and Δm as "change in hamburgers," and "change in milkshakes," respectively. Thus $MRS_{mh} = \Delta h / \Delta m$ shows the number of hamburgers that a milkshake will replace in Susan's weekly diet without changing her total satisfaction. The marginal rate of substitution is said to be diminishing because, as we move downward along I_1, each additional milkshake will replace fewer hamburgers than the previous one did.[3]

The shape of the indifference curve tells a great deal about Susan's preferences. For instance if the indifference curve is a right angle it means she would be unwilling to substitute one commodity for the other. She would purchase only one combination of goods, such as six hamburgers and four milkshakes. However if she perceives them to be good substitutes the indifference curve would be closer to a straight line. In this case she would be willing to interchange the goods at a nearly constant rate.

Indifference curves have three major characteristics. The first feature is that they are downward sloping to the right. This means that if a consumer gives up one commodity, the loss in satisfaction must be compensated for by additional units of the other commodity if utility is to remain constant along the indifference curve. The second characteristic is that indifference curves are convex to the origin. A requirement such as this is fulfilled if the marginal rate of substitution decreases as one moves along the indifference curve. If the indifference curve was not convex but concave (bending away from the origin) it would suggest that our consumer is getting equal satisfaction from giving up more and more of one commodity to obtain given amounts of another. This fact does not coincide with observed consumer behavior.

A third feature of indifference curves is that they can not intersect. Higher indifference curves are larger combinations of both goods and hence represent higher levels of satisfaction (Figure 3-2). Since we assume that the consumer is not satiated with goods, I_1, I_2, I_3 show progressively higher levels of satisfaction. Each consumer has an indifference map (family of indifference curves as demonstrated by Figure 3-2) showing that person's own tastes and preferences.

The Budget Line. What Susan can consume is determined by her money income. If she has $7.50 per week to spend on these two goods, and the price of hamburgers is $1.00 each and milkshakes

---

[3]Since utility along the indifference curve is constant, we may rewrite this relationship as $\Delta m \cdot MU_m = \Delta h \cdot MU_h$ where MU_m means the marginal utility per milkshake and MU_h the marginal utility per hamburger. Along I_l from point A to point B the units of change in hamburger times their MU must equal the units of change in milkshakes times their MU. The marginal rate of substitution is negative because the indifference curve slopes downward to the right. Ignoring sign, the equality $\Delta m \cdot MU_m = \Delta h \cdot MU_h$ can be rewritten as $\Delta h / \Delta m = MU_m / MU_h$. Thus we can note that the relative marginal utilities are the determinants of the rate at which two goods substitute for one another.

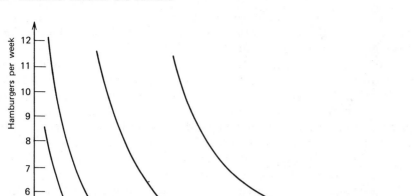

Figure 3-2. Susan's indifference map.

are $.50 each, then she could buy 7 ½ hamburgers ($7.50/$1) if her entire $7.50 budget were spent on hamburgers. If the total weekly income is spent on milkshakes, she could buy 15 ($7.50/$.50). It is also possible to buy other combinations of hamburgers and milkshakes with $7.50. You can see that if two-thirds of her income were spent on hamburgers and one-third on milkshakes, five hamburgers and five milkshakes could be purchased. These three possible combinations of $7.50 expenditures are shown in Figure 3-3. Connecting points *A, B,* and *C,* derives the *budget line* which shows all the possible combinations of hamburgers and milkshakes that the consumer can buy for $7.50. The slope of the budget line is a negative 7.5/15, or $-1/2$. Thus the slope of the budget line is equal to price of milkshakes (P_m) divided by the price of hamburgers (P_h), $-.50/1.00 = -1/2$.

Consumer Equilibrium. We now have both the consumer's preference system and the budget line. Putting them together permits an analysis of the combination of goods which will be purchased to maximize satisfaction or utility, and result in efficiency in consumption.

The rational consumer wants to get to the highest indifference

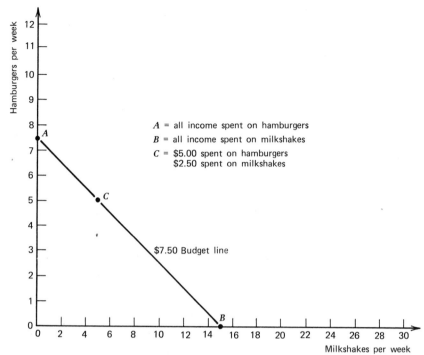

Figure 3-3. The consumer's budget line.

curve, given the budget constraint. From Figure 3-4, one can see that the optimal position of the consumer is at point B where the budget line is just tangent to indifference curve I_1. At that preferred point, the consumer is maximizing satisfaction (given $7.50 of income) by purchasing three hamburgers and nine milkshakes per week. This consumer would not be in equilibrium at point A or C, because by moving her purchases to point B, she could consume on indifference curve I_1 rather than attain less satisfaction on I_0. This consumer cannot consume at point D on I_2, because she does not have the income to reach that utility level.

The slope of the indifference curve (MRS) is equal to the ratio of the marginal utility of milkshakes to the marginal utility of hamburgers. Also we know that the slope of the budget line is equal to P_m/P_h. Hence the point of consumer equilibrium at point B is the same as saying that in equilibrium

$$MU_m/MU_h = P_m/P_h^4$$

[4] In this form, the equation shows that the rate at which these goods substitute *in consumption* (MU_m/MU_h) is identical to their rate of substitution *in the market* (P_m/P_h), a condition for equilibrium.

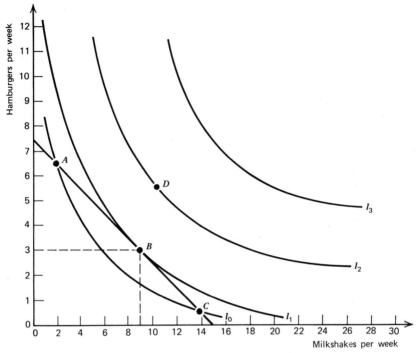

Figure 3-4. Consumer equilibrium in consumption.

Rearranging this equation, we have:

$$MU_m/P_m = MU_h/P_h$$

In this form one can see that this consumer's optimum is where the marginal utility from each good purchased is proportional to its price. Another way of stating the same condition is to say that the consumer is in equilibrium when the marginal utility per dollar spent on milkshakes is equal to the marginal utility per dollar spent on hamburgers. This condition must hold for all goods purchased for the consumer to be in equilibrium.

The Effect of Price Changes. Let us return to our example with Susan and her fixed income of $7.50 per week, with the price of hamburgers at $1.00 each and the price of a milkshake at $.50. Now let's assume the price of a milkshake drops to $.25. We can plot a new budget line representing the same amount of money income ($7.50). These two budget lines are shown in Figure 3-5.

As was mentioned previously, Susan will be in equilibrium consuming at the point where the budget line is tangent to the highest

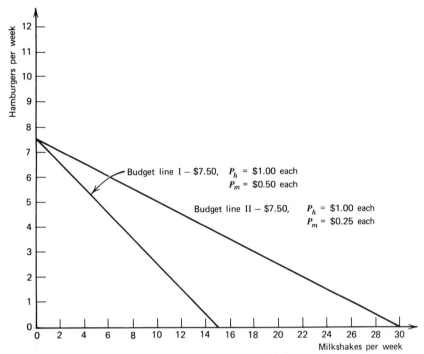

Figure 3-5.   A rotation of the budget line due to a milkshake price decrease.

possible indifference curve. This can be illustrated by adding Susan's indifference map to Figure 3-5, resulting in Figure 3-6. This figure shows that before the price of milkshakes dropped from $.50 to $.25 she was purchasing nine milkshakes per week. After the price of milkshakes fell to $.25 Susan is in equilibrium purchasing 15 milkshakes. She buys more milkshakes when the price decreases. The increase in the quantity of milkshakes purchased is due to the *substitution effect* and *income effect* of the price change. The substitution effect occurs when the price of milkshakes declines relative to hamburgers. Susan will substitute milkshakes for hamburgers because the price of milkshakes has fallen. When the price of milkshakes fell, this increased Susan's real income. This is called the income effect. The real income effect of a decline in the price of milkshakes means that Susan is now able to buy more of either or both of these goods even though her money income has not changed.

The Demand Curve.   The effect of a price change of a commodity, *cet. par.*, normally is to change the quantity demanded in the opposite

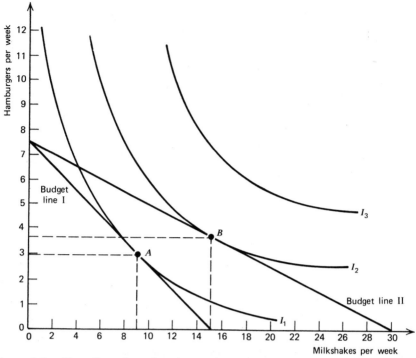

Figure 3-6. The effect of a price change for milkshakes.

direction. A *demand curve* shows the quantities of a good that consumers will buy at different prices for that good at a point in time, everything else unchanged.

We can derive two points on Susan's demand curve for milkshakes from Figure 3-6. Budget line I shows a price of milkshakes of $.50 and of nine milkshakes purchased (point *A*). Budget line II shows the price of milkshakes at $.25 with about 15 milkshakes purchased (point *B*). These points are plotted in Figure 3-7, making up two points on Susan's demand curve for milkshakes. Other points on the demand curve could be derived by varying the price of milkshakes (as in Figure 3-6) and deriving an equilibrium quantity purchased at each price.

The price of an item must fall for the consumer to be willing to purchase more of it, because each additional unit consumed adds less utility than the previous one yielded. Since the utility derived from additional units of a good declines, those additional units are worth less to the consumer, resulting in the downward slope of the demand curve.

The market demand curve for milkshakes is the horizontal

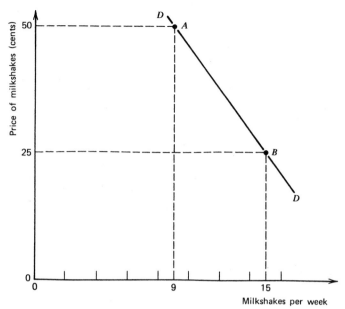

Figure 3-7. Individual demand curve for milkshakes.

summation of all individual demand curves for that good. The market demand curve is defined as the quantities of a commodity all consumers are willing to purchase at different prices, in a given period of time, holding all other factors constant.

An example of adding two individual demand curves for milkshakes to obtain the market demand curve for milkshakes is shown in Figure 3-8.

At a price for milkshakes of $.50 each, Susan purchases nine shakes; Joe buys none. Thus, one point on the market demand curve is represented by Susan's purchase of nine milkshakes at $.50. At $.25 per shake, Joe buys 10 and Susan buys 15 milkshakes. Thus, another point on the market demand curve at $.25 is a total of 25 milkshakes taken by the two consumers. Additional points are derived in a like manner.

Price Elasticity of Demand. The downward sloping demand curve gives rise to another phenomenon of considerable importance—a price-quantity relationship referred to as the "price elasticity of demand." Price elasticity of demand measures the responsiveness of quantity demanded to a change in price, *cet. par.*

Price elasticity of demand is computed as the percentage change in quantity demanded divided by the percentage change in price. A simple method to derive the price elasticity of demand over a small

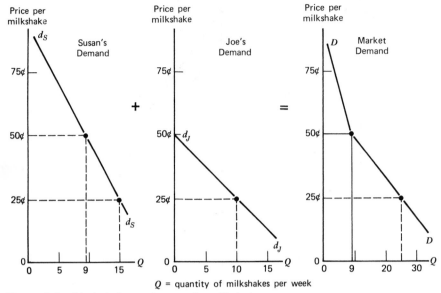

Figure 3-8. Market demand curve for milkshakes.

segment of the demand curve may be expressed by the following formula:[5]

$$E_d = \frac{(Q_1 - Q_2)/(Q_1 + Q_2)}{(P_1 - P_2)/(P_1 + P_2)}$$

The percentage of change in quantity demanded is represented by $(Q_1 - Q_2) \div (Q_1 + Q_2)$, and the percentage of change in price by $(P_1 - P_2) \div (P_1 + P_2)$.

To illustrate the use of this method in calculating elasticity, refer to Figure 3-9, where $Q_1 = 4$ billion bushels, $Q_2 = 5$ billion bushels. $P_1 = \$2.00$ per bushel. and $P_2 = \$1.25$ per bushel. By substituting these values into the formula,

$$E_d = \frac{\dfrac{4-5}{4+5}}{\dfrac{2.00 - 1.25}{2.00 + 1.25}} = \frac{-\dfrac{1}{9}}{\dfrac{.75}{3.25}} = -\frac{1}{9} \cdot \frac{3.25}{.75} = -.48$$

[5]This formula measures price elasticity between two points on the demand curve, and is called "arc" elasticity. Differential calculus would permit the determination of price elasticity at a specific point on the demand curve, called "point" elasticity of demand.

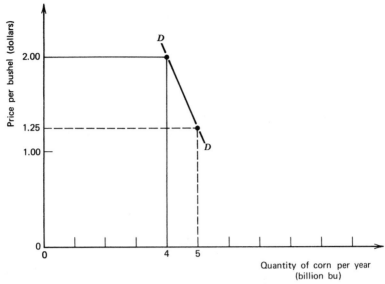

Figure 3-9.   An inelastic segment of a demand curve.

the price elasticity is computed to be −.48, or inelastic.[6] When the coefficient is less than one (ignoring the negative sign), demand is said to be inelastic, and when elasticity is greater than one (ignoring the negative sign), demand is elastic. When price elasticity equals one, demand is said to be of unitary elasticity.

If demand is *inelastic,* the quantity demanded changes relatively little compared to the change in price. A decrease of 75 cents in corn price, from $2.00 to $1.25 as shown in Figure 3-9, increases the quantity demanded from four billion bushels to five billion bushels. In spite of the apparently large increase in corn purchases, total expenditures still drop from $8 billion to $6.25 billion because of the inelastic demand. Were the price of corn to increase, on the other hand, total expenditures would increase because of the relative unresponsiveness of quantity demanded to these price changes.

Price elasticity of demand is called *elastic* when the change in quantity demanded is large relative to the change in price, as shown in Figure 3-10. At a price of 80 cents per dozen eggs, a consumer may be willing and able to purchase 20 dozen eggs per year for a total expenditure of $16.00. With a drop in the price of eggs to 70 cents per dozen, our consumer can buy 40 dozen eggs for an expenditure of $28.00.

[6]Since the demand curve slopes downward to the right, the coefficient of price elasticity will always be negative.

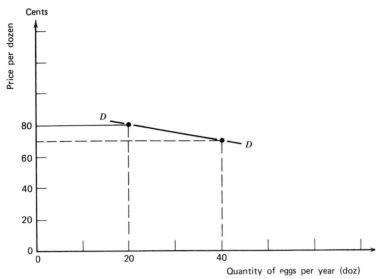

Figure 3-10. An elastic segment of a demand curve.

Likewise, if the price of eggs were to increase rather than decrease, total expenditures would fall because of the responsiveness of quantity demanded to price changes as indicated by the elasticity coefficient of -5.0.

Price elasticity of demand is termed *unitary* when the percentage changes in price and quantity demanded are the same. With unitary elasticity of demand, total expenditures do not change as price changes. This is because changes in quantity bought just offset the expenditures that would be gained (or lost) as the price increases (or decreases).

Elasticities are usually measured for only small price movements along a demand curve, with different elasticities at each point along any straight line demand curve. Demand is generally more elastic at higher prices and more inelastic at lower prices.

Price elasticities of demand for farm commodities vary widely. For example, the price elasticity of demand at the farm level for cattle is $-.68$; for calves -1.08; for eggs $-.23$; for vegetables $-.10$; and for wheat $-.03$.[7]

Factors that Influence Demand Elasticities.   Three primary factors influence the elasticity of demand:

[7]George E. Brandow, *Interrelationships Among Demands for Farm Products and Implications for Controls of Market Supply.* University Park, Pa.: Agricultural Experiment Station Bulletin 680, 1961.

1. whether good substitutes for the product are available;
2. whether or not there are many alternative uses for a product; and
3. whether the product is an important expenditure in a consumer's total budget.

The elasticity of demand for a product will tend to be greater the more substitutes that are available, the wider the range of uses of the product, and the more important the product is in the consumer's budget.

Most raw agricultural products have inelastic demands because there are few good substitute products for them. For example, different wheat varieties are used to make flour for bread, rolls, cakes, noodles, macaroni, and spaghetti. Some of these products could be made from flours ground from rye, corn, or barley, but in many cases the quality of such products is poor. Because of the poor substitutability of other flours for wheat flour, the price of wheat flour can be decreased or increased, prices of substitute flour unchanged, without causing consumers to shift rapidly to or from the use of wheat flour.

The greater the number of alternative uses for a commodity, the greater is its price elasticity. The demand for ground beef is relatively elastic because it can be used for such things as hamburgers, as a steak, mixed with extenders such as soybeans, or as an ingredient in a casserole. If the price of hamburger changes, large variations can occur in the quantity purchased.

The demand for automobiles, homes, furniture, television, etc., is elastic because they are large expenditure items and take a large portion of the family budget. When expenditures are large it tends to make consumers budget more carefully and shop for the best deal, taking into account the quality and price of substitute products. Therefore, a small change in price may be noticed by many consumers, causing a large change in the quantity taken.

So far, the discussion has been limited to a single demand curve and movements along that curve. Any movement along a given demand curve indicates a "change in quantity demanded" in response to a change in price. When the entire demand curve shifts for some reason, it is termed a "change or shift in demand."

Changes in Demand. A change in demand means that at any given price a larger or smaller quantity will be demanded. In Figure 3-11, the demand for butter has increased as indicated by the shift from demand schedule *DD* to demand schedule *D'D'*. Notice that along the original demand curve *DD*, at a price of 80 cents per pound for butter, consumers purchased 10 pounds per week. After the demand curve shifted to demand curve *D'D'*, consumers purchased

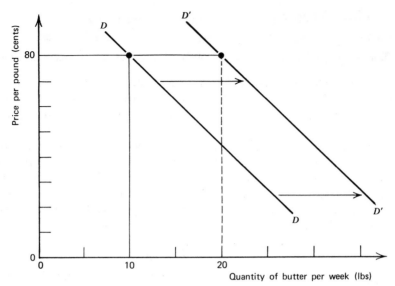

Figure 3-11. An increase in demand for butter.

20 pounds rather than 10 pounds per week even though the price remained unchanged at 80 cents per pound. Thus, when the demand increases, more units of a product will be sold at each price (or what amounts to the same thing, paying a higher price for the same quantity).

Conversely, if demand decreases, or shifts to the left, fewer units of a product will be demanded at each price as shown in Figure 3-12. If consumers originally were purchasing 10 pounds per week at 80 cents per pound, a decrease in demand to $D'D'$ causes them to buy only five pounds per week at that same price. Again note that consumers would purchase 10 pounds, but only at a lower price.

Whenever a demand curve is drawn it is assumed that many factors are held constant. When any of these factors change a shift in the demand curve results. These factors generally include changes in consumer income, population, tastes and preferences, related product prices, and peoples' expectations.

As disposable incomes increase, consumers have more money to spend on goods and services, resulting in increased demand for these items such as illustrated in Figure 3-11. A decrease in incomes due to such things as increased unemployment will shift the demand curve for most consumers to the left, as in Figure 3-12.

As the number of people increases, more housing, food, clothing, and services are needed. Therefore, as population grows so does the demand for these items (Figure 3-11). When population

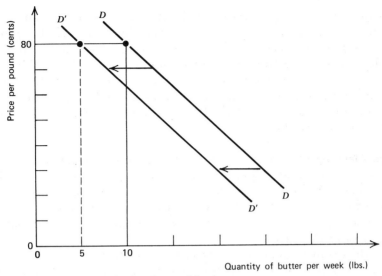

Figure 3-12. A decrease in the demand for butter.

drops in an area, the demand for these same items decreases, Figure 3-12.

Related products are classified as being *substitutes* or *complements*. The effect of relative product price changes may be seen, using feedgrains as an example. Barley and corn are substitute feedgrains. If an increase in the price of barley occurs for some reason, the quantity of barley consumed will decrease and the demand for corn will increase as consumers of barley shift to the relatively cheaper feedgrain.

If two products are used together such as bread and butter, we call these products complements. An increase in the price of bread will reduce the quantity of bread demanded and consequently reduce the demand for butter since less butter is used as bread consumption falls.

Tastes and preferences change slowly. Many of our tastes are developed as a result of our cultural environment, and may change over time because of experiences and education. Advertising and promotional efforts of business firms are an attempt to increase the demand for their products, and to make the demand curve more inelastic by developing brand loyalties. As people acquire less of a taste for a product, its demand curve will shift to the left. An example is the declining per capita consumption of fresh potatoes. At the same time, however, the per capita consumption of frozen potatoes is increasing.

Consumer expectations are difficult to handle in economics, but they play a significant role in the market behavior. If the general price level is increasing and is expected to continue to increase, people will increase their current demand for products. They will buy more now in the expectation that prices will rise further. This is especially true during periods of rapid inflation. On the other hand, if consumers expect prices to drop, they may postpone purchases until some future date.

Income Elasticity of Demand. The relationship between changes in consumer income and quantity of an item purchased is called an Engel curve. As income increases more or less of a commodity may be bought. A normal good is one in which consumers buy more of it as income increases. An inferior good is one that consumers buy less of as income increases.

A different Engel curve exists for each commodity and for each individual. Let's use food as an illustration. The quantity of food purchased increases as income rises, but at a decreasing rate. Thus, the proportion of income spent for food decreases as income increases (Figure 3-13). Other items such as clothing can be characterized by an Engel curve represented in Figure 3-14. The flattening curve shows that the quantity of clothing purchased changes substantially as money income rises.

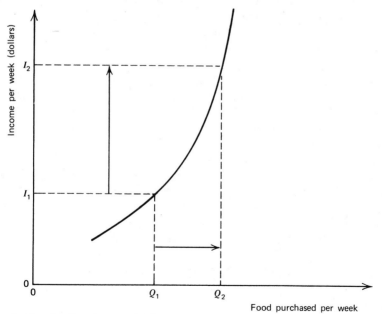

Figure 3-13. An Engel curve for food.

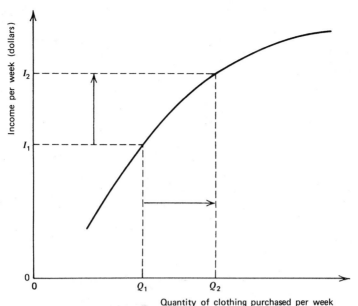

Figure 3-14. An Engel curve for clothing.

Income elasticity of demand is defined as a measure of the responsiveness of quantity of a good purchased with changes in income, holding all other factors constant. It can be expressed as the percentage change in quantity bought divided by the percentage change in income at any point along an Engel curve. When the income change is small a rough estimate of the income elasticity of demand can be made using the following arc income elasticity formula:

$$E_I = \frac{(Q_1 - Q_2)/(Q_1 + Q_2)}{(I_1 - I_2)/(I_1 + I_2)}$$

The arc income elasticity coefficient can be calculated from the Engel's function shown in Figure 3-15 over segment *AB*.

$$E_I = \frac{(10 - 30)/(10 + 30)}{(200 - 400)/(200 + 400)} = \frac{20/40}{200/600} = 2/4 \cdot 6/2 = 1.5$$

The income elasticity coefficient of steak is 1.5, meaning that a one percent increase in income results in a 1.5 percent increase in the quantity of steak purchased. Analyses such as income elasticity of demand are important in determining the impact of income changes on the purchases of farm food items. "The income elasticity

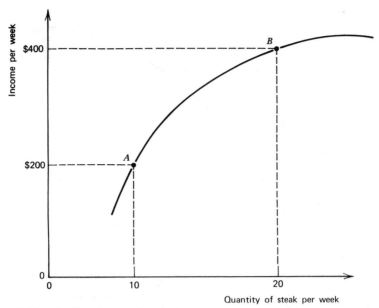

Figure 3-15. An Engel curve for steak.

for food in the aggregate, as well as for many individual food products, is thought to decrease as incomes increase."[8] Therefore income
elasticities will usually change over various income levels and can be
positive or negative. Positive income elasticities indicate normal
goods and negative income elasticities indicate inferior goods.

Cross Elasticity of Demand.   Cross price elasticity of demand is another
elasticity concept similar to price and income elasticities of demand.
Cross price elasticity is a measure of the responsiveness of the quantity demanded of good X to a change in the price of good Y, holding
all other factors constant.

Arc cross price elasticity of demand for commodity X with respect to a small change in the price of commodity Y can be illustrated with the following algebraic expression:

$$E_{xy} = \frac{(Q_{x_1} - Q_{x_2})/(Q_{x_1} + Q_{x_2})}{(P_{y_1} - P_{y_2})/(P_{y_1} + P_{y_2})}$$

If the cross elasticity coefficient from the above calculated equation is positive, the two commodities (X and Y) are called substitutes.

[8]William G. Tomek, and Kenneth L. Robinson, *Agricultural Product Prices.* Ithaca, N.Y.: Cornell
University Press, 1972, p. 31.

An example of substitute commodities are peanut and soybean oil. An increase in the price of soybean oil will decrease its quantity demanded and increase the demand and price of peanut oil. Therefore the increase in price of soybean oil and the increase in consumption of peanut oil are both positive making E_{xy} positive.

Commodities which have negative cross elasticities of demand are classified as being complementary commodities. Bread and butter provide an everyday illustration. If the price of butter increases the quantity of butter demanded decreases and the demand for bread would also decrease. Hence, as the price of butter increased the consumption of bread would decrease giving a negative sign to the cross price elasticity between these two complementary commodities.

The cross price elasticity of pork with respect to the price of beef is around +.15. The interpretation of this coefficient is that the quantity of pork purchased will increase .15 percent for each one percent increase in the price of beef, *cet. par.*

Commodities with high cross elasticities are very close substitute commodities, whereas coefficients close to zero show commodities that are unrelated. High negative coefficients represent strong complementary commodities.

Summary

Utility or satisfaction that a consumer receives from consuming goods and services is partly subjective in nature. We assume that human wants are insatiable. However, consumer's incomes are limited. Therefore, the consumer is attempting to purchase goods and services that will maximize satisfaction given that person's limited money income. Once the consumer is in equilibrium, it is possible to determine the quantities of a good purchased. By changing the prices of a good, and hence the consumer's budget constraint, additional price-quantity relationships can be found (review Figure 3-6). This price-quantity data can be plotted to derive the individual's demand curve for this product.

Individual demand curves for a product are added horizontally to obtain the market demand curve for a product.

Price elasticity of demand is a measure of the responsiveness of quantity demanded to a change in price, *cet. par.* It is calculated over a small segment of a given demand curve. When the elasticity coefficient is less than one in absolute value, demand is inelastic; when greater than one in absolute value, demand is elastic; and when price elasticity is equal to one, demand is unitary.

If demand for a product is inelastic, price and consumer expenditures vary directly. An increase in price increases consumer spending. A decrease in price decreases consumer expenditures on the product. On the other hand, if demand is elastic, price and consumer expenditures on the product vary inversely.

Income elasticity of demand is a measure of the responsiveness of quantity of a good purchased to changes in income.

How products are related can be determined by the cross price elasticity of demand. Commodities with negative cross elasticities are complementary. Commodities with positive cross elasticities of demand are substitutes.

Chapter Highlights

1. Consumers derive utility or satisfaction from the consumption of goods and services.
2. The concept of diminishing marginal utility is based on observations of consumers' market behavior. It states that as an individual consumes additional units of a commodity the amount of utility attained from each additional unit decreases, other things remaining equal.
3. An indifference curve shows all the different combinations of two goods that will give a consumer the same amount of satisfaction or utility.
4. The marginal rate of substitution is the rate at which one good can be substituted for another without changing the consumer's total utility.
5. Goods substitute for one another at a diminishing marginal rate because of diminishing marginal utility for each; it takes progressively more of one good to replace the satisfaction lost as successive increments of the other good are given up.
6. The budget line shows all the combinations of two goods that the consumer can buy with a given amount of money.
7. The consumer is at an equilibrium when an additional dollar spent on each good would return the same marginal utility per dollar, or $MU_a/P_a = MU_b/P_b$.
8. A change in relative prices will change the slope of the budget line and change the proportion of goods bought at equilibrium for the consumer.
9. Each tangency point between the budget line and an indifference curve identifies a point along the demand curve.
10. A demand curve is a schedule that shows, *cet. par.*, how many units of a good the consumer will buy at different prices for that good.
11. The market demand curve for a good is the horizontal summation of the demand curves of all individuals in the market for that good.
12. An individual's downward sloping demand curve for a commodity is caused by diminishing marginal utility.
13. A movement along a given demand curve is a change in quantity demanded.
14. Price elasticity of demand is a measure of the responsiveness of quantity demanded to a specific change in price.
15. The elasticity of a given demand curve for a product will depend on whether

or not good substitutes are available for that product, alternative uses for the product, and the importance of the product in the consumer's budget.

16. A change in demand is a shift in the entire demand schedule.
17. Factors that will shift the demand curve are changes in consumer incomes, population, tastes and preferences, related product prices, and expectations.
18. Income elasticity of demand is a measure of the responsiveness of quantity purchased of a good to changes in income, *cet. par.*
19. Cross elasticity of demand is a measure of the responsiveness of the quantity of one commodity to a change in price of another, *cet. par.*
20. Substitute commodities have positive cross elasticities of demand.
21. Complementary commodities have negative cross elasticity of demand.

Review Questions

1. Define utility. Is temperature measurable? Is utility measurable?
2. Indifference curves represent the tastes and preferences of a consumer. Can you add up indifference curves to show the tastes and preferences of a nation? Why, or why not?
3. Demand curves normally slope downward and to the right. Can you think of abnormal demand curves that have different slopes?
4. Given your knowledge of elasticity, why would legislators continue to raise the tax on products such as cigarettes and beer?
5. What is the difference between a change in demand and a change in quantity demanded?
6. Explain the factors that would shift a given demand curve.
7. Explain the meaning of a cross elasticity coefficient between bread and butter of -1.8.

Suggested Readings

1. Awh, Robert Y. *Microeconomics: Theory and Applications.* Santa Barbara, Calif.: John Wiley and Sons, Inc., 1976, Chapter 6.
2. Goodwin, John W. *Agricultural Economics.* Reston, Va.: Reston Publishing Company, 1977, Chapter 12.
3. Heyne, Paul T. *The Economic Way of Thinking.* Chicago: Science Research Associates, Inc., 1973, Chapters 2 and 3.
4. Leftwich, Richard H. *The Price System and Resource Allocation,* 6th ed. Hinsdale, Ill.: The Dryden Press, Inc., 1976, Chapters 5 and 6.
5. Samuelson, Paul A. *Economics,* 8th ed. New York: McGraw-Hill Book Company, 1970, Chapter 22.

4

PRODUCER DECISION-MAKING: SINGLE-VARIABLE INPUT FUNCTIONS

PRODUCER DECISION-MAKING: SINGLE-VARIABLE INPUT FUNCTIONS

Since the ultimate objective of all economic activity is the satisfaction of human wants, any activity or process that satisfies a human desire (either directly or indirectly, presently or in the future) can be considered production. Viewed in this light, production is a process by which resources are transformed into products or services that are usable by consumers.[1]

Producers face a threefold decision problem: (1) what to produce; (2) how much to produce; and (3) how to produce. The subject matter of this chapter relates most directly to the producer's second question. But we concentrate on its other side by considering what happens when the quantity of a resource used in production is changed. Our approach here is to simplify the rate of resource use problem by directing our attention to the input-output relationship between a single resource and its product.

Production may be a many-staged series of products, with the output from one process or stage being used as an input in a following stage until it reaches the form desired for final consumption. Such complexity is the rule rather than the exception. This may be made clear by recognizing the many processes carried on before a slice of bread can find its way to your dinner table.

The farmer uses a wide variety of resources as raw materials to produce the wheat which is an input for the miller, whose product is an input to the baker, whose product is an input for the retail grocer, whose product is the consumable good, bread, an input in the act of consumption, valued for the utility or satisfaction it yields to you the final consumer. And this description has not bothered to identify the roles played by brokers and dealers, wholesalers, the transportation and financial industries, and many others involved in transferring products from one stage to another all along the route from the farmer to the final consumer.

It was stated earlier that scarcity creates the need to economize. Because there are too few resources to produce enough goods and

[1]These are also called "inputs" or "factors of production."

services to satisfy all of our wants, we must economize on our resource commitments by choosing which of many alternative uses and combinations of resources will do the best job for us in meeting our wants.

Economists have defined a resource as a factor that can be used to produce a product which can satisfy a human want or desire. Since the number and variety of resources, and the complexity of resource interrelationships defies mental comprehension, we are forced to classify those resources and their relationships into generalized groupings.[2]

In the simplified example just mentioned of how resource services get transformed into consumable goods and services, each stage of production used a mixture of resources. At each step along the way decisions were made about which resources to use, quantities of each, and how much of the product to produce. At this point, we are unable to determine just how much each resource has contributed to the output and to the costs of obtaining the output. We need to establish the cause-effect relationships between the resources used and their product. This is most clearly accomplished by grouping resources on the basis of similarities in their special characteristics.

Physical Relationships

To make resource and product relationships as explicit and clear as possible, let's be a little extra careful for the moment. We can identify four basic categories of resources—land, labor, capital, and management[3]—each of which must be used in some combination with the other three before any product can be produced.

In the *land* group we put everything you ordinarily see in viewing the earth's surface. But there's more than this to our economic concept of land. We include not just the soil itself, but all of its physical characteristics and all of the natural environment that may influence the ability of land to yield a product.

In spite of the fact that we frequently find labor and manage-

[2]Because the universe is infinitely complex, and the human mind is finite, there is no way to study and understand the real world other than by classifying objects and things into groups that exhibit certain similarities. This is an abstraction from reality that is fundamental to all sciences, not only to economics. By abstracting we reduce the real world problems to manageable proportions, making possible meaningful predictions—the basic goal of all science.

For a more rigorous treatment of the scientific method, see, for example, George A. Stigler, *The Theory of Price,* New York: The Macmillan Co., 1946.

[3]This grouping accords with the view of resource earnings held by firm operators, with the payment to *land* called "rent," the earnings of *labor* its "wage," the earnings of *capital* its "interest," and rewards to *management* being "profit."

ment in one and the same person, particularly in the single proprietor firm, we will reserve for *labor* the strictly physical act of performing a task; and for *management* the sole responsibility of decision-making. Decision-making includes the entrepreneurial functions of risk bearing, organizing resources into productive sets, deciding on which resources to use, their forms, and when and how much of each will be used in production.

In the one remaining group, *capital,* we will toss every man-made thing that can be used to aid or enhance production. Capital is inclusive of such physical things as buildings, machinery, brood stock, seed, equipment and tools, physically improved resources (land clearing, drainage and leveling, for example) that are made more productive as a consequence of that improvement, and any action by which current consumption of production is deferred so as to make resources more productive in the future.[4]

Common observation tells us that different quantities and combinations of these four resources will produce different amounts of the product. Despite their versatility, some resources are totally incapable of producing certain things: given present technology, we don't find cotton being produced on the polar ice caps (land), nor would we expect a cement mixer (capital) to be of much use in polishing magnifying glass lenses. Within limits, however, most resources can be used to produce a variety of products and, in addition, many resources can be substituted for one another in production.

These characteristics, of relationships between resources and their products and between the resources themselves, are easily verified. That resources are productive can be demonstrated by changing the quantity of a resource used and observing that the quantity of product also changes. Further, whenever one resource is reduced in quantity and an increase in another resource prevents a decrease

[4]Not all economists agree with such a rigid specification of types or classes of resources as this. Some will go only so far as a three-way classification (land, labor, and capital).

The further we go in attempting to define specific attributes of individual resource categories, the more aware we must become of how one resource characteristic overlaps another. How, for instance, can we separate the original and indestructible gift of nature (land) from the improvements (capital) that have been made to the land resource over time by the succession of those who have managed and made use of it? The distinction between land and capital, in that resource, is made less useful, for some purposes, by the fact that the relative contribution of capital has been increasing through time. Similarly, the distinction between labor and management appears a bit artificial—even insulting to labor, one of the most important resources in any economy. Even in the simple act of digging a ditch, labor really is a combination of these two resource services, performing the physical work while also giving thought to where next to put the shovel point, how deeply, etc. No special inference is intended here, we wish only to separate as clearly as possible the basic functions of each resource type so that later identification of resource relationships may be more easily understood.

in the quantity of output, these two resources are substitutes for one another. These properties are basic to the theory of production and the economic decisions required as a consequence.

What this says is that output results from the particular set of resources used in some "functional" way. We call this the *production function*.[5] We can represent the relationship symbolically as

$$Y = f(X_1, X_2, X_3 \cdot \cdot \cdot X_n)$$

where Y stands for the physical quantity of product, or output, the symbolism $f(\ )$ means "results from," "depends on," or "is a function of," and the X's identify the different resources (inputs) used to produce that Y, where X_n refers to the last different input in the production function.

As we increase the amounts of the resources $X_1 \cdot \cdot \cdot X_n$, we find two general choices in their proportions, leading to two different results. Either we increase them in the same proportion[6] and experience one kind of production response, or we change the resource proportions and get a completely different response.

Constant Returns.   If we consider increasing all inputs in a constant ratio, we could just as well restate the function as $Y = f(X)$. Thus if one unit of this input is composed of, say, 100 acres of land, one year of labor, $5000 of capital, and one month of management time, then two units must be *exactly* twice as much of these *identical* resources, three units being three times as much, etc. And if one unit of this input X yields 100 units of Y, then two units of input X can yield nothing other than 200 units of Y, three units of X will produce 300 units of Y, etc., resulting in a constant relationship between X and Y, or *constant returns*.[7] Figure 4-1A shows this relationship graphically,

---

[5]Much like demand and supply curves, the production function is also a "schedule"—it shows how much output will be produced by a specific set of resources in a given period of time and state of the arts (or technology). See C. E. Ferguson, *Microeconomic Theory,* rev. ed., Homewood, Ill.: Richard D. Irwin, Inc., 1969, p. 116.

[6]If we don't do this, we can't even meet the implicit assumptions of graphics.

[7]Don't get trapped by "loose" thinking here. Each unit of our composite input X is an exact duplicate (in *every* way) of every other unit of that resource. For instance, the $5,000 capital component cannot be machine services in the first unit of X, fertilizer in the second, different types of seed in the third, pesticides or herbicides in the fourth. The land part of one unit of X cannot be "Grade A" land, for instance, with that in another unit being of a different quality, etc.

At this level of abstraction, we haven't even the liberty of saying "But if you continue doubling both X and Y you must eventually run out of space, if nothing else." Our definition of land includes the totality of the natural environment, including space which cannot be conceived of as being finite and limiting as land is being increased. Thus depleting land space would set up a different situation in which our resource proportions are being changed, failing thereby to fulfill our requirement that resource proportions are not changed.

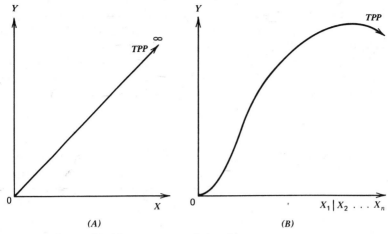

Figure 4-1. Generalized input-output relationships.

with the line of relationship (or function) labeled *TPP*, meaning "total physical product."[8] The relationship between the resource and its product is also called a "production function."

Now consider the other, more realistic choice open to us. As a producing firm changes the quantity of its output, it will change one or more of the resources, but it is not very likely that the firm will (or even can) change all of them. If a farmer decides to increase the output of a particular crop or livestock product, he may increase the amount of labor used, acres of land devoted to that product, fertilizers, machinery, or some combination of these but not all of the resources. Total land acres, buildings, or major machines, among other resources would not necessarily be changed. We then have some inputs that are *variable* inputs, and others that are held constant, or *fixed*.

Diminishing Returns. In the first instance, with everything varied and resource proportions constant, we are forced to conclude that the only result obtainable is a constant ratio of input to output. Here, because we are changing resource proportions, another natural phenomenon that we cannot escape becomes obvious. We cannot avoid a *changing* input-output relationship that seems so absolute

---

[8]We use the label *TPP* to emphasize the fact that, at this point, we are dealing only with physical relationships, and not values. Further, we draw *TPP* as a continuous (smooth) curve by assuming that the input *X* is divisible into as small an increment as desired. This may seem a bit unreasonable at first, but consider the resource labor. One eight-hour day may be regarded as a unit of labor, but that doesn't prevent the use of only one hour if that small an amount is desired. All other resource units, or their services, can be regarded as similarly divisible.

economists call it a law, a consequence only of changing input proportions. This relationship can be represented by the function

$$Y = f(X_1 | X_2, X_3 \cdot \cdot \cdot X_n)$$

where the vertical bar is used to indicate that the inputs to its left are *variable*, and those to the right of the vertical bar are held constant or *fixed*. This function is demonstrated graphically in Figure 4-1B, with the horizontal axis label indicating the general function.

The shape of the total product curve tells us what happens when we change the input proportions, making clear the physical basis of the *law of diminishing returns*[9]—the producer's exact counterpart of diminishing marginal utility in consumption. Our law states that as successive amounts of a variable input are combined with a fixed input in a production process, the total product will increase, reach a maximum, and eventually decline.

Let's use a hypothetical example to demonstrate this important principle. Assume a firm producing the product Y, using a resource X_1 that is variable, plus another set of resources $X_2 \cdot \cdot \cdot X_n$, all of which are held constant. Our production function then is $Y = f(X_1 | X_2 \cdot \cdot \cdot X_n)$, with the data given in Table 4-1, and plotted in Figure 4-2.

Given rigid adherence to the specific requirements of the law of diminishing returns, we can consider our data as typical of real world physical resource and product relationships. Plotting these data will result in a function that exhibits the characteristics stated in the law of diminishing returns.[10]

Marginal Physical Product. Beginning with no X_1 used, as we add successive increments of the variable input, its physical productivity is low at first because there is too little of the variable input relative to the fixed inputs.[11] Consequently, as we use greater amounts of X_1,

[9]Also referred to, with possibly a bit more clarity, as the "law of variable proportions," or "proportionality," strongly implying that changes in the shape of the *TPP* curve are the result of changes in the proportions between the resources used to produce that product.

[10]You might engage in an interesting bit of futility by trying to think of some real life situation where the law of diminishing returns proves to be wrong, but don't forget its strict, limiting requirements. And if hypothetical data don't "turn you on," a good exercise would then be to try to find some examples out of the wealth of production data available that meet the necessary conditions of the law. Facts dealing with the application of fertilizer on growing crops, of irrigation water use, of varying the amount of labor used to produce a variety of agricultural commodities, etc., should make the principle clear.

[11]There are few land-using examples in agriculture where the total product curve will actually begin at zero output when none of the variable input is present, because past management practices, resource substitutability, and the nature of the soil resource itself cause some of the varied input already to be in the soil. Agronomic experiments therefore make use of check plots with zero X_1, measuring "yield over check" to adjust for this.

Table 4-1 Hypothetical Data from the Function
$Y = f(X_1|X_2 \cdots X_n)$

(1) Variable input (X₁)	(2) Total physical product (TPP)	(3) Average physical product (APP)	(4) Marginal physical product (MPP)
0	0	0	
			7.5
10	75	7.5	
			17.0
20	245	12.3	
			19.0
30	435	14.5	
			12.5
40	560	14.0	
			8.8
50	648	13.0	
			6.2
60	710	11.8	
			4.3
70	753	10.8	
			2.9
80	782	9.8	
			1.8
90	800	8.9	
			1.0
100	810	8.1	
			−0.2
110	808	7.3	

we should expect its productivity to increase causing the total product curve to bend upward. In this part of the function, total product is increasing at an increasing rate, as the data in Table 4-1 show.

At some point along the curve,[12] *TPP* will begin bending away

[12]The point of steepest slope on the *TPP* curve (where *TPP* stops increasing at an increasing rate and begins increasing at a decreasing rate) is called the "inflection point"—labeled *A* in Figure 4-2.

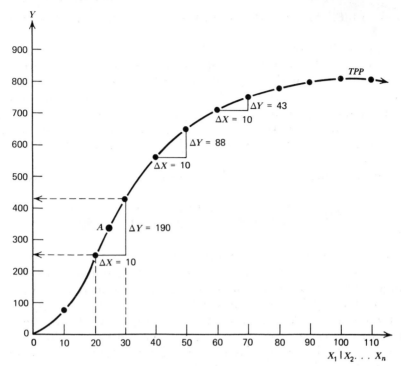

Figure 4-2. The total physical product curve.

from the Y-axis—increasing at a decreasing rate—because the variable resource has become more plentiful in relation to the fixed factors, and its productivity is relatively high.[13] Continued additions of X_1 will cause it to become excessive relative to the fixed inputs, losing more and more of its physical productivity because the fixed inputs become more and more limiting. Finally, using more X_1 can actually reduce output as can be noted in the data in Table 4-1.[14]

Because economic decisions are based on additions or increments of the variable input, a more meaningful definition of diminishing returns is based on the marginal product of the variable input X_1, because it is an *incremental* measure of resource productivity. We define *marginal physical product (MPP)* as the amount

---

[13]Let's postpone until the section on two-variable input analysis if one of the fixed factors, $X_2 \cdots X_n$, is used in different amounts from that set which generated the function we are using here.

[14]Excessive fertilizer applications will burn up a crop, too much irrigation water will drown it out, or put too many laborers doing a job and they will get in one another's way, etc.

Note carefully that the law of diminishing returns is not a case of step by step sequential additions of X_1, but either/or choices in its application where we may use one unit of X_1, *or* two units, *or* three units. We cannot use one unit of X_1, then add a second, then a third, etc.

added to total product when another unit of the variable input is used.

The *MPP* curve is derived from the production function [column (4) in Table 4-1, and plotted graphically as in Figure 4-3] and is a measure of the *slope* of the *TPP* curve. The shape of the *MPP* curve more clearly describes the changing nature of the total product curve. Total product increases at an increasing rate when *MPP* is increasing, increases at a decreasing rate when *MPP* is falling, reaches a maximum when *MPP* is zero, and falls absolutely when *MPP* is negative.

The formula by which *MPP* is derived can be shown as

$$MPP = \frac{\text{Change in output}}{\text{Change in input}} = \frac{\Delta TPP}{\Delta X_1} = \frac{\Delta Y}{\Delta X_1}$$

where the Δ symbol means change. When computed in this manner we are able to determine by how much *TPP* changes whenever a change (either an increase or decrease) is made in resource use, at whatever level of X_1 use from which we measure that change. Since our increments of X_1 (in Table 4-1) are in groups of ten, the computed *MPP* is *per unit* of X_1. As a result, the figures in column (4) of Table 4-1 are placed midway between the X_1 observations; likewise the plottings in Figure 4-3 are at the midpoints of the observations along the horizontal axis because the 10-unit groupings (and not just

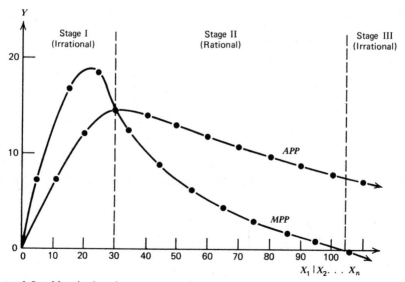

Figure 4-3. Marginal and average product curves, and the stages of production.

the tenth one in each increment of X_1) produced the change in output.

Average Physical Product. One further useful derivation from the production function is the *average physical product (APP)*, the formula being

$$APP = \frac{\text{Output}}{\text{Input}} = \frac{Y}{X_1}$$

The computed values [Column (3) of Table 4-1, and plotted in Figure 4-3] tell us how productive the variable resource is *on the average,* or *per unit* of X_1. If 20 units of X_1 produce 245 units of the product Y, the *APP* per unit of X_1 is 12.3, at 30 X_1 and 435 Y, *APP* is 14.5, etc. As *TPP* increases, *APP* also increases, but only to the point on the *TPP* curve where *MPP* and *APP* are equal. From that point on, as X_1 is increased, *APP* falls, and becomes zero only when *TPP* becomes zero.

These two curves, *MPP* and *APP*, define three zones or stages of production, in only one of which (Stage II) can we find an optimum use of the input X_1. The two other stages (Stage I and Stage III) are both labeled irrational because, given our assumption that the firm's objective is to maximize its net earnings over the cost of X_1 used, the firm can increase its net revenue by moving into Stage II from either of the other stages.[15] It is a necessary condition that we know of the existence of our two irrational zones, but we can eliminate them from any further consideration since an answer to the economic question of how much X_1 to use, and how much product to produce, is to be found only in Stage II.

Value Relationships

Up to this point our description has had a purely physical basis only. But economics is not concerned simply with the physical activities of producing something—that is a question of technical relationships. The economic concern is with economic feasibility—the manner in which human wants may be satisfied most efficiently, with

---

[15]We can make a preliminary (but positive) statement about Stage I that if it pays at all to produce in this stage it will pay even more to move into Stage II because the increment to output, whatever its value, is greater than the increment to cost. And in Stage III, the producer is incurring additional resource costs while at the same time reducing total output, so he is throwing away valuable product while increasing variable costs. Thus, given profit maximization as the firm's objective, both Stages I and III are irrational.

economic criteria as the foundation for judging what is efficient. We need to be able to answer questions such as "What does it cost?" "Is it worth it?" "Is there a better way of doing this?" We then are directed to comparing the values of products with the values of inputs used up in their production.

As a first step, a couple of assumptions will be useful (even a bit realistic): (1) there are so many firms producing this product that the actions of any one firm will have no influence whatsoever on either input or product prices; and (2) that the market does not differentiate one firm's product from that of another, that is, the firms produce a homogeneous product. Thus if a corn producer were to shut down completely or, alternatively, to produce the last possible extra bushel of corn, the market price of corn would not be affected. And provided that the corn meets certain quality standards, one producer's corn will not be discriminated against or offered a premium over that of other firms producing corn.

Value Product.　　Now let's inject some prices into our production information. Given the data in Table 4-1, and assuming that the market price of the resource X_1 is \$5.00 per unit, and the market price per unit of Y is \$1.00, what is the proper amount of X_1 to use so as to maximize profits? Table 4-2 provides the cost and value information to answer this question.

When we multiply the units of output (the TPP schedule) by the price of the product (P_y = \$1.00), we obtain *total value product* ($TPP \times P_y = TVP$) in column (2). The function now shows dollars worth of output produced by the different amounts of the input X_1 used.

Dividing TVP by the units of X_1 used derives *average value product (AVP)*, the average value of output per unit of X_1 at each level of use of that input—$AVP = TVP/X_1$.

Marginal value product (MVP) is derived by dividing the change in TVP by the change in the variable input, so we now are able to show how much additional value of output is produced by each additional amount of the variable input used—$MVP = \Delta TVP/\Delta X_1$.

Marginal Factor Cost.　　We require a concept that measures costs at the margin in the same way that MVP measures output value at the margin. That measure is *marginal factor cost (MFC)*. MFC is the amount that is added to total cost when one more unit of the variable input X_1 is used. Since the market price of X_1 is \$5.00 per unit, using another unit of that resource will add \$5.00 to total costs. Therefore $MFC_{x_1} = P_{x_1}$.

Table 4-2 Functional Relationships (from Table 4-1)
in Value Terms

(1) Variable input (X₁)	(2) Total value product (TVP)	(3) Average value product (AVP)	(4) Marginal value product (MVP)	(5) Marginal factor cost (MFC)
0	$ 0	$ 0		
			$ 7.50	$5.00
10	75	7.50		
			17.00	5.00
20	245	12.25		
			19.00	5.00
30	435	14.50		
			12.50	5.00
40	560	14.00		
			8.80	5.00
50	648	12.96		
			6.20	5.00
60	710	11.83	$MVP = MFC$	
			4.30	5.00
70	753	10.76		
			2.90	5.00
80	782	9.78		
			1.80	5.00
90	800	8.89		
			1.00	5.00
100	810	8.10		
			−0.20	5.00
110	808	7.35		

An optimum[16] can now be determined by locating the point on the production function where one more unit of the variable input adds to revenue just what it adds to costs, i.e., where $MVP = MFC$.

[16]By optimum we mean that one rate of X_1 use which yields the highest net return over the cost of X_1, given the fixed resource set.

Table 4-3 Checking the Net Revenue Productivity of the Variable Input X_1

Variable input (X_1)	Total revenue (TR)	Total cost of X_1 (TC_{x_1})	Net Revenue $(NR = TR - TC_{x_1})$
—	—	—	—
—	—	—	—
—	—	—	—
50	$648	$250	$398
60	710	300	410 Max. NR
70	753	350	403
—	—	—	—
—	—	—	—
—	—	—	—

Since MFC is $5.00, we must find a $5.00 point in the MVP schedule. That occurs at approximately 60 units of X_1.

If we were to use 70 X_1 instead, our value product per unit for the ten additional units of X_1 would be $4.30. But they cost $5.00 each so we would be losing $0.70 on each of them, a loss that can be avoided simply by using 60 rather than 70 units of X_1. And if we use only 50 units of X_1, the last 10 units of that resource added $6.20 each, which is $1.20 more than they cost, meaning that profit can be increased by using more X_1.

Our optimizing rule, of finding the point where $MVP = MFC$, said that by using 60 units of X_1 we would maximize the net difference between revenue and costs. Let's check that in another way, as in Table 4-3.

Relabel our TVP schedule from Table 4-2 as TR (total revenue), develop a TC_{x_1} column (meaning the total cost of X_1) by multiplying the amounts of X_1 used by $5.00, the price of a unit of X_1. Then subtract these cost amounts from the corresponding revenue figures to get net revenue (NR),[17] the amount by which revenue exceeds cost incurred for the variable input. Net revenue is maximized when 60 units of X_1 are used, which yields a TR of $710. If you compute the other values at both lesser and greater amounts of X_1 you will find that NR continues to fall in both directions away from the $410 maximum.

To graph our information, as in Figure 4-4, multiply the Y-axis

---

[17]This is nothing more than a net over the cost of the variable input but it still is the only relevant indicator in deciding how much X_1 to use, as will be discussed later. We can't call this figure profit because we have not identified the costs of the other (fixed) resources used to produce that income. However, at the point where net revenue is maximized, profit is also maximized, because fixed costs will not affect marginal analysis.

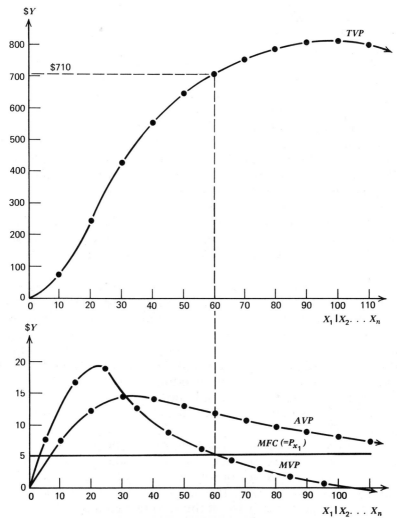

Figure 4-4.   Graphic determination of an optimum.

physical unit scale by $1.00, which gives dollars worth of output. We still maintain physical units of X_1 on the X-axis because we want to know what happens to costs and returns as different physical units of that resource are used.

The *TVP* curve maintains the same shape as the *TPP* curve we started with because it has been multiplied by a constant factor, $1.00, the price of a unit of output. The market price of Y does not change as a result of decisions made by this firm because of the competitive market condition we have assumed. And the same holds true for the shapes of the *MVP* and *AVP* curves because they are derived from the *TVP* curve.

Likewise, the price of the variable input X_1 does not change as a result of the producer's decisions either to use none of the resource, the maximum amount, or some amount between these extremes. Because of this market condition, we can graph *MFC* as a horizontal line with $P_{x_1} = \$5.00$.[18]

We now have a graphic picture of the search for the optimizing point where *MVP* = *MFC*. Given our assumed prices, *MVP* = *MFC* wherever the two lines cross. But this is true at two points along the *MVP* curve, so let's dispose of the one at less than 10 units of X_1 by adding the requirement that *MVP* must be declining and less than *AVP*, which forces us into Stage II. Drop a vertical line (from the point where *MVP* and *MFC* are equal) to the horizontal axis, and it shows 60 X_1; carry that vertical line up to the *TVP* curve and over to the *Y*-axis, and it shows $710. This is the optimum use of X_1.[19]

Adjusting to Price Changes.   Our assumption about unchanging prices was valid regarding individual firm decisions, but that doesn't mean that we are unable to cope with changing resource and product prices, or that we even expect them to remain unchanged. Change is a fact of life, in markets as in anything else. Changing economic conditions, in total market supply and demand cause frequent price adjustments in both resource and product markets. So our optimum is correct, not for all time, but only until another price change occurs, then an adjustment in X_1 use must again be made to find a new optimum.

It would seem obvious that as the price of the product increases, producers should increase their output to take advantage of the price change, and to reduce output when product price falls. Possibly not so clear, however, are the necessary changes in resource use that must be made as the price of the resource changes. Let's look at these two types of price changes, first to see why a product price change should cause the volume of output to be changed.

We need to go back to Table 4-2 (and Figure 4-4) and ask what happens to the *TVP* curve if P_y is $2.00, say, rather than $1.00. With product price doubled it should be clear that *TVP* will be twice as large at all levels of X_1 used. With that new *TVP* curve, *MVP* must

---

[18]We can say that $MFC = P_{x_1}$ because $MFC = (\Delta TC/\Delta X_1) = (\Delta X_1 \times P_{x_1})/(\Delta X_1) = P_{x_1}$.
[19]The increments in our production function do not permit a more accurate estimate of X_1 use than to say about 60 units, in spite of the fact that a mathematical derivation might result in exactly 62.5 X_1 as optimal. *MVP* is $6.20 between 50 and 60 X_1, and $4.30 between 60 and 70. An *MVP* of $5.00 falls somewhere between these two observations, closer to $4.30 than to $6.20, and therefore something more than 60 units of X_1, but that degree of accuracy is beyond our needs here.

also have increased. Its zero points (at $X_1 = 0$, and near 100 X_1) cannot change but all other points will be twice as high as previously. Given $P_{x_1} = \$5.00$, MVP now must equal MFC at a higher level of X_1 used, that is, at about 80 units. The optimal output is now $1,564 worth of Y, caused both by the product price increase and the greater amount of X_1 now being used.

If P_y were to fall to 50 cents, with P_{x_1} unchanged, optimal input use would drop to about 40 units. And if P_y were to fall even lower (about 34¢) so that maximum AVP falls to less than $5.00, the firm would cease production altogether. At maximum AVP less than $5.00, the firm would find no point in Stage II where $MVP = MFC$, so no matter what its fixed resource losses might be, there would be an additional loss on the variable resource that just makes a bad situation worse.[20]

The Firm's Demand for Resources. The effects of resource price changes on the rate at which resources are used are more easily noted than are the effects of product price changes. Begin with a price for X_1 of $19.00 per unit. Equating MFC and MVP results in approximately 25 units of X_1 used. However, 25 units of X_1 cost $475 and produces a TVP of about $325,[21] leaving a net loss of $150. Obviously this is not feasible. Given $P_y = \$1.00$, we can pay no more than $14.50 for input X_1 (its maximum AVP) and even that price will leave a zero net return over the cost of X_1. As the price of input X_1 falls below $14.50, the proper amount of X_1 to use is still found by equating MVP and MFC, with the results shown for selected price-quantity observations in Table 4-4, and plotted in Figure 4-5.

What we now have is a set of data that shows how the use of a resource must be changed as its price changes. We, therefore, have price-quantity data just as explained in the chapter dealing with the consumer's demand curve, and that is exactly what it is—the firm's *demand* for the variable resource. The firm's demand curve for X_1 then is the MVP of X_1 within Stage II. There is a maximum price of X_1 ($14.50 and 30 X_1 used) above which the firm will quit using the resource entirely, and a maximum amount of X_1 that can profitably be used even when the resource is free[22] to the user, with an optimum use of X_1 to be found at all possible prices between these two

[20]We will defer, until the chapter on costs, any consideration of what resource market price changes can be expected, and what alternatives may still be open to the owner of the fixed resources, should the product price fall so low.

[21]At 25 units of X_1 used, AVP is $13, so $TVP = \$13 \times 25 \ X_1 = \$325$.

[22]Even if X_1 were to be a free good, we could afford to use no more than about 100 units because nothing would be added to TVP by employing a greater amount of X_1. Using more than 100 X_1 actually reduces TVP (a phenomenon of Stage III) and is irrational.

Table 4-4 Deriving the Firm's Demand for Inputs

Price of input X_1	Quantity of input X_1 used
—	—
—	—
$14.50	30
—	—
10.00	40
—	—
5.00	60
—	—
2.00	80
—	—
—	—

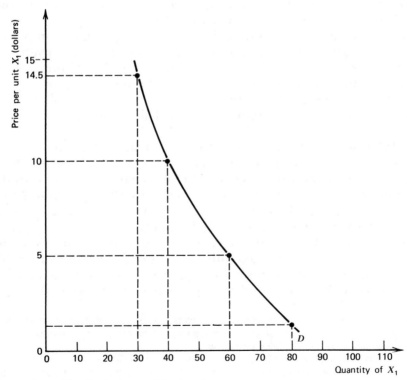

Figure 4-5. The firm's demand for inputs.

extremes. The firm's response to price changes thus fits the specifications of the law of demand—"quantity demanded varies inversely with price,"[23] as shown by the curve in Figure 4-5 labeled D.

To this point we have been discussing the simplest of functions, specifically: (1) a single-input function with nothing fixed, and its constant returns; and (2) a single-variable input function with fixed factors, and its diminishing returns.

Our analysis of the economics of production has necessarily been somewhat abstract, but this does no damage whatsoever to the validity or applicability of the concepts presented here. Note the simplifying (and correct) logic of the method—if this is true using one exemplifying input as the variable, with all others held constant, it must also be true for all other productive resources.

You should recognize that, no matter what separately identifiable resource each different X might represent, any one of those X's could be used as the variable input. The farmer who may be thinking about buying a nearby tract of land as an add-on, but hoping to get by without increasing other resources too (e.g., more or larger machinery, or more labor, etc.), really is looking at that tract of land as the variable resource X_1 with all others held constant. A rancher who is considering developing a tract of irrigated hay land may be dealing with a complex variable input by virtue of varying not only the capital investment, but more haying equipment may also be needed, with even an increase in the livestock herd size to take best advantage of the greater amount of forage to be available, with yet other resources held constant.

Summary

The major concern in this chapter has been the basic principles underlying (economically) proper choices. We have approached the question of how much of any variable resource to use within the framework of a single-variable input function.

Given the set of resources a firm uses to produce a good, it is convenient to classify these resources into four categories: land; labor; capital; and management. Then as we change any one of these resources we expect a corresponding change in the quantity of the product. The law of diminishing returns describes the effect on total output when the amount of a variable input is changed while all

---

[23]With the marginal productivity of a resource related to its price as the basis for the proper rate at which to use that factor as an input, what does this suggest to you regarding the consumer's use of a good to produce satisfaction (utility), and the comparable marginality of such use?

other resources are held constant. The production function is descriptive of this relationship.

As the price of a variable input falls, or its product price rises, it would appear logical that greater amounts of that resource would be used to increase the quantity of product produced; opposite changes should cause a reduction in the rate of resource use.

Such changes are based on the relationship between costs and values of an additional—marginal—unit of a variable resource. When the value output (MVP) of a marginal unit of that resource is greater than its cost (MFC), it pays more to use that unit than to not use it. Profit is increased (or losses decreased) by using that unit because more is added to revenue than is added to cost. If, however, MVP is less than MFC it pays to cut back the use of that resource. Profit is greater (or losses less) when that marginal unit is not used because costs are reduced more than is revenue by that reduction in resource use.

As we relate the quantities of a variable resource to different prices for that resource, we can note the special conditions in the demand for any good or resource. The higher its price, the less of any good or resource that will be used, and conversely. Plotting the pairs of price-quantity observations identifies the firm's demand for a variable resource. The Stage II portion (only) of the MVP curve of any variable resource is the firm's demand curve for that resource.

Chapter Highlights

1. Resources, production, and goods and services, are words or terms with economic meaning. In the process of using resources to produce goods and services, utility is created because human wants can be satisfied with them.
2. The universe of things and their relations one to another are far too complex for the human mind to grasp without a systematic abstraction and classification.
3. The relationship between resources and their product is called a production function.
4. A constant input-output relationship results when we do not change the make-up of the input unit formed from the four basic resources, land, labor, capital and management. This relationship may be summarized with the general function $Y = f(X_1 \cdots X_n)$, or simply $Y = f(X)$.
5. Diminishing returns are the inevitable consequence of changing proportions among the inputs used to produce something, a relationship described by the general function $Y = f(X_1 | X_2, X_3, X_4)$.
6. The law of diminishing returns states that "as successive amounts of a variable input are combined with a fixed input, the total product will increase, reach a maximum, and eventually decline."

7. Marginal physical product is the amount that is added to total product when another unit of the variable input is used. MPP measures the rate of change in the input-output relationship, and is obtained by dividing the change in total physical product (TPP) by the causal change in the variable input.

8. Average physical product is a measure of the average productivity of the variable input. APP is obtained by simply dividing total output by the number of units of the variable that produced the product.

9. Taken together MPP and APP define three stages of production in only one of which (Stage II) will an economic optimum be found.

10. When output is multipled by the price of the product we have total value product—$TPP \times P_y = TVP$. We then derive MVP and AVP in the same way as their physical counterparts were derived:

$$MVP = \frac{\Delta TVP}{\Delta X_1} \quad \text{and} \quad AVP = \frac{TVP}{X_1}$$

11. The amount that is added to total cost, when another unit of the variable input is used, is called marginal factor cost—MFC—which is the market price of that resource, so $MFC = P_{x_1}$.

12. Knowing both returns and costs at the margin permits us to determine the optimal rate at which to use the variable input. The optimum is determined by equating MVP and MFC. Too little of the resource is being used if MVP is greater than MFC; the opportunity to capture that excess of value over cost is needlessly forfeited. If MVP is less than MFC, the last unit of output cost more to produce that it is worth, and too much of the variable input is being used.

13. The MVP curve within Stage II is the firm's demand curve for the variable input, observed by noting the optimal quantity of the input used at each different price for that resource.

Review Questions

1. We could list separately identifiable productive factors in each firm by the hundreds, and more. What good reasons could there be for grouping them into four categories?

2. Discuss the meaning of a production function.

3. What causes conditions to be so absolute that we summarize them as the law of diminishing returns?

4. Is the labor used by a cotton farmer during growing season tillage operations the same resource as labor for harvesting?

5. "Obviously, a farmer should handle all the land within the farm in such a way that crop yields per acre are maximized." Comment.

6. On pages 84 and 85 the effect of changing the price of the product was described. With Table 4-2 as a starting point, recompute TVP and MVP using the two additional product prices discussed ($2/unit, and 50¢/unit). Construct a graph and plot these MVP curves, as well as the MVP curve when $P_y = \$1.00$/unit. What is the optimal rate to use X, at each of these prices, given $P_{x_1} = \$5.00$/unit? Do these adjustments in response to product price changes make sense?

Suggested Readings

1. Brehm, Carl. *Introduction to Economics.* New York: Random House, Inc., 1970, Chapter 5.
2. Bishop, C. E., and Toussaint, W. D. *Agricultural Economic Analysis.* New York: John Wiley & Sons, Inc., 1958, Chapters 4, 5, and 6.
3. Bradford, Lawrence A., and Glenn L. Johnson. *Farm Management Analysis.* New York: John Wiley & Sons, Inc., 1953, Chapter 8.
4. Ferguson, C. E. *Microeconomic Theory,* rev. ed. Homewood, Ill.: R. D. Irwin, Inc., 1969, Chapter 5.
5. Leftwich, Richard H. *Introduction to Microeconomics.* New York: Holt, Rinehart and Winston, Inc., 1970, Chapter 15.
6. Peterson, Willis L., *Principles of Economics: Micro,* 3rd ed. Homewood, Ill.: R. D. Irwin, Inc., 1977, Chapter 4.

Courtesy of Montana State University Photographic Services Department, Bozeman.

PRODUCER DECISION-MAKING: TWO VARIABLE INPUTS AND ENTERPRISE SELECTION

PRODUCER DECISION-MAKING: TWO VARIABLE INPUTS AND ENTERPRISE SELECTION

In the previous chapter we discussed the simplest production functions, specifically: (1) a single, composite, variable input function with nothing fixed, and its constant returns; and (2) a single-variable input function with other resources held constant. This functional relationship between a variable factor and its product is sometimes referred to as the "factor-product" relationship.

In deciding what to produce and how to produce it, the decision-maker is faced with two other choices. Few resources, if any, are so limited in their adaptability that they can only be used to produce one thing. This means that a choice has to be made as to what proportions resources should be combined to do the best job of producing the product. Such a choice deals with the relationships among resources, or the "factor-factor" relationship.

Another choice facing the producer is what enterprise or combination of enterprises will be the most profitable for the firm.[1] Agricultural production decisions are seldom so simple that the operator can choose a single crop or single livestock enterprise as the firm's only product. Crop farms typically produce two or more different types of grain crops; stock ranches frequently produce both livestock and grain or forage crops, or even two or more types of livestock. The relationship between enterprises is referred to as the "product-product" relationship.

These two general problem areas—factor-factor, and product-product—and the economic criteria for making those choices, will be dealt with in turn in this chapter.

The Two-Variable Input Function

What happens when two or more variable inputs are used? Should we not still be able to classify specific resources into groups as before,

---

[1]An enterprise is a specific crop or type of livestock from which products are obtained, e.g., cotton, wheat, beef cattle, hogs, or onions, etc.

developing: (1) the one type of function with nothing fixed; and (2) the other general type of function using two or more variable inputs with one or more inputs fixed, and discover the same two unavoidable types of input-output relationships?

Begin first with a function using all four general resources (land, labor, capital, and management) and call a given amount of each of labor and management a "unit" of X_1, and a given amount of each of land and capital a unit of X_2. If we vary both of our composite inputs, the function then is $Y = f(X_1, X_2)$. An infinite number of alternatives exist for the ratios in which these two variables can be combined, with a few of those alternatives sketched in Figure 5-1, plotting units of X_1 on the horizontal axis and X_2 on the vertical axis.[2]

Recall from our earlier discussion of graphics that no matter how one unit of X_1 is composed, two units of X_1 must be exactly twice as much of identical resources. The same holds true for X_2.

If, for instance, we move out from the origin along the heavily drawn ray (the 1:1 ratio between inputs) to the point where we have used one unit of each X_1 and X_2, a specific amount of output Y will be produced, two units of each input will be twice as far along the ray with Y being doubled, three units of each input will be three times as far along the ray with Y tripling, etc.[3] We can get no other result. All other rays will exhibit the same input-output characteristic but with different output rates. And any of these rays will generate input-output data[4] that plots a two-dimensional graph of the function $Y = f(X_1, X_2)$ with X_1 and X_2 combined in a ratio that differs from the X_1 and X_2 ratio along any other ray.

Isoproduct Contours.   Select one level of output along the heavy ray. Then locate the same amount of output along all other rays and connect those points with another heavy (arcing) line, labeled $Y = 200$. We now have a curve for which output is a constant 200 units at all points on that curve, known as an *isoquant*.[5] *Iso* is a Greek root

---

[2]As was stated in the previous chapter, all four general resources must be used to be able to produce anything, therefore both X_1 and X_2 must be used to produce the output Y. Thus, if we move out along the X_1 axis we are not using any X_2, so no output can result. The same holds true along the X_2 axis—no X_1, no product.

[3]Holding constant the proportion of X_1 to X_2 as we move outward along any ray, our inputs X_1 and X_2 could just as well be reidentified as an X input, with a functional notation of $Y = f(X)$, and with results exactly as in Figure 4-1A.

[4]A graph of the function for any of these rays would be similar to the one in Figure 4-1A, all having an identical shape but with the slope of the function determined by the ray selected for plotting.

[5]Variously referred to as an isoproduct contour, isoproduct curve, equal output contour, product-indifference curve, etc., all have the same meaning and are identical in concept to the consumer's indifference curve discussed in Chapter 3.

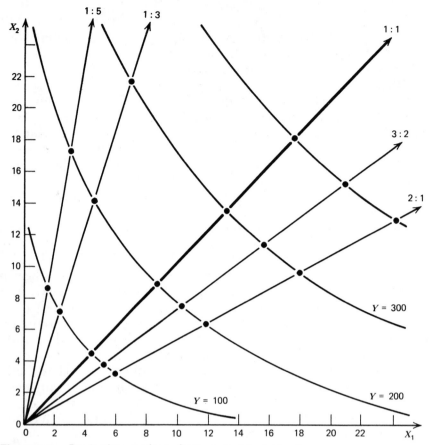

Figure 5-1. Production surface from a two-variable input function.

word meaning equal, so the word isoquant means a line of constant (or equal) quantity or product. The diagram now measures output vertically from the plane of the graph. This third-dimensional measure depicts and quantifies (in units of output) height above the plane in the same way, and with exactly the same intent, that a cartographer uses contours to show the surface elevation of a hill.

It should be clear that if nothing directed us to select the one particular ray used to describe the functional relationship that was discussed, nor were we forced to select the 200 Y isoquant, an infinite number of possible choices exists, in looking at either (or both) rays and isoquants. Put the point of your pencil anywhere in the quadrant space and a ray of specific ratio between inputs passes through that point. The *production surface* (diagrammed as a family of isoquants) can be visualized in the same way. In Figure 5-1, we could draw isoquants between those shown, and between those again, continuing to draw different isoquants between others until we have a solid surface so dense with isoquants that we would be unable to distinguish one isoquant from another. So isoquants are everywhere in our product space, each showing a different quantity of output.[6]

Note that a movement along an isoquant changes the ratio between X_1 and X_2 with quantity of output constant, while a movement along a ray changes output but holds the input proportion constant. Almost hidden in a movement along an isoquant is the old problem of diminishing returns, caused by changing the proportions in which the two variable inputs are combined. As we select rays closer and closer to the X_1 axis we are increasing the ratio of X_1 to X_2 with the result that X_1 becomes less and less productive. There simply is too much of that resource being used with any given amount of X_2. The same holds true for X_2 and its productivity as we select rays tilting closer and closer to the X_2 axis.[7]

Since there are relatively unproductive resource combinations toward the vertical and horizontal axes, we should expect to have to move farther out from the origin along those outer rays to locate some specific quantity of output. Nearer the extremes, inputs have been combined in a (physically) inefficient manner, while a better physical balance of inputs is established between those outer rays. All points along an isoquant are technically possible, but only one point along any isoquant is economically efficient, giving rise to the economic problem of having to select that one combination of inputs which will minimize the cost of producing that output.

What we have described is a characteristic of resource relation-

---

[6]A special characteristic of isoquants is that they do not intersect. Were an intersection of isoquants possible, it would mean that two or more different amounts of output could be produced by one level of input use. This is an impossible contradiction of the law of diminishing returns which, further, would destroy the meaning and predictability of any functional relationship.

[7]Even though these isoquants might be viewed as most typical of the real world when all inputs are varied, there are important (and realistic) exceptions based entirely on how the inputs are put together.

Visualize the type of production surface which would result if a unit of X_1 were composed of *ten* days of labor, *one* day of management, *$100* of capital, and *one* acre of land; and a unit of X_2 included *five* days of labor, *two* days of management, *$500* of capital, and *three* acres of land. Each of these inputs would be capable of producing output on its own (the other need not be present at all because all four of our basic resources are included in the unit of either input), therefore Y would rise continually on either axis rather than be zero along the axes. Note carefully, however, that such exceptions have nothing to do with proving invalid the law of diminishing returns, or proving that these are only hypothetical examples lacking real life observation or meaning. They result purely from a different arrangement of the inputs and the manner in which they are combined with one another, problems for which every producer must find answers in the everyday use of resources.

ships with special economic meaning—that of *resource substitutability*. Resources are able to substitute for one another when the use of one resource can be increased as a replacement for another reduced in amount and still yield a given amount of product. The ease or difficulty of substituting one resource for another is made apparent by the shape of the isoquant. Thus the shape of an isoquant is determined by the rate at which resources substitute for one another. Three basic types of resource relationships are discernible: (1) perfect substitutes; (2) perfect complements; and (3) imperfect substitutes.

Perfect substitutes are just that, perfectly able to replace one another without affecting output, and the isoquant for perfect substitutes must be a straight line, as in Figure 5-2, Isoquant *A*. An example of perfect substitutes would be in choosing between 20 percent nitrogen as X_1 and 40 percent nitrogen as X_2. Disregarding the effect that may exist because of the greater bulk of inert carrier in 20 percent nitrogen, it will substitute for 40 percent nitrogen at a constant 2:1 ratio.

Assuming no quality differences, irrigation water from one well (X_1) would substitute for irrigation water from another well (X_2) at a constant rate. Many other examples could be used. The firm's decision as to which resource to use with such a substitution relationship is easily made: use the cheapest one.

Resources that are *perfect complements* leave no room for choice in the proportion of their use. Perfect complements (B) must be used in a technically prescribed ratio. An additional amount of one resource or the other will add nothing to total product, so the decision problem is one of whether or not to use the *pair* of resources rather than their *ratio* of use.

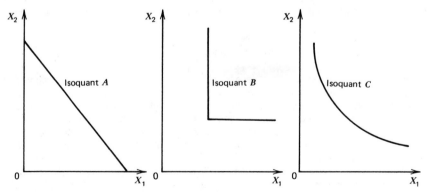

Figure 5-2. Isoquants for perfect substitutes (*A*), perfect complements (*B*), and imperfect substitutes (*C*).

An example of (nearly) perfect complements is a tractor and plow. A tractor with plow can turn so much soil in a given period of time. Adding more tractors will not increase output, nor will output be increased if more plows are added to your tractor.[8]

The third resource relationship is probably more typical of the kind of choice problem faced by the agricultural producer—the relationship categorized as *imperfect substitutes*. When resources are imperfect substitutes for one another, successive incremental reductions of X_2 will cause output to fall unless increasingly larger offsetting amounts of X_1 are added, as indicated by the curved isoquant (C) in Figure 5-2. Such isoquants are concave from above (convex to the origin) indicating that it takes larger and larger amounts of one resource to replace equal incremental reductions in the other resource.

For instance, one can use less and less land to produce a product, if that sacrifice of land is offset with more intensively applied capital, but continuous substitutions of capital for land would eventually be unable to maintain output.

Poultry producers use capital as a substitute for land when they build confinement facilities that reduce the need for land area. The western wheat farmer substitutes land for capital by using a larger land area rather than develop irrigation (or other capital intensive) facilities to produce that product.

Other substitution possibilities exist among the four basic resources, or among innumerable types or kinds of resources within each category. The limit of such substitution is where the *MPP* of a resource becomes zero. Thus no matter how much effort one might make, further additions of that resource could not prevent a reduction in output.

We are describing a specific characteristic of the *rate* at which resources substitute for one another, or the *marginal rate of substitution*.[9] The marginal rate of substitution of X_1 for X_2, ignoring sign, is indicated by the formula

$$MRS_{x_1 x_2} = \Delta X_2 / \Delta X_1$$

---

[8]Providing the tractor/plow technical unit was already proper as to load, speed of travel, quality of plowing done, etc.

Or maybe you'd prefer this example (no special mechanical adjustments, please!): right and left drive wheels on a standard two-drive-wheel tractor.

[9]Some prefer to refer to this as the *marginal rate of technical substitution (MRTS),* to indicate the technical nature of resource use in production, and to distinguish this from the same phenomenon in consumption where one good is substituted for another, the measure there referred to as *MRS.*

which can be read to be the number of units of X_2 that a unit of X_1 can replace without changing output,[10] and is, therefore, a measure of the *slope* of the isoquant. Since the isoquant for imperfect substitutes is a curving line, we face a *diminishing* marginal rate of substitution.

Viewed on a graph (Figure 5-3), a change in either input can be shown as a straight line in the direction of that change, such as the line segment from point a to point b showing a reduction in the amount of X_2 employed. Reducing X_2 without a compensating increase in X_1 will drop output to a lower isoquant (that runs through point b), the amount of that drop being the marginal product of that change in X_2, or ΔX_2 times MPP_{x_2}. An increase in the use of input X_1 equal to the distance b-to-c (measured along the X_1 axis) will increase output by $\Delta X_1 \cdot MPP_{x_1}$. Notice that as we have started the upper left portion of the isoquant we have a high ratio of X_2 to X_1. Therefore MPP_{x_2} is relatively low and MPP_{x_1} is relatively high, meaning that a given increment of X_1 replaces a relatively large amount of X_2. As we continue to add more and more X_1, its MPP falls (just as shown earlier in Figure 4-3) while the MPP of X_2 increases. Thus the vertical length of any line $a - b$ gets shorter and shorter (compare with $a' - b'$, and $a'' - b''$), the reason for calling it *diminishing MRS*.

Since these moves are being made *along* the isoquant, output is constant and any such move can be stated as $\Delta X_1 \cdot MPP_{x_1} = \Delta X_2 \cdot MPP_{x_2}$. With the slope of the isoquant equal to $\Delta X_2 / \Delta X_1$, these terms can be rearranged to $\Delta X_2 / \Delta X_1 = MPP_{x_1} / MPP_{x_2}$ showing that the slope of the isoquant ($MRS_{x_1 x_2}$) is also equal to MPP_{x_1} / MPP_{x_2}, the ratio of their marginal products.

Isocost Line. If a given amount of output is to be produced, we obviously can select any input ratio along the output contour so long as that contour line has a slope between zero and infinity, or between the horizontal and vertical. But of all those possibilities only *one* ratio can be best, or optimal, in terms of costs and returns. Any ratio other than that will cause us to spend too much on our resources to produce that output, therefore profits will be reduced. To find the proper ratio of resources, we must first relate their prices to their *MRS*.

Earlier (Figure 4-5) we looked at the firm's demand for a resource, so the problem hinges on viewing the whole set of resources this firm is using with a price-quantity demand curve for each re-

[10]The *MRS* for perfect substitutes would be a constant, for perfect complements it is zero, and for imperfect substitutes a number varying in magnitude.

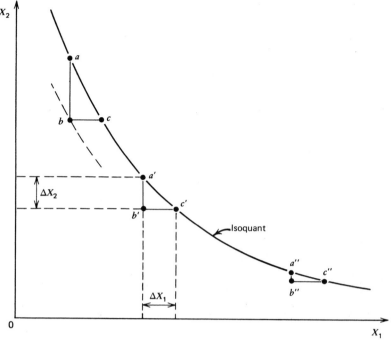

Figure 5-3. Illustrating diminishing marginal rate of substitution.

source. In this case our view is limited to just our two variable inputs [from $Y = f(X_1, X_2)$].

A clearer illustration of the problem makes use of an *isocost line*, which shows what amounts of these two resources can be bought for a given amount of money. Let's use $100, given $P_{x_1} = \$5.00$ per unit and $P_{x_2} = \$2.50$ per unit. As Figure 5-4 shows, we can spend all this money for X_1, all of it for X_2, or some combination of the two as indicated by the diagonal straight-line isocost. The line is a straight line because of an implicit assumption about the resource market: no matter what this producer does in allocating expenditures, by buying nothing of either input, or buying all he can of either or both, input prices will not be affected at all.[11] (This is only one set of

[11] Given $P_{x_1} = \$5.00$ and $P_{x_2} = \$2.50$, this $100 will buy 40 units of X_2, or 20 units of X_1, or any combination along the isocost line. If we use C to indicate the $100 cost level, then $C = P_{x_1} \cdot X_1 + P_{x_2} \cdot X_2$, where $(P_{x_1} \cdot X_1)$ is the amount spent on X_1 and $(P_{x_2} \cdot X_2)$ the amount spent on X_2, with total spending being their sum. Rearranging our terms we get $P_{x_2} \cdot X_2 = C - P_{x_1} \cdot X_1$, and $X_2 = (C/P_{x_2}) - (P_{x_1}/P_{x_2}) \cdot X_1$. Thus, X_2 is the unit quantity along the vertical axis, C/P_{x_2} is the vertical axis intercept, P_{x_1}/P_{x_2} the (negative) slope of the isocost line, and X_1 the unit measure along the horizontal axis. Our cost line formula is identical to the straight line formula $Y = a - bX$. We thus have an incremental measure of slope (P_{x_1}/P_{x_2}) showing how these resources substitute for one another in the market.

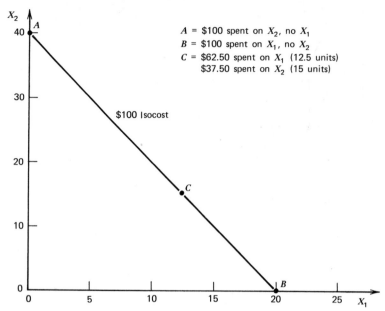

Figure 5-4. Illustration of cost allocation possibilities.

assumptions about pure competition—the topic of a later chapter—but not at all atypical for most producing firms in American agriculture, as they purchase resource inputs.)

The Least Cost Combination. Individually, Figures 5-3 and 5-4 show us, respectively, what happens to output as we change resource proportions, and what amounts of the two resources can be purchased with a given dollar outlay. To minimize the cost of producing a given output (or what is the same thing stated in a different way, to maximize output from a given cost outlay), we must combine the type of information each provides us with, as shown graphically in Figure 5-5.

Given output and resource prices, we optimize the ratio of the inputs X_1 and X_2 by finding that one point along the entire isoquant where the slopes of the two curves (isoquant and isocost) are equal. This is another way of saying that for any given output the producer will find an optimum ratio in the use of these resources by equating their *MRS in production* with the *rate at which they substitute in the market*. Resource prices tell what they are worth to other users in the competitive market, so the producer must use them in such a way that they each are worth *just that much* at the margin in order to make optimal use of those resources.

With the slope of the isocost line determined by the ratio of

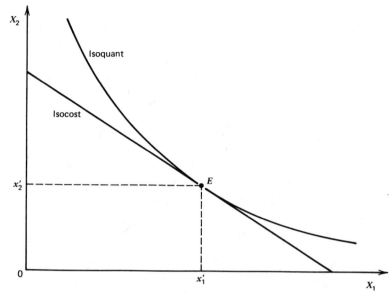

Figure 5-5. Optimizing resource combinations to minimize costs.

market prices (P_{x_1}/P_{x_2}) we equate this ratio with the slope of the isoquant (MPP_{x_1}/MPP_{x_2}).[12] When $P_{x_1}/P_{x_2} = MPP_{x_1}/MPP_{x_2}$ the slopes of the two curves are equal (at tangency point E). We have minimized the resource cost of producing that output, called the "least cost combination" and have found that input ratio $(0\text{-}x_1'$ of X_1 and $0\text{-}x_2'$ of $X_2)$ at which an additional dollar spent on either variable input will yield the same output or value of product.[13]

In our constant returns case $[Y = f(X_1X_2)]$, nothing is inferred about a profit-maximizing rate of using *both* of these variable resources. Rather, our attention has been directed to the question of minimizing the unit cost of producing a given level of output—the factor-factor decision. We have not yet asked whether that would be the most profitable output. Profit maximizing is a question dealing with the volume of output, which involves an expansion or contraction along the expansion path.

The question of optimizing input proportions is determined along an *expansion path* as shown in Figure 5-6. Given input prices,

[12]$MRS_{x_1 x_2} = \Delta X_2/\Delta X_1 = MPP_{x_1}/MPP_{x_2}$ and, when equated with their price ratio, can be re-written as $MPP_{x_1}/P_{x_1} = MPP_{x_2}/P_{x_2}$.
[13]You might verify this by choosing any point along the isocost curve toward either axis from point E. Another isoquant of lower output runs through that point. So a given dollar outlay produces less and less output as different proportions of the inputs are selected farther and farther away from the equilibrium point E.

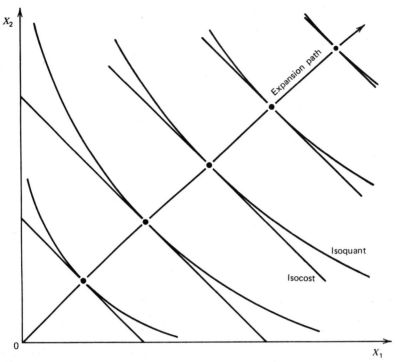

Figure 5-6. Path of expanding plant scale.

an equilibrium proportion can be decided for each and every level of output (any Y) where the marginal rate of substitution between inputs equals their price ratio (as was shown for a single isoquant in Figure 5-5). Connecting these points develops an expansion line showing the optimizing ratio between inputs for any desired output, or scale of operation.

The optimum proportions are determined when each of the variable resources is used to the point at which its addition to value of output just equals its addition to costs. If the MVP of a resource exceeds its price (its MFC), the amount of that resource used should be expanded. Use should be reduced if MVP is less than price. When these criteria are met for all variable resources, the ratio of inputs is at an optimum, and

$$\frac{MVP_{x_1}}{P_{x_1}} = \frac{MVP_{x_2}}{P_{x_2}} = \cdots = \frac{MVP_{x_n}}{P_{x_n}}$$

The effect of prices in prescribing resource use (resource allocation) is made more evident by noting how equilibrum points and the expansion line change as either or both resource prices change. Suppose, for instance, that the price of input X_2 increases to $10 per unit. The dashed line labeled (2), Figure 5-7, is the new $100 isocost curve. That sum can still buy 20 units of X_1 but only 10 units of X_2, so it is a flatter line than our original isocost and will therefore shift the point of tangency to a different ratio of inputs. With relative prices now changed the producer would be prompted to cut back on the use of the resource X_2 whose price has risen. The $100 isocost line would be tangent at a lower level of production and different input ratio (point E'). On the other hand, a price fall for X_2 means that more of this resource can now be bought with $100, the isocost line would be steeper and tangent to a higher isoquant than the one shown.

Another isocost curve, labeled (3) shown as the steeper dashed line, demonstrates the combined effect of a doubling in the price of input X_1 to $10 per unit and a fall in the price of X_2 to $1 per unit. A variety of other prices, isocost curves, and isoquants can be postulated with the resulting changes similarly identified.

Note that to here our considerations of resource use optimizing

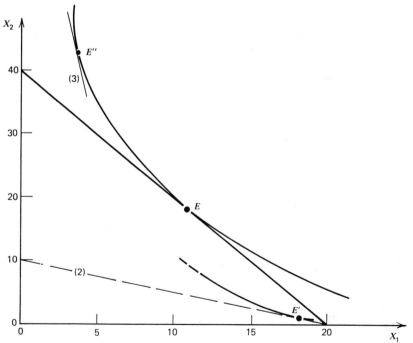

Figure 5-7.   Illustrating the effect of resource price changes.

has been limited to the two-variable input function $Y = f(X_1, X_2)$ with the four basic resources included in these two variables. The production surface has been that as described by Figure 5-1. We also portrayed a single-variable input function with fixed factors, and developed appropriate data (Table 4-1), with no logical contradiction between constant returns and diminishing returns.

Consider Figure 5-8, which more fully projects the production surface from $Y = f(X_1, X_2)$, the two-variable input function that was first shown in Figure 5-1. Since constant returns are unique to varying all resources in a constant proportion, and diminishing returns come into play when one or more resources in a production activity are held constant, both of these phenomena should be demonstrable from this constant returns production surface if, as we claim, there is no logical inconsistency between the two concepts.

Fix X_2 at the 5-unit level and vary X_1; the function now is $Y =$

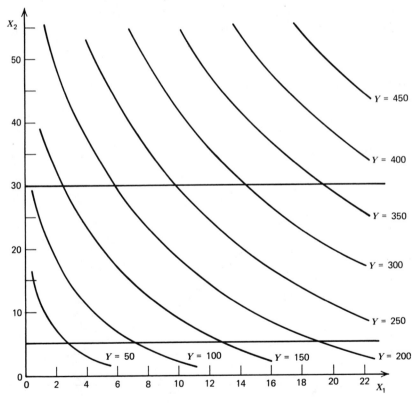

Figure 5-8. A two-variable input function.

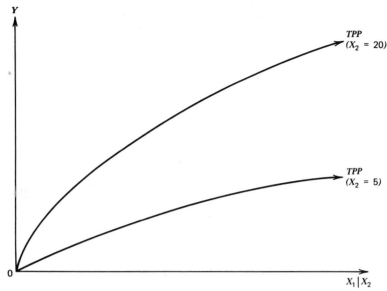

Figure 5-9.   Subfunctions of two-variable input function.

$f(X_1|X_2)$. Diminishing returns are evident in the curvature of the function in Figure 5-9, as the data plot the *TPP* curve of X_1 variable with X_2 fixed at five units.[14] Multiplying output by the price of the product (as was done in Table 4-2) makes it possible to determine an optimum amount of X_1 to use by locating the input level at which *MVP* = *MFC*. Fixing X_2 at a different level causes a different production function as identified where X_2 may be fixed variously at 10, 15, 20, units, etc., with as many different functions as there are possible numbers of units of X_2.[15] It should be clear that individual units of the variable resource are made more (or less) productive as the quantity of the other resource is increased (or decreased), demonstrating the substantial dependence of resources on one another for their productivity. The different production functions that may be identified also illustrate the importance to the producer of productivity limitations imposed when an inadequate scale of operations is established.

[14]Visualize slicing down through the production surface at the fifth unit of X_2 and parallel to the X_1 axis, then turning the exposed side of that cut so that you are looking at the third dimension of the model—a single-variable input subfunction of the two-variable function surface.
[15]The results would be similar if, on the other hand, X_1 were fixed at any level and X_2 were varied. We would just be cutting slices through the production surface in a direction parallel to the X_2 axis.

The Diminishing Returns Surface

Earlier we held that a more realistic view of producer options would be one in which some resources would be fixed and a few others could be varied. This, in general, is the sort of thing the above section dealt with but where all resources were packaged into a two-variable input function.

Suppose we take a somewhat different approach with the four basic resources, calling labor the variable input X_1, capital in all its different forms the variable input X_2, and land (X_3) and management (X_4) as the resources held constant.[16] We have exactly the same basic resources (with different unit packages, however) as in the constant returns case—exactly the same firm, if you wish—but now the function has something fixed before we even begin considering production alternatives.

With $Y = f(X_1, X_2 | X_3, X_4)$, a set of output quantities must result such as those shown in Figure 5-10. These numbers then permit a plotting of isoquants that gives the production surface an appearance such as that in Figure 5-11 (rather than as Figure 5-8, the constant returns case). The reason for this is that no matter in what ratios we may expand the use of the two variable resources, their proportion to the fixed inputs X_3 and X_4 is being changed and we can't escape diminishing returns. The diagram must reflect this in all directions in the quadrant space, rather than just when moving parallel to either axis as in the constant returns case. Furthermore, since there are fixed inputs (X_3 and X_4), those fixed resources becoming limiting. As more of X_1 and X_2 are used there is a maximum output (916 Y) that can be produced by these resources. Total physical product falls away from that maximum in all directions as the quantities of X_1 and X_2 are increased individually or together.

Diminishing returns are indicated by the spacing of the isoquants. Their increased spacing farther out in the quadrant results from diminishing MPP. Progressively greater amounts of the variable resources are required to produce the increment to product represented by the more distant isoquants.

To confirm the general shape of the production surface, fix X_2 at different levels. We demonstrate this with X_2 fixed at two levels only—10 units and 40 units. Varying X_1 with $X_2 = 10$, for instance,

---

[16]Land, a fixed resource, for an ordinary crop/livestock ranch, may itself be a composite of given acreages of many different types of land—dry rangeland; grazed forest land; unimproved meadowland for grazing; improved meadow hayland; irrigated hayland; tilled dry cropland; irrigated cropland; etc.—each separately identifiable with an X of its own, each with different productivities and resource combinations that enable it to produce a valued product.

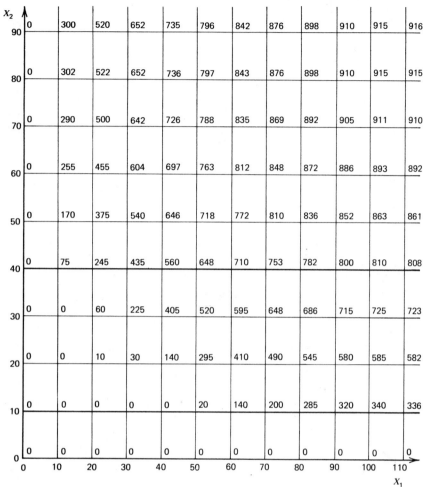

Figure 5-10. Production data derived from the function,
$Y = f(X_1 X_2 | X_3 X_4)$.

will cause output changes from 0 to 20 Y, then 140, 200, etc., rising
to a maximum of 340 units of output. From that point (where
$MPP_{x_1} = 0$), total product actually declines with additional amounts
of X_1 used because its MPP is less than zero. The 340 Y isoquant
must therefore bend away from the horizontal axis at amounts of X_1
used beyond 100 units.

The same holds true for all other isoquants with X_2 held fixed at
other levels. The $X_2 = 40$ subfunction (our source of the data for the
production function used as the primary example of diminishing
returns in Chapter 4) performs in a manner similar to the one just

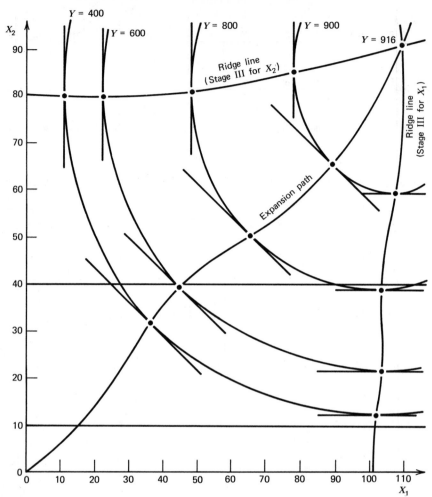

Figure 5-11. Production surface illustrating diminishing returns.

discussed. With $X_1 = 0$, output is zero, rises at a rate determined by the marginal productivity of X_1 up to a maximum Y of 810 units, and declining from that point as greater amounts of X_1 are applied.

The heavily drawn line rising vertically from the X_1 axis is called a *ridge line*. This line connects all points of zero *MPP* of the input X_1, thus separating Stage II from Stage III for all subfunctions with only X_1 varied.

Similar results are obtained when X_2 is varied, while X_1 is fixed at different levels. All isoquants eventually bend away from the vertical axis. Stages II and III for X_2 are separated by the horizontal ridge line that connects all the points where isoquants reach and pass the vertical (i.e., points of $MPP_{x_2} = 0$).

The expansion path is determined in the same way, and with the same meaning, as was done in the constant returns case. Numerous expansion paths that extend outward from the origin are possible, bounded at the extremes by the axes and the ridge lines, as determined by the ratio of the prices for X_1 and X_2. If the price of X_1 were zero (i.e., a free good) and that of X_2 some positive number, the expansion line would follow the vertically rising ridge line; and if X_2 were free with a positive price for X_1, the expansion path would follow the horizontal ridge line. With any positive price for both resources the expansion path would lie somewhere between the ridge lines. The specific location of the expansion path within the area is determined, as in Figure 5-7, by the points at which the slopes of the isocost and isoquant curves are equal ($P_{x_1}/P_{x_2} = \Delta X_2/\Delta X_1$).

Recognize that as only one of these inputs is varied, we are dealing with subfunctions of that resource set which generated the production surface, with the same solution to the problem of optimality as discussed in Chapter 4. So there really is no need to maintain fixed resource identification—we could just as well call all the nonvaried resources an input X_2, with the relevant function then being $Y = f(X_1|X_2)$. The reason for ignoring fixed resources in this way will become clearer in Chapter 6. We pay no attention to fixed resource costs because they have nothing to do with deciding how much of a variable resource to use. The value productivity of a variable resource and its price are the only determinants of that.[17]

When all resources are variable as in $Y = f(X_1 \cdots X_n)$, where X_n may be the tenth different resource, the 100th, or an even greater number, we used $Y = f(X_1, X_2)$ as sufficiently descriptive of the particular input-output relationship. The larger function would simply be too cumbersome to describe and comprehend, and it would be no more able than the simpler form to answer meaningful economic questions. Where one or more resources might be variable with the remaining resources fixed, such as $Y = f(X_1 \cdots X_g|X_h \cdots X_n)$, X_g might be a large number of resources and X_n much larger still. And the simplifying fact is that resource proportions are being changed, so diminishing returns cannot be avoided. Thus, we can use a much simpler appearing function, $Y = f(X_1|X_2)$, for the single-variable input type; and with two-variable inputs, $Y = f(X_1X_2|X_3X_4)$. These two general functions are correctly and fully descriptive of the economic meaning of resource-product relationships.

[17]Restudy Table 4-2 and Figure 4-4 to make this point clear.

Product-Product Relationships in Combining Enterprises

In the single enterprise case just discussed, the solution to the question of how much to produce was relatively simple and straightforward. One optimizes by expanding variable resource use to where the last unit applied just pays for itself, $MVP_{x_1} = P_{x_1}$.

The solution to the question of how to produce that product is a bit more complicated because it involves choosing among two or more variable inputs: we adjust resource proportions so that $MPP_{x_1}/P_{x_1} = MPP_{x_2}/P_{x_2} = \cdots = MPP_{x_n}/P_{x_n}$. Along the expansion path each variable resource must be used to the point at which the last unit applied just pays for itself, or

$$\frac{MVP_{x_1}}{P_{x_1}} = \frac{MVP_{x_2}}{P_{x_2}} = \cdots = \frac{MVP_{x_n}}{P_{x_n}} = 1$$

This equating of resource costs and value of output at the margin has pushed the rate of resource use for all inputs to that one point along the expansion path where the firm's profits have been maximized, given that single enterprise as the firm's only product.

Few operators are so fortunate that they can push resources to the point where $MVP = MFC$ for each resource in all their possible uses. The more usual case is rooted in scarcity; there just aren't enough resources available to the firm. Consequently, the decision problem also involves choosing those enterprises which will most contribute to the firm's profits.

Combining Enterprises. A third choice—what to produce—is often a very complex decision. Grain farmers seldom are so specialized that they can ignore the profit potential offered by other types of crops, or in some cases, adding a livestock enterprise. Stock ranches most frequently find that adding forage or grain crops will enhance the firm's earnings.

Land and other resources are usually sufficiently versatile that they can be put to a number of different uses. So the decision boils down to one of combining two or more enterprises to maximize profits from the resource set available to the firm.

Just as the choice in the rate and proportion of resource use is optimal only so long as resource and product prices remain unchanged, so also is the enterprise combination proper only until product prices change. Shifts in demand for the firm's products will change the relative profitability of enterprises, and will require adjustment in emphasis.

Except for the occasional complete reorganization of a farm or ranch, year-to-year enterprise changes may not appear especially severe. But widespread enterprise adjustments in response to changing economic conditions have taken place over longer periods of time. Changes in technology and product prices have forced many farmers to make sharp adjustments from earlier production efforts.

Ohio has slipped far from its once prominent position in the sheep industry. Cotton, once produced exclusively in the South, has shifted so that much of its production is in irrigated land in the arid Southwest. Few farmers in Aroostook County, Maine, trouble themselves with raising wheat, since they have become especially well known for potatoes. Yet an 1838 report of a study of the Aroostook territory concluded that "the staple crop is, and must ever be, wheat."[18]

The Firm's Production-Possibilities.   In order to illustrate the principle of enterprise choice we must again back away from the complexity of real life problems. Begin with a farm that has a given amount of each of the resources land, labor, capital, and management. The operator must choose what product(s) to produce from a number of possible enterprises, adopting only those that will contribute toward maximizing the firm's profits. It is not unlikely that an operator may have a dislike for some particular enterprise. A dislike for handling hogs, milking cows, or caring for poultry, etc., may be so strong that the individual knowingly sacrifices higher earnings in favor of a more pleasing enterprise.

In spite of the fact that the farmer will face choices involving a large number of potential crop and livestock enterprises that *could* be produced, let's simplify the problem to one of deciding between just two enterprises. Suppose this is a 320-acre farm with the operator deciding whether to produce only grain sorghum or soybeans, or some combination of the two. The product output information for these two enterprises is shown in Table 5-1. To maintain consistency with our earlier use of the label Y to indicate a product, we will call grain sorghum Y_1, and soybeans Y_2.

The table demonstrates the principles of "sacrifice" and "cost." In order to produce more grain sorghum, the acreage devoted to producing soybeans must be reduced. Soybeans are sacrificed and therefore are a cost of any additional grain sorghum produced.

Given full utilization of this firm's resources, our farmer could devote all of the farm's resources to producing soybeans in which

---

[18]By 1930, 85 percent of all farms in Aroostook County were classified as potato farms. Cited in John D. Black, et al., *Farm Management,* New York: The Macmillan Co., 1947, p. 136.

Table 5-1 Enterprise Combination Possibilities

Choices	Y_1 Grain Sorghum (bu)	Y_2 Soybeans (bu)	$MRPS_{y_1y_2}$ $(=\Delta Y_2/\Delta Y_1)$	Total Revenue When	
				$P_{y_1} = \$1.00$ $P_{y_2} = \$5.00$	$P_{y_1} = \$2.50$ $P_{y_2} = \$3.75$
A	0	7500		\$37,500	\$28,125
			$\frac{500}{2000} = 0.25$		
B	2000	7000		\$37,000	\$31,250
			$\frac{650}{2000} = 0.33$		
C	4000	6350		\$35,750	\$33,812.50
			$\frac{775}{2000} = 0.39$		
D	6000	5575		\$33,875	\$35,906.50
			$\frac{1025}{2000} = 0.51$		
E	8000	4550		\$30,750	\$37,062.50
			$\frac{1450}{2000} = 0.73$		
F	10000	3100		\$25,500	\$36,625
			$\frac{3100}{2000} = 1.55$		
G	12000	0		\$12,000	\$30,000

case output of that crop would be 7500 bushels. But with all the land and other resources used to produce soybeans, there are none available for grain sorghum, so the output of that crop is zero. The other extreme allocation devotes all the resources to producing grain sorghum (12,000 bushels), with zero soybean output.

For ease in visualizing the decision problem and its consequences, we have set up only seven different output proportions, Choices A through G. In addition to the one-product-only resource allocations (A and G) with their resulting values of production, five other possibilities are shown. The operator could produce some of both enterprises (any one of B through F), with the total value of the products produced changing as a result.

The full range of these possible allocations is called the firm's *production-possibilities*.[19] The production-possibilities show all the possible combinations of the two products, Y_1 and Y_2, that can be produced, given the set of resources in the firm's control. Since this is a case of, first, assuming full utilization of the firm's resources, then using those resources in one enterprise or the other, costs are constant; they do not change with different allocations of resources to the two enterprises.

Note carefully the effect of changing relative product prices on

---

[19]Sometimes also called the "product-transformation curve," that demonstrates the rate at which one product can be transformed into the other.

the amounts of each one produced, and the logical basis of the statement that prices allocate resources. When relative product prices change, we *must* respond by adjusting resource quantities devoted to the different products or needlessly suffer a loss in the firm's profits.

When the price of grain sorghum (Y_1) is \$1.00 per bushel, and soybeans (Y_2) are \$5.00 per bushel, the farm's net income is maximized by producing only soybeans (choice A). No other allocation will yield as much income. Attempting to produce any amount of grain sorghum, given these prices, will serve only to reduce total revenue and profits by the same amount because total costs, whatever their level may be, are unchanged. Therefore, any increase or decrease in total revenue will increase or decrease profits by the same amount.

If, on the other hand, prices were \$2.50 per bushel for grain sorghum and \$3.75 per bushel for soybeans, a different allocation of resources would be required. Profits would be maximized with resources allocated to produce 8000 bushels of grain sorghum and 4550 bushels of soybeans. Total revenue would then be a maximum, \$37,062.50, and any other allocation would simply throw away potential earnings. And if the price of grain sorghum were to rise to say \$5.00 per bushel, with soybeans still \$3.00, one would not produce any soybeans at all. Producing only grain sorghum (12,000 bushels) would maximize the firm's earnings.

In the table we have shown output Y_1 in increments of 2000 bushels to aid in understanding the computations we must make, and their economic meaning. This information is also graphed in Figure 5-12 to aid in visualizing the relationships between enterprises.

Start at point A with zero Y_1 and 7500 bushel of Y_2, then change to point B with 2000 bushels of Y_1; product Y_2 drops from 7500 to 7000 bushels. An increase of 2000 bushels of Y_1 causes a reduction of 500 bushels of Y_2 because resources have been shifted from producing Y_2 to Y_1. We have substituted Y_1 for Y_2.

The *marginal rate of product substitution (MRPS)* measures the differing rates at which either of these products will replace (substitute for) the other. That calculation tells us the amount by which one product output is decreased in obtaining a unit increase in the alternate product. If we divide the reduced Y_2 by the 2000 bushel increase in Y_1, we have the marginal rate of product substitution of Y_1 for Y_2. The formula for this determination is

$$MRPS_{y_1y_2} = \frac{\Delta Y_2}{\Delta Y_1}$$

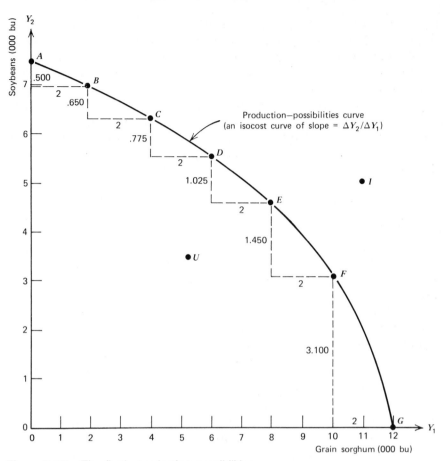

Figure 5-12.   The firm's production possibilities.

which reads "the marginal rate of product substitution of Y_1 for Y_2."[20] This calculation is a measure of the slope of the production-possibilities curve between two points on the graph, or between the same two sets of data in Table 5-1.

In going from A to B, $MRPS_{y_1 y_2} = 500/2000 = 0.25$, which means that (within the A–B range) one bushel of Y_1 will replace 0.25 bushels of Y_2. Since costs are unchanged, one bushel of Y_1 added has the same production cost as 0.25 bushels of Y_2 given up.

In moving from B to C, the $MRPS_{y_1 y_2} = 650/2000 = 0.33$, a greater sacrifice of Y_2 per bushel of Y_1 added than in going from A

[20]The marginal rate of product substitution of Y_2 for Y_1 simply measures these changes in a counter-clockwise direction: $MRPS_{y_2 y_1} = \Delta Y_1/\Delta Y_2$, giving a set of numbers that are the reciprocals of those measuring the $MRPS_{y_1 y_2}$, the sign being ignored in both cases.

to *B*. As we continue to move clockwise along the production-possibilities curve, more and more of Y_2 must be given up for each additional unit of Y_1. Diminishing returns causes proportionately more resources to be used for each increment of Y_1 added.[21] What this also says, is that the opportunity cost of producing additional amounts of Y_1 increases. The more resources that are committed to producing Y_1, the greater are the sacrifices of Y_2 given up to get those greater amounts of Y_1. This characteristic causes the production-possibilities curve to bulge outward from the origin.

The production-possibilities curve is sometimes also called a "frontier" because it identifies the maximum output for each and every combination of the two products that the firm's resources can produce. It is a frontier because it identifies the boundary between what is and what is not possible. The firm's resources are incapable of producing more goods than those indicated by the production-possibilities curve. Any combination outside the curve, such as the one labeled *I*, is impossible. Only an increase in the overall productivity of the firm—from a new technology or a greater quantity of resources, or both—will push the curve further out into the quadrant space.

A point such as *U* is possible, however. At any point *U*, some resources are idle, or unemployed, so production of both products is less than what is possible. It is an inefficient organization.

As we consider the *MRPS* derivations, we are unable to decide which quantities of those that could be produced would provide the greatest net return to the firm. This can be determined only after taking into account the effect of product prices.

At $P_{y_1} = \$1.00$ and $P_{y_2} = \$5.00$, the market says that it takes five bushels of Y_1 to equal the value of one bushel of Y_2; one bushel of Y_1 is worth 0.20 bushels of Y_2. Given these prices, producing at *B* instead of *A* means that $2,500 worth of Y_2 has been sacrificed to gain $2,000 of Y_1. An unnecessary loss of $500 has been incurred. Whatever the profit level that would have obtained at *A*, the firm is $500 worse off at *B*, and worse off still at other points farther down the curve.

The seven output choices (*A* through *G*) with only two pairs of product prices was a necessary abstraction from all the real life production and price possibilities. We would be hard pressed to

---

[21]The previously mentioned cause of diminishing returns—changing resource proportions—may not be so obvious here. But other factors take their toll. It is unlikely that other resources would be of equal productivity in both enterprises, so yields will decline as more and more (increasingly less productive) resources are shifted to either enterprise. And as cropping intensity grows, up to the instances of continuous cropping, yield-reducing problems of plant nutrient availability, weeds and crop diseases also increase.

compute all the revenue capabilities were we to expand the number of different price combinations to the number that might occur. A full accounting of all output and price possibilities would cause the choices to balloon to an impossibly large number. We need a simplifying rule capable of incorporating both ratios of production and prices into the decision mechanism.

The Firm's Revenue Possibilities.   Just as in consumer and producer choices among things used to produce utility or goods, we need to compare the rates at which goods substitute for one another in consumption or production with their rate of substitution in the market. And just as an objective-maximizing rule could be given in each of those cases, a similar rule should determine the profit-maximizing allocation of the output from two different enterprises. Figure 5-13 adds the price dimension to our choice problem.

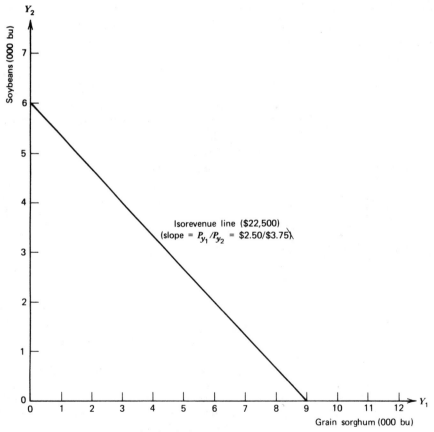

Figure 5-13.   Prices and the firm's isorevenue.

An *isorevenue line* shows all the possible combinations of two products sold that will bring the same total revenue. The isorevenue line is a straight line because of an assumption regarding this firm's size in relation to the market for its products; it is too small to have any influence on price regardless of the firm's production and marketing decisions. If this firm produced and sold all it could produce of either Y_1 or Y_2, and none of the other product, neither product's price would be affected. Thus, if this firm produces and sells 9000 bushels of Y_1 at \$2.50 per bushel, revenue is \$22,500. That same revenue could be obtained from 6000 bushels of Y_2 at \$3.75 per bushel. A straight line drawn between $6000\,Y_2$ and $9000\,Y_1$, describes all the possible combinations of these two products that will bring a total revenue of \$22,500. Such quantity pairs as $5000\,Y_2$ and $1500\,Y_1$; $3000\,Y_2$ and $4500\,Y_1$; and $1500\,Y_2$ and $6750\,Y_1$ are readily identifiable from among the many others along the isorevenue line that would total \$22,500 in revenue.

Note that the slope of the isorevenue line is determined by the ratio P_{y_1}/P_{y_2}.[22] Since it would take 9000 bushels of grain sorghum to equal the value of 6000 bushels of soybeans, the isorevenue line has a slope of 1:1.5. Each unit measured along the vertical axis equals the value of 1.5 units measured along the horizontal axis, a direct result of these product prices.

For any higher or lower product prices, with their ratio unchanged from the \$2.50 and \$3.75, we could draw a great many other isorevenue lines of identical slope anywhere in the quadrant space. For each even slightly different ratio of prices another similar number of isorevenue lines, all of different slope, could be drawn.

If P_{y_1} were to rise to \$3.00 per bushel, given $P_{y_2} = \$3.75$, only 7500 bushels of Y_1 would have to be sold to return \$22,500. And with Y_2 still at 6000 units, the isorevenue line is now steeper than the one drawn in Figure 5-13. Given any increase in P_{y_1} relative to the price of Y_2, the slope of the isorevenue line is increased; a reduction in P_{y_1} relative to P_{y_2} will reduce (or flatten) the slope of that line.

Optimizing Output.   We can now put these two sets of information together and determine that *one* allocation of resources to these products that will maximize the firm's profits, as in Figure 5-14. With axis labels the same as in Figure 5-12, but scales expanded to aid in reading quantities, we plot the data for the production-possibilities curve. The ratio of the first pair of prices used in Table 5-1 ($P_{y_1} = \$1.00/\mathrm{bu}$ and $P_{y_2} = \$5.00/\mathrm{bu}$) results in Isorevenue line *I*.

---

[22]That P_{y_1}/P_{y_2} is the determinant of the (negative) slope of the isorevenue line is proved in the same way as was shown earlier in this chapter (in footnote 11) for the slope of an isocost line.

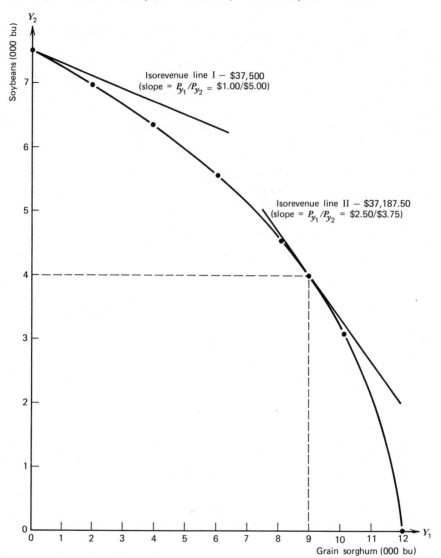

Figure 5-14. Optimizing the firm's output.

With this specific isorevenue line there really is no clearly seen point of tangency, but being the only output proportion available, the firm's optimum is at point A. As can be confirmed by the data in Table 5-1, no greater revenue can be obtained than by devoting all the firm's resources to producing soybeans only, worth $37,500. Any other proportion simply reduces total revenue without a reduction of costs, so profits suffer as a consequence.

As product prices change, so that the price of Y_1 rises relative to the price of Y_2, the point of tangency between the isorevenue line and the production-possibilities curve rotates clockwise along the production-possibilities curve. When the isorevenue line slope increases, less Y_2 is produced while the output of Y_1 is being increased.

Such a change in price ratios is shown by Isorevenue line *II*. Assume the price of Y_2 has fallen to \$3.75 per bushel while the price of Y_1 has risen to \$2.50 per bushel. As the slope of the isorevenue line is determined by P_{y_1}/P_{y_2}, this change in product prices causes Isorevenue line *II* to be steeper than Isorevenue line *I*. With these price changes, the revenue producing capabilities of the two products also changes, depending upon the magnitude of price changes. The point of tangency now falls between points E and F on the production-possibilities curve. At this point, sufficient resources have been shifted from producing Y_2 to producing Y_1 that the output proportions are now about 4050 bushels of Y_2 and 8800 bushels of Y_1. These quantities at the given prices produce a total revenue of \$37,187.50, which is greater than the revenue at either point E or point F.

We stated earlier that equating the $MRPS_{y_1 y_2}$ $(\Delta Y_2/\Delta Y_1)$ with their price ratio (P_{y_1}/P_{y_2}) would be an optimum in that no greater revenue could be earned from this set of resources. When we have located the point at which $\Delta Y_2/\Delta Y_1 = P_{y_1}/P_{y_2}$ the rates of substitution at the margin for both production and the market have been equated. Their opportunity costs in production are now identical to the values the market puts on these products. Costs at the margin equal revenues at the margin. And because of the curvature of the production-possibilities curve, any movement from the point of tangency would cause more to be sacrificed in value of the product given up than is obtained from the value of the other product's increased output.

Thus far, we have considered only one specific set of resources. What happens when the resource base itself is changed? For instance, an increase or decrease in available labor and management may come about through the occasion of marriage, divorce, or death. Some of the owned land may be sold to acquire other resources. The operator may rent more land, or lose the lease on some of the presently used acres. Some labor may be lost as offspring grow and leave the farm to other pursuits.

Each of these changes, among a great many other possibilities, will cause the firm's total output capabilities to change. And they may or may not result in proportionate increases or decreases in total resources. When resource proportions change there may also be changes caused in the shape of the production-possibilities curve as well, each different set of resources having its own specific production-possibilities curve.

The Expansion Path. How the firm optimizes output as the production-possibilities curve expands may be viewed as a question of firm growth. The path along which a firm expands (or contracts) its output optima, given product prices, is shown in Figure 5-15.

Suppose that instead of the resource set we have been using, as shown by the more heavily drawn production-possibilities curve, we had started with a firm having fewer of some or all the resources land, labor, capital, and management. The output of soybeans and grain sorghum would be reduced if this farm had only 160 acres of land, say, and would be able to produce even less with 80 acres of land. The production-possibilities curves for these smaller sizes of the firm would lie within the heavier drawn curve for the 320-acre farm. For each different level of available resources there will be a different production-possibilities curve, only three of which we have sketched in the diagram. Given just one pair of product prices there will be only one most profitable combination of outputs for each production-possibilities curve. The line drawn through these points is called the *expansion path*, showing the revenue (and profit) maximizing proportions of Y_1 and Y_2 as the firm expands or contracts output when the firm's size is changed.

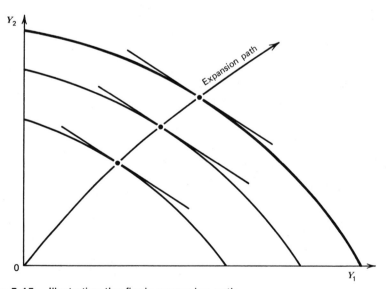

Figure 5-15. Illustrating the firm's expansion path.

To summarize, let's use the symbolism $MVP_{x_1}^{y_1}$ to mean the marginal value product of resource X_1 in the production of product Y_1, and $MVP_{x_1}^{y_2}$ to mean exactly the same for that resource in another product Y_2. The resource allocation problem has been solved for resource X_1 when, for two products,

$$\frac{MVP_{x_1}^{y_1}}{P_{x_1}} = \frac{MVP_{x_1}^{y_2}}{P_{x_1}} = 1$$

Since P_{x_1} is unchanged, this relationship can be stated simply as $MVP_{x_1}^{y_1} = MVP_{x_1}^{y_2}$. The resource X_1 has been allocated to its most profitable use because no reallocation of that resource among products Y_1 and Y_2 will increase its value productivity.

With this set of relationships true for each and every variable resource in all possible enterprises, the firm is earning its highest possible profit. Any reallocation of resources between the different enterprises within that firm will reduce its profits.

Some, impatient to get on with cost analysis, may feel we have been tediously long in identifying the physical and economic relationships in production. Too frequently, however, the student misses the firm ground of cost analysis in the production function. In dealing with the question of what happens to costs when output is changed, we forget too easily that the only way the operator can change output quantity is to reallocate variable resources between two or more enterprises. Thus the need exists to lay the foundation carefully for the next chapter's analysis of costs.

Summary

A two-variable input function, with other resources fixed, is used as the simplest device with which to describe the solution to the problem of how to produce. The physical response to changing proportions of the variable inputs results in the isoquants. The slope of isoquant shows the marginal rate at which these resources substitute for one another—$MRS_{x_1 x_2} = \Delta X_2 / \Delta X_1$.

The slope of an isocost line (P_{x_1}/P_{x_2}) is determined by the ratio of market prices for X_1 and X_2. Equating their marginal rate of substitution with their price ratio $(\Delta X_2 / \Delta X_1 = P_{x_1}/P_{x_2})$ derives the cost-minimizing ratio for these two inputs. Combining variable resources in this ratio results in an equal value of output per added dollar of cost for each resource.

An optimum (maximum profit point) has been reached along

the expansion path when the difference between total value output and total cost of the variable resources is maximized.

A production-possibilities curve for two products (enterprises) is used to describe the solution to the question of what to produce. That line of relationship is drawn convex from above to reflect diminishing returns as more and more of the firm's resources are devoted to one or the other enterprises.

The slope of the production-possibilities curve is indicated by $\Delta Y_2/\Delta Y_1$. When the ratio is equated with the ratio of the product prices ($\Delta Y_2/\Delta Y_1 = P_{y_1}/P_{y_2}$), the firm's profits are a maximum. The firm's resources can produce no more than the quantities indicated by that point of equality. Increasing the output of either of these products would cause a reduction in the output of the other, also with a reduction in total value output and profit.

Chapter Highlights

1. A producer faces three production choices: (1) factor-product—how much to produce; (2) factor-factor—what resource combination to use; and (3) product-product—what product(s) to produce.
2. Constant returns to scale means that output increases in a direct (constant) proportion to the increase in inputs.
3. Diminishing returns are the result of changing resource proportions.
4. An isoproduct contour (or isoquant) shows the different combinations of inputs that will produce the same quantity of output.
5. The marginal rate of substitution shows the rate at which one resource can be substituted for another without changing the level of output. *MRS* is thus a measure of the slope of the isoquant.
6. An isocost line shows the different combinations of resources that can be bought with a given cost outlay.
7. The least cost combination is determined at that point where the isocost line is tangent to an isoquant. At that point,

$$MRS_{x_1x_2} = \frac{\Delta X_2}{\Delta X_1} = \frac{P_{x_1}}{P_{x_2}}$$

8. The firm's profits are maximized along the expansion path at that point where the *MVP*-to-price ratio is one, and is equal for all resources.
9. A production-possibilities curve shows all the combinations of products that a firm can produce given its resources and technology.
10. The marginal rate of product substitution (*MRPS*) is shown by the slope of the production-possibilities curve, which also shows the opportunity cost of producing more of either product.
11. The isorevenue line shows all the combinations of products sold that will bring the same total revenue.

12. A firm will maximize profits by producing that combination of products where the isorevenue line is tangent to the production-possibilities curve.

13. The proper (profit-maximizing) scale of the firm is determined along the expansion path.

14. The production function provides the basis for the firm's costs.

Review Questions

1. Draw an isoquant to show how a farmer in your area can choose between commercial fertilizer and a legume crop to provide nitrogen for a growing crop. By adding an isocost line to your diagram, show how that person can determine the proper amount of each to use.

2. Show how the decision in review question 1 would be changed if the price of nitrogen fertilizer or the cost of raising alfalfa changed.

3. Imagine two farms in a particular type-of-farming area of your state with equal land acres and identical soils in their farms. Should these farms have the same crop and livestock enterprises to maxmize their profits? Why, or why not? What affects the decision of what enterprises to include in the firm, and the relative sizes of each?

4. Given a farm with its two major enterprises being cotton and corn/livestock. Suppose that by shifting more of its resources to cotton, a reduction of $4000 worth of corn and $5000 worth of beef permitted an increase of 12,000 pounds of cotton. What was the cost of that additional cotton? If the farm price of cotton were 85¢ per pound, would this have been a profitable change?

5. In what way is an isoquant (an isoproduct contour) similar to an indifference curve?

Suggested Readings

1. Bishop, C. E. and W. D. Toussaint. *Agricultural Economic Analysis.* New York: John Wiley & Sons, Inc., 1958, Chapters 9 and 10.

2. Bradford, Lawrence A., and Glenn L. Johnson. *Farm Management Analysis.* New York: John Wiley & Sons, Inc., 1953, Chapters 9, 10, and 11.

3. Brehm, Carl. *Introduction to Economics.* New York: Random House, Inc., 1970, Chapter 7.

4. Castle, Emery N. and Manning H. Becker. *Farm Business Management: The Decision-Making Process.* New York: The Macmillan Co., 1962, Chapter 12.

5. Ferguson, C. E. *Microeconomic Theory,* rev. ed. Homewood, Ill.: R. D. Irwin, Inc., 1969, Chapter 6.

6. Leftwich, Richard H. *Introduction to Microeconomics.* New York: Holt, Rinehart, and Winston, Inc., 1970, Chapter 7.

7. Peterson, Willis L. *Principles of Economics: Micro,* 3rd ed. Homewood, Ill.: R. D. Irwin, Inc., 1977, Chapter 5.

6

Courtesy of Northern Manufacturing Company, Havre, Montana.

PRODUCTION COSTS, SUPPLY, AND PRICE DETERMINATION

PRODUCTION COSTS, SUPPLY, AND PRICE DETERMINATION

A firm's costs are incurred by using valuable resources to produce its product. Individual firms can change their total output only within the restraints imposed on them by the resources under their control. Hence the concentration on resource relationships in Chapters 4 and 5, as one element affecting a firm's costs. The other factor affecting production costs is the values of the resources used, an important part of this chapter's discussions.

We begin by identifying costs, as viewed by economics, by studying the methods by which costs are measured, to make intelligent production decisions. It is necessary to combine consumer valuations of a good (treated in Chapter 3) as expressed by the market demand curve with producer costs as demonstrated by the market supply curve. These two curves together—demand and supply—are the determinants of the equilibrium market price for all goods bought and sold in the open market. Changes in these prices are signals to consumers and producers to adjust their consumption and production, reestablishing their optimal positions.

In a market economy, prices are the signals guiding decision makers to do those things that will be to their own best advantage. As was shown in Chapter 4, when the price of a product increases or decreases, operators are being told by the market to increase or decrease their output of that good. Likewise, when resource prices change, resource cost changes force adjustments in the rates of resource use.

The operator of a firm develops plans and carries them out on the basis of expected future product prices, resource costs, and technical production relationships. A resource mix should be used to produce such output quantities that the difference between revenues and costs is the greatest possible. But what cost items do we tally up to derive the true costs of any operation in order to examine a firm's economic profitability? Because the economic meaning of a number of cost identifying terms differs from common usage their special meanings must be made clear.

Identification of Costs

All production costs can be divided into two general groups, *explicit* and *implicit* costs.[1] An explicit cost has been incurred when money is spent to hire labor, repair machinery, buy seed, fuel, or other things for which cash expenditures are made. These expenditures have been made to enhance product output, but a simple totaling of all such money spent is inadequate when trying to determine the costs of production, since explicit costs account for only about one-third of all costs on a typical American family-operated farm.

For all variable resource services purchased,[2] their costs are explicit, incurred directly to buy or hire those resources, with each being paid its market price. In Figure 4-4 we considered use of a variable resource X_1 whose market price was $5, meaning that others stood ready to buy that resource for $5 per unit. The market price reflects a resource's alternative employment opportunities which must at least be matched by the buying firm to be able to obtain any of that resource.

Resources also are used during the year for which there is no cash outlay in that same period of time, and it also is necessary to determine that type of resource cost. One such type of cost is for a resource lasting for two or more years. For instance, a $25,000 tractor may be purchased with the full purchase price paid on delivery, or stretched out over the useful life of that asset, but since it will last for several years the $25,000 cost cannot be charged against one year's operations. The cost of the tractor must be allocated in such a way that the flow of its costs matches the flow of its services over the tractor's productive life. If this isn't done properly, costs will be over- or understated and apparent losses or gains also erroneously computed.

Another type of implicit cost is that incurred for the operator's own labor and management which, because of circumstances, must accept whatever is left after other resources have been paid. Some even look on that leftover reward as something akin to profit, but this would be quite inconsistent with last chapter's four-way classification of resources. Worse, this says nothing about the economic worth or value contribution of labor and management and provides no information for determining the true costs of production.

---

[1]These costs are sometimes referred to as "direct" and "indirect," "cash" and "noncash," or "operating" and "overhead," with the same basic meaning intended.

[2]Since one's own labor and management may be used in varying amounts, and certain fixed resources may be rented for cash, we are not able to state that explicit costs and the costs of all variable resources used are the same thing.

Opportunity Cost. Common practice in appraising the cost of owned land gets closer to the economic meaning of implicit costs (not just for land, but for all owned resources). Taxes paid on owned land are correctly viewed as an explicit cost. But what about the value of one's investment in that land? Surely a cost exists which somehow relates to the value of that resource. The land, whatever its market value might be, may be owned free and clear, but most operators feel that an investment interest charge should be made as a cost in the use of that land. This reflects the basic foundation on which resource costing must rest by asking the question, "What would this investment earn if it were allocated to an alternative use?"[3] Thus, alternative earnings possibilities have very much to do with the cost of using that land.

Suppose your land could be sold for $500 per acre and that this money could be invested in a land mortgage (a loan even to the buyer of your land) at eight percent per year. The annual interest yield would thus be $40 per acre, so if your present use of land returns only $25 per acre you simply are throwing away $15 per acre, a cost in the purest sense. This cost concept is a simple one that economists refer to as *opportunity cost* (or alternative cost). It considers the value of other opportunities foregone as a cost. So the cost of using any asset is the value of output from a different, forfeited use.

Now, if your land is capable of producing either corn or wheat, and a commitment of $100 cash costs will yield $300 worth of corn or $200 worth of wheat per acre, what is the cost of producing wheat? Not the $100 spent to raise wheat! It is the $300 worth of corn sacrificed (the value of a foregone alternative) that is the true cost of producing wheat.

Maybe you are raising your own hay for livestock feed. Even though you may have made no direct payment to someone in producing that hay you still wouldn't price the hay at zero cost to your livestock, because at least one alternative is to sell it. Therefore, the opportunity cost for the hay is its selling price when fed to your livestock.

The same is true for all the firm's owned resources. Returns for each resource, in any use, must equal the next best alternative for each of them or the resource is being used inefficiently and more profitable earnings are being bypassed. So we may go even further and state that opportunity costs are the true costs of production.

A summary view of owned-resource costs would then run something like this: if I could be paid $5,000 for my labor and manage-

---

[3]Whatever the alternative investment might be, it must be one of equal risk in order to arrive at a realistic estimate of alternative earnings.

ment doing this same work for someone else, and my land investment could earn $15,000 if the money value of the land were loaned to someone else, and if the value of machinery, buildings, brood stock, and other capital assets could earn $10,000 in another use, each of these amounts is the opportunity cost of that particular resource type, and their sum ($30,000) is the full opportunity cost of the present use of these resources.

Profit. The reason for our hesitancy to mention profit may now be made more clear. From whatever viewpoint, the word profit carries the implication of a surplus of receipts over expenses. Thus, an accounting profit has been made when all operating costs (direct expenditures for labor hired, rentals, and other purchased inputs) and overhead costs (taxes, insurance, depreciation, etc.) are exceeded by revenues so that a net balance remains.

A bookkeeping profit, however, is not necessarily the same as an economic profit. A net surplus of revenue over expenses in the corn-wheat example just mentioned, is possible even if only wheat is produced, yet an economic loss is incurred because a higher return (with the same costs) from corn production was forfeited. An *economic profit* (or *pure profit*)[4] has been made when a firm's revenues exceed the total of its explicit and implicit (opportunity) costs. From the standpoint of any resource, an economic profit is the amount by which its net earnings exceed the payment required to attract it to (or keep it in) its present use. This concept of profit thus includes what might be called "normal profits" as a cost to the firm since each resource is priced to the firm at its opportunity cost.

Fixed and Variable Costs. After looking at the true meaning of costs, it now becomes necessary to make a different classification of costs—one that coincides with the fixed and variable resources as categorized earlier in the production function.

We will call *variable* those costs which increase or decrease as output changes, and *fixed* those costs incurred for the resources which do not change as output is changed. Our costs now include both explicit and implicit costs, and the sum of variable and fixed costs are the total costs of the firm's operations.

This arrangement of resources and their costs permits an emphasis clarifying just how the costs of production affect the firm's output. We now are able to demonstrate the operator's response to market price changes.

---

[4]Resource economists have traditionally used yet another term, "economic rent," as we will do in Chapter 11, with exactly the same meaning as economic (or pure) profit.

Length-of-Run · In order to emphasize the source of production costs, look back to the discussion (in Chapter 4) of how some resources come to be fixed and other variable. Two possibilities were discussed in relation to the law of diminishing returns.

One possibility was that we simply could choose any desired functional relationship by classifying some resources as fixed and others as variable, then handling them accordingly, and noting the outcome. There's nothing wrong with this; it is scientifically correct. But you might consider this an unexciting exercise with little real-life application.

The distinction between fixed and variable resources need not be an arbitrary one, however. Whether resources are fixed or variable is an everyday circumstance of the planning process *all* producers face, one that is related to the passage of time, yet not dependent upon days, months, or years as basic to the distinction.

Many farmers plan their cropping season operations during the preceding months. And each has a set of expenses that would continue at the same (fixed) level whether the farm produces to its maximum output or shuts down completely. These expenses are rightly regarded by the operator as fixed.

Other expenses would be variable because of choices available in the rates of use for such resources as labor hired, machine use, seed, fertilizers, pesticides, and herbicides, etc. These are all variable expenses since the amounts of each of them can be varied. And whether their number is large or small they will influence the *length-of-run* of the production function, and the consequent cost function.

Length-of-run is a planning concept reflecting that there exist differences in one's ability to change input use. Some resources cannot be changed during one span of time; but those same resources may not be fixed given a longer period of time. We may then look at two extremes of length-of-run with innumerable possibilities between.

The Short-Run. One length-of-run we might call the *immediate short-run,* meaning right now, a time span so short that *no* resource changes can be made. Everything, therefore, is fixed. A truck gardener, for example, may have completed harvesting, and have the produce ready for sale. The operator faces the problem of disposing of that produce in as short a time as possible to prevent spoilage losses. Nothing can be done to change the quantities of resources used or the amount of produce to be marketed.

A somewhat longer time-period is involved when a producer considers what to do next year. Certain changes might be made in the use of land without changing total land acres. The acreage of a particular crop might be changed, resulting in some other resource cost changes but with the large majority of costs still remaining unchanged.

An even longer period might be one covering the next two, five, or even ten years. A change in total land acres may or may not be planned, with no change planned for certain capital improvements, and with some machinery and equipment being replaced. The production function still has some resources fixed and some variable, but with more resources varied than in the examples just given. What we are considering then, is just different short-run periods, some being shorter or longer than others, and still within the framework of the law of diminishing returns, a short-run concept itself.

Figure 5-10 may be used as an explanation of two different short-run functions. The two-variable function that yielded the production surface would itself be a short-run function; the subfunction slice of that surface, with a single-variable input, would be an even shorter length-of-run with costs of production affected accordingly.

The Long-Run.   The other extreme, the *ultimate long-run,* is then a period so long that everything may be varied. The quantities of all resources may be changed, including management itself, either by special training to make it more capable of directing the planned operation, or by hiring the service. In its strictest application this length-of-run gives rise to the special constant returns function described in Figure 4-1A where all resources are varied. Thus the distinction between the long run and any shorter run hinges upon whether or not there are fixed factors in the function. Since there may be an infinite number of possibilities between now and some period far into the future, we may summarize by simply saying that the *long-run* is a period of time so long that everything is variable, while in the *short-run* one or more of the factors cannot be varied.

Short-Run Costs of Production.   To maintain sight of the specific relationships between the production function and the costs of production, we will retain an example from the previous chapter, using the (short-run) functional information from Table 4-1. Those data came from the production surface with two variable inputs (Figure 5-10) in which the input X_2 was fixed at 40 units, yielding a subfunction of the general form $Y = f(X_1|X_2, X_3 \cdot \cdot \cdot X_n)$. As the production relationships were analyzed all measures were *input oriented,* with averages and marginals derived on a per-unit-of-input basis. Since the input X_1 was the independent variable, units of X_1 were measured along the horizontal axis, and output, the dependent variable, along the vertical axis.

We switch now to an *output oriented* set of measures, all of which are derived from the production function, generating cost information in which output has become the *independent variable* plotted along the horizontal axis, and input X_1 (now) the *dependent variable* plotted along the vertical axis.

Figure 6-1 is a graphic demonstration of the reciprocal nature of production and cost functions (Table 4-1 data). Earlier, output quantities were determined in a manner equivalent to saying, "If 10 units of X_1 are used, how much output will be produced?" The same question is apparent for all other input levels. Arrows pointing upwards from the X-axis to the production function, then to the Y-axis, demonstrate this for selected input levels. Cost analysis requires only that the question be restated as, "If a certain amount of product is to be produced, how many units of the variable input X_1 must be used?" Arrows pointing from the Y-axis to the production function, then to the X-axis, demonstrate the cause-effect nature of this.

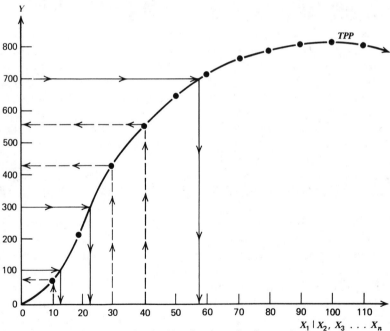

Figure 6-1. Illustrating the physical basis of production and cost relationships.

With output as the independent variable measured along the horizontal axis (using 100-unit increments for convenience only), the physical basis of the cost of producing each output quantity becomes clear. The physical basis is the amounts of X_1 used in producing those output quantities, as shown in the first two columns of Table 6-1.

When dollar amounts are computed for each observed quantity of output and input, given the same prices as were used in the earlier production example (P_y = $1/unit, and P_{x_1} = $5/unit), we can determine total revenue and total costs for each level of output.

Production costs (the three remaining columns in Table 6-1) include expenditures for the variable input, the costs of the fixed resources, and the total of these costs. Multiplying each quantity of X_1 used, at the different levels of output, by the market price of X_1 gives *total variable cost (TVC)*, the total spending for the variable input. Note that the first 100 units of output required 11.6 units ($58.00 worth) of X_1 with variable resource requirements per unit of output declining through 400 units of output, then rising to 32.2 units ($161.00 worth) required for the last 100-unit increment of output, a consequence of diminishing returns.

Since we have used the data from Table 4-1 (which was a subfunction slice of the production surface in Figure 5-10, with X_2 fixed at 40 units), the cost of X_2 is a component of fixed costs. At $2.50 per unit of X_2, this cost item amounts to $100. Assuming that the implicit opportunity costs of all *other* fixed resources amount to $50, *total fixed costs (TFC)* now are $150. This $150 cost is a constant for all levels of output.

Table 6-1   Short-Run Costs
(with X_2 Fixed at 40 Units)

Output (Y)	Input (X_1)	Total Variable Cost (TVC)	Total Fixed Cost (TFC)	Total Cost (TC)
0	0.0	$ 0.00	$150.00	$150.00
100	11.6	58.00	150.00	208.00
200	17.6	88.00	150.00	238.00
300	22.8	114.00	150.00	264.00
400	28.0	140.00	150.00	290.00
500	34.5	172.50	150.00	322.50
600	43.9	219.50	150.00	369.50
700	57.8	289.00	150.00	439.00
800	90.0	450.00	150.00	600.00
810	100.0	500.00	150.00	650.00

Total cost (TC) for this firm is the sum of its total variable cost and total fixed costs which, because of the increasing variable cost, also rises as output is increased. These cost measures are graphed in Figure 6-2.

The firm's *total revenue (TR)* is derived by multiplying the price of the product ($1 per unit) by the units of product, at each output level. *TR* plots as a straight line because of the market assumption that prices will not change as a result of this one firm's production decisions.

With all costs included, subtracting *TC* from *TR* shows the firm's net revenue at each level of output, as in Table 6-2. These net values can correctly be called *pure profits* because all production costs have been included. Since *TC* is a curving line (resulting from changes in productivity of the variable input as increasing amounts of that resource are combined with the fixed resource), there can be only one optimum output, 700 units of output with a profit of $261. Profits will be reduced by producing any output other than 700 units. Graphically (Figure 6-2), this is where the vertical distance between the *TR* and *TC* curves is a maximum. Any movement away from 700 *Y* will reduce that vertical difference and, therefore, reduce profit.

It was stated earlier that fixed costs have no influence in deter-

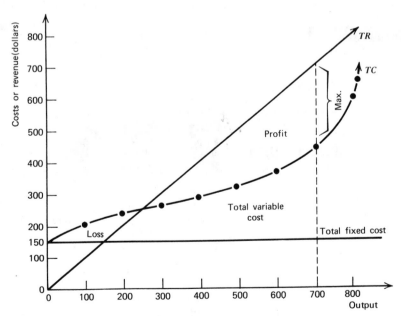

Figure 6-2. Short-run costs and revenue.

Table 6-2   Revenues, Costs, and Profits

Output (Y)	Total Revenue (TR)	Total Cost (TC)	Profit	
0	$ 0	$150.00	$−150.00	
100	100	208.00	−108.00	
200	200	238.00	− 38.00	
300	300	264.00	36.00	
400	400	290.00	110.00	
500	500	322.50	177.50	
600	600	369.50	230.50	
700	700	439.00	261.00	Maximum
800	800	600.00	200.00	
810	810	650.00	160.00	

mining the optimum level of output. The correctness of this can be illustrated here. On the graph, imagine that fixed costs are zero: the total cost line will simply shift downward by $150 without changing its shape or slope, and the profit-maximizing output remains unchanged at 700. Increase fixed costs to $500: now there is no net profit, only net losses. What can be done?

The first temptation might be to say "Quit!," maybe hoping that market conditions will improve later. But shutting down production would result in forfeiting *any* possible return on fixed costs, with a loss totaling $500. As levels of output greater than zero are considered, losses are reduced until we reach 700 units of output with losses minimized at $89.00, so an *optimum* output may be said to be "that output quantity at which profits are maximized or losses minimized." And this optimum output has been determined without regard to fixed costs.

Measuring Per-Unit Costs and Returns.   An analysis such as the foregoing reveals aggregates of returns, costs, and profits. But market signals, being given only in dollars per unit of products and resources, require a further breakdown so that our information is in the same form. When put in the same unit measures as provided by the market, the operator can then determine whether the market price of the product is high enough to make it worth it to use valuable resources to produce that commodity, and what quantity produced will be an optimum.

Four additional cost measures are required to complete analysis on a per-unit-of-output basis—*average variable cost (AVC), average fixed cost (AFC), average total cost (ATC),* and *marginal cost (MC).* Each of these unit cost measures is derived from its total counterpart, as

Table 6-3 Short-Run Costs and Returns per Unit of Output

Output (Y)	AVC ($= TVC \div Y$)	AFC ($TFC \div Y$)	ATC[a] ($= TC \div Y$)	MC ($= \Delta TC \div \Delta Y$)	MR ($= \Delta TR \div \Delta Y = P_Y$)
0	$0.00	$0.00	$0.00		
				$0.58	$1.00
100	0.58	1.50	2.08		
				0.30	1.00
200	0.44	0.75	1.19		
				0.26	1.00
300	0.38	0.50	0.88		
				0.26	1.00
400	0.35	0.38	0.73		
				0.33	1.00
500	0.35	0.30	0.65		
				0.47	1.00
600	0.37	0.25	0.62		
				0.70	1.00
700	0.41	0.21	0.63	$\dashrightarrow MC = MR$	
				1.61	1.00
800	0.56	0.19	0.75		
				5.00	1.00
810	0.62	0.18	0.80		

[a] Numbers do not add exactly, because of rounding error.

shown in Table 6-3 and graphed in Figure 6-3. Each computation furnishes the producer with useful information on the types and amounts of costs, all on a unit-of-output basis.

Average variable cost (AVC), the amount spent on the variable input per unit of output, is derived as

$$AVC = \frac{\text{Total variable cost}}{\text{Output}} = \frac{TVC}{Y}$$

Since the variable input is relatively unproductive when only a small amount of that resource is being used, the cost of the variable input per unit of output produced will be relatively high. As the productivity of that resource increases with greater amounts used, *AVC*

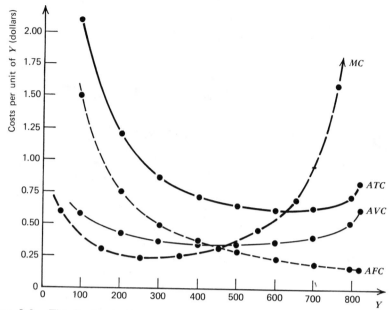

Figure 6-3. The firm's short-run cost curves.

must fall, describing a U-shaped curve, as graphed, that is the reciprocal of the APP_{x_1} curve.[5] AVC falls to its minimum at the output
quantity where APP_{x_1} is a maximum and rising thereafter as greater
amounts of output are produced, becoming vertical at the firm's
maximum output (810 Y when $X_2 = 40$).

  Average fixed cost, the costs of the fixed resources per unit of
output, is derived as

$$AFC = \frac{\text{Total fixed cost}}{\text{Output}} = \frac{TFC}{Y}$$

AFC is a declining curve with increased output because a constant
(TFC) is being divided by an increasingly larger number (Y), up to
the maximum output of 810 units. For this firm, given its specific
resource organization, AFC can fall no lower than \$0.18 because an
output greater than 810 units is impossible without first increasing
the fixed resources in the firm.

---

[5]That changes in the productivity of the variable input give AVC its specific shape can be verified
by looking at the source of each measure of TVC and output. TVC equals the units of X_1 used,
times the price of X_1 ($TVC = X_1 \cdot P_{x_1}$). Units of output produced equals the units of X_1 used
times its APP ($Y = X_1 \cdot APP_{x_1}$). So by substitution, $AVC = TVC/Y = (X_1 \cdot P_{x_1})/(X_1 \cdot APP_{x_1}) =
P_{x_1}/APP_{x_1}$. With APP_{x_1} divided into a constant (P_{x_1}), AVC must trace a U-shaped path, clearly
demonstrating the reciprocal relationships between AVC and APP.

Average total cost (ATC), the total cost of all the resources used per unit of output produced, is the sum of *AVC* and *AFC,* and is computed as

$$ATC = \frac{\text{Total cost}}{\text{Output}} = \frac{TC}{Y} \text{ or } = \frac{TVC + TFC}{Y}$$

Graphically, *ATC* is equal to the combined heights of *AVC* and *AFC.* Since both of these curves are high and falling beginning with the lowest output levels, *ATC* must also be high and falling through that same general range of output. Its minimum point occurs at a greater amount of output than for minimum *AVC* because *AFC* continues to decline as output is increased. A point is reached, past the point of minimum *AVC,* where the increase in *AVC* is just equal to the decrease in *AFC.* At that point (600 *Y*) *ATC* must be at its minimum. *ATC* will rise from that level of output because *AVC* is rising, becoming vertical at the maximum output of 810 units. Like *AVC, ATC* also traces a U-shaped curve between zero and maximum output.

The seventh and final cost concept, *marginal cost,* looks at production costs in the same incremental manner as was done in the last chapter to determine the marginal productivity of a variable input. Marginal cost *(MC),* is defined as the change in total costs when output is changed by one unit, and is determined by

$$MC = \frac{\text{Change in total cost}}{\text{Change in output}} = \frac{\Delta TC}{\Delta Y} \text{ or } = \frac{\Delta TVC}{\Delta Y}$$

Remember that the output observations in Table 6-1 are in 100-unit groupings therefore ΔY is 100 for each observed change, except for the last increment of only 10 units of *Y.* With the *change in output* (100) divided into the *change in total costs* accompanying that output change, the computed cost value is then on a per-unit-of-output basis. Note that in computing *MC* we can use either ΔTC or ΔTVC because they are one and the same. Since fixed costs cannot be changed, the only element of change in *TC* is the change in *TVC.*

The reason for the specific shape of the *MC* curve can be made more clear by looking at the physical basis of production as indicated by the marginal product of the variable resource. Since the productivity of the variable input increases when more of that resource is used, from zero X_1 up to its maximum *MPP, MC* must be falling at the same time. No matter what the output produced by the first unit of X_1, given P_{x_1} unchanged, if a second unit yields more product than the first unit, the cost per unit of producing that additional output must fall—*MC* must decline so long as *MPP* increases. The same reverse relationship must hold when *MPP* is declining: smaller and smaller increments to output with each (equal) increment to input must cause *MC* to increase. Where *MPP* is a maximum, *MC* is a minimum; and where *MPP* is zero, *MC* becomes vertical.[6]

The Search for an Optimum.   In the previous chapter, the question of how much of the variable input to use was answered after developing incremental measures of value productivity per unit of input (*MVP*), and cost (*MFC*). Once having determined the *MVP* schedule, and the level of input use at which increments to revenue and cost were equal (*MVP* = *MFC*), the optimum input use is determined (Figure 4-4).

Our problem now is to determine that one *output* level at which increments to costs and revenue are equal. The one additional concept needed to make this determination is *marginal revenue (MR)*. Marginal revenue can be defined as the amount added to total revenue when an additional unit of output is produced and sold.

As assumption about the market—that this producer's decisions will have no effect on the price of the product[7]—simplifies the problem of optimizing output. Because P_y remains constant whether this operator decides not to produce at all, or expands output to the maximum, the market price can be plotted as a horizontal line in Figure 6-4. In algebraic symbols,

$$MR = \frac{\Delta TR}{\Delta Y} = P_y^{\,8}$$

Given P_y = $1.00, each additional unit sold will add $1.00 to total revenue (the definition of *MR*). Since costs at the margin change (according to the *MC* curve) as output is changed, the oper-

---

[6]This relationship between marginal cost and marginal product may be restated in a similar manner as was done for *AVC* and *APP*. Since ΔTC ($=\Delta TVC$) equals ΔX_1 times the price of X_1, and ΔY equals ΔX_1 times MPP_{x_1}, by substitution

$$MC = \frac{\Delta TC}{\Delta Y} = \frac{\Delta X_1 \cdot P_{x_1}}{\Delta X_1 \cdot MPP_{x_1}} = \frac{P_{x_1}}{MPP_{x_1}}$$

With MPP_{x_1} divided into a constant (P_{x_1}), *MC* must trace a U-shaped path that is a reciprocal of the *MPP* curve.

[7]The market assumption we make here is not at all unrealistic: it simply says that this producer's firm is so small a part of the total market that decisions either to increase or decrease output will not be noticed by the market, i.e., market price will not change as a result of this firm's decisions. As you might observe, very much of this nation's agricultural output is produced in this type of market. Whether it be grain crops, livestock, poultry, or numerous other commodities produced by large numbers of farms, the decision of producers, acting individually, cannot affect the market price of their product.

[8]Because $\Delta TR = \Delta Y \cdot P_y$, by substitution $MR = (\Delta Y \cdot P_y)/\Delta Y$. Since the ΔY's cancel, we are left with the identity $MR = P_y$.

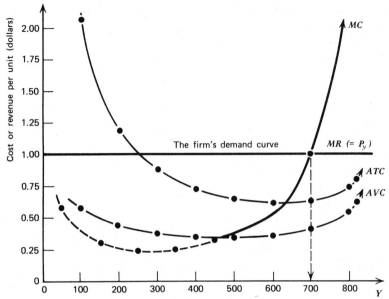

Figure 6-4. Short-run costs and returns per unit of output.

ator must find that one output level at which $MC = MR$.[9] At that output (700 Y), profits are a maximum (or losses a minimum).[10]

The Firm's Short-Run Supply Curve.   With a product price of $1.00 per unit, we discovered that the profit-maximizing output would be 700 Y. But what of the many other possible prices for this product? In the absence of strict price controls, there is no reason to expect price to be locked in at $1.00 only.

What would you as a producer do if the market price were to rise, say to $1.50 per unit? By applying the rule, produce to where $MC = MR$, you would find a new optimum output between 700 and 800 Y. You would employ a greater amount of the variable input to produce more Y, to where $MC = 1.50, because that would be more profitable than just maintaining the previous level of output. In-

---

[9]For any output level to be an optimum, MC must be increasing.

[10]This can be checked against the data in Tables 6-2 and 6-3. Profits are a maximum of $261 at 700 Y, where MC ($= 1.00) $= MR$ ($= 1.00), and would fall to $230.50 if output were reduced to 600 Y—a needless forfeiture of $30.50 profit. Further reductions of output make that difference even greater, with further unnecessary sacrifices of profitability. Increase output to 800 Y and MC ($= 1.61) exceeds MR by $0.61, an unnecessary loss of $61.00 on that 100-unit increment.

So the $MC = MR$ optimizing rule forces adjustments in output because of inequalities in costs and returns at the margin. If MR at any level of output exceeds MC, that inequality simply tells the operator that an additional surplus can be captured and added to his profits if he will just increase output. The opposite signal is equally forceful when MC exceeds MR.

stead of P_y = $1.50, make it $2.00, $4.00, or $10.00, and the optimum output will be greater still (but don't forget that the fixed resource structure of this firm prevents any output greater than 810 Y).

Let the price fall to $0.50 per unit and we must find that output level where MC also is $0.50 per unit ($MC = MR$ at 600 Y).[11] At that output, ATC is $0.62, meaning that costs per unit total $0.12 more than the item brings in the market. Now you're losing $72.00. Should you just quit? No, at that output TVC is $219.50 while TR is $300. There is a net return of $90.50 over variable costs to apply toward fixed costs, and losses are minimized at 600 Y.

How about a market price for Y of $0.30? At that price $MC = MR$ at 400 Y. But at this output AVC is $0.35 so you would be spending more for the variable resource (TVC = $140.00) than you get back from its product (TR = $120.00), for a net loss of $20.00 on variable costs alone. This loss, in addition to the $150.00 fixed costs (a total of $170.00) is worse than your losses would be if you stopped producing entirely.

Note that at 500 Y, AVC is a minimum of $0.35. At any product price less than that, out-of-pocket variable costs cannot even be covered because more would be spent on the variable resource than the product can be sold for. So we have found the minimum price below which this firm can't afford to produce—it pays more not to produce at all. At all prices greater than this, output will be determined at the level where $MC = MR$. We now have a *price-quantity schedule* that is the firm's short-run *supply curve:* the MC curve above minimum AVC is the firm's supply curve showing how much Y will be produced at all possible prices for this product, as indicated by the heavily drawn segment of the MC curve in Figure 6-4.

As market price may fluctuate from a price that is equal to this firm's minimum AVC, to any level greater than that, the firm finds its profitability affected accordingly. Note that earlier in this chapter we priced all the fixed resources to this firm at their opportunity costs, the only meaningful measure of the *true* costs of using resources to produce something. When we tally up the out-of-pocket *explicit* costs for the variable resources used with the *implicit* costs of the fixed resources, then subtract this from total revenue, a balance exists that can be called *economic profit*. This profit can be negative, zero, or positive. A zero profit then is simply a situation where the present use of resources is neither more nor less profitable than the next best paying alternatives for those resources. Economic profit is thus a surplus, being either greater or less than the return necessary

[11] It's really more like 575, but we'll use 600, because numbers are handy for an output of 600.

to attract or keep these resources in their present use. If a zero profit can be expected to keep these resources in their present use, either a negative or positive profit, on the other hand, should trigger adjustments within this firm in the quantities of resources it uses.

If the market price is greater than AVC but less than ATC, the firm will be incurring a loss. How long can it continue to do so? Until fixed asset depreciation has continued to the point where those assets must be replaced, or that the opportunity costs (alternative earnings) of the fixed assets cause these resources to be shifted to alternative, higher paying uses. At that time some or all of the fixed resources are no longer available to produce the product—either worn out and unproductive, or shifted elsewhere—reducing output below that possible from the original function. This will reduce productivity of the variable resources, increase unit costs of production, leaving production even more unprofitable, and squeezing this firm (with its present resource organization) out of the market.

The existence of a net surplus over full production costs and the changes this will cause are more easily visualized than the consequences of a deficit. Figure 6-5 shows a situation where price is greater than ATC. The firm's optimum output is $0-q_1$ (where $MC = MR$). Total revenue for the firm is the rectangle $0-b-c-q_1$ (price of $0-b$ times the quantity $0-q_1$) while total costs are only $0-a-d-q_1$. The shaded rectangular area $a-b-c-d$ is therefore a surplus (economic) profit. The operator would be encouraged to increase the scale of the operation by adding to the fixed resources and using a greater amount of the variable resource to take best advantage of this profitable situation.

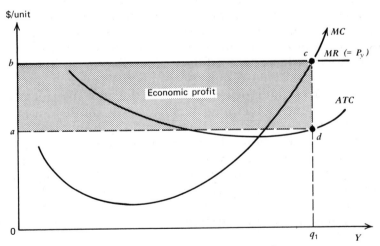

Figure 6-5. Production costs, revenue, and economic profit.

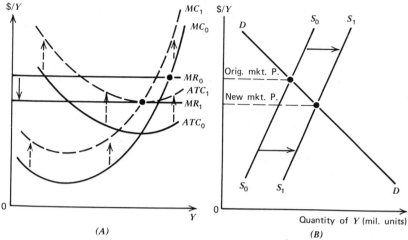

Figure 6-6. Final adjustments in firm costs, market supply, and price in response to economic profit. (A) The firm. (B) The market.

Such a situation may be unique to this one firm only, but it also could be somewhat general in a competitive industry. If so, the market for this product will cause other producing firms to adjust similarly, and attract others into the market, having an effect on both resource costs and product price, eliminating the economic profit. The final effects of these changes are shown in Figure 6-6 demonstrating market changes (B) as well as those for the individual firm (A).

As potentially competing firms see the profitability of this and similar firms, the prices of the variable resources will likely increase (more firms wanting and bidding for the existing supply of these resources, and others being attracted to this use only if their price and expected returns will increase and exceed their present returns). This will cause an upward shift of the firm's AVC and MC curves, resulting also in an upward shift of the ATC curve.

At the same time, the supply of fixed resources will find their prices bid up by the activities of the new firms coming into the market as well as by the existing firms wishing to expand the scale of their operations. This will cause an upward movement in AFC, and another source of upward pressure on ATC.[12] These two sets of

[12]Here's how: Suppose an operator had priced his own management at $5000 per year (the next best paying alternative use of this resource). The $5000 cost is built into the firm's fixed cost structure. Suppose now that someone else wishing to get into this type of business also can see the way clear to hiring this operator to do the same management job, but at a payment of $10,000 per year. Our operator's opportunity cost for his management, in the existing firm, has now gone up, with corresponding upward changes in TFC, AFC, and ATC.

forces will result in this firm's ATC moving upward to the new position shown in Figure 6-6A.

As more resources are committed to producing this product (new firms coming in, plus the expansion of existing firms), the price of the firm's product will be forced downward. Expanding resource use (both fixed and variable) means that the market output will expand as shown by the shift in supply from S_0 (original supply) to S_1 (new supply) in Figure 6-6B. Given demand unchanged, the new market price for this product will be lower than the original price, as determined by the intersection of the market supply and demand curves.

The consequences of all this is that, with costs being pushed upward and market price moving downward, our firm's original economic profit has been squeezed out, and it is now just normally profitable.

Changes such as these presuppose a number of qualifications, which we will treat in Chapter 7. We have dealt here only with a market situation in which the producer, and all others in this market, are too small to have any influence whatever on market price. Along with this has been an implicit assumption that the individual is free to choose from among alternatives as market prices change. Our intent is not to describe a particularly desirable market, but simply to hold all other factors constant so that the effects of certain decisions can be isolated and attributed to that decision alone. The effects of market restrictions, by whatever source or cause, will be treated in Chapters 7 and 8 where specific market conditions can be handled separately.

Market Supply

Market supply curves differ from demand curves in that they are determined by producers' costs and they normally slope upward and to the right rather than downward to the right. A supply curve is defined as the amount of a good or service producers are willing to offer for sale at different prices, *cet. par.* The market supply curve is determined in the same manner as is done for a market demand curve. An individual firm's output response to price changes was described (Figure 6-4, and related text) as being determined by the intersection of the firm's MR (the product's market price) and MC curves. Thus the MC curve above minimum AVC is the firm's supply curve.

All the firms producing a good for the market are the source of the market supply of that good. Individual MC curves are summed

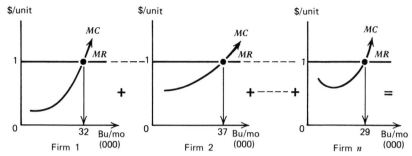

Figure 6-7. Supply curves for all firms producing Good A.
Firm 1. Firm 2. Firm *n*.

horizontally to obtain the total amount of that good those firms are willing to produce for the market at all possible prices. A graphic description of this procedure is shown in Figures 6-7 and 6-8.

In Figure 6-7, three separate firms *1, 2,* and *n* and their respective *MC* curves are used to represent the number of firms in this market. With one price shown ($1.00), each firm decides its output quantity by equating price (*MR*) and *MC*. The quantity for each firm (plus other firms not shown) becomes the total market supply at that price (Figure 6-8). The shape and slope of the market supply curve is determined by the quantities each firm would produce at all other prices.

Using wheat as an example, assume a situation as indicated in Figure 6-9. The market supply curve shows that wheat producers are willing to produce 500 million bushels of wheat at a price of $1.00 per bushel and two billion bushels at a price of $4.00 per

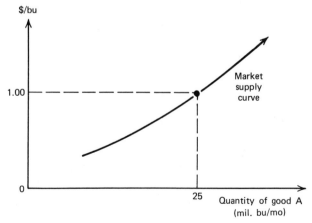

Figure 6-8. Market summation of firms' supply curves for
Good A.

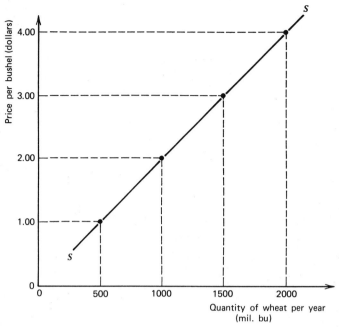

Figure 6-9. A market supply curve.

bushel. This illustrates the concept that as wheat prices increase, producers are willing to commit more resources to wheat production and increase the output of wheat. This direct relationship between price and quantity produced exists due to the increased resource costs of increasing output. Given the resources and technology available to them, producers seek to maximize their returns within the legal framework in which they operate. This does not mean that everything a person does as a supplier of goods and services is related to profit, but only that it is an important influence. Other motivating factors are prestige, tradition, religion, etc.

Changes in Market Supply. Movement along a supply curve is called a "change in quantity supplied," while a change in supply is a shift in the entire supply schedule. An increase in supply is shown in Figure 6-10 by a shift from SS to $S'S'$. This movement could be precipitated, for instance, by good growing conditions or by an improvement in technology (new crop variety that increases yield per acre). Other factors that could cause this shift include: a reduction in resource prices (making it profitable to use more of them); a reduction in relative prices of other products (causing producers to increase their output of this commodity); or changes in institutional constraints such as increased acreage allotments under a farm program.

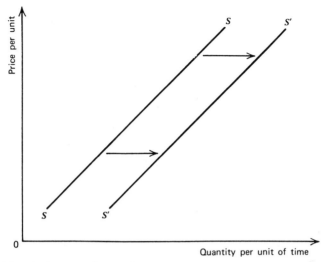

Figure 6-10.   An increase in supply.

On the other hand, a decrease in supply could be caused by such things as drought or crop diseases or opposite changes in the supply shifters mentioned above. The impact of these factors would be to shift the supply curve to the left as in Figure 6-11 so that fewer units of product are supplied at each price.

Elasticity of Supply.   Price elasticity of supply and demand are calculated with the use of the same algebraic expression:

$$E_s = \frac{(Q_1 - Q_2)/(Q_1 + Q_2)}{(P_1 - P_2)/(P_1 + P_2)}$$

Price elasticity of supply is defined as a measure of the percentage change in quantity supplied in response to a percent change in price, *cet. par.* A supply elasticity of .4 for cotton in the short run means that the quantity supplied increases 0.4 percent with a one percent increase in the price of cotton. The sign on the price elasticity coefficient is usually positive since the supply curve is normally positively sloped.

A perfectly vertical supply curve has a zero elasticity coefficient. A zero supply elasticity coefficient means the quantity supplied is not responsive to price changes. If the supply elasticity is between zero and one, the supply elasticity is referred to as being *inelastic.* The percentage change in quantity supplied is less than the corresponding percentage change in price. A supply elasticity coefficient

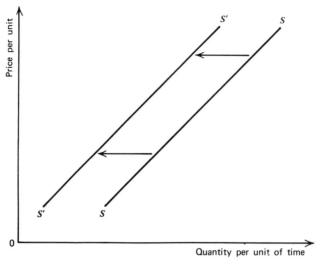

Figure 6-11.   A decrease in supply.

greater than one defines an *elastic* supply. When the percentage increases in supply and price are the same, the coefficient is 1.0. That supply elasticity is called *unitary.*

Supply elasticities are highest for those crops and livestocks where production adjustments are relatively easy to make, such as in potatoes, eggs, and poultry. Low supply elasticities are encountered for fruit, wheat, tobacco, cotton, feedgrains, and milk.

Price Determination

Individual demand curves for a product are added up to derive the market demand curve; individual supply curves for a product also sum horizontally to derive the market supply curve. The demand curve reflects the desires of the consumers while the supply curve indicates the motivations of producers. These two curves interact as in Figure 6-12 to determine market price.

Equilibrium in the Market.   At the point where the demand curve, (DD), intersects the market supply curve (SS), the quantity demanded (Q_0) by consumers equals the quantity supplied by producers (Q_0). This occurs at the equilibrium price, P_0. At equilibrium, all buyers of this product who are willing to pay price P_0 for the commodity could buy the amount they wanted, and all producers who supplied quantity Q_0 could sell their product at P_0, the price they needed to receive in order to produce quantity Q_0. There are no shortages or surpluses in the market; the market is in *equilibrium.*

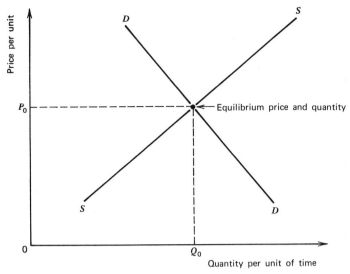

Figure 6-12. Price determination in a market.

Market Disequilibrium. There is a tendency for equilibrium to exist unless demand shifters or supply shifters cause price to change from the equilibrium position. If such changes occur, a new equilibrium will be formed.

A price such as P_1 in Figure 6–13 is not an equilibrium and will cause a surplus to exist. At P_1 producers will wish to sell Q_2 but consumers are willing to buy only Q_1, leaving a surplus (Q_1 to Q_2) in the market at this price. Producers who want to sell this surplus must

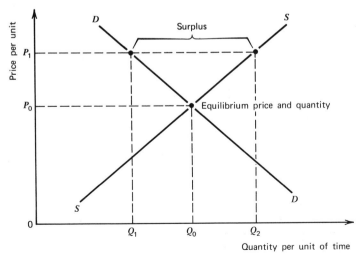

Figure 6-13. Disequilibrium in the market: A surplus.

yield to the downward pressure on their asking price. Only when the price falls to the equilibrium price P_0 will consumers purchase all that suppliers want to sell.

On the other hand, if a price is initially established below equilibrium, at price P_2 (Figure 6-14), suppliers will supply only quantity Q_1, but consumers want quantity Q_2 as shown by the demand curve. Therefore, there is a market shortage equal to Q_1 to Q_2. In order for consumers to purchase the short quantity supplied, they must bid the price up to P_0. Only at the equilibrium price (P_0) is the amount producers supply equal to the amount consumers demand.

An example of this situation existed during the World War II, when rationing was put into effect. Many items such as sugar, shoes, and tires were rationed in order to meet the needs of the public, as well as the war effort. Ceiling prices were established by the government at prices below the equilibrium level as at P_2 in Figure 6-14. This resulted in "black market operations" because at price P_2 producers would supply quantity Q_1, but for quantity Q_1 consumers were willing to pay price P_3. Thus, many rationed items were sold on the black market at prices higher than the price ceilings set by the government.

Using the preceding analysis, the effect of changes in supply or demand may be determined. The impact on the United States of the 1974 oil embargo can be shown in general terms (Figure 6-15). Approximately 20 percent of the United States' crude oil supply came from the Arab States. Figure 6-15 shows the American supply (*SS*) and demand (*DD*) for crude oil prior to the embargo. The

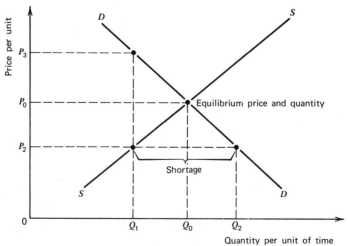

Figure 6-14. Disequilibrium in the market: A shortage.

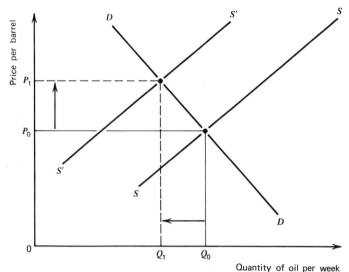

Figure 6-15. Impact of a supply shift on equilibrium price.

equilibrium price was P_0 and the quantity consumed was Q_0. The oil embargo cut off Arab oil shipments to the United States and caused the supply curve to shift to $S'S'$. The result was a new equilibrium at P_1 and Q_1. Consumers now had to pay price P_1 for oil and received only quantity Q_1 rather than Q_0.

A change in the demand schedule occurred with the 1972 sale of wheat to Soviet Russia. Russia purchased about 400 million bushels of wheat which caused an increase in the world wheat price from $2.00 per bushel to about $4.00 per bushel. The United States

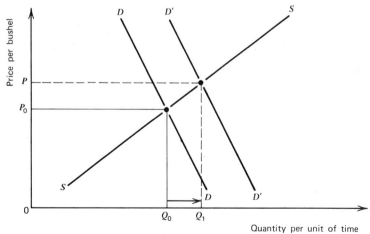

Figure 6-16. Impact of a demand shift on equilibrium price.

was unaware of the total volume of wheat Russia intended to buy. It was assumed that the purchases were for feedgrains in order to increase livestock production. Instead, because of poor weather conditions in the Soviet Union, wheat was needed and purchased for human consumption. The poorer quality Russian wheat was then used for feedgrain purposes in the Soviet Union.

Before the wheat deal, the equilibrium world price was at price P_0, as shown in Figure 6-16, and the quantity consumed was Q_0. The Russian purchase increased the demand for wheat from DD to $D'D'$. This increased the price of wheat to P_1 and increased the quantity consumed to Q_1.

Summary

The true costs of production are opportunity costs. Opportunity costs arise because using resources to produce any output causes a sacrifice of other goods that could have been produced with those resources.

Production costs can be quantified only after recognizing the specific resource relationships upon which any product output is based. We began the analysis of a firm's costs by again using a single-variable production function as a point of departure. Given the rigid tie between production functions and cost functions, we made use of the production function data in Table 4-1 (and graphed in Figure 4-2) as the starting point.

Short-run cost curves are defined within a given period of time. Each of these curves (*AVC, AFC, ATC,* and *MC*) shows which cost items change, and their directions (increasing or decreasing) as the firm changes its rates of resource use and output.

The firm optimizes its rate of output by producing a quantity of output that is determined by the point at which *MC* and *MR* are equal. The point of minimum *AVC* determines the lowest price at which the firm will produce for the market. From that point upward the *MC* curve is the firm's supply curve. As price may rise above minimum *AVC* the firm is experiencing a loss until price equals *ATC*. Higher prices will result in economic profit for the firm (*NR* in excess of all opportunity costs or, what is the same thing, in excess of all explicit and implicit costs).

As firms in an industry earn economic profits, other firms will enter the industry, bidding up the prices of both variable and fixed resources in those firms. With more firms producing, market output will increase (a market supply shift). Given demand unchanged, price will fall and cause economic profits to decline.

If, on the other hand, firms are earning negative economic profits, some firms will leave the industry. As firms leave there will be an output reducing shift in market supply causing price and economic profit to rise. Thus long-run market equilibrium can be described as one of zero economic profits.

Chapter Highlights

1. Product supply results from the use of resources, giving rise to two general types of costs: (1) explicit costs—direct or cash costs paid for resources bought or hired; and (2) implicit costs—indirect or noncash costs of the owned resources.

2. Opportunity costs are the true costs of production. In a free market, the payments to variable resources must at least equal their best paying alternative in order to obtain the services of these resources. Fixed resources are being used inefficiently if they are not earning at least as much as they could in the next best alternative.

3. What we ordinarily like to call "profit," economics includes as a cost of production. So if receipts exceed the full costs of production, there is a surplus, called "economic (or pure) profit."

4. The shapes of the cost curves are determined by the firm's production function.

5. The short-run stems from a production function with one or more fixed resources.

6. The longer run is derived from a production function that has a larger proportion of resources that are variable. The ultimate long-run is when all resources are variable.

7. Economics utilizes seven cost concepts: *TVC, TFC, TC, AVC, AFC, ATC,* and *MC.*

8. Two concepts are especially useful in determining an optimal output: *MC* which is defined as the change in total costs when output is changed by one unit; and *MR* which is defined as the amount added to total revenue when an additional unit of output is produced and sold.

9. Since the price that the competitive firm gets for its product does not change as it adjusts output, the firm's demand curve is its *MR* curve.

10. The firm's profit-maximizing output is determined by the point at which *MC* = *MR*, an output which can also be determined by using the *TR* and *TC* curves.

11. In the short-run, a firm will shut down operations if it cannot at least cover its variable costs.

12. The short-run supply curve of the competitive firm is its *MC* curve above minimum *AVC.*

13. The existence of economic profit will cause present firms to expand output (by increasing firm size), and will also attract new firms into the industry both of which cause the market supply curve to shift to the right and market price to fall.

14. Factors that shift a supply curve are: changes in growing conditions (weather); technology; resource prices; product prices and profitability of substitute products; and institutional constraints.
15. Individual demand curves for a commodity are added horizontally to derive the market demand curve. Individual supply curves are summed in the same manner to derive the market supply curve.
16. Equilibrium market price and quantity are determined by the interaction of market demand and supply curves.
17. At market equilibrium all buyers of a commodity who are willing and able to pay the equilibrium market price will obtain the amount of product they desire. Also, all sellers will supply the amount purchasers want at that price.
18. A new market equilibrium will be established if any of the demand or supply shifters change.

Review Questions

1. What is the economic meaning of costs?
2. Suppose that you maintain a full set of books for your firm, which meet minimum requirements for recording income and costs. In what way are your book's costs different from economic costs?
3. What is the special meaning of each type of cost (*TVC, TFC, TC, AVC, AFC, ATC,* and *MC*)?
4. Suppose you are the operator of a firm with the following short-run schedule of output and total cost:

Output	Total Cost
0	$10,000
1000	15,000
2000	25,000
3000	40,000
4000	60,000
5000	90,000
6000	130,000

   a. What is your firm's total fixed cost? total variable costs? average variable costs? average total costs? marginal cost?
   b. How much of this product would you produce at a market price of $2.50 per unit?
   c. How much (if any) economic profit would you earn if the market price were $10 per unit?
5. Many people think that profits are wrongly taken from consumers. Justify an economic profit as a reward for producing something which society wants so strongly that you were able to claim that amount as yours. Did you cheat your hired labor to get that economic profit? Did you cheat your customers?
6. Are economic losses (negative economic profits) wasteful? Is this in any way a use of the wrong resources to produce the wrong product, thus "wasting" society's resources?

7. Obviously, shifts in supply and demand can counteract one another when both curves shift or accentuate the impact of the other's change. Draw several graphs with increasing and decreasing shifts of both supply and demand, and analyze the effects on equilibrium price and quantity.

Suggested Readings

1. Bishop, C. E. and W. D. Toussaint. *Agricultural Economic Analysis.* New York: John Wiley and Sons, Inc., 1958, Chapters 7 and 8.
2. Bradford, Lawrence A., and Glenn L. Johnson. *Farm Management Analysis.* New York: John Wiley and Sons, 1958, Chapter 12.
3. Brehm, Carl. *Introduction to Economics.* New York: Random House, Inc., 1970, Chapter 6.
4. Gwartney, James D. *Microeconomics, Public and Private Choice.* New York: Academic Press, Inc., 1977, Chapters 6 and 7.
5. Leftwich, Richard D. *Introduction to Microeconomics.* New York: Holt, Rinehart and Winston, Inc., 1970, Chapters 8 and 9.
6. Peterson, Willis L. *Principles of Economics: Micro,* 3rd ed. Homewood, Ill.: Richard D. Irwin, Inc., 1977, Chapters 5 and 6.

Courtesy of the University of Nebraska, Lincoln.

COMPETITION AND THE MARKET

COMPETITION AND THE MARKET

This chapter deals with the competitive conditions in a market in order to explain a firm's pricing and output decisions. The competitive model is presented so that other noncompetitive models can be examined. The role of scarcity and rationing and the manner in which they influence competition is also discussed.

The problem of scarcity is basic to much of the topical material of this book for a reason: because of scarcity some means of allocating (rationing) limited resources among their alternative uses, and of distributing limited goods and services among those desiring them, must be devised. There simply are too few of the desired things to fully satisfy all of our desires, thus we have scarcity and the need for rationing. The criteria by which the allocation problem is solved only reflects the fact of scarcity which, in itself, is the cause of competition.

Rationing can be accomplished in a number of ways, any of which require discriminatory criteria, by discriminating against those who, no matter how strong their desire for the particular good, are unable to meet requirements to get it. If rationing is done administratively, the basic criteria may simply be sex, age, height, weight, family size, agility, willingness to wait in line, level of education, or any of a great many other possibilities and combinations. The point is that specific criteria are established (somehow, or by someone); then those eligible will compete in whatever manner is required to gain their share of that desired item, whatever it might be.[1]

But scarcity and rationing are hardly the only causes of competition. A Robinson Crusoe, alone on an island, will expend effort to improve fishhooks, for example, if the expected benefits of that ef-

[1]Should a large, heavy person get more food than a small person? Should an adult get less milk than a child, with the needs of all those under five years of age, say, being met first? If individuals performing the most difficult physical labor get more of certain foods than others not so employed, there will be competition for jobs, with their performance in those jobs designed to continue employment, depending on the degree of scarcity and the amount of discrimination in their favor.

fort exceed the sacrifices required to gain benefits. If improved fishhooks ("capital," with cost measured as the value of other desired things foregone while producing fishhooks) will reduce the time spent in fishing, and permit more time to be spent in other activities (an overall increase in desired goods), the benefits are determinable. The worth of these benefits (and sacrifices) will be influenced by the values of what Crusoe considers to be good or bad; desirable and undesirable. Thus, the system has not been the cause of competition. Given the freedom to choose between alternatives, the driving force is the individual's own set of preferences and desires, and the relative scarcities of the desired things, not someone else trying to outdo him.

The Function of Price

An isolated Robinson Crusoe causes no concern for others. Crusoe alone gains or suffers from his decisions. Only his well-being is improved or worsened by what is done. By economizing on scarce resources, including his time and abilities, an optimal balance is achieved between the sacrifices made to achieve desired benefits.

But this is too simple and private a problem. Proper or improper rates of resource use and product output impact only on Crusoe's own well-being, with no one else affected in the process. When a number of people are involved—when the decisions made, and the efficiency with which any one person operates, have an effect on the well-being of others—the problem becomes one of organizing the economic system and ordering decisions in such a way that undesirable effects on others are minimized or eliminated. One answer to this need for controlling individual actions is a "market," as was discussed earlier.

In a free enterprise economy the market is decentralized, with decisions being made and carried out by individuals responding to their preferences and market prices, rather than by conscious direction from elsewhere in the system. In such a market-oriented economy, prices play a key role in directing the allocation of resources among alternative uses and in causing the produced goods to be divided among consumers according to their individual preferences.

When a good becomes more scarce relative to the demand for it, the price of that good will increase. A price increase is the market's signal to both producers and consumers that changes are required. Penalties are inflicted on those who make the wrong decisions or who simply refuse to change: producers needlessly forfeit potential profits, and consumers find increased sacrifices of other desired goods, as their penalty for not making the proper adjustments in their purchases.

An increase in the relative price of a good conveys to both buyers and sellers the information that this good is now more scarce than it was formerly. No individual needs to know why the good is now more scarce, nor does the individual necessarily need to contemplate how that increased scarcity can best be alleviated. The message of increased scarcity, as transmitted by price alone, suggests the solution. Individual buyers who now value the good lower than does the market, are induced to reduce purchases by shifting more spending to acceptable substitutes. Thus, demand for the good falls because marginal utility per dollar spent has fallen and causes the spending shift. Resource owners are encouraged by the prospect of increased profits to divert resources from other goods because the marginal revenue per dollar of resource commitment is now enhanced. The supply of the good is increased. The market is thus an efficient clearinghouse bringing order out of conflicting desires, by giving the appropriate price signals to all who by their actions are able to help correct the problem. As the market functions efficiently it is then possible for prices to be efficient indicators of the relative values of all things traded in the market. But if the market itself is not efficient (if it is unable to reflect changes in market forces because of restrictions stemming from the ability of individuals, groups or government actions to regulate prices or production), the ability of prices to indicate values correctly is diminished.

Market Classification

As we consider how prices of goods and services are determined, and how earnings of all types of resources are established, it is necessary to look more carefully at different types of markets within which all economic activity takes place, where price is used as the rationing device. It is in this area that economic efficiency has its roots.

Some firms appear to be at the mercy of the market, with fluctuating prices seemingly unrelated to the production activities of those firms; many agricultural producers fall within such a market situation. It is a market characterized by a high degree of competition between producing firms.

Numerous other industries appear to be made up of firms which seem able to manipulate price to their advantage. A market such as this is loosely referred to as being "monopolistic" to some degree. Competition between these firms appears to be minimal, or

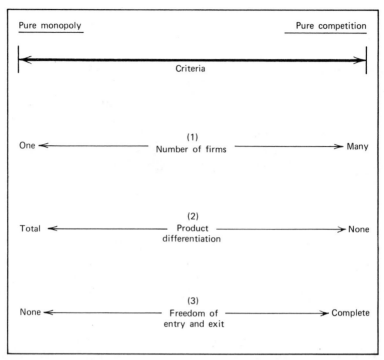

Figure 7-1.   Criteria extremes for classifying markets.

even absent, because there are so few firms in that industry.[2] A pure monopoly, in fact, is defined as a single seller.

Since economic efficiency involves production of goods and services in the quantities and proportions that people want, and that with a minimum of resource expenditure, we may classify markets in a way having some usefulness in making judgments about the efficiency with which a system operates. Extreme opposites (models), based on the degree of competition between firms in a market, are generalized in Figure 7-1. The market situation within which the firm operates, and the firm's reactions to those conditions, form the basis for this classification.

Given identifying characteristics, firms may be found anywhere along a continuum ranging from the purely competitive firm at one extreme to the pure monopolist firm at the other, with its particular

[2]Don't let the discussion mislead you into thinking that the labels and distinctions used here apply only to producing firms. Identical conditions may also be applied to the buyer's side of the market. If, for instance, there is only one buyer for an industry's output, we would call that firm a monopsony (rather than monopoly). Purity on both sides of the competitive market occurs when there are many buyers as well as sellers.

location along the continuum depending upon the degree to which the firm fits some or all of the criteria.[3]

Pure Competition. The necessary conditions for the existence of pure competition are: (1) many firms in the industry; (2) a homogeneous product; and (3) individual freedom to enter or leave the industry.

The actual number of firms that it takes to constitute *many* is relative. We simply need to realize that it means so many of them that no individual firm can have any influence whatsoever on the market price of its product as a result of its own decisions and actions. If a firm is a small part of the total market, then whether it produces the maximum amount that it is capable of producing, or shuts down completely, the market will not be affected. The firm's output is such an insignificant bit of the total market supply of that product that it cannot affect the market price.

Many farms and ranches in the United States fit this requirement. Producers of grain, livestock, and many other food and feed products are especially incapable of influencing price by their individual actions. And they frequently are used as examples of a highly competitive industry, unable on their own, to do anything about the prices they get for their products in the market place.

A *homogeneous product* may be achieved either by uniformity in all physical characteristics of the product as it leaves producing firms, or by the market classifying and separating the product into distinctive groups according to specific grades and standards. In either case there will be no favoring or discriminating against any firm's product in the market. Product homogeneity eliminates the possibility of buyers preferring one firm's product over that of another.

Any attempt by the individual firm to obtain a premium for its product would be futile because the market can obtain all of that good it wants from other producing firms. Any attempted discounting of the price of one firm's product would be rejected because the firm could sell all of the product at the going market price. The reduced price would only reduce revenue. Pure competition thus results in the products of competing firms being perfect substitutes for one another.

Homogeneity by grade-standardization is evident in many agricultural product markets. Specific grade standards are sufficiently precise that the buyer need not even see and inspect the commodity

---

[3]The words "pure" and "perfect" are sometimes loosely used synonymously in these market descriptions. But for pure to become perfect requires two additional criteria: (1) perfect mobility (of all goods and services); and (2) perfect knowledge and foresight (for all decision makers).

being purchased. All firms able to deliver the particular grade of product will receive the market-determined price for their product at the time of the transaction, because the market is indifferent as to who produced it.

The third condition, *freedom of entry and exit,* permits the individual firm to enter or leave a market as its own costs and returns might dictate, without other restrictions or encouragement of any kind. Such freedom permits the firm to produce or not, or to produce more or less, as its own decision criteria and objectives might direct, without restrictions beyond the pure force of market price. Thus, if the firm sees an opportunity to profit by switching from corn to wheat, for instance, it may do so without restraint or direction either from other firms in the market or by governmental institutions.

Given the three criteria for pure competition, a firm operating in such a market may be described as being a *price-taker:* price is taken as given, with no opportunity for influence by the individual firm. The firm competes by organizing its mix of land, labor, capital, and management to establish the rate of resource use and product output that will maximize its net revenue.

This characteristic of the firm in pure competition is significant to the larger (social) objective of an efficient economic system. Even though the *market* demand curve slopes downward to the right, the *firm's* demand curve is horizontal (i.e., perfectly elastic). Because of this, the product price will not change as a consequence of the individual firm's decision-making; price is beyond the firm's influence. It is a boundary on the firm's options: the firm recognizes its inability to affect or manipulate the price of its product. It concentrates instead on the area in which individual control may be exercised with beneficial results—achieving an economic optimum in the firm's productive activities. This is one reason why you see farm or ranch operators spending so much of their time and effort in direct management activities and so little (individually) in economic activities "beyond the farm gate."

Pure Monopoly. At the other extreme of our continuum is the pure monopolist which may be type-cast as a *price-searcher.* This firm, unlike those in pure competition, need not accept price as given. It "searches" for that price for its product which will balance its rate of output (and sales) with its cost structure so that its profitability is maximized.

The classification as a pure monopoly hinges on the three basic criteria in Figure 7-1. Where there must be many firms in pure competition, monopoly, in its purest extreme means there is a single firm selling the product. The *market* demand curve and the *firm's* demand curve are one and the same, which adds another dimension to the monopolist's decision-making and market powers.

Being the only firm producing and selling its product, the monopolist has no competitor producing a similar good—that firm's product is differentiated from all others—so competition in that product market is absent. This carries with it some incorrect implications about a monopolist's pricing policies.

A monopolist appears to have a strangling control over the price that its product may command in the market place. But that strength cannot be so absolutely exercised. The power to set the price at any level *does* exist; however, an unconcerned use of that ability would require that the demand for its good also be perfectly inelastic.[4] Granted that an uncontrolled monopoly is free to set its product price at any level it might wish. But if the monopolist is profit oriented (and not just flexing muscle in a demonstration of its market power), it will recognize that a price too high for the product will impose its own penalty by causing so large a reduction in sales that profits are being forfeited.

Without the ability to protect and maintain its unique position, a monopoly could not be continued for long. Given the market's price

---

[4]The elasticity of demand for any good reflects, among other things, the availability of acceptable substitutes for that good, ranging from the perfect substitutes (perfectly elastic demand curve for a homogeneous product) of pure competition to the complete opposite of *no* substitutes whatever. The monopolist's perfectly inelastic demand curve would graph as a vertical line which says that a given quantity of that good will be demanded no matter what the price might be. But this is a real-life impossibility since consumers would have to possess infinite incomes to pay the infinitely high price which such a demand curve shows a pure monopolist could charge for his product.

We are misled if we attempt to base the meaning of substitutes on the similarity of physical characteristics, or of the desires satisfied, by two different goods. Rather, it must be remembered that sacrifices of other goods means that the higher price of *any* good (monopolist's product, or otherwise) the more of other goods that must be sacrificed if one is to continue buying it.

No matter how strong our desire for a good may be, the economics of its consumption prevents us from consuming a specific quantity of that good on the basis of some physical criterion. For example, we may have an intense desire for baked goods made from wheat, and might even convince ourselves that we absolutely must have some of that product, no matter what (a good without substitutes, having an apparently perfectly inelastic demand curve). Then imagine if you will, the price of wheat going higher and higher. Eventually, the physical fact of life (that other goods can, maybe in lesser degree, satisfy that need) and the economic fact of life (that its cost, in terms of other goods sacrificed has gotten too high to be worth buying any more of it) will force us to accept a substitute made from oats, barley, corn, rye, or some other cereal grain, or even a synthetic substitute. Our preferences may lean strongly toward consuming a wheat food, but our bodies need only food that provides the proper nutrition, not necessarily wheat. Therein lies the basis for a demand curve that is anything but vertical. We are forced to the realization that there are substitutes for everything, and that the monopolist's perfectly inelastic demand curve is an economically impossible fiction.

signals, a highly profitable business could expect competitors to appear from elsewhere in the system in the expectation of higher profits for them. Those competitors must be kept out, and they may be by a variety of devices (legal and otherwise) that prevent others from becoming established in the monopolist's market.[5]

Conceivably, a monopolist could prevent competitive entry by other firms if it enjoys what may be called a natural monopoly. A natural monopoly would exist where the firm owns or controls the only available source of a necessary resource used in the manufacture or production of the good that it sells in the market.[6] Unless prohibited by law, the firm could protect its monopoly position simply by refusing to share its supply of this ingredient with any other firm.

Many other means of preventing entry also exist, some with powers developed by the firm, and others actually granted by the government. Economies of scale may prevent entry of new firms in the monopolist's market. Large initial investment outlays for fixed capital items may rule out potential firms because they simply can't amass sufficient capital. And the technology of production may be such that a very large-scale operation is the only possibility, preventing another from beginning as a small firm, then growing larger as it succeeds in its efforts. For whatever internal reason, the ATC curve may fall through such a wide range of output that smaller firms can not compete. The declining ATC curve may also be over such a wide range of output that the single firm is capable of supplying the entire market demand without experiencing rising average costs. Competitors are thus kept out of the market because the monopolist is able to price its product below any other firm's costs of production.[7]

The firm may hold a patent on the production process with exclusive use of that process being granted and protected for a period of years by the government, under the conditions of its patent laws. Franchise or license fees to operate may also be set so high,

---

[5] In terms of the monopoly model itself, the method by which entry is prevented is immaterial. The theoretical elimination of competition is essential, however, to permit an analysis of the specific operation of a pure monopoly and its effects in the economy.

[6] An example of this was the market power that the Aluminum Company of America had in the aluminum industry, through its control of 90 percent of the nation's bauxite supply. See John Ise, *Economics,* New York: Harper and Brothers, 1946, p. 135.

[7] In such a situation, fostering (or requiring) competition from other firms would be an economic waste in that the product cost to consumers would be greater with two or more competing firms than with the single monopoly producing the commodity. Public utility companies are frequently used as examples of this type of situation. Granting them exclusive market rights prevents the economic waste involved in competitively duplicating facilities.

or the number so restricted, as to prevent other firms from competing in that market.

To this point in the discussion, we have quite rigidly defined and described two opposite market types which we would not even expect to find (in their pure forms) in the real world. Then why study them? Must we now admit to a kind of academic pretension that has simply been toying with a set of artificial concepts that are without real-life meaning? Hardly. Their usefulness becomes apparent when they stand as benchmarks, or yardsticks, against which we may measure the efficiency of markets and firms as they use valuable resources to produce want satisfying goods and services.[8] These pure models make clear the manner by which firms search for an optimum in their operations, and the social effects in terms of resource allocation, production, and prices.

The Efficiency of Pure Competition

The efficiency with which the competitive market determines production decisions in the short run was presented in the chapters on production and costs. When the firm has established the rate of output at which its profits are maximized, as in Figure 7-2A, given the assumed market conditions of pure competition, no adjustment to a higher profit level is possible without first changing the number and mix of resources within the firm's control, or improving the technology of using those resources. With all firms in the market at their optima the resulting price is an equilibrium price because quantities demanded and supplied are equal (Figure 7-2B). At that price, firms are willing to supply just the amount that consumers are willing and able to buy. This situation is called an equilibrium because the firm is not encouraged, by expectations of greater profits, to make any changes in its present operations. An equilibrium situation is sometimes referred to as being one of "normal profits." Profits are normal because each resource within the firm is earning a return that is neither greater nor less than its next best employment possibility (its opportunity cost). No firm is encouraged to enter or leave the industry because earnings are neither better nor worse than they would be elsewhere in the system. Resources are thus efficiently allocated.

We may summarize the pure market's adjustment solution to

[8]Although we limit ourselves here to the price effects of these two market types, other, broader, social evaluations may also be made in which the point of concern is directed toward the efficiency of existing or proposed economic policies, programs, institutions, or even the organization of an economic system itself.

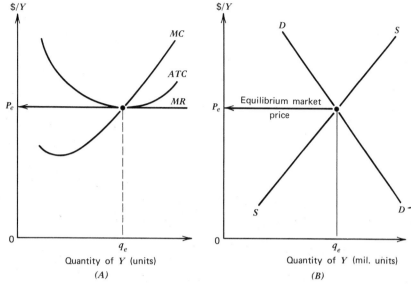

Figure 7-2. Equilibrium for the firm and the market. (A) The firm. (B) The market.

the questions of resource allocation, production rates and prices by studying the individual firm's solution to its own problems under conditions of disequilibrium. Either of two types of disequilibrium is possible: (1) firms are experiencing the surplus earnings of economic rent; or (2) they are incurring losses—negative economic rent. These situations are shown in Figure 7-3 *A* and *B*.

Longer-Run Changes Caused by Economic Rent. Since the firm's ATC curve includes a normal rate of return (profit) as a cost of production, any return per unit of output that is greater than ATC at that output is therefore an excess or surplus over costs. It is a surplus in that it exceeds the expected return that had previously attracted each of the firm's resources into its present use, and is greater than the return needed to keep the firm and its resources in their present employment.

Suppose the firm shown in Figure 7-3A is a wheat farm that, under its current costs and product price conditions, is producing 5000 bushels of wheat per year. Because the firm is a price-taker, its demand curve is its MR curve and the optimum output for the firm is 5000 bushels, as that is the output at which this firm's MR and MC are equal. At this level of output, however, the firm's total costs per unit of output are only P_2 while its revenue per unit is P_0; it is earning a surplus equal to P_2 to P_0 (measured along the vertical

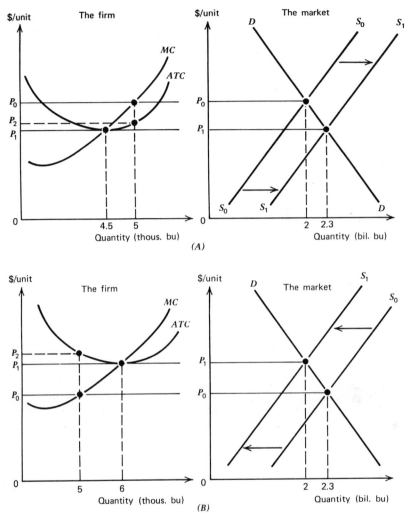

Figure 7-3. From short-run disequilibrium to longer-run adjustments. (A) Economic rent and shift in supply as firms enter the industry. (B) Economic losses and shift in supply as firms leave the industry.

axis). If this firm is typical of others in the industry, the pure market will cause longer-run changes to be made by individual firms, all acting on their own initiative, that will eliminate this surplus.[9] This rate of return exceeds the earnings of other firms elsewhere in the

[9]To present a more easily recognized picture of longer-run market adjustments, another set of market forces has been disregarded here: when new firms enter the industry, their effect is not

system, which will encourage them to shift from their present employment to wheat production in the expectations that they, too, might reap such earnings. As other firms enter the wheat market, the wheat supply curve shifts to the right from the original supply (S_0) to the new supply (S_1). Given the demand for wheat (D), the increased supply causes the new equilibrium price (P_1) to be lower than the original price (P_0). Firms will continue entering the market until the price of wheat has fallen to the point where price (MR) equals the firm's MC at minimum ATC, a longer-run equilibrium position. Economic rent has now been eliminated and consumers are supplied with the amount of wheat they are willing and able to buy at a minimum opportunity cost to them. No other good or service more valuable than the last unit of wheat produced has been sacrificed to produce that last unit of wheat.

This equilibrium is the economic efficiency that is so much to be desired. With all industries so structured (i.e., pure competition), and each at an equilibrium, society's costs for all of its goods and services are minimized; the system is efficient in that no greater output of any good or service can be obtained from the available resources without having to sacrifice something else more highly valued by consumers.

Longer-Run Adjustments to Losses.   When firms in an industry are earning less than normal returns (i.e., not covering their full opportunity costs) in the short run, as in Figure 7-3B, changes will be made that are opposite in directions from those just discussed. In the market, supply and demand are equal at P_0. But for the price-taking firm, a product price of P_0 is not sufficient to cover all costs. The short-run loss-minimizing output for the firm is 5000 bushels when price is P_0. At 5000 bushels of output, the firm is losing an amount per bushel of wheat that is equal to the vertical distance (measured along the vertical axis) from the point where MR and MC are equal up to the ATC curve (P_0 to P_2). Since the firm's ATC curve is the sum of all per-unit opportunity costs of the resources used to produce wheat, a longer-run adjustment for this firm is to shift some or all of its resources to other uses—such as a shift of land from producing wheat to alternative crops or other uses that will

---

solely on the market price of the product (the result of a shift in the market supply), but also affects the prices of resources within the industry as well. New firms will be bidding for resources already in the industry and, excepting the possibility of a perfectly elastic input supply curve, will increase the existing firms' resource costs because of their now increased opportunity costs (as discussed in Chapter 6). Thus there are two simultaneous changes occurring: product price falls, and costs increase.

yield greater returns than wheat.[10] As firms carry out these changes, the market supply curve for wheat shifts to the left causing the market price of wheat to rise until a new equilibrium price (P_1) is reached. At this price level all opportunity costs are once again just fully covered, and firms are experiencing zero economic rent.

Longer-Run Market Supply Curves. To more clearly focus our attention on the direction of changes in market supply, straight-line market supply curves were used in Figure 7-3 *A* and *B*, with no change in the slopes of those shifting curves. Let's now examine more carefully the market supply changes that would result as firms make their longer-run adjustments to economic profits or losses.

The firms' short-run *MC* curves sum horizontally to form the market supply curve. But when firms react to economic rent by changing the fixed resources used, those short-run cost curves are no longer the relevant length-of-run for either those firms or the market. As the length-of-run is increased, the firm's *MC* curve becomes more elastic because a greater proportion of the firm's resources is variable than in the shorter run.

Figure 7-4 shows the different market supply curves that result from different length-of-run production and cost functions for the firms that make up the industry.

The basis for defining length-of-run is the proportion of resources that can be varied by the producing firm. So the longer the length-of-run for the firms, the greater will be the elasticity of the market supply curve.

A perfectly inelastic market supply (S_1) occurs when no changes in resources can be made by the producing firms because the time period is too short to make resource and product changes—the immediate short-run. Its opposite is the ultimate long run which is so long a time period that everything is variable, resulting in the perfectly elastic market supply curve (S_4).

Many intermediate length-of-run possibilities, and their consequent supply elasticities are possible, depending upon the proportions of the resources that are variable for the firm. If firms are able to vary only a few of their resources a relatively inelastic market supply curve (such as S_2) results. However, if more resources are variable, the market supply curve is more elastic (S_3).

[10]The recent shifting of rangeland from livestock to wheat production, by some ranch operators in areas of the West, is a vivid demonstration of how producers react to changes in relative prices. As the price of beef fell between 1973 and 1977, the relative profitability of wheat increased to the point where it paid to plow up some of that rangeland and use it to produce wheat instead. No matter how optimistic beef producers' longer-run expectations might have been, short-run losses were forcing some operators to make such an adjustment.

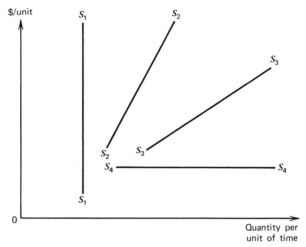

Figure 7-4. Length-of-run and market supply.

Summary

Markets are classified by the number of firms in an industry; whether or not products are differentiated; and the entry and exit conditions of the firms. A purely competitive market is one in which there are many firms in the industry, a homogeneous product is produced, and each firm has the freedom to enter or leave the industry. A firm operating in a purely competitive market is described as being a price-taker. The firm's demand curve is perfectly elastic or horizontal. The firm cannot influence price by the amount of product it sells. Remember, however, that the market demand curve in a competitive industry slopes downward and to the right.

A monopolist on the other hand is a single firm selling the product. The market demand curve and the firm's demand curve are identical. Entry is blocked or restricted in some way.

Firms in pure competition are more efficient than are monopolies. In pure competition, firms can only make a normal profit in the long run because firms can enter or leave the industry. Entry conditions influence the supply of the product to insure that only a normal profit is made. However, in monopoly this may not occur.

Chapter Highlights

1. Scarcity causes rationing by discriminating: (1) through the market where those able to pay for the goods are the ones who get them; or (2) by using nonmarket criteria that direct goods and services to those who get them.

2. Competition is caused by scarcity and not by the economic system, or by someone else.
3. Market prices are signals, which direct production and consumption decisions.
4. The conditions necessary for "pure competition" are: (1) many firms; (2) a homogeneous product; and (3) complete freedom of entry and exit.
5. A purely competitive firm is called a "price-taker."
6. The market demand curve slopes downward to the right. The firm in pure competition faces a horizontal (or perfectly elastic) demand curve, while the pure monopolist's demand curve is the market demand curve.
7. The conditions necessary for a "pure monopoly" are: (1) a single seller; (2) a differentiated product; and (3) no freedom of entry.
8. A pure monopolist is called a "price-searcher."
9. Market models such as pure competition and pure monopoly are useful in evaluating the economic efficiency of an industry.
10. Purely competitive firms in equilibrium, with zero economic rent, are economically efficient because the costs of society's goods and services are minimized.
11. The concept of length-of-run derives from the resource-use options available to producing firms in a market, affecting market supply elasticity.

Review Questions

1. What is the role of prices in a free enterprise economy? What happens if prices are changed artificially?
2. Define pure competition. Is agriculture a purely competitive industry? Discuss.
3. Do firms such as General Motors and Ford operate in a competitive market? Why or why not?
4. Why do firms like to become price searchers? Explain how a firm might become a price searcher.
5. What is a "normal profit?" Are normal profits made in agriculture? Explain.
6. Does the length-of-run of firms influence the elasticity of the market supply curve? Why?
7. Draw the firm and industry demand curves for a firm producing a product under purely competitive conditions.
8. Draw the industry demand and supply curves for a product. Now draw another diagram showing the competitive firm's demand and cost curves for the same product.
9. How does competition reduce the cost of goods to consumers?
10. How does competition increase the quality of consumer goods?

Suggested Readings

1. Hirshleifer, Jack. *Price Theory and Applications.* Englewood Cliffs, N.J.: Prentice-Hall, Inc., 1976, Chapters 9, 10, and 11.

2. Leftwich, Richard H. *The Price System and Resource Allocation,* 6th ed. Hinsdale, Ill.: The Dryden Press, 1976, Chapter 7.
3. Quirk, James P. *Intermediate Microeconomics.* Chicago, Science Research Associates, Inc., 1976, Chapter 8.
4. Samuelson, Paul A. *Economics,* 8th ed. New York: McGraw-Hill Book Company, 1970, Chapter 25.
5. Watson, Donald S., *Price Theory and Its Use,* 4th ed. Boston: Houghton Mifflin Company, 1977, Chapters 13 and 14.

Courtesy of Montana State University Photographic Services Department, Bozeman.

IMPERFECT COMPETITION AND MARKET REGULATION

IMPERFECT COMPETITION AND MARKET REGULATION

Given the criteria for pure competition, we can draw important conclusions regarding the economic efficiency with which an economy so organized could operate. Such a system constitutes an ideal in that no greater efficiency in the organization of an economy can be visualized. Thus, it is useful as a standard of performance for appraising other market types.

The Pure Monopoly.   We defined a monopoly in Chapter 7 not only on the basis of its failure to meet the requirements for pure competition but that it stands at the opposite end of the continuum with special criteria of its own.

As we considered decision-making principles in pure competition, it was necessary to distinguish between the market's demand curve and the firm's demand curve. No such need exists in the case of pure monopoly because the monopoly firm and market are the same. The market demand curve *is* the pure monopolist's demand curve.

Since the market demand curve is always downward sloping, the simple criterion for profit maximization, of equating the firm's costs and returns at the margin ($MC = MR$), cannot result in an efficient allocation of resources for society. An important difference from pure competition is the problem a monopoly faces in selling its products. While the market will take all of the price-taker's output at the market price, the only way a monopolist can sell more output is to reduce the price of the product. The monopolist's marginal revenue and demand are thus two different curves, and are the underlying cause of resource misallocation in that market.

Let's look at a hypothetical set of data appropriate to a monopolist's market that demonstrates the relationship between price and sales, Table 8-1. The downward sloping demand curve is evident in that more of this good will be purchased by consumers only if its price is reduced.

Since we define marginal revenue as the amount by which total

Table 8-1   A Monopolist's Demand and Revenue

Price per Unit = AR	Quantity Demanded	Total Revenue	Marginal Revenue
$6	2	$12	
			$4
5	4	20	
			2
4	6	24	
			0
3	8	24	
			−2
2	10	20	
			−4
1	12	12	
			−6
0	14	0	

revenue increases when another unit of product is sold, we derive *MR* by (first) determining the firm's total revenue schedule (*TR*). *TR* is simply derived by multiplying the price times the number of units sold at that price.[1] Marginal revenue is then computed by determining the change in *TR* that accompanies each change in output and sales: $MR = \Delta TR / \Delta Q$. These schedules, $D (=AR)$, and *MR,* plot as shown in Figure 8-1. Since demand is a declining schedule, and the price at each quantity demanded applies to all units sold and not just to the last unit, *MR* lies below the demand curve and is more steeply sloped than *D*.

We now superimpose on the same graph a set of cost curves necessary for decision-making. As in the data for Table 8-1, the actual numbers used are of no special importance, so long as they properly reflect the total market price-quantity relationships. The numbers used to demonstrate the firm's costs are also, in themselves, unimportant, so long as they are sufficiently realistic as to portray a firm subject to the law of diminishing returns, and one capable of supplying the entire market demand for the commodity. These conditions are all met by the curves drawn in the graph.

[1] Because elasticity of demand reflects the responsiveness of quantity demanded to a change in the price of the product, we note that *TR* is not a constant function of units sold, but increases throughout the range of the demand curve where its elasticity coefficient is greater than one, to a maximum *TR* at the point where price elasticity of demand is unity, and actually declines with further price reductions. This relationship between revenue and units sold causes an additional problem for the monopolist—the effect of price on sales prevents an equating of price and *MC* as in pure competition, as well as the effect of the level of output on the firm's production costs.

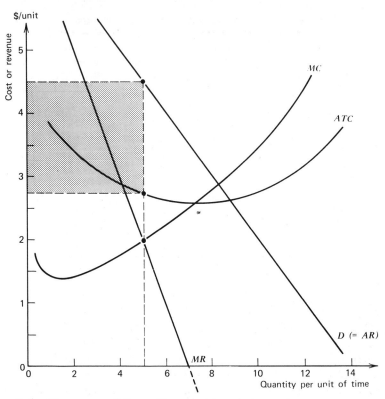

Figure 8-1. The monopolist's profit-maximizing choice.

The Profit-Maximizing Monopolist. Whether the firm be in pure competition or monopoly, its production decisions are based on its costs and returns at the margin. While the price-taker can influence only its costs by the decision the firm makes—price is taken as a given and is beyond the firm's influence—the monopolist's decisions affect both its costs and price. Both firms, however, find an optimum at that output where marginal revenue and marginal cost are equal.

Any unit which adds more to revenue than it adds to costs is a profitable unit to produce and sell, no matter what we might have classified that firm to be; profits are greater from the sale of that unit by the difference between MR and MC than they would be without that unit. The monopolist maximizes profits in exactly the same way as the pure competitor—expand output and sales until that quantity is reached at which $MR = MC$. Any inequality between MR and MC dictates an adjustment in output, with equilibrium for the firm occuring only at the point where $MR = MC$.

The monopolist, depicted by the graph, discovers an optimum

at five units of output. That many units will sell in the market for $4.50 per unit, the number that consumers are willing to buy for that price, as shown by the demand curve. But the cost of producing those five units is only $2.75 per unit, so this firm obtains a surplus over all costs (economic rent) of $1.75 per unit (the difference between AR and ATC). Total revenue for this firm is the rectangular area under the demand curve ($4.50 × 5 units), whereas total cost is the rectangular area under the ATC curve ($2.75 × 5 units), with the lightly shaded area being the economic rent at this output ($1.75 × 5 units).

Since market demand is given, being determined by the consumers' demand functions, its location, shape and slope are independent of the firm or firms serving a market. Thus the location of the demand curve in the graph space, with respect to the location of the firm's cost curves, need only be such that it is apparent this firm can supply the market's demand for the good in question.

One might shift the D and MR curves right or left to reflect a larger or smaller demand for the good, relative to the size of the firm, and we will find the same profit possibilities as for any other type of firm—economic rent may be positive, zero, or negative depending upon demand and production costs.

If we increase the size of the market, by moving the demand curve farther and farther to the right, economic rent to the firm increases. Were a situation of this sort to occur in an actual market, either potentially competitive firms would have to be faced with such excessively high production costs that their entry into this market is impossible or, barring that, other restrictive devices would have to be employed to protect the market for this monopolist.

As shown in Figure 8-2A and B, we can identify two separately unique situations in the monopoly case that result in: (1) zero economic rent for the firm; and (2) minimized production costs, out of an almost infinite number of demand possibilities.

In Figure 8-2A, the firm is sufficiently large relative to the total market, that the demand curve is tangent to the ATC curve somewhere along the downward sloping portion of that curve. In such a situation the price that consumers are willing to pay for this good, and the firm's cost of producing it, are both the same at the optimum output, q_e, and there is no economic rent for the firm.

A number of possibilities could cause this situation to exist. For one thing, the firm may have been serving a larger market at the time its facilities were constructed, and now finds that the demand curve has shifted to this position. A further shift to the left would cause this firm to leave the market eventually, as some or all of its fixed resources would find greater earnings elsewhere (because of

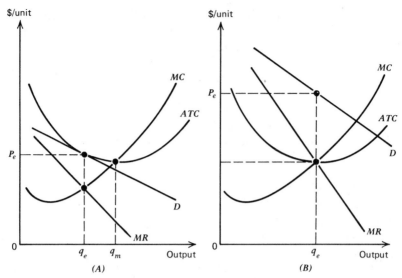

Figure 8-2. Zero economic rent and minimum *ATC* possibilities. (*A*) Zero economic rent. (*B*) Production at minimum *ATC*.

the failure to cover their opportunity costs). The word "eventually" requires emphasis because short-run resource fixity means that no changes can be made in these unprofitable resources during this length-of-run. As long as price is greater than *AVC*, the firm faces two choices: (1) continue to produce until its fixed resources are no longer of use, which will force this firm to withdraw from the market, or (2) reorganize its fixed resources so as to reduce its unit costs of production, both of which require more time than the short-run defines.

Another possibility might be that the firm, given this demand curve as its beginning market, built this particular scale of plant in the expectation of sufficient future growth of its market (a later shift in the demand curve to the right) that it would soon begin capturing economic rent while also protecting its monopoly position.[2]

Figure 8-2*B* describes another possible market situation in which both the demand curve and the firm's size are such that the *MR* curve passes through the *ATC* curve at its minimum point.

[2]Examples of a shrinking market demand can be found in certain low demand-high cost facilities such as airports, rail lines, etc., that have been abandoned in spite of public service commission attempts to perpetuate those operations. The demand-growth expectation is more frequently observed in city water or sewer systems, electric power plants, etc., where, because of the long lead time for planning and construction, and the large capital outlays required, the plant is presently overbuilt in the expectation of a larger population to serve (sometime) in the future.

Equating *MR* and *MC* to determine the firm's optimum output (q_e) means that the cost per unit of good produced, in terms of resources used, has been minimized. Even this circumstance does not maximize social preferences, however. Misallocation of resources and social waste are still present.

Efficiency Comparisons

We stated previously that pure competition leads to an efficient allocation of resources and their products by finding that one equilibrium level of output at which the value of an additional unit produced for consumers is just equal to the value of other goods sacrificed to get that additional unit. Any divergence from this market–type leads to misallocation and is therefore inefficient. To demonstrate the reason for this we need to review the basic meanings of the demand and marginal cost curves, as in Figure 8-3*A* and *B*.

The demand curve shows the amounts of a good that consumers will buy at various prices; it also implicitly reflects the values of other goods that must be sacrificed in order to buy these quantities. Thus in Figure 8-3*A*, the area under the demand curve between a pair of points such as *a* and *b* (between 150 and 250 units) represents the value of satisfactions to be derived from those 100 units of the good. If, as we have stated, a monopolist always produces less

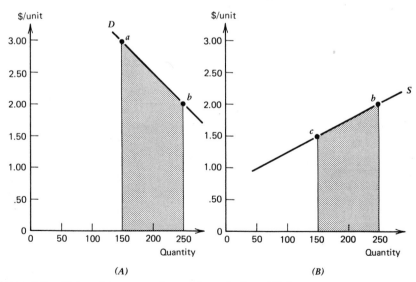

Figure 8-3. Values in consumption and production. (*A*) Demand and consumer valuation. (*B*) *MC* and producer values.

than a price-taking firm, and that output also at a higher price, the value of goods *not* received by consumers (the area under the demand curve between 150 and 250 units) amounts to $250, the shaded area in the figure.

The area under the *MC*, on the other hand, represents the value of other goods that would have to be given up to produce those 100 units, since the *MC* curve is the opportunity cost (the value of alternative outputs sacrificed) of producing each unit of this good. That value amounts to $175, the shaded area under the *MC* curve in Figure 8-3*B*.

Although in pure competition the *MC* curve is the firm's supply curve, and the horizontal summation of the *MC* curves of all the firms in the industry is that market's supply curve, no such clear identity between *MC* and *S* exists in a monopoly, because the pure monopolist *is* the industry and price is always greater than *MR* for that firm because of its downward sloping demand curve. Thus, as Figure 8-4 shows, an industry of price-takers would find an equilibrium (point *b*) at 250 units and a price of $2.00 per unit. But given freedom to determine its own production and pricing policies, the monopolist finds *MR* and *MC* are equal at 150 units at a price of $3.00 per unit, the price consumers are willing to pay for 150 units of the good. Thus consumers are forced to give up 100 units of a good worth $250 to them while the value of other goods that would have been sacrificed to produce those 100 units amounts to only $175. Society has thus incurred a net loss of $75, the area of the

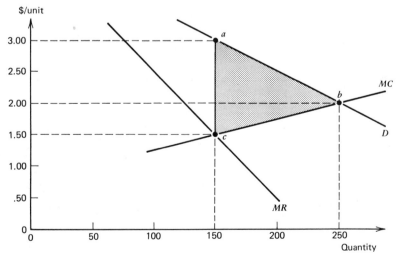

Figure 8-4. Monopoly's misallocation and waste.

shaded triangle (a-b-c), which is the difference in the two areas described separately in the previous figure.[3]

The waste of misallocation in monopoly is that the resources which could have been used to produce an additional 100 units of this good, worth $250 to consumers, have been forced into lower-valued alternative production.

This conclusion is valid for any market deviation from the conditions of pure competition. Because the demand curve is less than perfectly elastic, *MR* is less than market price, and the firm produces a lower optimal output with a higher price than would be the rule in pure competition, which forces consumers to sacrifice some of this preferred good for other, less desired goods.

Imperfect Competition in the Market.   For purposes of theoretical clarity we have, to this point, ignored the large middle ground between pure competition and pure monopoly. The workaday world is not to be found at either of these two extremes, with firms, instead, falling somewhere along the continuum in Figure 7-1, between these two rigidly defined models, in situations exhibiting some (but not all) of the characteristics specific to one extreme or the other.

The label "imperfect competition" is used here to cover a wide variety of real-life possibilities. Although correctly including pure monopoly we will limit ourselves in the discussion that follows to the general area covering a great many possibilities from a situation with two or more firms exhibiting some degree of competition, however limited that might be, toward the other end of the spectrum with a large number of competing firms that do not, however, meet all the requirements of pure competition.[4]

The word "imperfect" indicates a lack of conformity to the conditions for pure competition. And this departure causes definitional problems. To define an industry from the immense variety of goods available to consumers is arbitrary, at best; a distinction must be made for similar goods somewhere along a scale from *exactly the same* to *totally different,* that says, these two products are sufficiently alike to be viewed as competing goods in Industry $\bar{X}$, but a third product is so different that it cannot be included in that industry.

---

[3]We could have drawn the *D* and *MC* curves as curving lines, to more correctly reflect diminishing marginal utility in consumption and diminishing marginal productivity in production, but this would have added nothing and reduces our ability to estimate the areas (and values) involved.
[4]Technically more correct distinctions (within this imperfect competition grouping) are made as between "monopolistic competition" and "oligopoly," based upon the number of firms in the market, ease of entry and exit, the degree of product differentiation, and each firm's expectations of other firm's retaliation to their product pricing decisions.

Because of wide differences in the number of sellers, that may range from a few to many, the degrees of product differentiation and control over price, and the manner in which firms respond to these situations, we are forced to search for common characteristics where differences are a matter of degree only.

Similarities in these firms' operations can be noted, particularly in that the competing firms' demand curves are interdependent, causing each firm to take other firms' possible actions into account when making their decisions.

Suppose Figure 8-5 represents the market position of Firm A in an imperfectly competitive market. Its demand curve will have a slope between the vertical and horizontal (the greater the number of good substitutes for its product the less steeply sloped the demand curve will be). With interdependent demand curves, any change in the price of Firm B's product will cause Firm A's demand curve to shift because B has now attracted some of A's customers, and will call for retaliatory action by A to recapture its share of the market.[5]

Given Firm A's beginning situation indicated by D and MR, and the later situation by D' and MR', let's assume this shift of demand has been caused by Firm B cutting the price of its product and that this has resulted in A losing some of its customers to B. Firm A was originally at an equilibrium with its product selling for price p_e with q_e units being sold. Firm A can no longer maintain its price at p_e because that would cause its sales to fall to q_n. Firm A will be encouraged to drop its price to p' because its MR (from the new demand curve, D') at price p_e is greater than MC. We cannot conclude, however, that q' will be optimal (i.e., that $MR = MC$ at q') because this price change will have brought back some or all of its original customers (and maybe even some others besides, depending upon whether p' is less than B's price). Our vagueness here is caused by the addition of a second element to Firm A's optimizing decisions. When the firm's change in TR results from a *shift* in its demand curve, as well as a movement *along* the curve, we are unable to indicate clearly what Firm A's MR will be until both demand curves are clearly specified (requiring additional, and more tenuous, assumptions about the consumers in this market).

Such competition by price results in what is often called "cut-throat competition" which, if continued, can be so destructive as to drive some (or a large number) of the competing firms out of the market. When price competition is so severe that firms in the market will avoid using price as a means of competing with one another, a

---

[5]This sort of competition by price leads to the price wars seen in a number of industries, such as the gasoline price wars of local filling stations, for instance.

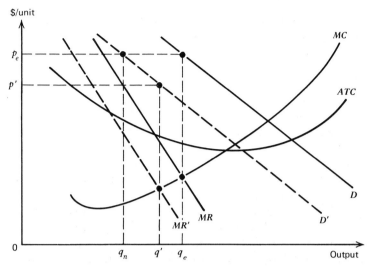

Figure 8-5. Price-competition with interdependent demand curves.

second characteristic of the imperfectly competitive market is evident—that of "nonprice competition." Nonprice competition is engaged in when a firm advertises to create a real (or imagined) special image about its product in the minds of consumers. If buyers can be convinced that a firm's product has a special characteristic not to be found in competing products, the advertiser has effectively shifted the firm's demand curve to the right and made it more inelastic in the process, giving the firm a greater degree of control over its price.

Other types of nonprice competition take the form of product design, improving its serviceability, or making it more appealing or more easily recognized by the consumer. These changes are the outcome of research and market development expenditures which become important components of a firm's costs, in preference to the more immediate response from competing firms that can be expected when direct price competition is attempted.

Some improvements may only be illusory, at best, yet "Foaming Bubbles Soap" may find difficult an early response to the "New, New, Improved Suds" of one of its rivals if its own improved variety is not ready to be marketed. Until that response materializes, a market advantage has been obtained for the initiating firm's product.

On the other hand, improvements may be significant additions in that they become more desirable products of greater value to the users. One person's frills may be another's necessities. But such innovations as the change from the steel wheels of earlier model tractors to the softer-riding rubber tired equipment of today with its power steering and hydraulically controlled attachments are more than just conveniences. The transformation from the tractor operator's direct exposure to the elements, to the much more comfortable tractor of today with its sound (and air) conditioned cabs with radio and other conveniences, are hardly undesirable changes for many of today's operators. As one firm has added certain attachments and conveniences that have attracted a larger share of the market, other firms have been forced to follow suit with their own improvements.

Firms in an imperfectly competitive market may also offer different kinds and amounts of special services in addition to the good itself—"specials" such as free delivery, postage-paid shipping, or allowing charges without interest for a specified period of time, etc.

Because potential MR per unit is so large, relative to MC for each firm in an imperfect market, there is strong incentive to act alone in determining price and output policies. Yet, the consequences of retaliatory pricing by competing firms are severe. Thus, these firms are encouraged to seek alternative solutions such as the nonprice competition just discussed, or to act in collusion so as to avoid competing by price. Aside from the illegality of acting in consort to set market prices and divide the market among the firms in the industry, widened differences between MR and MC carry the seeds of destruction for such arrangements because of the attractiveness of larger gains to be reaped by breaking away from the group. And the larger the group, the more difficult it would be to maintain discipline among members because the group is unable to adequately reward individual firms for acting in the interests of the whole rather than their own.

When the structure of markets in an economy is such that price competition is weakened, society has cause for concern because of the undesirable consequences of the noncompetitive behavior of producing or marketing firms. If a high degree of competition cannot be obtained from the functioning of the firms in the market, such markets will fail to allocate resources efficiently and their regulation by the government is sought, in the hope of eliminating those undesirable effects. How that regulation is best carried out and in what particular segments of these markets to place the greatest control so as to be of benefit to the public is the subject of much continuing debate, and the topic of the following section.

Public Regulation of Markets

Through much of this nation's history many markets have fallen under the domination of a single large firm or a few relatively large firms. We characterize a market noted for the small number of firms in that market as "oligopolistic."

The greater the size of such firms the greater is their opportunity to exert a special influence in the market. As wealth becomes concentrated in the hands of a few people or firms in the marketplace, their ability to control or manipulate the market for selfish purposes is enhanced and the benefits to be obtained from competition also threatened.

The Growth of Firms.   Some business firms have been able to grow with their market (both in absolute and relative terms) internally or externally, or by a combination of these methods. "Internal" growth is indicated by the increased value of a firm's capital that permits the construction of additional facilities and increasing business volume as the market for its products has grown. "External" growth has occurred when, through purchase or other means, a formerly independent firm becomes merged with another. As firms are so absorbed, growth is achieved through a change in asset ownership, with many different avenues by which such growth is accomplished.[6]

Three distinct periods of business mergers have been identified by students of industrial organization: 1898–1903; 1926–29; and 1940–47,[7] followed more recently by a fourth that took place during the 1960s. Each period had its basic emphasis on horizontal, vertical, or conglomerate combinations, each its industries in which the activity was most intense, and each with its type of vehicle most often used to combine firms.

Horizontal mergers are combinations of firms in the same industry. An example is a dairy distributor taking over a competing distributor. A vertical merger is one that involves two or more firms in different production or marketing stages within the same industry. For instance, a tractor tire manufacturer combining with a firm producing tire cord. Conglomerate mergers are among firms in unrelated industries. An apple packing company merging with a cotton processor is a good example.

The first merger period has received particular attention be-

---

[6]We will loosely categorize this latter type of growth as a "merger," although technical distinctions are more correctly made between one firm's assets being acquired by another through lease or purchase, the consolidation of two or more firms into a new firm, or the holding company with its parent and subsidiary structure: See, J. Fred Weston, The *Role of Mergers in the Growth of Large Firms,* Berkely, Calf.: University of California Press, 1953, p. 3. For a discussion of the growth of agricultural cooperatives by merger and other means see Leon Garoian and Gail L. Cramer, "Cooperative Mergers: Their Objectives, Success, and Impact on Growth," Corvallis, Oreg.: Oregon Agricultural Experiment Station Bulletin 605, February 1969.

[7]Weston, op. cit., p. 9. This does not mean that no mergers were formed prior to or following the dates specified, only that the consolidations were much greater in number during those years.

cause this cycle "gave to America its characteristic twentieth-century concentration of control."[8] Many of today's very large industrial corporations were formed at that time primarily by purchasing the stock instruments of competing firms. To name but a few, mergers in steel, copper, tobacco, meat packing, chemicals, and farm machinery saw the organization of U.S. Steel, Anaconda Copper, American Tobacco, Swift, duPont, and International Harvester.

Few of the large horizontal combinations of the early merger period resulted in monopolies, but it is evident that it did increase concentration in their respective markets.

In the second merger period (1926–29) more firms were involved than during the earlier period, yet the effect on industry concentration was less than the former. The second period mergers occurred in less concentrated industries and involved many small firms.

One difference from that earlier period was that the merged firm's capital assets were acquired, rather than their stocks as in the first period. And while expansions during the first period were primarily horizontal (acquiring competing firms), mergers in the 1920s were both horizontal and vertical (expansion backward into materials supplies, and forward into consumer goods manufacturing and distribution outlets).[9]

Most of the merger activity of the 1920s took place in the food industry, public utilities, banking, petroleum, and chemicals instead of the heavy industries of the first period.

The third merger period (1940–47), although widespread, occurred primarily in the metals industries, textiles, food, liquor, and petroleum. Most of the firms absorbed were quite small, with little measurable impact on industrial concentration.[10]

The latest merger period (1961–69) was characterized by Blair as "the explosive emergence of the 'new conglomerate' of the 1960s."[11] Expansions in this period were of both the horizontal and vertical varieties, with the latter involving many combinations into industries that were completely unrelated to the industry of the parent company.

Ling-Temco-Vought, one of the "go-go" conglomerate holding companies, expanded rapidly during this period picking up a number of large firms in a variety of industries having no product-

[8]Paul T. Homan, "Trusts: Early Development," *Encyclopedia of the Social Sciences,* 15:114, 1935; cited in J. Fred Weston, Ibid., p. 31.

[9]John M. Blair, *Economic Concentration, Structure, Behavior and Public Policy,* New York: Harcourt Brace Jovanovich, Inc., 1972, p. 264.

[10]Weston, op. cit., p. 61.

[11]Blair, op. cit., p. 285.

line relationships that might encourage such a combination. One of the companies within the Ling-TV conglomerate, for instance, was Wilson and Company, itself a conglomerate that was well known in meat packing, sporting goods, and pharmaceuticals, among others. Wilson's array of products was aptly characterized by someone recently, as ranging "from meat balls to golf balls to goof balls."

The Antitrust Laws

The institution of government is an integral part of all human activity, devising the rules within which we act. Regulative institutional devices within a democratic system develop slowly, after the fact, and legislated reactions to undesirable business practices are no exception.

By the mid-1800s, state laws permitted the incorporation of business firms in limited form. With further legislative actions by a number of states to make incorporation easier (liability limited to the value of the shares of stock held by the owners, free transferability of those shares, one vote per share, and voting by proxy), the ability to manage the affairs of the corporation rested in the hands of directors elected by the stockholders. In addition to numerous other liberalizing laws passed by one or more of the states, New Jersey made an important change in its laws (in the 1880s) that gave corporations the right to own the stock instruments of other corporations. With reciprocity among states honoring the institutions created by any one of them, businesses incorporated under New Jersey's more liberal corporation law could operate nationwide.[12] The door was now opened for drastically reorganizing the structure and operational methods of business firms.

Public resentment and reaction to the development of large trusts and business combines following liberalization of the incorporation laws became so intense that both political parties, during the 1888 presidential campaign, expressed their intent to remedy the situation.[13] Two years later, the U.S. Congress produced the Sherman Antitrust Act, the foundation of the United States' business regulatory policy. The first two sections of this Act contain the primary weapons against monopoly and other restrictive business practices.

Section 1 makes it illegal to act in restraint of trade (either interstate or internationally) by conspiring with other individuals or firms to do so, whether by contract, the formation of a trust, or other

[12]Harry L. Purdy, M. L. Lindahl, and W. A. Carter, *Corporate Concentration and Public Policy*, New York: Prentice-Hall, Inc., 1942, p. 47.
[13]Ibid., p. 302.

means. It forbids restraining trade through price fixing arrangements, or controlling and sharing industry output by collusive agreement.

Section 2 makes it illegal to monopolize interstate or international trade, or even to attempt to do so, by combining or conspiring with others to monopolize the channels of trade. This section forbids the use of economic power to exclude competitor's from the market.

Except for a few early landmark decisions where dissolution of the offending firms was ordered, deficiencies appeared in the Act, and in its application. Enforcement was not pressed with equal vigor by succeeding administrations, and when proceedings were instituted, decisions of the court made differing interpretations of the law.

A Supreme Court decision in 1911 adopted the "rule of reason" that resulted in a great deal of criticism. That rule softened the interpretation of trade "restraint" by questioning whether agreements that restrained trade were "unreasonable." A firm might, by virtue of internal growth made possible by large-scale economies, become dominant in an industry, yet be immune to prosecution. But a strict interpretation of the law would cause the same size of operation to be subject to prosecution if it resulted from a combination of competing firms.[14]

Even though court action under the Sherman Antitrust Act continued, a number of large firms also were formed during the same period of time. Monopolistic business combines and trusts once again became a political issue with both major parties proposing changes in federal antitrust policy during the 1912 presidential campaign. After much controversy over the content of the proposed legislation, two important measures were enacted in 1914—the Federal Trade Commission Act, and the Clayton Act.[15]

Given broad powers, the commission was charged with the responsibility of investigating business organization and practices, and with carrying out the provisions of the Clayton Act.

While the Sherman Act was general in its identification of what actions were illegal, the Clayton Act was made specific. Section 2 prohibits discrimination between purchasers of a firm's products (except where differences in price are caused by differences in the grade, quantity, or quality of the commodity sold), tie-in sales (i.e., preventing later sellers from also dealing in a competitor's product), and interlocking directorates. Section 7 of the act also prevents a company from holding stock in competing companies, or the com-

---

[14]Ibid., pp. 332–34.
[15]Ibid., pp. 360–61.

bining of two or more companies, where such ownership or combination might create a monopoly or reduce competition.

Although the Clayton Act prohibited corporate mergers by means of stock acquisitions which might reduce competition between the merging firms, no such ban was made clear regarding the acquisition of another firm's assets. That loop-hole was plugged in 1950 with passage of the Cellar-Kefauver Anti-Merger Act.[16]

Agricultural Bargaining

As any part of the market system for agricultural products becomes more concentrated, the power of large firms in the market to influence the prices of farm products also increases. Dominance of a market by one or a few large firms gives them a manipulative ability that may not only raise consumer prices, but widen the market spread by lowering farm prices as well.

Earlier (in Chapter 7) we used a set of criteria as a theoretical model to describe specific market structures, with one extreme of the continuum representing price-takers, and varying degrees of price-searching toward the opposite extreme of the pure monopolist.

The more typical agricultural situation has frequently been one of a large number of farmers facing a single buyer for their products. The theoretical and practical outcome of such a market situation is that producers are forced to accept the price of their product as "given," yet the monopsonist has sufficient market power to be able to hold down the offered price.

Historically, these "middlemen" have handled large volumes of agricultural products, and in attempting to maximize the profitability of their own operations, buy less of the product at a lower price to the producer than would be the case where both buyers and sellers were price-takers. Agricultural producers, consequently, have been pressed to actions in two directions. On the one hand, they have long felt the need to "fight fire with fire" by organizing themselves into groups to offset this disparity in market strength. On the other, many farm people have been strong supporters of antitrust and other legislation designed to prevent individual firms from attaining market power, and to protect them from unfair practices in their markets.

Fears that the Sherman Antitrust Act might be broadly inter-

[16]Louis B. Schwartz, *Free Enterprise and Economic Organization,* 4th ed., Mineola, N.Y.: The Foundation Press, Inc., 1972, pp. 136, 170–71.

preted to include agricultural organizations as well were not unfounded. Words and phrases in that act, such as "every" person, "every" contract, and a 1911 Supreme Court decision in the Danbury Hatter's case specifically including agricultural organizations under the Act,[17] did nothing to dispel farmers' fears of that possibility.

That the Congress intended to give agricultural associations (limited) freedom to operate in a manner which would be illegal for industrial firms has been made clear in a later series of statutes beginning with the Clayton Act, one of the most important measures providing farm organizations a degree of immunity from the Sherman Act.

Section 6 of the Clayton Act permits agricultural organizations to be formed for the purposes of mutually buying supplies or selling products for their members, but with the provision that they may not issue capital stock nor may they be operated for profit.

A number of cooperatives, however, had issued capital stock in organizing prior to passage of the Clayton Act. The Congress then passed the Capper-Volstead Act (1922) to clarify that section of the Clayton Act as it applied to agriculture.

This Act allows producers to establish "marketing agencies in common" with or without stock, provided:

1. That they are operated for the mutual benefit of their members,

2. That they do not deal in the products of nonmembers to an amount greater in value than such as are handled by it for its members,

3. That they conform to one or both of the following requirements:
    a. That no member of the association is allowed more than one vote because of the amount of stock or membership capital he owns, or
    b. That the association does not pay dividends on stock or membership capital in excess of 8 percent per year.[18]

The Capper-Volstead Act does not provide cooperatives with blanket immunity from the antitrust laws. Yet an agricultural cooperative could gain control over a substantial share (even 100 percent) of the total supply of a commodity without being prosecuted for being a monopolist. How that cooperative gained its control, and how it operates in the market are important determinants of whether or not it would be challenged in court.

Such market control would be illegal if the cooperative were to be developed as a combination or conspiracy with noncooperative

[17]Ibid., pp. 311–12, 320–21.
[18]Ewell P. Roy, *Cooperatives: Today and Tomorrow,* Danville, Ill.: The Interstate Printers and Publishers, Inc., 1964, pp. 215–16.

firms. If the cooperative was properly organized under the Capper-Volstead Act, it would be illegal to use its market power to enhance the prices of its products. Further, the cooperative may not use its power to restrain trade by use of predatory practices designed to eliminate competitors. Any such actions would make the cooperative subject to legal action under the same antitrust laws as any other monopolizing firm.

A number of other acts favorable to agricultural organizations have been passed by the Congress. These laws were enacted to protect agricultural producers and their associations from the superior powers of firms handling their products, or to give them a better balance of market power as they deal with large firms in their markets. Most notable of these laws are the Packers and Stockyards Act of 1921, the Cooperative Marketing Act of 1926, the Robinson-Patman Act of 1936, and the Agricultural Marketing Agreement Act of 1937.[19]

The Packers and Stockyards Act reinforced antitrust laws regarding: livestock marketing; making certain stockyards public utilities; regulating the buying and selling of livestock; service charges and commission rates. The larger meatpacking companies had previously agreed to divest some of their interests ranging from stockyard ownership to railroad terminals, refrigeration, and market news services. That ownership structure had provided them with the ability to discriminate successfully against the smaller packers.

The Cooperative Marketing Act permits farmers, agricultural associations, or federations of such associations to acquire, exchange, and disseminate a variety of price and market information.

The Robinson-Patman Act governs such activities as price discrimination between dealers of commodities and promotional allowances or services in kind for a firm's agents.

The Agricultural Marketing Agreement Act deals with marketing orders, especially important in such commodity areas as fruits, vegetables, and milk. Grower-producer agreements are permitted for fresh and processed classes of these commodities, resulting in a better control of product quality and a more orderly flow through the marketing channels.

These acts (including Capper-Volstead) are of special significance to agriculture in that they assign to the Secretary of Agriculture authority to issue cease and desist orders in cases of violation. The secretary's orders may be backed by resort to district courts for enforcement of penalties, should that become necessary.

---

[19]Dale C. Dahl and Winston W. Grant, eds., "Antitrust and Agriculture," Conference Proceedings, Agricultural Experiment Station Misc. Report 137, St. Paul, Minn.: University of Minnesota, 1975. pp. 2, 23, 35, 45–49.

Two economic objectives are evident in our antitrust laws as they apply to agriculture. These laws are protective devices for agriculture, because of the relative market weakness of individual producers as they face large firms handling their products. And food, itself, is viewed as being so essential to a healthy people and economic system that it deserves special measures to insure an abundant supply at reasonable cost to consumers.

An agricultural bargaining association, if it is to be effective in increasing its farmer-members' incomes, must be able to control or influence those variables that determine whether a firm is a price-taker or price-searcher. This means that it must either be accepted by processors as the bargaining agent for all growers of that commodity, or gain control over production and supply to the extent that processors will treat them so.

But control over total supply is very difficult to achieve and almost impossible to maintain. Seldom can all growers of a commodity be convinced that they should join the bargaining association. Unless some method is used to restrict production through grower contracts, or other legal means, it is difficult to control supply through membership maintenance. And in the absence of special power over members, it is difficult to keep them in the group. A further difficulty is caused by their inability to control the production and supply of substitutes, and imported quantities of that good.

Success in bargaining for the members of the association carries its own weakening forces. Given a low price for a product, growers may willingly become a part of the association. As product price is increased, through the actions of the group, some of its members may be tempted to "go it alone" because the original cause of group action has passed. Furthermore, the now higher price is, in itself, a divisive factor. It is a strong incentive for each producer to expand production and thus the total market supply of that product. If the higher price came about through agreements to reduce output, this would cause a loss of members and weaken the association in the very area where it had based its market strength.

As a consequence, bargaining associations have not been very successful in the longer term. In spite of this, they have been a balancing power and a beneficial force in improving the degree of competition in many of the markets for agricultural commodities.

Summary

A monopolist maximizes profit by producing that rate of output where $MR = MC$. For this rate of output, the monopolist will charge that price as shown by the demand curve. A monopolist misallocates resources because the firm produces less output and charges a higher price than would be the case in a competitive industry. As a consequence, consumers are forced to sacrifice some of the monopolist's product for other less desirable products.

Government regulation has been necessary to prevent firms from monopolizing markets. The Sherman Antitrust Act, the Clayton Act, and the Federal Trade Commission Act are examples.

Agricultural producers have formed agricultural bargaining associations or encouraged national legislation to give farmers market power. These attempts have been marginally successful because it has been difficult to maintain control of the total supply of a product, the supply of substitute products, and imports from other countries.

Chapter Highlights

1. A pure monopolist is the only seller in a market; barriers to entry prevent competition from others.
2. The monopolist's demand curve and the market demand curve are the same.
3. The monopolist's marginal revenue curve lies below the demand curve because market demand curves always slope downward to the right.
4. The monopolist maximizes profit in the same manner as a purely competitive firm by producing the output at which $MR = MC$.
5. A monopolist's selling price always exceeds MC at equilibrium output. (Prove this with a diagram.)
6. A monopoly is subject to the law of diminishing returns just as is any other firm.
7. A monopoly is inefficient because the value to society of the last unit produced by the monopolist is always greater than its opportunity cost to society.
8. The term "imperfect competition" covers all those market possibilities which do not meet the conditions of pure competition.
9. In imperfect competition one firm's optimizing depends on its competitor's price policies because their demand curves are interdependent.
10. Imperfectly competitive firms avoid price competition, whenever possible, because of demand interdependencies.
11. Public regulation of markets is intended to protect the public by preserving competition in market.
12. Firms grow by either internal or external expansion, or both.
13. Antitrust laws are designed to prevent monopolistic firms from driving out competitors and to protect consumers from unfair pricing.
14. Agricultural producers form bargaining groups to counterbalance buyers' market power.
15. Special acts by Congress provided bargaining groups with limited immunity from the antitrust laws.

16. Agricultural bargaining groups face difficulties in maintaining continued member cooperation.

Review Questions

1. Explain why a monopolist's marginal revenue and demand curves are two different curves.
2. Does a monopolist always make excess profits? Draw a graph of this situation.
3. What is imperfect competition? How does imperfect competition differ from pure competition?
4. Why do some firms compete on "nonprice factors" rather than on price? Discuss.
5. Explain the four business merger periods in the United States. What happened to the structure of American industry during the first merger period?
6. What are horizontal, vertical, and conglomerate mergers?
7. Why have antitrust laws been passed? Are these laws performing their function?
8. What factors must farmers analyze if they want to form farm marketing organizations to improve their prices? Can farmers control these factors? Can the government control these factors? Explain.

Suggested Readings

1. Alchian, Armen A. and William R. Allen. *Exchange and Production: Theory in Use.* Belmont, Calif.: Wadsworth Publishing Company, Inc., 1969, Chapters 7 and 17.
2. Bain, Joe S. *Industrial Organization.* New York: John Wiley and Sons, Inc., 1959, Chapter 1.
3. Dahl, Dale C. and Jerome W. Hammond. *Market and Price Analysis: The Agricultural Industries.* New York: McGraw-Hill Book Company, 1977, Chapters 13 and 14.
4. Moore, John R., and Richard G. Walsh, eds. *Market Structure of Agricultural Industries.* Ames, Iowa: The Iowa State University Press, 1966, Chapters 1–14.
5. Samuelson, Paul A. *Economics,* 8th ed. New York: McGraw-Hill Book Company, 1970, Chapters 25 and 26.
6. Vernon, John M. *Market Structure and Industrial Performance: A Review of Statistical Findings.* Boston: Allyn and Bacon, Inc., 1972, Chapter 6.

Courtesy of Doug Warren, Editor, Montana Agricultural Experiment Station, Bozeman.

MARKETING
AGRICULTURAL
COMMODITIES

MARKETING AGRICULTURAL COMMODITIES

Agricultural marketing is a large subdiscipline in agricultural economics. In 1976, the cost of marketing food amounted to $116 billion, while the cost of producing farm food products was $55 billion. Of the $172 billion spent by consumers for domestic farm food products, approximately one-third was returned to producers while two-thirds of that amount was for marketing costs.

Marketing costs include those associated with assembly, transportation, processing, and distribution of farm food to consumers. The cost components of marketing (sometimes called the "marketing bill" or "marketing margin") are shown in Table 9-1 in billions of dollars. The table indicates that the major components are labor (accounting for about one-half of the total), packaging (accounting for 13 percent) and transportation (amounting to eight percent). Increases in the marketing bill have been due primarily to two factors: (1) greater volume of food marketed; and (2) increases in the cost of providing these services. Over the last two decades the cost of additional marketing services has accounted for about three-fourths of the rise in the marketing bill, while increases in the costs of marketing larger quantities accounted for about one-fourth. The dollar amount of marketing services actually declined slightly during this period.

What is Marketing?

The term "marketing" has a variety of meanings. To housewives it means shopping for groceries and all other household needs. From the point of view of farmers or ranchers it means selling their commodities. From the perspective of the handler of a commodity, it means storing the commodity, transforming the product into a form that consumers want, shipping it to retail outlets, and promoting its sale. All of these things are part of the marketing process.

The American Marketing Association has defined marketing as the performance of business activities that direct the flow of goods

Table 9-1 Cost Components of the Marketing Bill
for Farm Foods, 1960-76 (Billions of Dollars)

Year	Labor	Packaging Materials	Transportation	Corporate Pretax Profits	Business Taxes	Depr.
1960	19.7	5.4	4.1	2.1	1.3	1.5
1965	23.3	6.2	4.2	3.0	2.1	2.0
1970	32.3	8.5	5.2	3.6	2.9	2.5
1976	54.3	15.0	9.6	8.3	4.6	3.9

Year	Rent	Advertising	Bad debts	Interest	Other[a]	Total
1960	1.1	1.3	.7	.2	7.2	44.6
1965	1.6	1.9	1.1	.4	8.2	54.0
1970	2.3	2.0	1.5	1.1	9.3	71.2
1976	3.6	3.3	2.4	1.7	9.3	116.0

Source: Terry Crawford and Fenton Sands, The Bill for Marketing Farm Food Products, ERS-20, August 1973; and the Handbook of Agricultural Charts, USDA, 1977.

[a] Includes utilities, fuel, etc.

and services from producer to consumers or final user. In agricultural marketing, the point of production (the farm or ranch) is the basic source of supply. The marketing process begins at that point and continues until a consumer buys the product in the supermarket or until it is purchased as a raw material for another production phase. However, marketing also includes input supply firms that serve the farms and ranches. Thus, marketing consists of those efforts that effect transfers of ownership and which create *time, place,* and *form utility* to commodities. Time utility is added to commodities by storage. Place satisfaction is added to commodities through transportation services. Finally, form utility is added to a commodity through the processing function. By the creation of these utilities, marketers are productive and add value to raw agricultural commodities that consumers want.

Since consumption is the purpose and end result of production and marketing activities, it is necessary for marketers to focus their activities toward satisfying consumer wants and needs. It is difficult to successfully market something consumers do not desire, even with massive promotional endeavors.

How Marketing Developed

The existence of marketing is a direct result of specialization of production in our economy. Initially most families were self-sufficient, or nearly so. They produced most of the products they needed on their small acreages. They ground their own flour and baked their own bread; spun their fibers; butchered their meat and stored it for later use. As time passed, people discovered that their different resource endowments and talents allowed them to produce some things better than others. Along with this realization came increasing demands for various goods and services as population grew and society became more affluent. Increased demands made specialization profitable. As the individual farmer specialized, a surplus was produced that could be exchanged for goods and services that no longer were produced or provided on the farm. As the law of comparative advantage states, it is beneficial to the producer to specialize in the production of the good that person can produce more cheaply, and then exchange the surplus output for the surplus output of other producers. In this way, producers and society as a whole benefit because more commodities are available at lower costs.

In the early days, money was not used as a medium of exchange. Barter—exchanging goods for other goods—served society well. For example, a farmer might exchange a sack of potatoes for a wheelbarrow of coal. As people specialized and produced fewer products, it became more difficult to meet with producers of each of the goods needed; bartering became too costly. Let's illustrate the problems of a barter system using an example of five persons each specializing in producing different goods needed by each of the others. Ten separate exchanges must be made in order that each of

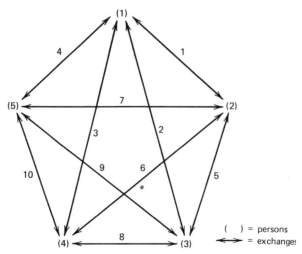

Figure 9-1. Bartering transactions among five specialized producers.

the five producers obtains the five products involved (Figure 9-1). If 20 people exchange 20 different goods, then 190 separate exchanges are necessary. Thus, increased specialization brings about money as a medium of exchange in order to simplify the exchange process. Marketing is the direct result of specialization and trade.

Markets and the Market Economy

In any economic system, regardless of the type of political or social structure, there are four basic decisions that must be made. The system must somehow determine: (1) what goods and services are to be produced and in what quantities; (2) how to allocate available resources (the inputs of land, labor, capital, and management) to obtain the largest output or national product; (3) what production methods should be used; and (4) how national output should be divided among the population. In most capitalistic countries these decisions are made through an intricate system of market prices that are reflected through the marketing system from consumers to producers. Before going into detail on how this is accomplished, a definition of a market is essential.

A *market* consists of buyers and sellers with facilities to communicate with each other. It need not be a specific place, although some people refer to markets in this sense, such as commodity markets and auction markets. Markets may be local, regional, national, or international. The only requirement is that the forces of demand and supply, via the communication between buyers and sellers, determine market price.

In a market economy, every scarce commodity commands a price and that price is market determined by the product's demand and supply curves. For example, examine the consequences of an increase in the demand for beef in America. When consumers go to their grocery stores and purchase more beef, they indicate to the grocer that they prefer that product over other goods their money could have bought. These dollar "votes" are cast when consumers purchase the available beef. The grocers must then purchase more beef from the packers. The packers need more beef to supply retailers' increased needs, so they buy more from the feedlots, and the feedlots need more animals, so stock ranchers increase the size of breeding herd, etc. This sequence of market relationships, as sketched in Figure 9-2, is much abbreviated as you might easily recognize. A large number of other suppliers also detect and respond to changes in the demand for their products or services. As consumers purchase more meat, the demand curve for meat shifts

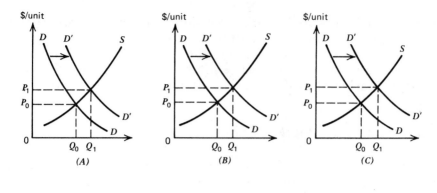

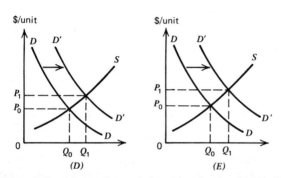

Figure 9-2. Market interrelationships for beef. (*A*) Retail. (*B*) Packers. (*C*) Feedlots. (*D*) Cow-calf operators. (*E*) Feedgrains.

which increases the price of meat at the retail level. This higher price is noticed by meat packers as their orders increase. Consequently packers demand more slaughter cattle and offer higher prices. This signal is passed back through the market to feedlots, feedgrain producers, and cow-calf operators. In a competitive system producers increase output in response to higher prices because they can improve their earnings by doing so. It is the profit motive that makes the market system work.

It is easy to see how our economy answers the question of what and how much is produced—it is determined by profitability. Firms will produce those goods from which they can make a profit. They will not produce a commodity if their information indicates they will lose money producing that good.

A competitive market system allocates resources to produce a good at its lowest cost. A producer who does not do so will find earnings declining, even to the point of being forced out of business by competitors. When people sell the services of their labor or other resources, they receive compensation in the form of wages or salaries, rent, interest, or income in general. With this income, they purchase goods and services. In a free enterprise system the allocation of resources to production determines the distribution of income which in turn determines how much of the total output each member of society will receive. This system is very complex, but it does work well and without the extensive planning that occurs in such command economies as Russia and China.

The Marketing Process.   Success by individuals and firms in achieving their own operational goals contributes to success in society's larger goal of economic efficiency in the total system. Marketers must accomplish many specific tasks, all of which are contained in two general aims. One requirement they must fulfill is to determine demand and changes in demand for products in order that the movement of commodities through the marketing system may be expedited. The second is to achieve efficiency in the marketing process by improving pricing and operational efficiency.

If consumers' wants change, the resulting changes in demand require that management make the necessary decisions regarding business investments, operational procedures and products handled so that future consumer desires will be met. Fluctuations in demand can drastically affect the profitability of an operation, making it necessary to anticipate those changes.

A first step in the marketing process is to ascertain what consumers want. To estimate sales, a firm must consider such sales-influencing factors as: general economic conditions; population in the market area; incomes; the price of the product; and the prices of substitute or complementary products. Another factor affecting sales is the amount of advertising and promotional effort used in persuading consumers to want the product. Estimates of probable sales may then be compared with the firm's anticipated costs of marketing the product to derive an estimate of profitability, the bottom line in deciding for or against the project.

The Efficiency of Markets.   Although we moved toward answering questions of economic efficiency by applying concepts of production and cost economics to commodity producing firms, economic analysis is not so severely limited. Identical product and resource relationships also exist in firms involved in the marketing process, and the methods of analysis are equally appropriate here.

Marketing efficiency is measured by comparing output and input values. Output values are based on consumer valuation of a good, and input values (costs) are determined by the values of alternative production capabilities. Therefore, markets are efficient when the ratio of the value of output to the value of input throughout the marketing system is maximized.

Any change that reduces marketing costs per unit of output is desirable, but if it also reduces consumer satisfaction it may not be an improvement in marketing efficiency. Conversely, a cost increase need not cause efficiency to fall if the value of output (consumer benefits) has increased as much or more than costs.

Since consumer satisfaction cannot be measured directly, changes are analyzed in terms of "technical" efficiency and "pricing" efficiency.

Technical efficiency is concerned with the manner in which physical marketing functions are performed to achieve maximum output per unit of input. Technological changes can be evaluated to determine whether they will reduce marketing costs per unit of output. For example, it is relatively simple to investigate the costs of a new apple packing machine that may handle more apples per day while also reducing labor costs.

Pricing efficiency is concerned with the accuracy, precision, and speed with which prices reflect consumer demands and are passed back through the market channels to producers. Pricing efficiency is thus affected by rigidity of marketing costs and the nature and degree of competition in the industry. Activities that may improve pricing efficiency are improvements in market news and information, and competition.

The primary reason for firms to increase their marketing efficiency is the expected income improvement; for society, the basic goal of economic efficiency requires marketing efficiency.

Approaches to the Study of Marketing

The study of marketing involves various approaches. The most common are the functional, the institutional, and the market structure approaches.

Functional Approach. The functional approach studies marketing in terms of the many activities that are performed in getting farm products from the producer to the consumer. These activities are called functions. They are performed by cooperative and private marketing firms.

Using the functional approach, it is feasible to "cost" these functions and to compare them against others doing the same job or against standards of performance. The following functions are widely accepted for classification purposes: (1) exchange—buying and selling; (2) physical—processing, storage, and transporation; and (3) facilitating—standardization, financing, risk-bearing, and market information. Most of these functions are performed in the marketing of nearly all commodities.

Exchange functions take place throughout the market channel and include buyers bidding for the supplies of commodities and sellers offering commodities at the best price they think they can attain. The buying function also includes locating supplies of the commodity and assembling them for shipment. The selling function can vary depending upon what stage of the market channel the product is in. It involves packaging, labeling, advertising, promotion and all other merchandising activities.

Physical functions add form, time, and place utility (value) to commodities. Processing adds form utility to a product by taking, for instance, live beef and transforming it into T-bone steaks, liver, chuck roasts, etc. In agricultural marketing the processing function encompasses all those manufacturing activities that require agricultural products as raw materials.

Storage adds time utility to a product by holding it from harvest or production and distributing it on the market over time as it is needed. For example, flour millers maintain large stocks of grain, and producers carry inventories of spare parts for machines and of gasoline and oil for their equipment. This storage function occurs at all levels in the marketing channel.

Transportation adds place utility to a commodity. The fact that oranges are grown in Florida and California is of little value to consumers in New York or Wyoming if the oranges are not shipped from producing to consuming areas. Transportation includes moving commodities from the farm to processing or wholesaling facilities and from these facilities to their final destination. Costs incurred in the preparation of goods for shipment and in the loading of goods can be a significant portion of total transportation costs.

Facilitating functions improve the performance of the marketing system by increasing operational and pricing efficiency.

Standardization is the establishing of grades and of quality criteria for a commodity. This function makes it possible for buyers to know exactly what they are buying without personal inspection of the goods. Through standardization, buyers know, for instance, what is dark northern spring wheat of ordinary protein. Therefore, the costs of exchange activities are greatly reduced because buyers do not have to travel to look at a specific bin of wheat, or to telephone to receive a verbal description of it. When standardization is employed, the accepted quality characteristics must be enforced. This is usually the job of an agency of the state or federal government, so that the standards can be enforced impartially.

Financing is necessary throughout the marketing process because someone must own a commodity as it moves through the marketing stages. And there is a lag between the time someone buys and sells a commodity. Money tied up in commodities is money that could be in other investments, therefore, interest foregone is a real cost of financing the purchasing and storing of a commodity. If the marketer borrowed the funds to purchase and hold commodities, that person's financing cost is the interest paid on the borrowed funds.

The risk-bearing function falls on the commodity owner who is faced with possible losses due to physical or market risks. Physical risk is the risk of loss due to quality deterioration or destruction. Physical losses can be caused by moisture, heat, wind, fire, hail, etc., and can be reduced or eliminated through the use of insurance (such as the federal disaster payments or coverage by insurance companies). Whether or not one buys insurance depends on the probability of physical loss and the cost of insurance. Market risk is the risk borne, by commodity owners, of a possible adverse price movement.

Farmers' and merchandisers' losses due to price movements, that occur while holding inventories can be reduced by using the futures market. The futures market allows them to hedge their cash position, reducing price risk.

Market information involves collecting, analyzing, and disseminating information. In the USDA most data are collected by the Economics, Statistics, and Cooperatives Service, the Federal Market News System, and the Consumer and Marketing Service. Market information is necessary for the smooth operation of the price system. If buyers and sellers are well informed about the factors that affect supply and demand, prices will be established that more nearly clear the market.

Institutional Approach. The institutional approach examines the activities of business organizations or people involved in marketing. These middlemen can be classified as follows: (1) merchant middleman (retailers and wholesalers); (2) agent middlemen (brokers and commissionmen); (3) speculative middlemen; (4) facilitative organizations; and (5) food processors.

Middlemen perform the operations necessary to transfer goods from the producer to the consumer, because of the benefit of specialization and scale that exist in marketing as well as in production. Rather than producers conducting all of the marketing functions, middlemen, through specialization and division of labor, reduce total distribution costs.

Retail organizations usually purchase products for resale to consumers. In the food business, grocery stores are an example of a retail operation. These retail *merchant middlemen* purchase from wholesalers taking title to the products they handle. Wholesalers buy commodities from processors and sell to industrial users or to retailers. There are different types of wholesalers, but their primary function is to hold inventories, package products in lots that meet consumer needs, prepare lots for shipment, and make arrangements for transportation. Wholesalers also provide credit to retailers, offer merchandising assistance, and assume some of the risk the retailer would have to take if the retailer purchased directly from manufacturers.

Agent middlemen can be distinguished from merchant middlemen in that they do not take title to goods. These agents engage in negotiations that transfer the title of products from seller to buyer. To successfully accomplish this task, they must have a special knowledge of the product and the markets they serve.

Brokers perform the duty of bringing buyers and sellers together. The broker may represent either side of a sale, but usually represents the seller. The broker's fee ordinarily is based on the amount of the sale. Brokers represent grain or livestock firms, food processors, fruit and vegetable shippers, and other producers and handlers of agricultural commodities.

Commissionmen for agricultural producers are primarily interested in grain, livestock, and fresh fruits and vegetables. They have more authority than brokers in the selling of products. Any product consigned to them, is sold at the best price available. They collect on the sale of the product, deduct their expenses and remit the balance to the seller. With more decentralization in the marketing of agricultural commodities (less going through terminal or central markets) the use of brokers and commissionmen has declined. Much of the decentralization has been a result of direct buying by retail chains and processors from large country buyer-suppliers.

Speculative middlemen take ownership of and hold commodities, thus assuming the risk of loss due to unfavorable price fluctuations. They take ownership of the commodity and attempt to make a profit from uncertain price movements. As an example, some speculative middlemen are called scalpers, daytraders, or floor brokers on commodity exchanges.

Facilitative organizations such as trade associations, are institutions that provide general industry data, or that provide physical facilities for marketing such as grain exchanges or auction yards. These organizations may also guide the rules of trading so that competitive pricing results.

Processors transform raw agricultural products into different final products. Almost all agricultural products are processed to some degree between production and consumption.

Market Structure Approach. Market structure analysis emphasizes the nature of market competition, and attempts to relate the variables of market performance to types of market structure and conduct. Market structure is a description of the number and nature of participants in a market. Examples of such dimensions include: the number and size distribution of buyers and sellers in the market; the degree of product differentiation; and the barriers to potential entrants.

Market conduct deals with the behavior of firms. Firms that are price-searchers are expected to act differently than those in a price-taker type of industry. Price-searchers can determine their selling prices or the quantity of output they will sell. In addition, they could use their market power to weaken or eliminate competitors. Market performance is a reflection of the impact of structure and conduct on product prices, costs, and the volume and quality of output. If the market structure in an industry resembles monopoly (one seller, few substitute products, barriers to entry) rather than pure competition, then one can expect poor market performance.

Marketing Margins

The difference between the price that consumers pay for the final good and the price received by producers for the raw product represents marketing costs, or the marketing margin. Consumer demand for a product is called "primary demand." The demand for a product at the farm level is a "derived demand," meaning it is derived from consumer demand. In Figure 9-3, the vertical distance A-B is the marketing margin, the difference between the retail price (P_r) and the farm price (P_f) for a given quantity (Q_0) marketed. If output increases to Q_1 the marketing margin is C-D, which is the difference between the retail price (P'_r) and the farm price (P'_f).

Note that with the marketing margin constant, the vertical distance between the two demand curves remains unchanged. If the marketing margin were to increase with greater output and volume handled, C-D would be greater than A-B; if the marketing margin declines with increased production, C-D would be less than A-B.

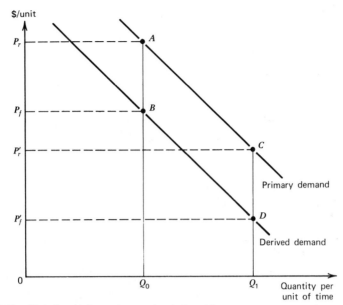

Figure 9-3.   Retail and farm demand relationships.

On the supply side, the supply curve at the farm level is primary since all food production is based on farm raw products. The derived supply curve is at other market levels and is primary supply plus the marketing margin as shown in Figure 9-4. If marketing costs are a constant amount then the marketing margins are shown at output level Q_0 as A–B and at output level Q_1 as C–D, and A–B equals C–D.

Figures 9-3 and 9-4 have been combined to produce Figure 9-5. The derived supply curve and primary demand curve determine the *retail* price. The primary supply curve and the derived demand curve determine the *farm* price. The difference between the retail price and the farm price is the marketing margin. Under competitive conditions the effect of changes in marketing costs on retail prices and farm prices can be determined.

Suppose, for instance, an improvement in transportation technology causes transportation costs to decline. The effect of this decrease will be a reduction in the marketing margin. On the graph, this translates into a downward shift in the derived supply curve and an upward shift in the derived demand curve. Thus, retail price falls and farm price increases resulting in a smaller marketing margin.

Statistics showing the farmers' share of the consumers' food dollar are based on an aggregate market-basket of food. The farmers' share of the cost of that basket has varied over time, amounting

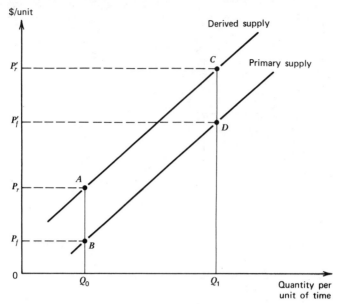

Figure 9-4. Retail and farm supply relationships.

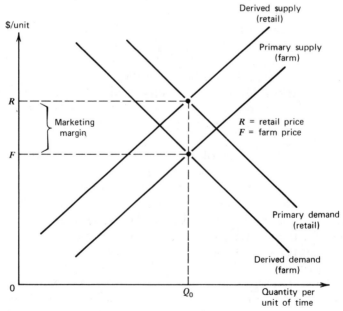

Figure 9-5. Market determination of farm and retail prices.

to 47 percent in 1950, to 39 percent in both 1960 and 1970, and to 40 percent in 1976. Another way to state these statistics is to say that in 1976, farmers received 40 cents out of every dollar the consumer spent for food and the marketers received 60 cents.

The share of the consumers' food dollar varies widely by food group. For every dollar spent by consumers in 1976 for poultry, the farmer received 55 cents; for meat products, 54 cents; for dairy products, 51 cents; for fruits and vegetables, 20 cents; and for bakery and cereal products, only 15 cents. There is a tendency for the farmers' share of the consumers' dollar to move up and down with commodity prices because marketing margins are relatively inflexible.

Many people look at the farmers' share data and think the marketers are taking financial advantage of producers. Before such a statement can be made, one must analyze the marketing activities performed and their costs. The farmers' share of the food dollar will normally reflect the amount of processing necessary, the perishability of the product, the bulkiness of the product relative to its value, and the seasonal nature of production.

The Futures Market

Futures markets such as the Minneapolis Grain Exchange, the Chicago Board of Trade, and the Chicago Mercantile Exchange operate to facilitate the marketing of agricultural products. These exchanges have been in existence since the mid-1800s and their purpose is to provide a place in which the activities of buyers and sellers determine the prices of commodities. At these exchanges traders buy and sell "futures contracts." Futures contracts are written documents calling for the future delivery of a commodity of a specific grade at a particular time and place. All terms and conditions are specified in the contract and are standardized by the futures exchange. Commodity futures contracts are bought and sold as if they were physical commodities.

Futures contracts are dated for the month of expiration, or when delivery must take place. In 1964, the Chicago Mercantile Exchange established live beef futures. These beef cattle futures expire around the twentieth day of the following months: February, April, June, August, October, and December.

Trading in a contract begins about a year in advance of the delivery (or expiration) date. For example, the buying and selling of the December 1978 contract started in November of 1977. It will terminate about the end of the third week in December 1978. Trading contracts with different delivery months can be compared to buying and selling in different markets. If a person buys a June contract, that buyer must meet the requirements of the contract by either accepting delivery immediately after June 20, or selling a June contract sometime before the June contract expires. Buyers and sellers need not be concerned about the other party to the contract because the particular exchange is responsible for clearing the transaction through its clearing house.

Chicago Mercantile Exchange rules call for a minimum delivery unit of 40,000 pounds of choice live steers, weighing from 1,050 to 1,150 pounds if the yield estimate is 61 percent, or weighing from 1,050 to 1,250 pounds if yield is estimated at 62 percent. Other yields and weights are acceptable at standard discounts. This *contract unit* represents approximately 35 to 40 head of fat cattle. Delivery on a live beef futures contract is possible at Omaha, Nebraska, and other specified locations.

When persons who are not members of an exchange buy or sell futures contracts they pay a broker who acts as their agent. A "round turn" is one purchase and one sale (or vice versa) of a specific contract, such as the purchase and later sale of a June 1978 contract.

Futures Price Quotations.   A futures market generates prices. If competitive conditions exist, the futures market generates prices reflecting today's best available estimates of the prices to be received during the respective delivery months. However, as new information arrives minute to minute, this estimate will change too, as you notice everyday in the futures price quotations in your local newspaper. The open, high, low, close, and previous close are given for each contract. An example of the price information that is released is illustrated below in Table 9-2 for April 24.

In these price quotations, the first trade of the day (April 24) on a June contract opened at $45.05 per cwt. The highest trading price for a June contract during the day was $45.60, and the lowest price

Table 9-2   April 24 Futures Price Quotations, Live Steers ($/cwt.)

Month	Open	High	Low	Close	Previous Close
June	45.05	45.60	44.95	45.50	44.75
August	46.70	47.45	46.70	47.40	46.50
October	46.00	46.55	45.90	46.45	45.65
December	46.25	46.40	46.00	46.25	45.70
February	45.60	46.25	45.60	45.80	45.55
April	—	—	—	45.50	45.10

was $44.95. The last trade of the day (the closing price) for a June contract was $45.50, and the previous close (the last trade made on April 23) for a June contract was $44.75.

The Hedging Process

Hedging is one way an individual or firm could use the futures market.[1] In the standard example of "insurance hedging," the hedger establishes a position in the futures market that is opposite from the position held in the cash (product) market. To illustrate hedging, assume that a cattle feeder with 40 head of steers determines in October that a selling price of $47 per cwt in the following June is needed to cover all costs including a normal rate of return on the investment. If the feeder is fearful that the market price will be less than $47 at the time at which the steers are ready to be sold, that person may wish to sell a futures contract provided it can be sold at or above $47 per cwt. If the feeder sold steers in June for $43 per cwt, and if the futures and cash market prices have moved up or down together, that person would also be able to buy back the futures contract at the same time at $43 per cwt. Thus, the feeder would make $4.00 per cwt on the futures transaction which would balance the $4.00 per cwt loss suffered on feeding operations. This is illustrated in the following example.

	Cash market	*Futures market (June contract)*
October	desired selling value 1,000 # @ $47/cwt = $470	sell 1,000 # @ $47/cwt = $470
June	sell 1,000 # @ $43/cwt = $430 −$40	buy 1,000 # @ $43/cwt = $430 +$40

The cattleman ended up with $470 for each steer, $430 from the sale of the steer and $40 earned from the futures transaction. This is what is called a perfect hedge and is a simple view of hedging.

Usually a feeder selling a futures contract as a hedge against a price decline on cattle in the feedlot will sell cattle on the local market and buy back futures at the same time. If the futures price is above the local cash price by more than the cost of making delivery

[1]Robert F. Bucher and Gail L. Cramer, "Beef Cattle Futures: A Marketing Management Tool," Montana Agricultural Experiment Station Bulletin 663, Montana State University, Bozeman, August 1972.

the feeder can deliver cattle by shipping them to Omaha, or they can sell the cattle at home and buy cattle in Omaha for delivery on the futures contract.

In actual practice feeders far from the delivery point do not deliver their own cattle on the futures contract. They buy back the futures contract and sell their cattle at home, or wherever the return is highest.

The price of cattle in the cash market will not always differ from the price of the futures contract in the futures market by the same amount. Economic conditions affecting the cash market do not exactly equal those influencing the futures market. However, because of speculative activity, the cash market price of fat steers at the time when a futures contract matures or expires, will be very close to the price of that futures contract. While it is impossible to completely eliminate price risk, it is possible to reduce that risk through the use of the futures market.

Hedging Cattle Fattening Operations. At the time of purchasing feeder cattle, the feeder hedges those animals by selling a beef futures contract that expires at the time the fattened cattle will be ready for market. This hedge only establishes an approximate selling price. The feeder must first estimate whether the approximate selling price will be profitable.

A feeder should know (or determine) certain facts to decide whether or not to hedge. These facts include the following:

1. The initial cost of feeder cattle at the feedlot (per cwt)

2. The best estimate of total cost of weight gain (per cwt)

3. The current price of the futures contract for the month in which cattle will be sold (per cwt)

4. The estimated "basis," which is the difference between prices of live cattle at the local selling point and the futures contracts at the time fat cattle will be sold, or the cost of delivering cattle to Omaha (per cwt)

5. The cost of hedging (per head).

The cost of feeder cattle includes the purchase price, the buyer's commission, transportation costs, and any other expenses incurred in securing cattle for the feedlot. If the feeder raises his own calves or yearlings the cost is the price for which the calves or yearlings could have been sold. For ease in estimating the effect of hedging, feeder cattle costs are used in terms of "cost per cwt."

A feeder's best estimate of "cost of gain" can be calculated using the previous year's feeding records as a benchmark. Cost of gain includes the costs of feed fed, interest on the value of feed, interest on the value of the calf, death loss, bedding, hired labor, fuel, marketing costs, and any other variable costs.

The current price of the futures contract for the month in which cattle will be sold can be found on the market page of some newspapers, or by calling a broker handling futures contracts.

The cost of shipping fat cattle from Billings, Montana and selling them in the Omaha market is approximately $2.45 per cwt. (Freight of about $2.00 and yardage commission and inspections of about $.45.) The cost of shrink must be added to this cost. If shrink is three percent and the fat cattle price is $45, the shrink cost is $1.35 per hundredweight.

A feeder who plans to sell cattle at Billings in June will be concerned about the basis, or the June difference between fat cattle price in Billings and the price of the June futures contract. Past records show that this varies from almost nothing to −$2.73 (i.e., Billings fat cattle price at $2.73 under futures). Therefore, some feeders use the cost of transporting and selling cattle in Omaha, about $2.45 per cwt, as an estimate of the basis. Then if the June difference between Billings fat cattle and futures is less than the cost of shipping to Omaha, they will sell their cattle in Billings. If the difference is larger they will ship the cattle to Omaha and sell there.

The cost of hedging includes the $50 broker's commission per contract, plus interest on $1000 margin over the length of the contract.[2] Assuming interest at eight percent and eight months as the life of the contract, hedging cost per head can be estimated as follows:

Commission (round turn)	$50.00
Interest on margins $1000 × .08 × 8/12 of year	$53.33
Total	$103.33
Hedging cost per head ($103.33 ÷ 40 head/contract)	$2.58

The following is a description of estimating possible profits and of executing a hedge. It is based upon the assumption that the feeder is planning to sell cattle at Billings, with costs estimated for an October to June feeding period.

The following assumptions will be used in the example (dollars

[2]This margin is the security deposit that must be deposited with the broker when the futures is sold.

are rounded to the nearest whole in order to keep the arithmetic simple):

1. Cost of calves (400 lbs) at the feedlot in October $50.00/cwt

2. Cost of gain (600 lbs)   27.00/cwt

3. Current (October) price of June futures   45.00/cwt

4. Expected basis at Billings, Montana   2.00/cwt

5. Cost of hedging   3.00/head

The Six Steps of Hedging. The process of hedging a cattle fattening operation breaks down into six steps as follows:

1. Estimate the potential feeding profit.

2. Determine the number of contracts to sell.

3. Arrange financing.

4. Place the order to sell futures ("place the hedge").

5. Record the order.

6. Place the order to buy back the futures ("lift the hedge").

With the required knowledge, the feeder can estimate the total cost of a 1000 pound fat steer by computing the necessary cost items (1 through 4) as shown in Table 9-3. The sale value of that 1000 pound steer may be calculated by subtracting the estimated basis ($2.00 per cwt) from the current price ($45.00 per cwt) of the June futures contract and multiplying the resulting $43.00 per cwt by 10 cwt, (the weight of the finished steer) as shown in item 5. By subtracting item 4 from item 5, the estimate of profit is $65.00 per head (item 6).

The feeder can now decide whether to run the risk of a price decline or to hedge. The risk can be shifted by selling the June futures contract at the time the calves are put in the feedlot. If a price decline occurs the feeder will sell the cattle for less than the

Table 9-3   Profit Estimate Made in October

1. Cost of calf 400 lbs × $50/cwt	$200.00
2. Cost of gain 600 lbs × $27/cwt	162.00
3. Hedging cost per head	3.00
4. Total cost of 1000 lb fat steer	365.00
5. Sale of 1000 lb fat steer × $43/cwt	430.00
6. Estimated profit per head	65.00

amount estimated, but will be able to buy back June futures for less than the initial sales price. The loss on the cattle on the cash market will be offset by the gain on the futures transaction so that the $65.00 feeding profit will be "locked in."

Related to the chance of gain is the chance of loss. In certain situations, a feeder may want to minimize a loss. Suppose a feeder has cattle on feed and estimates that a $5.00 per head loss would result if hedged, and further is convinced that beef prices are going lower and a loss greater than $5.00 per head could result. The $5.00 loss can be "locked in" by hedging, thus avoiding a greater loss.

To determine the number of contracts to sell, the feeder must first determine how many fat cattle will equal the contract weight of 40,000 pounds (for the Chicago Mercantile Exchange Contract). The feeder can determine the number of contracts required by dividing the total number of cattle to hedge by the number of cattle per contract. For example, 100 head of cattle divided by 40 head per contract equals 2.5 contracts. Since one-half of a contract cannot be traded, this feeder would sell two contracts and leave 20 head of cattle unhedged. A rule suggested for hedging is "never hedge cattle you do not have" because that would be simply speculation.

Memory often is short, so the feeder should write down the details of the futures transaction. This memo should include:

1. Brokers name, address, and telephone number.

2. Number and name of contracts sold (for example, "2 June—live beef.").

3. Price limit of the order (if the broker sells the order at or above the desired price he will confirm the execution of the sale).

4. Date of sale, price of sale, and margin paid to broker.

The hedge may be lifted by buying back the contracts any time up to contract maturity. It usually is done before the tenth day of the month of maturity. The hedge must be lifted by the nineteenth of the contract month unless the feeder wants to deliver cattle in Omaha to satisfy the contract. Feeders avoid making delivery for several reasons. One is that many of the delivered fat cattle will not meet contract requirements. For example, cattle not acceptable in the contracts include heifers, dairy steers, steers of other than British breeds, steers of less than 1050 pounds weight, packages of steers that grade "good," and packages of steers that vary too much in individual weights. So even though a feeder may have cattle in Omaha to deliver, one still may have to sell cattle in the Omaha market and get a buyer to purchase other steers to make up the delivery package. Therefore, feeders ordinarily sell their cattle wherever they can get the best net return over freight and selling costs, and make the necessary futures market transactions so as to avoid making a contract delivery.

If convinced that beef prices were going to continue rising, a feeder probably would not hedge, but if that were done the hedge might be lifted before the cattle were fat. Of course, when the hedge is lifted under these conditions the feeder would suffer a loss in the futures market which would be balanced by a gain in the cash market. However, if prices continued to rise the feeder would get the benefit of the rise that occurred between the time the hedge was lifted and the fat cattle were sold. On the other hand, if prices fell after the hedge was lifted the feeder would lose money on the cattle with no balancing gain on futures contracts.

Some hedging guidelines:

1. Calculate an acceptable profit.

2. Know basis of market.

3. Keep banker informed of hedging plans.

4. Do not hedge cattle not owned (this is speculation, not hedging).

5. Lift hedge by buying contracts before tenth day of contract month.

Pitfalls to avoid:

1. Locking in losses instead of profits because of unknown or undetermined costs or because a basis discount is used that is too small.

2. Being unable to meet margin calls because banker did not know of hedging plans.

3. Getting trapped into selling in an erratic futures market just before delivery date.

Speculation. Cash or current prices reflect current supply and demand conditions. The futures market reflects current best estimates of demand and supply in the specified futures month. Typically, agricultural producers use the futures market to hedge against price movements by selling futures contracts. This selling of contracts exerts a downward pressure on futures prices. Balancing producers' sales are purchases of contracts by people on the long (buying) side of the market. Some of these people may be exporters, processors, or speculators.

Exporters may hedge their future deliveries too. If they buy contracts to hedge then someone must have sold a contract. It may be a speculator who thinks prices are going to fall or a producer who is hedging a crop. Regardless of the amount of hedging that is occurring, adequate speculative activity is required. Speculation helps create the volume of trading to allow producers to get into and out of contracts, to keep the market competitive, and to keep the average cost of futures transactions as low as possible.

To economists, speculation is not gambling. A gambler takes unnecessary risks, risks deliberately created. Therefore, the gambler serves no useful purpose to society. The speculator assumes a risk that is already present. For example, when cattle feeders buy cattle to feed, they face the risk that prices of fat cattle may drop to a point at which they will suffer large losses. Unavoidable price risks exist. Someone must assume these risks because they are part of our economic environment. The only question is whether the cattle feeder will assume the risk or transfer it to a speculator through hedging operations.

Decentralized Markets

Few agricultural products are produced in a single location; rather they are produced in many different areas, each of which, frequently, also has a local market for the product. Producers usually sell their products in the local market where they can receive the highest net price, after taking into account transportation and handling costs (transfer costs).

If the product is produced and sold in a competitive economic environment, a producer can be aware of what products will bring at many different markets. This is because a competitive market provides adequate market news information. The producer can determine the farm price by subtracting transfer costs from the quoted market price.

Using the ideas of market price and transfer costs a "price surface" can be constructed, as in Figure 9-6. Suppose the figure represents a local area market for hogs, with the price of hogs at $50.00 per cwt in the central market (M). The farm price at any location is equal to the central market price less the appropriate transfer costs, and is shown by a specific isoprice contour. The isoprice contours (the concentric circles) show that the net farm prices are equal at equal distances from the central market for a given quality and quantity of the product marketed. Thus, hogs produced at a distance of A–M miles in any direction from the central market (M), bring a net farm price of $46 per cwt. Similar calculations can be made for other distances from the central market.

With two or more markets for a single product, the producer

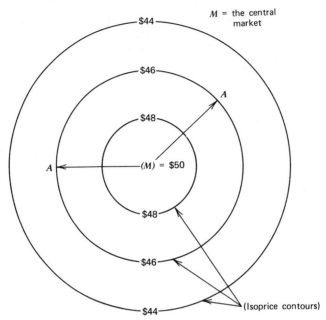

Figure 9-6.   A geographic price surface.

will ship to that market at which he can receive the highest market price less transfer costs. Therefore, one can see why market news information is so important to producers. It would be impossible for a producer to make rational marketing decisions if he were not aware of different geographical market prices. As long as goods can flow freely between competitive geographic points, markets will be related to each other by transfer costs. However, lags do exist in commodity flows and producers can take advantage of these lags.

How Markets Are Related.   Intermarket competition forces the market prices at two distant markets to differ most of the time by transfer costs for a given quality product. Assume transportation costs between markets A and B are $1.00. If, as in Figure 9-7, their prices differ by more than $1.00, buyers will purchase the product in market A at $3.00, spend $1.00 in getting the product to market B, then sell it in market B at $5.00, leaving a profit of $1.00 per unit. How many times have you seen a farmer market hay in another community because that price is greater than the local price by more than the cost of delivery? This buying and selling action will increase the demand in market A and increase its price, and selling it in market B will shift the supply curve and lower its price there. These transactions (called "arbitrage") will continue, until the possibility for such

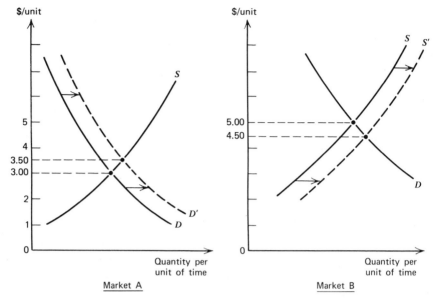

Figure 9-7. Spatial equilibrium in two markets.

profit is eliminated and the price differences between markets again equals the transfer costs. This action shifts the quantities of goods from one market where the good is less highly valued to another where it is more highly valued. Thus, the two markets now do a better job of allocating goods between consumers than could be done if it weren't for people who are willing to undertake whatever risks may be involved in these transactions.

Marketing Orders and Agreements.   Marketing orders and agreements were first established to make more orderly the marketing of milk and milk products, fruits, vegetables, and nuts. Through orderly (controlled) marketing it was thought that agricultural producers could even out the flows of sales of commodities on the market through the marketing year, increasing producers' net prices and therefore their incomes. These programs originated in the Agricultural Adjustment Act of 1933, and were clarified and modified under the Agricultural Marketing Agreement Act of 1937.

A "marketing agreement" is voluntary while a "marketing order" is mandatory. An agreement is a contract that is endorsed by the Secretary of Agriculture and the handlers of a particular commodity. This contract is binding only on those who sign it. These marketing agreements are exempt from the antitrust laws. A marketing order, on the other hand, is binding on all handlers of a commodity in a production or marketing area if two-thirds of the producers, with at least one-half of the volume of the commodity, approve the order through a referendum vote.

Most milk marketing orders attempt to protect farm income through classified pricing plans and by fixing minimum prices handlers must pay producers for various classes of milk. For example, prices of milk for fluid uses are set at a higher level than those for manufacturing uses.

Commodity marketing orders attempt to protect farm income by specifying the quality and quantity of a commodity that may be shipped, by prohibiting unfair methods of competition and unfair trade practices, and by establishing marketing research and development programs to promote the products.

Marketing orders are usually more effective than marketing agreements because agreements are only binding on those who sign them, whereas marketing orders, once approved, are binding on all handlers. This prevents the individual from undermining the agreement by acting in a personal rather than group interest.

Summary

Marketing is concerned with those productive activities that add time, place, and form utility to agricultural commodities. The existence of marketing is a result of specialization and trade in the economic system.

A market need not be a place. A market consists of buyers and sellers with facilities to communicate with each other. A well-organized market enhances the quality of communication between buyers and sellers so market prices can be determined. These prices in turn, guide producers' production decisions and consumers' purchasing decisions.

Efficiency is highly regarded in our society. Market efficiency can be measured by comparing the value of output to the value of inputs.

Three approaches to the study of marketing are the functional, institutional, and market structure. The functional approach analyzes marketing activities such as the exchange, physical, and facilitating functions that must be performed. The institutional approach examines the organizations or people involved in marketing. The market structure approach stresses the nature of competition in markets.

A marketing margin is the difference between the price consumers pay for the final product and the price received by producers for the raw product. Margins vary widely among agricultural commodities because of such factors as: the amount of processing that is necessary; perishability of the product; bulkiness of the product; and the seasonal nature of production. Large marketing margins may not mean that marketers are taking financial advantage of producers and consumers.

Futures markets determine prices for many agricultural commodities. They can be used to forward price commodities through hedging operations.

Marketing orders and agreements were established in the 1930s to even out the flow of products on the market. The purpose of orderly marketing is to increase producers' net prices and, therefore, their incomes.

Chapter Highlights

1. Marketing costs are those costs incurred in assembling, transporting, processing, and distributing farm food to consumers.
2. The major marketing costs are for labor, packaging, and transportation.
3. Agricultural marketing starts with production and continues until a product is sold to the final consumer. Thus, marketing also includes the input-supply firms that serve farmers and ranchers.
4. Marketing developed as a result of specialization and trade.
5. All economic systems must answer the questions of: (1) what and how much to produce; (2) how to allocate resources or inputs; (3) what production methods to use; and (4) how the product is to be rationed.
6. A market consists of buyers and sellers with facilities to communicate with each other. Markets may be local, regional, national, or international in scope.
7. In a market economy, market prices guide most production and consumption decisions.
8. There are three general approaches to the study of marketing: (1) functional approach; (2) institutional approach; and (3) market structure approach.
9. Marketing is production because it adds form, time, and place utility (or satisfaction) to agricultural commodities.
10. The marketing margin for a commodity is the difference between the retail price and the farm price.
11. The farmers' share of the consumers' food dollar reflects the costs of providing marketing services. Marketing services vary from one commodity to another.
12. Futures markets are important forward price discovery mechanisms that are used to price many farm products.
13. Futures contracts are standardized.
14. Hedging is establishing a position in the futures market that is opposite from the position one has in the cash (or product) market.
15. Speculators who take the opposite side of futures contracts are imperative in

the futures market. In addition they increase the volume of contracts traded to allow producers easy entry and exit from the market and keep the cost of hedging low.

16. Speculation in futures markets is not gambling.
17. A basis is the difference between cash and futures prices.
18. The basis is affected by economic influences; it is not fixed, but is continually changing.
19. In a perfectly competitive market, the farm price of a commodity at any location is equal to the market price minus transfer costs.
20. Marketing orders and agreements are used to even out the seasonal variations in marketing patterns. Their purpose is to increase producers' prices and incomes.

Review Questions

1. Why have marketing costs been increasing? What factors are causing marketing costs to rise?
2. How did markets develop? What role did specialized production and trade have in this development process?
3. Define a market. Why can markets be local, regional, national, or international in scope?
4. What is marketing efficiency? Are all changes that reduce marketing costs per unit of output an improvement in marketing efficiency? Explain.
5. Explain the three approaches to the study of marketing problems presented in this chapter. Is one approach preferred to the others?
6. Does a decrease in the farmers' share of the consumer dollar spent for farm food mean that marketers are taking financial advantage of producers? Discuss.
7. On January 28, the local cash price for winter wheat is $3.50 per bushel and the March future at Kansas City is $3.70 per bushel. On March 4 you deliver your winter wheat to your local elevator and the cash price is $3.45. The March future on March 4 is $3.80. What price would you obtain for your wheat if you hedged your wheat on the March basis as of January 28?
8. What is the "basis?" Calculate the basis for a commodity produced in your area. You can find the futures price information in the *Wall Street Journal* and obtain the local cash price from your local auction, elevator, or first handler.
9. Why would you expect intermarket competition to force market prices at two distant markets to differ only by transfer costs? Do you assume competitive markets?

Suggested Readings

1. Dahl, Dale C. and Jerome W. Hammond. *Market and Price Analysis: The Agricultural Industries.* New York: McGraw Hill Book Company, 1977, Chapters 7–10, 12, and 13.
2. Heyne, Paul T. *The Economic Way of Thinking.* Chicago: Science Research Associates, Inc., 1973, Chapter 8.

3. Hieronymus, T. A. *Economics of Futures Trading for Commercial and Personal Profit.* New York: Commodity Research Bureau, 1971.

4. Kohls, Richard L. and W. David Downey. *Marketing of Agricultural Products,* 4th ed. New York: The Macmillan Company, 1972, Chapters 1, 5, 6, 7, 9, and 16.

5. Moore, John R. and Richard G. Walsh, eds. *Market Structure of the Agricultural Industries.* Ames, Iowa: The Iowa State University Press, 1966. Chapter 15.

6. Shepherd, Geoffrey S. and Gene A. Futrell. *Marketing Farm Products,* 5th ed. Ames, Iowa: The Iowa State University Press, 1969, Chapters 1 and 2.

7. Tomek, William G. and Kenneth L. Robinson. *Agricultural Product Prices.* Ithaca, N.Y.: Cornell University Press, 1972, Chapters 6 and 12.

10

Courtesy of the Bozeman Production Credit and Federal Land Bank Associations.

FINANCIAL PICTURE OF AGRICULTURE

FINANCIAL PICTURE OF AGRICULTURE

This chapter discusses the financial position of agriculture, sources of farm credit, the banking system, and how to compute simple interest rates. The vitality of agriculture depends upon managers who understand finance and can apply it to the farm and ranch business.

A balance sheet gives you some idea of the present financial position of an individual or business. It is the result of all past transactions. A balance sheet is divided into *assets, liabilities,* and *net worth*. Assets are items of money value owned by a business. Liabilities are items of money value owed by a business, and represent creditors' claims against the assets. Net worth is the excess of assets over liabilities and represents the owner's residual claim to assets.

The value of all farm assets increased from $315 billion in 1970 to $671 billion in 1977. In 1977 real estate (land and buildings) accounted for $497 billion, nonreal estate assets (equipment, livestock, crops) $141 billion, and financial assets, $33 billion. Debt in agriculture was less than 16 percent of assets, or $102 billion. Most of this debt is split between real estate and nonreal estate loans (Table 10-1). Farmers' equity or ownership is $569 billion.

The average farm in the United States has real estate worth $181,000, nonreal estate worth $51,000, and financial assets amounting to $12,000 (Table 10-2). Total assets increased in nominal terms from $8000 in 1940 to $244,000 in 1977. Over this same time period, claims on those assets increased from $1,580 to $37,119. Thus proprietor's equity increased from $7000 to $207,000 per farm. As can be seen, farmers are in a good financial position on the average. However. these data do not give direct information on the profitability of farming.

Sources of Farm Credit

Most farm credit has been used to finance farm expansion and higher production cost items such as farm machinery and motor vehicles. In 1977, outstanding nonreal estate loans secured by farm assets totaled $45 billion. Commercial banks supplied 52 percent, production credit associations 28 percent, The Farmers Home Administration four percent, and individuals and others 16 percent.

Federal land banks supplied 33 percent of all outstanding real estate debt, life insurance companies 13 percent, commercial banks 12 percent, the Farmers Home Administration six percent, and individuals 36 percent. Individuals remain the major source of funds for land transfers. The Federal Land Bank is the largest institution involved in the land mortgage field. The total real estate debt outstanding as of January 1, 1977 was $56.4 billion.

The Farm Credit System

The farm credit system, which includes federal land banks, federal intermediate credit banks, production credit associations, and banks for cooperatives, is supervised by the Farm Credit Administration in Washington, D.C. The Farm Credit Administration is an independent agency within the executive branch of the federal government. The Federal Farm Credit Board is composed of 13 members, 12 who are appointed by the President of the United States and one member who represents the Secretary of Agriculture. This board sets policy for the Farm Credit Administration and appoints the governor or chief executive of the Farm Credit Administration. The underlying principle of operation is one of providing short, intermediate and long term credit to producers on a cooperative basis.

Farm Credit Districts

There are 12 Farm Credit Districts in the United States, including Alaska, Hawaii, and Puerto Rico (Figure 10-1). Within each district, there is a district farm credit board and three banks. These banks are the Federal Land Bank and its Federal Land Bank associations, the Federal Intermediate Credit Bank and its related Production Credit Associations, and a Bank for Cooperatives. The District Farm Credit Board is the board of directors for all three banks in the district. This board is composed of seven members, two borrowers from each of the three banks and one individual who is appointed by the governor of the Farm Credit Administration.

Federal Land Banks. The Federal Land Banks were organized under federal charter established by the Federal Farm Loan Act of 1916. There are 12 Federal Land Banks in the United States, one in each

Table 10-1 Balance Sheet of Farming Sector, January 1, Selected Years, 1940–77[a]

Item	1940	1950	1960	1970	1975	1977
				Billion dollars		
ASSETS						
Physical assets:						
Real estate	33.6	77.6	137.2	215.9	378.7	497.2
Nonreal estate:						
Livestock and poultry	5.1	12.9	15.2	23.5	24.6	29.1
Machinery and motor vehicles	3.1	12.2	22.7	32.3	55.7	72.3
Crops stored on and off farms[b,c]	2.7	7.6	7.7	10.9	23.3	21.9
Household equipment and furnishings	4.2	8.6	9.6	9.7	15.3	17.4
Financial assets:						
Deposits and currency	3.2	9.1	9.2	11.9	15.1	15.9
U.S. savings bonds	.2	4.7	4.7	3.7	4.3	4.4
Investments in cooperatives	.8	2.1	4.2	7.2	10.5	12.8
Total	52.9	134.7	210.6	315.2	527.5	670.9

continued

Table 10-1 *continued*

Item	1940	1950	1960	1970	1975	1977
CLAIMS		Billion dollars				
Liabilities:						
Real estate debt	6.6	5.6	12.1	29.2	46.3	56.4
Nonreal estate debt:						
Excluding CCC loans	3.0	5.1	11.5	21.2	35.2	44.7
CCC loans[d]	.4	1.7	1.2	2.7	.3	1.0
Total liabilities	10.0	12.4	24.8	53.0	81.8	102.1
Proprietors' equities	42.9	122.3	185.8	262.1	445.6	568.8
Total	52.9	134.7	210.6	315.2	527.5	670.9
Debt to asset ratio[e]	18.9%	9.2%	11.8%	16.8%	15.5%	15.2%

Source: "Balance Sheet of the Farming Sector 1977," Economics, Statistics, and Cooperatives Service, USDA, Agricultural Information Bulletin No. 411, October 1977, p. 2.

[a] Data for 50 states beginning with 1960.

[b] Commodity Credit Corporation was established in 1933 to carry out government price-support policy (See Chapter 12 for further details).

[c] All crops held on farms including crops under loan to CCC, and crops held off farms as security for CCC loans. On January 1, 1977, the latter totaled $397 million.

[d] Nonrecourse CCC loans secured by crops owned by farmers. These crops are included as assets in this balance sheet.

[e] Computed from unrounded data.

Table 10-2 Balance Sheet of the Farming Sector:
Average per Farm, Current Prices, January 1, Selected
Years, 1940-77 [a]

Item	1940	1950	1960	1970	1975	1977
				Dollars		
ASSETS						
Physical assets:						
Real estate	5,297	13,739	34,610	73,085	134,853	180,661
Nonreal estate:						
Livestock and poultry	808	2,283	3,848	7,949	8,750	10,566
Machinery and motor vehicles	482	2,154	5,739	10,934	19,851	26,280
Crops stored on and off farms [b,c]	420	1,344	1,952	3,697	8,287	7,944
Household equipment and furnishings	663	1,524	2,419	3,334	5,453	6,314
Financial assets:						
Deposits and currency	510	1,607	2,313	4,025	5,363	5,803
U.S. savings bonds	39	836	1,177	1,266	1,542	1,586
Investments in cooperatives	131	364	1,071	2,438	3,744	4,647
Total	8,350	23,851	53,129	106,728	187,845	243,801

continued

Table 10-2 *continued*

Item	1940	1950	1960	1970	1975	1977
			——Dollars——			
CLAIMS						
Liabilities:						
Real estate debt	1,037	988	3,049	9,879	16,484	20,504
Nonreal estate debt:						
Excluding CCC loans	473	912	2,909	7,166	12,545	16,247
CCC loans[a]	70	305	294	906	114	368
Total liabilities	1,580	2,205	6,252	17,951	29,143	37,119
Proprietors' equities	6,770	21,646	46,877	88,777	158,702	206,682
Total	8,350	23,851	53,129	106,728	187,845	243,801
Debt to asset ratio	18.9%	9.2%	11.8%	16.8%	15.5%	15.2%

Source: "Balance Sheet of the Farming Sector 1977," Economics, Statistics, and Cooperatives Service, USDA, Agricultural Information Bulletin No. 411, October 1977, p. 4.

[a]Total values divided by total number of farms. Data for 50 States beginning with 1960.

[b]Commodity Credit Corporation was established in 1933 to carry out government price-support policy (See Chapter 12 for further details).

[c] All crops held on farms including crops under loan to CCC, and crops held off farms as security for CCC loans.

[d]Nonrecourse CCC loans secured by crops owned by farmers. These crops are included as assets in this balance sheet.

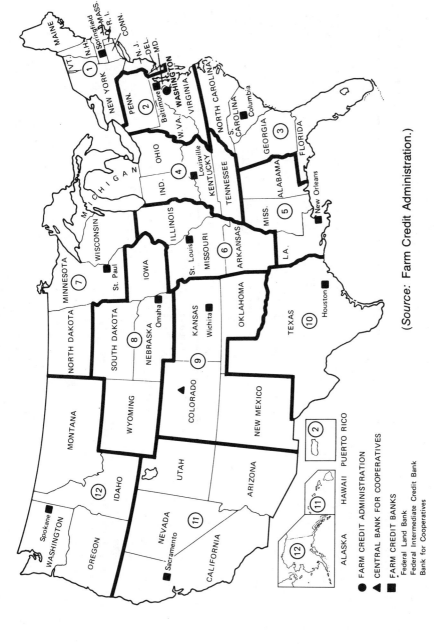

(*Source:* Farm Credit Administration.)

Figure 10-1. The farm credit system districts.

ALASKA HAWAII PUERTO RICO

● FARM CREDIT ADMINISTRATION
▲ CENTRAL BANK FOR COOPERATIVES
■ FARM CREDIT BANKS
  Federal Land Bank
  Federal Intermediate Credit Bank
  Bank for Cooperatives

Farm Credit District. These banks make long term loans secured by first mortgages on real estate through more than 500 local Federal Land Bank Associations. The federal government provided initial financial support to these banks, but by 1947 the federal support was repaid and now the banks are entirely owned by their borrowers.

The Federal Land Bank in each district supervises the Federal Land Bank Associations in their district. The producer actually borrows funds from the Federal Land Bank Association, but the loan is transferred directly from the Federal Land Bank to the borrower. The Federal Land Bank delegates the authority to the Association to make and service all loans, but supervises the activities of the associations. Voting members of these associations select a board of directors and employ a manager.

When farmers borrow from the local association, they are required to purchase capital stock or participation certificates in the local association equal to five percent of the loan. The local association then buys the same amount of capital stock or certificates in the district Federal Land Bank. District bank and local association stock and certificates are refunded to the borrower when the loan is repaid.

The Federal Land Bank obtains funds through the sale of bonds in the national money market with the size of any bond issue being dependent on the estimated money needs of the 12 land banks. In addition to bond issues, the banks can borrow from other financial institutions with the Farm Credit Administration's approval.

The Federal Land Banks make loans with a range of five to 40 years for maturity. Loans may not exceed 85 percent of the appraised value of borrowers' collateral.

Interest rates are determined by the bank boards subject to the Federal Credit Administration's approval. Banks primarily use two types of interest rate programs. One is the fixed rate, where the borrower pays a designated rate for the entire time of the loan. The second type uses a variable interest rate in which interest rates can rise or fall over the length of the loan depending on the cost of money to the Federal Land Bank.

The Land Banks, after providing for reserves and operating expenses, may distribute earnings to the local associations in the form of dividends. These local associations in turn, may decide to pass their dividends on to their member patrons.

Production Credit. The production credit system was established under federal laws in 1923 and 1933 to provide short term and intermediate term loans to farmers, ranchers, harvesters of aquatic products and rural residents. The federal intermediate credit banks were first authorized by the Farm Credit Act of 1923. These 12 banks were intended only to discount short term notes that farmers had given to various financial institutions. Farmers and ranchers did not make use of the credit banks, so short and intermediate credit remained a problem. Therefore, in 1933, Congress authorized local production credit associations.

The relationship between the Federal Land Bank and the federal land bank associations is similar to the relationship between the federal intermediate credit banks and the production credit associations. The 12 Federal Intermediate Credit Banks discount loans for, and make loans to, the production credit associations. They also supervise some of the production credit associations' operations which are usually educational in nature, including such functions as helping on problem loans and developing credit standards.

The federal intermediate credit banks obtain funds in the same way as the Federal Land Bank, by selling bonds in the national money market. This provides the production credit associations with a dependable source of credit at current interest rates.

Today there are more than 400 production credit associations throughout the United States with 1500 full-time offices. Members with voting stock in the production credit associations elect a board of directors from its members and employ a staff to conduct business affairs.

Ownership of the federal intermediate credit banks is by the local production credit associations through purchases of capital stock and certificates issued by the bank. Every production credit association borrower must purchase stock in the association equal to five percent of the loan and may be required to own as much as 10 percent. When these loans are repaid, the stock or certificates are not returned for this would weaken the financial structure of the production credit association. Therefore, most members retain their stock and use it again when they need another loan. If a member does not borrow for two years that stock is converted to nonvoting stock, which leaves active members in control of the production credit association at any given time.

Loans to borrowers are made by the individual production credit association, with producers' notes and mortgages then used as collateral to borrow from the district Federal Intermediate Credit Bank. In 1971, the Farm Credit Act was passed that provides participation agreement in making and servicing loans between federal intermediate credit banks and production credit associations. This provision facilitates the making of large loans as producers become fewer and larger by spreading risks.

The interest rate policy is much the same as for the federal land banks. Many production credit associations use the "fixed-interest spread," adding their costs of making and servicing loans and requirements for reserves to the amount they must pay for money from the Federal Intermediate Credit Bank.

Banks for Cooperatives.   The 12 district banks for cooperatives service the credit needs of agricultural cooperatives. Also there is a Central Bank for Cooperatives in Denver, Colorado, that participates with district banks on large loans. The Farm Credit Act of 1933 established the organization and initial capitalization for these 13 banks.

The board of directors of the Central Bank for Cooperatives is composed of one director elected from each district farm credit board and one additional member appointed by the governor. The banks for cooperatives are owned by current and former borrowing cooperatives. A cooperative's equity in its district bank is acquired by: (1) purchasing shares of stock when a loan is made; (2) purchasing additional shares of stock in proportion to interest paid on borrowings; and (3) net savings of the banks, which may be distributed to the cooperative in stock as patronage refunds or allocated surplus. These banks may issue other stock for investment purposes, with dividends limited to no more than eight percent per year.

The banks for cooperatives obtain most of their loan funds through the sale of debenture bonds backed by borrower collateral. These bonds are sold by a Fiscal Agency in New York City. Other funds are obtained from borrowing from other farm credit banks, commercial banks, and other financial institutions.

Any association of farmers, ranchers, or producers or harvesters of aquatic products, or any federation of such associations, may be eligible to borrow from a bank for cooperatives. To be eligible to borrow a cooperative must have at least 80 percent of its voting control with agricultural producers, and the cooperative must do at least 50 percent of its business with its members. No member shall have more than one vote, and dividends on stock or membership capital must be restricted to eight percent per year.

Loans to eligible borrowers are made to finance long term assets or working capital. Most loans are made for constructing, remodeling or expanding facilities, or purchasing land, buildings or equipment.

Interest rates vary from district to district depending on the type and length of the loan. Short term loans usually carry a lower rate of interest than longer term loans. As the cost of money in the money market rises or falls, the rate to cooperatives also rises and falls.

The farm credit system in the United States has been very successful. All original equity capital supplied by the government to establish the farm credit system was repaid by 1968. This producer owned and controlled organization is providing access to the major money market for all producers. Therefore, producers have the advantage of maintaining competition with local commercial banks in obtaining loanable funds at the lowest possible rates. In 1975, the system had $30 billion loaned to 850,000 producers. Loans outstanding have increased 130 percent since 1969.

Farmers Home Administration

The Farmers Home Administration is an agency of the United States Department of Agriculture located in Washington, D.C. This agency has 42 state offices covering all 50 states plus Puerto Rico and the Virgin Islands. All rural counties are served by over 1700 offices normally located in county seat towns. This organization was established to assist beginning producers and other farmers and ranchers with limited resources who are unable to obtain credit from the farm credit system or commercial lenders. These credit programs have been expanded to include help in providing new employment and business opportunities, improve the environment, assist in acquiring homes, and improve the quality of life in rural America.

The Farmers Home Administration primarily provides two types of loans. One is a guaranteed loan handled by a private lender. Farmers Home Administration guarantees to limit the loss on the loan to a specified percentage. The second type, is a direct loan by the Farmers Home Administration. Loan funds are obtained from insured notes backed by the government. Also Congress authorized the Farmers Home Administration to provide grants for rural development planning, pollution abatement and control, and facilitate business and industry.

Types of loans made by the Farmers Home Administration:

1. Farm ownership loans

2. Farm operating loans

3. Farm emergency loans

4. Irrigation and drainage loans

5. Grazing association loans

6. Resource conservation and development loans

7. Watershed loans

8. Indian land acquisition loans

9. Soil and water conservation loans

10. Recreation enterprise loans

11. Youth loans

12. Community facility loans

13. Business and industrial loans

14. Individual homeownership loans

15. Repair and rehabilitation housing loans

16. Rental and cooperative housing loans

17. Farm labor housing loans

18. Homesite development loans

19. Self-help technical assistance grants

The maximum amount that can be borrowed, the repayment schedules, and the terms of the loan differ according to the type of loan.

The Banking System

Agriculture and agricultural financial institutions do not operate in isolation from conditions in other sectors of the economy. The agricultural sector must compete for available funds with public and private borrowers from all segments of the economy. While both monetary and fiscal policies influence the availability of loanable funds to agriculture, monetary policy is of greater concern here.

Fiscal policy is the government policy regarding expenditures and taxation. Thus, the government can increase expenditures of such agencies as the Farmers Home Administration and increase loanable funds, or restrict credit by cutting budgets. Also, of course, tax levels influence the amount of money available to producers to invest in their operations. Fiscal policy changes affect the flow of funds to financial institutions and therefore affect loanable funds. These changes also influence business activity and savings. A tax decrease tends to stimulate incomes, employment and savings, while a tax increase will have an opposite impact on the economic system.

The ability of banks to create or destroy money as they perform their usual business has a great deal to do with the performance of the economy. Given their potential impact throughout the system, the activities of the banking industry must be coordinated so as to inhibit wide swings in prices and employment levels.

Monetary policy is an effective tool for attempting to meet the national goals established by Congress and the President of maintaining price stability and full employment. To do so requires that the flow of bank credit and the supply of money maintain a certain stability because of their effects on incomes, employment and savings. By regulating the supply of money and therefore the terms on which people borrow money, monetary authorities can stimulate or retard business activity. The federal reserve system which was established by the Federal Reserve Act of 1913, is the principle organization that regulates monetary policy in the United States.

There are 12 federal reserve bank districts serving all 50 states, with one bank in each district plus 24 branch banks (Figure 10-2). All of these banks are part of the Federal Reserve System. Each bank has nine directors, six elected from member banks and three appointed by the Board of Governors of the Bank System.

The federal reserve system has a membership of over 6000 commercial banks which control about 80 percent of the commercial bank assets, but only comprise about 40 percent of the approximately 15,000 banks in the United States. While these member banks operate for profit, the system does not. In its operation the reserve system does earn money, but all income over expenses and reserves is transferred to the U.S. Treasury.

The supervision of the federal reserve system is handled by a board of governors. This board consists of seven members appointed by the President of the United States and confirmed by the Senate for a 14-year term. These members are full-time employees whose primary function is to formulate national monetary policy and supervise its execution.

The federal reserve system regulates the supply of credit through controlling the supply of money. There are four basic ways this control occurs. These are regulating member bank reserve requirements, conducting open market operations, adjusting the rediscount rate, and using various selective controls.

1. *Member Bank Reserves.* The Federal Reserve has control over the volume of money and the interest rate by regulating the amount and use of member bank

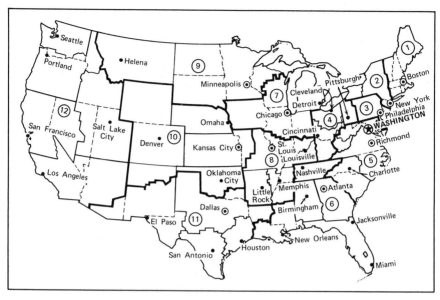

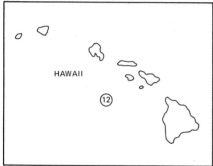
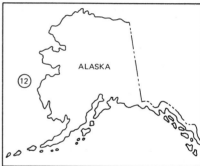

(*Source:* Board of Governors, Federal Reserve System.)

LEGEND

▬▬▬ Boundaries of Federal Reserve Districts	⊙ Federal Reserve Bank Cities
─── Boundaries of Federal Reserve Branch Territories	● Federal Reserve Branch Cities
✪ Board of Governors of the Federal Reserve System	● Federal Reserve Bank Facility

Figure 10-2. Districts in the Federal Reserve System.

reserves. The required reserve is the percentage of a bank's demand deposits that the Federal Reserve requires these banks to keep in reserves. The reserve requirement can vary between 7 and 14 percent of demand deposits in country banks, 10 to 22 percent for city banks and 3 to 10 percent on time or savings deposits. As long as banks have excess reserves they can continue to loan or invest funds. But if the Federal Reserve increases the reserve requirement, it means that member banks have less excess reserves, which restricts the amount of credit the bank can extend. For example, assume a local bank in Burns,

Oregon has demand deposits of $50,000. If the reserve requirement is 10 percent, that bank can make loans or investments up to a total of $45,000.[1] If the reserve requirement is increased to 14 percent, the maximum amount it can lend or invest is reduced to $43,000. Also, if the reserve requirement is lowered, the amount of credit available to borrowers can be increased. Changes in the reserve requirement are an infrequently used tool of the federal reserve system. Day to day operations of the money supply are handled through open market operations.

2. *Open Market Operations.* Open market transactions are controlled by the Federal Open Market Committee, which buys and sells government securities, i.e., bonds, in the open market. This committee has 12 members, 7 from the board of governors and 5 of the presidents of the federal reserve banks. By purchasing or selling securities, the federal reserve system can influence the volume of member bank reserves. For example, assume the federal reserve system buys bonds from commercial banks worth $100,000. The system receives the bonds and the banks get dollars in the form of deposits. The deposits increase reserves, so more loans can be made. Remember, bankers are in business to make money and they don't want to lose interest on money by leaving it idle. Thus, by increasing the supply of loanable funds, there is a tendency for the interest rate to fall and this may lead to additional borrowing.

The reverse occurs if the open market committee decides to decrease member reserves. In this case, the government sells bonds in the open market. People or businesses buying these bonds reduce their bank demand deposits by paying for the bonds, and therefore bank reserves are reduced. This policy tightens credit, tends to increase interest rates, and causes reduced borrowing.

3. *The Rediscount Rate.* When a member bank runs short of money, it can borrow from its district federal reserve bank just as we borrow for an automobile when we lack cash to pay for it. The rate of interest charged by the federal reserve bank is called the rediscount rate. It is termed the rediscount rate because when a member bank borrows money, it must have collateral that is usually loan notes from customers. These notes then are discounted at the "Fed window" at a set rediscount rate.

---

[1] An individual bank can lend or invest its excess of reserves. The entire commercial banking system, however, can create money by a multiple of its excess reserves. If the reserve requirement is 20 percent, then 80 percent of any new deposit can be loaned. So if a commercial bank receives a new deposit of $10, the banking system can create $40 in additional deposits (for a total of $50). Money creation is accomplished with a reserve requirement of 20 percent as follows: The 1st bank receives $10 and loans $8, which is deposited in the 2nd bank; the 2nd bank can loan $6.40, which is deposited in the 3rd bank; the 3rd bank can loan $5.12, which is deposited in the 4th, etc. This process can be repeated until the banking system has recorded new demand deposits of $50.00. A formula is used to calculate the total amount of new demand deposits in the banking system. The formula is:

$$\text{Total new demand deposits} = \frac{\text{New Deposit}}{\text{Reserve requirements}}$$

In the above example, the total new demand deposits = $10/.20 = $50.

By raising the rediscount rate, the Fed discourages borrowing by member banks and their customers because the cost of borrowing money is increased. On the other hand, by lowering the rediscount rate the Fed encourages member bank borrowings. However, the rediscount rate is relatively unimportant in controlling the volume of money, because the Fed does not loan funds except for short periods of time.

4. *Selective Controls.* The Fed also uses many selective controls and moral suasion to induce member banks to follow bank policy. For example, they regulate the amount of interest banks can pay on various types of savings programs. They control margin requirements on stocks and bonds. Also, from time to time, the Fed has used its authority to regulate consumer installment credit. Such control may deal with down payment requirements, the maximum length of loan, and the rate of interest to be paid.

Federal Reserve Bank activities affect the federal farm credit system because bonds sold by the system must be purchased by commercial banks and other investors. If the Fed wants to reduce the volume of funds available, it means that commercial banks have less reserves to purchase farm bonds, and producers must pay a higher rate of interest on borrowings.

Commercial Banks

There are about 15,000 commercial banks in the United States. These banks are corporations chartered under federal or state law. They are stock organizations that are owned by the people who have invested in them. The stockholders elect a board of directors that determine bank policy and employ a staff to operate the bank. Thus, a commercial bank is a private business, but it is supervised by many federal and state (public) agencies. This regulation is required to insure the safety of depositor's funds, and that member banks follow the national regulations of the Federal Reserve System.

Most commercial bank loans to agricultural producers are of a short term nature for production expenses. These expenses are for fertilizer, cattle, feed, seed, fuel, labor, and so forth. Loans of longer duration are made for machinery and equipment, but little mortgage money of a long term nature is available from commercial banks. As of 1977, commercial banks provided about 52 percent ($23 billion) in nonreal estate loans to agriculture and about 12 percent ($7 billion) in real estate loans.

Interest rates commercial banks charge depend on the demand for loans, policy of the Fed, rates charged by competitors, and their excess reserves. Also important is the risk involved and the management capacity of the borrower. Usually banks are competitive with production credit associations and other lending institutions. But it is necessary for producers to shop for credit like shopping for any other commodity. The interest rate is the price of money and large savings are often possible if one can borrow at lower rates.

Many banks have agribusiness or agricultural departments that specialize in agricultural credit needs. They employ skilled agricultural representatives that understand agriculture. Most of these specialists can analyze the farm business and provide information and guidance in assisting producers so they use capital wisely and are able to meet their repayment schedules.

Life Insurance Companies

Life insurance companies finance about 13 percent of the real estate loans, or about $7 billion. In 1950, life insurance companies provided more than 25 percent of the mortgage money to agriculture. In recent years, however, the Federal Land Bank has become more competitive.

Life insurance companies are in the business to sell life insurance. As people pay on their policies, companies accumulate large sums of money. Such funds are used in all types of investments to produce income for their policyholders. Most of their investments are made in the nonfarm economy, but insurance companies do diversify their portfolios and invest in long term credit to agriculture.

There are two types of insurance companies: stock companies and mutual companies. Mutual life insurance companies are cooperatives. Many do not issue capital stock and there are no stockholders. Those who purchase insurance from these companies own the assets of the company. The company provides insurance at cost. If the premiums paid by policyholders cover all expenses with reserves left at the end of the year, these reserves are credited to policyholder accounts as dividends. Mutual companies issue about 60 percent of all life insurance sold. Stock life insurance companies are organized as private stock ventures. They are controlled by stockholders who operate the business for the profit of investors. Therefore, the stockholders share in the gains or losses from the enterprise.

Most life insurance companies that are fairly large have field representatives located in branch offices around the country. They hire highly trained agriculturalists to procure and service loans.

Farm mortgage loans fit the nature of the insurance business. Most policyholders have held their insurance policies for over 40 years. Also most farm mortgages are repaid over 20–25 years although some of their loans may be for shorter time periods. In terms of dollar amounts, insurance companies have been making much larger loans than commercial banks or the Federal Land Banks. The average farm mortgage loan made in 1975 by life insurance companies was $314,529 while it was $71,673 for Federal Land Banks.

Interest Rates.   An interest rate is the price of borrowing money. A producer who wants to borrow money must be able to compare interest rates among the alternative lenders. The 1969 Truth in Lending Act requires that lenders specifically inform borrowers of the total finance charges and the annual percentage rate of interest.

Suppose a farmer borrows $10,000 for one year at a cost of $600. The true interest rate that is being paid can be approximately estimated for *short-term* loans by the use of the following formula:

$$i = \frac{2 \cdot N \cdot C}{P(T + 1)}$$

where:

i = annual simple interest rate

C = total cost of loan

N = number of payments per year (twelve if monthly, one if annually)

T = total number of payments

P = the amount of the loan advanced

Substituting our figures into the formula:

C = $600

N = 1

T = 1

P = $10,000

$$\text{Therefore, } i = \frac{2 \cdot 1 \cdot 600}{\$10,000\,(1 + 1)} = .06 = 6 \text{ percent}$$

In this example, six percent is the simple or actuarial interest rate. It is the interest on the average loan balance for the year.

Now let's suppose that $10,000 is borrowed for one year to be repaid in 12 monthly payments. The total interest charge is still $600. Therefore you are paying back $10,600 over 12 months. This add on method is used in financing machinery and equipment.

$C = \$600$

$N = 12$

$T = 12$

$P = \$10,000$

Thus,

$$i = \frac{2 \cdot 12 \cdot \$600}{\$10,000 \, (12 + 1)} = \frac{14,400}{130,000} = .11 = 11 \text{ percent}$$

In a last example, suppose that $10,000 is borrowed for one year to be repaid in 12 montly payments. The interest charge is $600, however, the $600 interest charge is deducted from the loan at the beginning. The producer receives $9,400, but must pay back $10,000 over the year. This discount method is used in personal loans as follows:

$$i = \frac{2 \cdot 12 \cdot \$600}{\$9,400 \cdot (12 + 1)} = \frac{14,400}{122,200} = .118 = 11.8 \text{ percent}$$

With both the add on and discount interest, the rate paid is associated with the original balance not the average balance.

One needs to shop for money to borrow as you would for a tractor, because there is usually a large difference in finance charges among lending institutions. The particular interest rate paid will be influenced by the cost of funds to the lending institution, risk of default on the loan, cost of servicing the loan, and possibly state and federal laws.

Summary

The general financial picture of agriculture is shown by the balance sheet. This financial statement shows all assets, liabilities, and net worth. Agriculture's assets totaled $671 billion in 1977. Claims against these assets amounted to only $102 billion. Thus, farmers have substantial amounts of assets that they own. The debt to asset ratio per farm was 15.2 percent in 1977.

Agricultural producers borrow production funds from commercial banks, life insurance companies, individuals, the Farmers Home Administration, and the farm credit system.

The farm credit system is composed of the federal land banks, federal intermediate credit banks, production credit associations and banks for cooperatives. This farm credit system is farmer owned and controlled. Federal land banks make long-term loans for real estate. The production credit associations, however, fulfill short-term credit needs for production items.

The Farmers Home Administration of the U.S. Department of Agriculture was established as a lender of last resort. It was an agency to help finance beginning producers with limited resources. Now this agency is involved in financing rural development projects and rural housing.

The federal reserve system was established by the Federal Reserve Act of 1913 and is the principle organization that regulates monetary policy in the U.S. This system has 6000 member banks which control about 80 percent of the commercial bank assets. It regulates the supply of money available by controlling: (1) member bank reserves; (2) open market operations; (3) rediscount rates; and (4) selective controls.

The interest rate is the price of borrowing money. The 1969 Truth in Lending Act requires that lenders inform borrowers of all finance charges and the annual percentage interest rate they would pay. Interest rates do vary, thus, it is important to be able to compute simple interest rates so they can be compared among alternative lenders. Quoted interest rates may differ because lending institutions obtain loanable funds at different costs, the risks of loss vary among borrowers, and the costs of serving loans differ.

Chapter Highlights

1. Assets, liabilities, and net worth are shown on a balance sheet.
2. Farm assets amounted to $671 billion in 1977. Land is the major asset owned by the farm business.
3. Agricultural debt is $102 billion, less than 16 percent of assets.
4. Farmers and ranchers own most of their farms. Net worth was $569 billion in 1977.
5. Farm credit is available from the farm credit system, life insurance companies, commercial banks, Farmers Home Administration, and individuals.
6. The federal farm credit system includes the federal land banks, federal intermediate credit banks, production credit associations, and banks for cooperatives.
7. The farm credit system is farmer owned, although it started with government assistance.

8. The Farmers Home Administration assists farmers with credit if they are unable to attain funds from the farm credit system or other commercial lenders.
9. National monetary policy is established by the Federal Reserve System.
10. The federal reserve system influences the national money supply by: (1) regulating member bank reserve requirements; (2) conducting open market operations; (3) adjusting the rediscount rate; and (4) using selective credit controls.
11. Commercial banks provide most of the nonreal estate loans to agriculture.
12. Life insurance companies primarily finance the purchase of real estate.
13. An interest rate is the price of borrowing money.
14. The simple or actuarial interest rate is based on the average loan balance over the period of the loan.

Review Questions

1. What is the general financial condition of agriculture? Does the balance sheet give a complete financial picture of agriculture?
2. What are the sources of farm credit? Which of these sources provide short-term credit?
3. The farm credit system was established as a cooperative credit system initially funded by the U.S. government. At present, who owns the farm credit system?
4. Where does the farm credit system borrow the money it loans to farmers and ranchers?
5. Are farm loans granted by the Farmers Home Administration? What type of loans do they handle?
6. Explain the difference between government monetary and fiscal policy.
7. How does the federal reserve system regulate the supply of credit available by controlling the money supply?
8. Why should you "shop" for farm credit? How can you compare the costs of borrowing money from different financial institutions?

Suggested Readings

1. Hoag, Gifford W. *The Farm Credit System.* Danville, Ill.: The Interstate Printers and Publishers, Inc., 1976.
2. Hopkin, John A., Peter J. Barry, and C. B. Baker. *Financial Management in Agriculture.* Danville, Ill.: The Interstate Printers and Publishers, Inc., 1973, Chapters 4 and 5.
3. Nelson, Aaron G., Warren F. Lee, and William G. Murray. *Agricultural Finance,* 6th ed. Ames. Iowa: The Iowa State University Press, 1973, Chapters 19–25.
4. Stokes Jr., W. N. *Credit to Farmers.* Washington, D.C.: The Federal Intermediate Credit Banks, Farm Credit Administration, 1973.
5. Willis, James F., and Martin L. Primack. *Explorations in Economics.* Boston: Houghton Mifflin Company, 1977, Chapter 12.

Courtesy of Doug Warren, Editor, Montana Agricultural Experiment Station, Bozeman.

NATURAL RESOURCES

NATURAL RESOURCES

The word "resource" was used earlier (Chapter 4) as meaning any good or service that can be used to produce a good capable of satisfying a human want. A "natural" resource is simply a resource provided by nature, a good existing in the universe, yet not limited solely to physical things.[1]

Such phenomena in nature have no value until they have been discovered and an economic use has been found for them. Natural resources, then, are a function not only of their physical existence, but also depend upon our knowledge of them and the technology of use plus our ability to make economic use of them as sources of want satisfying goods and services. It is quite possible that we have discovered economic uses for only a minute fraction of resources in and on the earth and its surroundings. How much remains to be discovered? How many new uses can be discovered?

Of the wide array of resources around us, the one that most typically comes to mind when the term natural resource is used is *land*—land from which we derive our food and fiber, space over which to transport people and goods, building materials, space for homesites, for recreation and aesthetic purposes.

Other natural resources are the *water* that exists in lakes, streams, rivers, or in underground channels and reservoirs; *minerals* in their many types, locations, and varying concentrations; and self-propagating *plant and animal life,* all of which are of immense usefulness to mankind. And if plant and animal life are properly included, how can we ignore *humans,* who, with their labor and other productive abilities, are probably the most important of all natural resources?

A Natural Resource Classification. Rational answers to questions of which resources to use, when to use them, and how rapidly to use them are made more difficult because of the characteristics exhibited by these resources.

We may pump the oil from an underground basin, at a rate

---

[1]Were we to be too restrictive in this we would have to find a special definitional slot for such phenomena as wind, tides, and the energy of the sun.

determined by the costs of getting the oil out of the ground and the value of the pumped oil, but what do we do when the well runs dry? We may have used this resource wastefully by a too-rapid pumping rate. This is quite a different problem from capturing a benefit from the flow of the wind. If its velocity has not been diminished, nor its quality fouled in the process of its utilization, there has been no reduction or depletion of that resource. Not using this energy source may constitute "waste," since failing to use the wind's power when it is available is a resource-use forever lost.

These are examples of the special characteristics of certain natural resources. Some are fixed in quantity, and using them depletes the amounts remaining. We call these *fund* (or stock) resources to reflect the fact that their quantities are fixed in their natural state.[2] Many of our natural resources are of this type: coal, oil, natural gas, sand and stone, iron ore and other minerals, and similar natural deposits that are nonrenewable resources whose use forever reduces their remaining quantities.[3]

Other natural resources such as sunlight, wind, rain, tides and flowing water, are called *flow* resources. Their present use does not prevent possible future use because the available quantity is constantly being replenished. If, in using the wind's power, heat energy from the sun, or the flow of water in a stream does not disturb their continued flow, the amounts available for other uses is left undiminished.

A simple fund or flow classification does not adequately serve to describe all natural resources, however. Many other important resources exhibit some characteristics of both these groupings. Growing, maturing plants (the flow) may be harvested without damaging the productivity of the parent stock (the fund). The product flow can be maintained indefinitely, increased or decreased, depending on the harvesting rate and the manner in which both the fund and flow are managed. This special characteristic has led some authorities to identify these resources as either a subcategory of fund and flow resources, or separately as *biological* resources.

Our forests, ranges, livestock, fish, and wildlife yield an annual product which may be taken without harm to the productive source

---

[2]Natural processes may very well be continuing the formation of additional amounts of certain fund resources, but at a rate insignificant when compared with existing stocks or present rates of use.

[3]Even though depletable in their natural form, exhausting a fund resource need not mean it is gone forever; many natural resources may be reused. Steel processed from iron ore that is fabricated into automobiles, then junked, may be reclaimed for further use. Disposing of solid wastes in landfills may even provide a future bonanza by having concentrated many scarce materials that may later be extracted and reprocessed to be used again.

of that output. Yet each can also be used in ways that may either enhance or diminish the quantity (and productivity) of that fund resource, with production increases or decreases following changes in uses or use rates.

Forest cutting can be so intensive in one period of time that future yields are reduced, even eliminated entirely. Rangeland can be overgrazed to the extent that grass regrowth and production declines in later years. Ranchers may sell off brood stock, in addition to young stock, and find total output reduced until the breeding herd is again restored. Fish and wildlife harvesting may be carried on at a rate which also causes a reduction in the fund part of those resources, from which the flow is derived, even to the point of extinction, as in the case of the Dodo bird, the California grizzly bear, or the Carrier pigeon.

Even the soil itself, although viewed most frequently as a fund resource, also has some of the characteristics of a flow resource. Management practices may have the deliberate objective of reducing, maintaining, or improving the level of plant nutrients held in the soil, depending upon whether current practices use those nutrients at a greater, equal, or lesser rate than their inflow to the soil. Much like a savings account in the bank, the present balance of those nutrients is the result of both additions to and subtractions from that account, as well as any original amount.

The importance of economic criteria in the above examples, and in similar decision problems with many other natural resources, cannot be ignored. It should be clear that the physical facts of resource existence, and their capabilities to satisfy human wants, do not establish the criteria by which those natural resources are used; physical conditions can only set the limits within which correct answers are determined. In the utilization of any natural (or other) resource we cannot escape making choices as to whether or not to use a resource, the rate at which to use it, and the purpose of its use, causing them to be economic questions requiring economic criteria for their solution.

Resource Inventories. Of all the natural resources that exist, what do we know about them? How much of each is there? How much do we use? How much can we use? Are there better uses for them? Will there be adequate supplies in the future? What will be the effects of increasing or decreasing our rates of use? And of what importance are the numerous "if" conditions that must be dealt with in projections into the future?

Attempts at identifying the amounts of specific natural resources that we now have, and may or may not have in some future

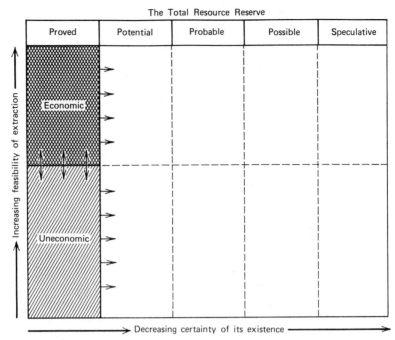

The Total Resource Reserve

Figure 11-1.   A natural resource inventory classification.

period, are not, in themselves, necessarily confusing; interpretational liberties taken with technically developed terms frequently make them so, however. Such resource reserve labels as "proved," "known," "potential," etc., carry special meanings that require a clear understanding of their basic intent and assumptions upon which they are based.

Take, for instance, the abstraction shown in Figure 11-1, a conceptual framework that can be applied to any natural (or other) resource. The area of the box itself demonstrates the total physical quantity of a specific resource as it exists in the natural state.[4] The horizontal axis measures the certainty with which the existence of the total amount of the resource is known. Those concerned with geologic structures and formations, and the quantity of the resource contained at various locations and depths of the earth's surface have, in some cases, identified and determined specific quantities of the

[4]The following categorization of resource reserves is based on Speir Collins, "Reserves, Reserves, Reserves," in *Petroleum Today,* 1976/two, Washington, D.C.: American Petroleum Institute, pp. 26–29. This classification, and the diagram in Figure 11-1, are quite similar, but with reserves labels similar to Vincent E. McKelvey, "Mineral Potential of the United States," *The Mineral Position of the United States, 1975-2000,* Eugene N. Cameron, ed., Madison, Wisc.: The University of Wisconsin Press, 1973, pp. 67–82.

deposits; in others, sheer speculation may suggest that the resource might be there, and our degree of certainty is so indicated as we move further to the right in the diagram.

The mere fact of physical presence, however, is insufficient. We must be able to take the resource from its present location, with whatever refining and processing is required, and get it marketed. If this can be done without sacrificing other, more valuable, goods and services, it is economically feasible; if not, its high costs would cause the resource to be unutilized. We indicate this along the vertical axis, with the degree of feasibility increasing as we move upward along the axis.

Extraction and related technology make up an important contribution in this distinction. A primitive technology, based primarily on hand labor, for instance, may prevent any use of this resource. As capital investment in improved technology makes possible the movement of sufficient quantities of the resource-bearing material, costs per unit of the extracted product fall low enough that it becomes feasible to utilize the resource, as indicated by the line running horizontally through the diagram. The more technology is improved the farther downward the line will be pushed, reflecting the fact that it has become possible to reach to deeper levels or to lower concentrations for the resource, as indicated by the downward-pointing arrows.[5]

The other important element in determining economic feasibility is price. As the price of the extracted product increases (or decreases), the horizontal line is shifted downward (or upward), indicated by the upward- and downward-pointing arrows. The higher the price the deeper we can go in extracting the resource, and the lower the concentrations that can be utilized. A falling price, on the other hand, will make uneconomic the harvesting of this resource at the depths and concentrations that formerly were feasible.

That part of the total resource stock that is called the *proved reserve* depends upon past production and exploratory work that has been done to determine the size and content of each deposit. How much of the resource there is in such deposits (the area in the diagram labeled "Proved") is known with considerable certainty. But price, costs and technological factors, as just discussed, limit the usable portion of the proved reserve to the shaded part labeled

[5]This effect is demonstrated in the petroleum industry. Early technology that depended upon (natural) well-pressure could recover approximately 20 percent of the crude oil in place; the technology of water injection increases that recovery to about 30 percent; tertiary methods using chemicals adds more to the amount recovered, with higher-cost special polymers (still in the research stage) expected to increase the amount recovered even more. (Reported in *Business Week*, June 14, 1976, pp. 31–32.)

"Economic." In spite of knowing with certainty how much (physically) exists, the "Uneconomic" portion[6] is presently unavailable for use because taking the resource from its deposit and getting it to market costs more than it is worth.

With population increases, and possible new uses for the resource, the demand curve for the resource will shift to the right, causing its price to rise, *cet. par.* Not only does this cause additional quantities of the proved reserve to become economic, the higher price will encourage more intensive searching for new sources and further effort at improving the technology of detection, as well as its extraction, causing a shift of the vertical boundary to the right. Proved reserves are thus expanded in spite of the fact that past and current use has constantly been withdrawing from the physical quantity originally available.

Somewhat less certain are *potential reserves.* Depending on the type of resource, estimates are developed from outcroppings, test drillings or other samplings, production data, and projections from geologic evidence.

Because an unexplored area may closely adjoin a producing area, inferences may be drawn as to the quantity that might be found. Such reserves are called *probable.* And at an even greater degree of uncertainty are the *possible* reserves, with their estimated quantities being based upon underground structural similarities with a producing area nearby.

The most uncertain of all are the *speculative resources.* The lack of geologic testing in an area forces this speculation, as with the question of finding oil under the U.S. East Coast Continental Shelf. Seismic studies reveal different formations from those in producing areas, but oil still is believed to be trapped in certain locations under that Shelf.

Resource Supplies.   Having some knowledge of the physical amounts of various resources that are present is of value only as a limit. The *physical supply* of any resource may be defined as the total quantity provided by nature.[7] But that would include the total area of the diagram in Figure 11-1 which, for most natural resources has little relationship to the amounts used. The concept of greatest relevance is that of *economic supply,* the part of the physical supply that is used for want satisfaction. We could attempt to equate this physical quantity with the economically feasible portion of the proved reserve (the

---

[6]Also referred to as "paramarginal" or "submarginal," depending upon how much price would have to increase to make extraction profitable.

[7]Raleigh Barlow, *Land Resource Economics,* 2nd ed., Englewood Cliffs, N.J.: Prentice-Hall, Inc., 1958, pp. 19–20.

amount economically available for human use), but this is a total concept—the sum of both the amount actually used and the amount unused. If we limit ourselves to meaning that amount of the resource actually used within some time-period (annually, for instance), we have been pushed to considering the equilibrium quantity, a single point on the supply curve of that resource.

With this view of economic supply, we can more readily recognize the importance of both supply and demand upon how intensively we use our natural resources, and at what rates they are being consumed in the production process. These two concepts are fundamental to understanding changes that occur in our economic reserves. They make clear that expansions and contractions of the economic supplies of natural resources are caused by resource price changes, which are the result of changes in either or both supply and demand functions.

Natural (or other) resources in themselves, have no value; they are valued, and command a price, only because they are capable of producing goods and services people want and are willing to buy. The demand for a resource is thus a *derived demand*—it is derived from the fact that the resource can produce something else, the demand for which gets reflected back to the resource itself. Hence, the demand for land depends on (is derived from) the intensity of our demand for the products of land—food and fiber, aesthetics, etc., and not just because it is "land." We must now consider how this (or any other) resource's value-creation ability is reflected by the market in such a way that its economic value productivity is correctly demonstrated when a price has been paid by someone to gain control over its use.

Resource Values. In order finally to arrive at a dollar value of a resource (its per unit "price," "market price," "market value," "selling price," "productive value," etc., all of which mean the same thing),[8] we must determine the costs and returns arising with the use of that resource, and the net returns resulting from its use.

Resource productivity surely must affect the price one is willing to pay. If the best use of a tract of land could return no more than a zero net income in the future, how much would you be willing to pay for it? Would you be willing to pay more if the net return

---

[8]Although these words *mean* the same thing, the specific dollar amounts can be (and are) very different for different people. For some people, the value to them exceeds the market determined price for a good and it is a bargain for them, while for others the market price is too high for them to buy it.

were $10,000 per year? How much more? Or, if the net return were to be a negative amount, would you pay anything at all for that resource (i.e., pay good and valuable dollars for the privilege of losing money!)?

Note the emphasis on *future,* rather than past or current, returns. Something is worth money only because it can produce a net return in the future, and the higher the net return the greater its market value. You may own a $50,000 herd bull, prized for the value of the offspring, and you may have "made a bundle" from him over the past few years. Now suppose that he became totally impotent yesterday, and that fact is known to all possible buyers; today that bull is worth only what the slaughter market says he's worth, no matter what his net value productivity has been in the past, because of his inability to produce future income.

There should be (and there is) a systematic method with which to derive answers to such questions of "worth," rather than having to rely only on outright guesses.[9]

Recall the discussion in Chapter 4 on the *MVP* of a resource where one more unit of a resource is worth only what it can produce, giving rise to the demand curve that was shown in Figure 4-5. That is the value of a unit of the resource per unit of time (e.g., annually), an easily understood phenomenon for anything that is used up in a one-time use or application. But what if the resource, such as with most natural resources, does not just disappear with one use but can be used again and again, even indefinitely? The net returns earned by that resource occur as an annual flow throughout its productive life, and the valuation process appears to be more complex. The theoretical basis (from Chapter 4) still is applicable, however, but we can simplify it here.

Suppose that you presently operate a farm or ranch, and that a nearby tract of land is offered for sale. You might carefully estimate the amount by which your annual receipts would be increased by buying the land, and the amount by which your costs also would be increased.[10] Suppose, further, that after properly deducting all the increased costs associated with using this tract of land, the annual

---

[9]Successful decision-making ought to have a better foundation than sheer guesswork, since guesses have a nasty habit of being wrong about half of the time.

[10]The costs included would be all those costs associated with using this resource *except* a return on the investment. You would thus have tallied up all the tillage and other production costs, insurance, taxes, and the costs of all the other resources that are combined with this resource to produce a salable product, including the opportunity costs of your owned and unpaid labor, management, and capital.

net income to land alone is $20 per acre, and that this will continue indefinitely.[11]

Twenty dollars received today is worth just $20 because it will buy $20 worth of goods and services right now. But what about next year's $20? And each additional $20 farther and farther into the future? What are all those $20 amounts worth right now? We must determine what each of those $20 is worth now to get at one lump-sum figure that says "this is what it's worth now." Pay less than this amount and you got more than you have bargained for; pay more and you will have made some unnecessary sacrifices to get the resource.

Our opportunity cost concept is useful here: Suppose that the next best alternative use of your money to pay for the land is to deposit it in a savings account in your local bank that will pay interest at five percent. A deposit of $400 at five percent will yield that same $20 per year for as long as you wish (assuming the five percent opportunity continues), therefore, net earnings limit its present value to $400 per acre. You couldn't pay more than $400 per acre or you would be sacrificing greater alternative earnings elsewhere.

We need a formalized expression which adjusts ("discounts") future sums of money back to their present values, a process referred to as the "capitalization" of earnings. This capitalization approach may seem complex but this is exactly what the market has done when it has determined the market price of any good.

The comparison just given said, in effect, "I have a sum of money ($400) which, if invested at five percent, will yield $20 per year." The resource valuation approach is just the opposite, saying, "This resource will earn a net return of $20 per year, what is it worth today?"

We will use P as a symbol for present value, A for the amount to be received in the future (with subscripts 1, 2, 3, etc., to signify the year in which the amounts occur), and r as the opportunity rate used for discounting. So we have $P + Pr = A_1$, where P is the unknown (the present value), Pr which determines the first year's earning on that amount, and A_1 the amount that can be withdrawn after one-year (which includes the original amount).

We know the A_1 (the $20), so we must solve for P. Factoring out the common term P from the above equation we have $P(1 + r) =$

---

[11]Predicting a specific number into the distance future may not seem very realistic, but a world of certainty is the only starting base we can use. We can make any later adjustments we wish for uncertain yields, prices, and costs over time. This will do nothing, however, to help us understand the meaning of resource "value," and the process by which this is accomplished.

A_1. Transposing, we have $P = A_1/(1 + r) = \$20/1.05 = \$19.05$, the value *today* of next year's $20.

What about the second year's $20: The present value of that is the amount which would grow to $20 if deposited today and left for two years. P deposited today is increased by 1.05 after one year, and after two years is increased again by 1.05, or, $P(1 + r)(1 + r) = A_2$. The formula for the second year becomes $P = A_2/(1 + r)^2 = \$20/(1.05)^2 = \$20/1.1025 = \$18.14$, which says that at a five percent discount rate, $20 to be received two years hence is worth $18.14 today.

As we consider more and more years into the future, the process becomes more and more difficult to handle. For n years the equation becomes

$$P = \frac{A_1}{(1 + r)} + \frac{A_2}{(1 + r)^2} + \frac{A_3}{(1 + r)^3} + \frac{A_4}{(1 + r)^4} + \cdots + \frac{A_n}{(1 + r)^n}$$

Carrying out these computations for as many years as our tract of land will last would be extremely tedious. For any resource which will last for a long, long time into the future ("in perpetuity"), the formula sums algebraically to $P = A/r$. Thus, $P = \$20/.05 = \$400$, the present value of the resource able to yield a perpetual net return of $20 per year.[12]

Resource Conservation. To some, the conservation of natural resources is accomplished by a willful reduction in the rate at which these resources are used, leading to the conclusion that conservation and saving (nonuse) are one and the same. And to this is frequently added the admonition that we must "save for future generations." Doing this leads, however, to an untenable contradiction of terms.

---

[12]This method works well for our perfectly certain world, but in real life we cannot be that exact. Predicting yields, prices, costs, and interest rates 10, 50, or 100 years into the future becomes highly uncertain. On the other hand, how accurate is the actual market price of a long-lived asset? It can be correct only if a perfectly competitive market (which doesn't exist) has determined that price. The degree of inaccuracy depends upon imperfections in the market, which results from all the frailties of human beings and their institutions.

In using the capitalization approach, the nearer to the present the greater the importance of A, and the less important is r; and the farther into the future the less important A becomes, while the relative importance of r increases. Compare the 100th-year $20 with that of the first year, and you'll notice that estimating errors out there are quite unimportant. Twenty dollars to be received 100 years from now is worth only $0.15 today as compared with next year's $20 worth of $19.05 today. The present value of a perpetual annual stream of $20 is $400, and the 100th-year's contribution is only $0.15 out of that total. Thus the farther into the future a return occurs the smaller becomes its contribution to present value.

Faithful adherence to this dictum must result in perpetual nonuse because we are unable to specify which generation in the near or far-off future may have the privilege of use.

Resource saving may be cloaked in economic sounding phrases such as "efficient use," "wise use," "use without waste," etc., but these confuse rather than clarify the meaning of conservation.

To save resources so as to have a larger quantity available in the future is of questionable value because new discoveries (or new technology yet unavailable) may result in very large increases of usable reserves, or new alternative sources of the same service. And who can foretell with any certainty what shifts might occur in the uses to which presently known reserves might be put? The Northern Great Plains (especially North Dakota, Montana, and Wyoming) are endowed with many billions of tons of low sulphur coal. Coal is a natural resource supply that is becoming more valuable as other traditional sources of heat energy are being depleted.[13] To save this coal for some vague future period would be a gamble which predicts that a much better or cheaper energy source (even solar energy) will not be discovered—one which could make these coal deposits worthless—and thus a sheer economic waste of a (presently) valuable natural resource.

To obtain compliance with noneconomic criteria is difficult even with government action "in the name of society"—a government decision process that appears much less bound by the costs of its actions. This appears to be true, partly because a government's planning horizon is so much longer than for individuals or firms, and it can therefore "afford it" while individuals cannot. But this is erroneous thinking. Given whatever the values and costs to society might be, the fact that these might be hidden (for a time) doesn't mean a wrong decision wasn't made.

The conservation of natural resources is an important part of the basic economic problem of dealing with scarcity by making the proper choices, accomplished only by weighing economic alternatives. As consumers economize in their consumption choices, they have maximized the benefits to be obtained from their spendable incomes; and as producers economize in their production choices, the basic requirements of efficiency in resource conservation have been met.

Economic efficiency in resource use dictates that we use our resources at the time, and at the rate, and in those uses where their

---

[13]Strippable coal (with less than 150 feet of overburden) in this general area is estimated to be in excess of 50 billion tons; in *North Central Power Study*, Volume I, Washington, D.C.: U.S. Department of the Interior, Bureau of Reclamation, October 1971, p. 9.

contribution to consumer satisfaction is the greatest. The present value of their net returns will then be maximized. And their opportunity costs for other less profitable uses will also be maximized, thereby preventing wasteful use. We are then, using no more of those resources than is necessary to produce the mix and quantities of all those products that consumers will buy (which minimizes the real costs of those goods). This achieves part of the saver's basic objective on its only supportable basis, economics.

Recognizing conservation as an economic problem directs our attention to the act of responding, consciously or unconsciously, to prices and costs in the use (or nonuse) of those resources. The problem with natural resources is not simply that a fund resource is depleted with use and that we later will regret its absence. The problem is that the value of services will be lost when the resource is gone *unless* another source of that service has been discovered in the meantime.

We have optimized natural resource conservation when we have so distributed the rates at which those resources are used that we have maximized the present value of the future stream of their net social benefits. The economic meaning of conservation takes the future into account by answering the question: What is the best rate at which to utilize any resource so as to maximize net social benefits over time? Answering this question forces a comparison of values between different time periods, the only basis for deciding what to do with any natural resource. So what we are saying is that the question of economic efficiency encompasses the question of conservation; that *resource conservation cannot be viewed as something separable from the economics of resource use.*

When we compare the values of two different periods we find ourselves making use of the type of information discussed above in the valuation section. Since a dollar in the future is not worth the same as a dollar in hand right now, we are forced to ask: why not? And we get around, finally, to an admission that human nature is the cause: *we prefer goods now rather than in some future period.*

Given a choice of having a dollar now versus getting that dollar a year (or more) from now, we will choose possession today rather than later. We would choose to have that dollar now because we could either use it to gain whatever present satisfactions can be obtained by buying a desired good now, or invest that dollar in an interest earning opportunity (a savings deposit, for instance) and have it grow to some larger amount and therefore able to yield more satisfaction later. This preference for goods now rather than later is called our "time preference," or "time impatience."

Individual time preferences can be (and are) widely different, ranging, at any given instant, from those who will lend (invest) money now so as to enhance their future consumption, to those who borrow against the future so as to be able to consume now in preference to waiting until later. Our time preference can thus be expressed as a *rate* at which future values are discounted back to the present.

Exchanging present and future goods is facilitated by the existence of money and financial markets; exchanges being the *reason for* the existence of those markets, rather than the other way around. The market offers an interest rate for savers, or charges borrowers, permitting us to conduct transactions which demonstrate our preferences. The borrower, by the act of borrowing, has said, "I want the goods this money can buy *now* strongly enough that I'll pay the interest premium to escape having to wait until I have the cash in hand." Whatever the interest rate paid, the borrower has exhibited a sufficiently high time preference that made consumption now "worth more" than the value of that satisfaction later, with the difference in present and future values being equal to the amount of the interest paid.

The only difference between individuals and society in this attribute is the magnitude of the time preference and the length of time that is relevant. One cannot easily make (and carry out) plans for, say, 100 years from now; that's too far into the future and would thus be severely discounted, encouraging earlier use and consumption rather than later. Society, however, can expect (plan for) a much longer life span, which results in a lower discount rate and a postponement of use to a more distant future.

Agriculture's Natural Resources

Those who concern themselves with the productive uses of land sooner or later raise the question of whether we may run out of agricultural land in some future period. In spite of the serious concern over an impending food crisis, U.S. agriculture's problem has been just the opposite for more than 50 years. Rather than finding food costs increasing as a result of agricultural inadequacies, the problem has been one of being able to produce more than can economically be marketed.

An overview of trends in the nation's developing agricultural industry helps focus on the changes that have occurred over a long period of years (Table 11-1). Sharp increases in output have occurred in a manner that could appear to have resulted from fortu-

Table 11-1 A Growing U.S. Agriculture

Year	U.S. Population	Number of Farms	Farmland (Acres)	Index of Output
	------------millions------------			(1960 = 100)
1800	5	—	—	—
1850	23	1.5	—	—
1900	76	5.7	839	41
1920	106	6.4	956	56
1940	132	6.1	1061	66
1950	151	5.4	1162	81
1960	179	3.7	1176	100
1970	203	3.0	1107	111
1975	214	2.8	1088	122

Sources: Compiled from annual issues of *Agricultural Statistics* (1946–75), and *Statistical Abstract of the United States (1946)*, both U.S. Government Printing Office, Washington, D.C.; and *Changes in Farm Production and Efficiency*, Economic Research Service Statistical Bulletin No. 561, Washington, D.C., 1976. Earlier statistical output series were converted to a 1960 index base and are not strictly comparable because of changes in the output mix over time.

nate accidents rather than as conscious responses to changing economic conditions.

The opening of the continental United States to westward settlement added many millions of acres of productive land. As population grew from about five million to more than 75 million during the 1800s, probably three-quarters of a billion acres of agricultural land were also added. By 1920, the effects of land settlement programs and World War I food needs had increased the amount of land in farms to over 950 million acres.

Two important changes in agriculture contributed to the large growth in output. First, the development of mechanical power made possible a conversion from animal power, which became especially rapid during the pre-World War II period. Then, from about the 1930s, scientific discoveries in improving soil fertility, controlling weeds and plant diseases, genetic improvement of plants, and better management practices have all combined to create a large reservoir of productive capacity. The volume of total output has been almost tripled since 1900, with only about a 30 percent increase of land in farms.

Except for short periods of national crisis, returns in agriculture have been relatively low. This, coupled with improved off-farm opportunities both pushed and pulled farmers to other pursuits. Farm numbers declined by more than 50 percent from their 5.7 million in 1900, and by over 60 percent from the high reached in the mid-1930s.

Food production capability, roughly 50 percent higher from 1950 to 1975, is influenced by many factors. Land, people, water, energy, minerals, capital, and climatic conditions are integral parts of the production process.

The total set of resources used in agriculture is far from constant. Quantities and proportions of resources are frequently adjusted in response to economic and other conditions. Technological improvements in the use of one type of resource, with their resulting cost effects, cause increased usage of some resources while the use of others is reduced—the type of resource substitution discussed in Chapter 5.

Other cost effects come from competitive forces outside of agriculture, such as increased urban or recreational demand for land. With the increased price of land from such demand shifts, producers are forced to substitute other resources for land in order to remain competitive in their product markets. Higher wages elsewhere draw labor out of agriculture, and become a cause of increased agricultural labor cost, resulting in the substitution of capital and other inputs for labor. Industrial competition for water is viewed as a threat to agricultural use of that resource. And given the rate of output of energy and mineral resources that are of use in agriculture, the greater their use elsewhere in the economy the higher become their costs to agriculture. The increased competitive demand for resources, both within and outside of agriculture shows up in higher resource costs, shifts in resource use, and changes in agriculture's relative income position. The following note some of the broader changes that have occurred for major resource categories.

Land. The total land area of the United States presently amounts to nearly 2.3 billion acres (Table 11-2). Of this total, agriculture used more than one-half in 1974 (including 180 million acres of forest land grazed). Occasional remeasurement and increases in reservoirs constructed account for the 9-million acre decline in total land area since 1954.

Through the two decades shown, total cropland was held at about one-fifth of all land uses, declining by five million acres in the last five-year period but still slightly above the 1954 acreage.

The 598 million acres of grassland pasture and range on which livestock grazed in 1974 made up more than one-fourth of all land

Table 11-2   Trends in Land Use for Major Uses,
Selected Years, United States, 1954–74

Type of Use	1954	1959	1964	1969	1974
	----------million acres----------				
Cropland[a]	466	458	444	472	467
Pasture and range	634	633	640	604	598
Forested land[b]	727	728	727	723	718
Special uses[c]	143	151	168	178	192
Other[d]	303	301	287	287	289
Total	2273	2271	2266	2264	2264

Source: Data compiled from *Agricultural Statistics* (1975); *Our Land and Water Resources,* Misc. Pub. No. 1290, May 1974; *Major Uses of Land in the United States,* Agric. Econ. Report No. 247, Dec. 1973; and H. Thomas Frey, *Major Uses of Land in the United States* (preliminary estimates for 1974), Working Paper No. 34, Economic Research Service, U.S. Department of Agriculture, Washington, D.C., August 1977.

[a] Includes cropland harvested, idle, fallow, crop failure, and cropland used for pasture.
[b] Both public and private, exclusive of forest land devoted to parks, wildlife preserves, etc., but including forest acres grazed.
[c] Urban uses, farmsteads, highways and roads, parks and preserves, military installations, airports, and railroad rights-of-way.
[d] Desert, swamp, and other areas of little (present) agricultural use.

uses for that year. Though declining only slightly in the last five-year period, a total of 36 million acres have been shifted to other uses since 1954. These lands provided about 70 percent of all grazing, with the balance being from forest land grazed and cropland used only for pasture.

Within the "special uses" grouping are acres dedicated to uses which, by their nature, prevent agricultural use. Although their total acreage changed by 49 million acres during the 20 years shown, not all that land was removed from agriculture. The largest change within this category has been in land devoted to recreation and wildlife. A sizable portion of the change resulted from 10 million acres of Alaskan public land being reclassified as a wildlife preserve.[14]

[14] *Our Land and Water Resources.* Washington, D.C.: Economic Research Service, U.S. Department of Agriculture, Misc. Pub. No. 1290, May 1974, p. 10.

During the 20 years shown by these data, population grew by about 50 million, increasing the nonagricultural demand for land. Not only were greater acreages used for residences, industrial and commercial establishments, but additional acreages were also required for highways, roads, and airports.

Much recent concern stems from the appropriation of agricultural land for urban and urban-related uses. These uses occupied more than 60 million acres by 1974, an increase in excess of 500,000 acres per year over the 20-year period.

Economic efficiency of land use means that higher-valued uses (those with the greatest present value of discounted future net returns) will displace lower-valued uses. As urban and urban-related uses take cropland from farms, pasture land, for instance, will be pushed out by cropland, and pasture land will, in turn, "bump" other lower-valued uses. This process is not especially visible in the data in Table 11-3 but it has been occurring through time.

The listing of total cropland disguises land losses to other uses. Total acres shows only what is available for a variety of crop-related uses, not acreages used. Changes in cropland harvested more directly reflect operator responses to market and other conditions. Between 1959 and 1964, acres from which crops were harvested declined by 25 million acres. Productivity gains caused output to grow more rapidly than did the markets for many crops, and required increased acres to be idled under the federal farm programs. By 1969, program-idled land totaled 51 million acres so that cropland neither harvested or pastured increased by 20 million acres.

Table 11-3 Trends in U.S. Farm Land Use, Selected Years, 1954–74

Land Use	1954	1959	1964	1969	1974
	----------million acres----------				
Total cropland	466	458	444	472	467
Cropland harvested	339	317	292	286	325
Cropland pastured	66	66	57	88	84
Other[a]	61	75	95	98	58

Sources: Data compiled from *Agricultural Statistics (1975); Our Land and Water Resources,* Economic Research Service Misc. Pub. No. 1290, May 1974; and *Major Uses of Land in the United States,* Agric. Econ. Report No. 247, December 1973, all U.S. Government Printing Office, Washington, D.C.

[a] Includes land in fallow, soil building cover crops, failure, and idle.

During the five-year interval from 1969 to 1974, the change in cropland harvested was a sharp response to the release of 41 million acres of land from program restrictions and the large increase in grain sales abroad.[15] The acreage of crops harvested in 1974 was more than 13 percent greater than for 1969.

Water.   Given present technology, only a very small part of the world's physical supply of water is usable. It is from the less than one percent not in the oceans or in frozen polar ice caps that we derive the water used for life support.

Within the continental United States, about 4700 million acre-feet[16] of water falls as precipitation annually, providing water for growing plants, for streams and lakes, and underground aquifers. Of that amount, less than one-third is available for use by human direction, the other 70 percent escaping naturally by evaporation or transpiration from plants. The balance, about 1425 million acre-feet, is the natural runoff from which our economic water supply is derived (Table 11-4).

As our population has grown and agriculture has increased its output to meet the expanding demand for food, the amount of water withdrawn for use has increased greatly. Total withdrawals have more than tripled over the 115 million acre-feet taken in 1940. But withdrawal does not mean that much water has disappeared, however. Through the years, consumption (i.e., disappearance by evaporation, transpiration, or incorporation in products) has averaged only six to seven percent of the total amount of water withdrawn. The difference between withdrawals and consumption is the amount returned to the surface or ground water sources for subsequent use.

Although urban uses of water have increased rapidly, especially since 1960, households use only a very small proportion of total urban use. The largest nonagricultural users of water are industrial and steam-electric generating plants. Since much water is used for cooling, rather than becoming a part of their products, these users have low rates of consumption.

More than 35 percent of all the water withdrawn in the United States is for agricultural uses, with about 95 percent of agricultural withdrawls being used for irrigation. Because of its high consumption rate, agricultural uses of water amount to more than 80 percent of total American consumption.

---

[15]Ibid., p. 3.

[16]An acre-foot of water is one acre covered by water to a depth of one-foot, amounting to approximately 325,900 gallons of water.

Table 11-4 Water Availability and Use,
Selected Years, 48 States, 1940-75

Year	Annual Runoff[a]	Total Withdrawn	Consumption			Acres Irrigated (million)
			Total	Urban	Rural	
		----------------million acre-feet----------------				
1940	1425	115	38	3	35	18
1950	1425	171	52	4	48	26
1960	1425	256	65	7	58	34
1965	1425	270	78	10	68	38
1970	1425	327	87	13	74	42
1975	1425	370[b]	98[b]	17[b]	81[b]	45[c]

Source: Data compiled from *Our Land and Water Resources* Economic Research Service Misc. Pub. No. 1290, May 1974; *Our Nation's Land and Water Resources,* ERS-530, August 1973; and *Agricultural Statistics (1975),* U.S. Government Printing Office, Washington, D.C.

[a] Compare Alaska's runoff of about 650 million acre-feet per year.
[b] Authors' estimates for 1975 based on population growth, per capita consumption rates in earlier years, and acres irrigated with adjustments for proportion irrigated by sprinklers.
[c] Preliminary estimate in George A. Pavelis, "Natural Resource Capital in American Agriculture," NRED, Economic Research Service, U.S. Department of Agriculture, Washington, D.C., Working Paper No. 37, September 1977, p. 16.

In the 35 years from 1940 irrigated land has increased by two and one-half times to 45 million acres,[17] making up about 10 percent of all cropland by 1975. This also means that, except for the effects of improved water management practices adopted in the interim, agriculture used about two and a half times as much irrigation water in 1975 as in 1940. In the face of restricted or depleting supplies, such practices as canal and ditch lining, greater application and waste water control, and the increasing use of sprinkler irrigation systems should have reduced per acre water requirements somewhat.

An average of more than 750,000 acres of irrigated land has been developed annually over the 35-year period. For many of those years the primary growth was provided by government-sponsored irrigation projects. Of the 133 million acre-feet of water withdrawn in 1975 for agriculture, about 20 percent was supplied by the

[17]Preliminary estimates in George A. Pavelis, "Natural Resource Capital in American Agriculture," Washington, D.C.: NRED, Economic Research Service, U.S. Department of Agriculture, Working Paper No. 37, September 1977, p. 16.

Bureau of Reclamation from their storage reservoirs. About nine million acres were irrigated in that year with water from this agency, with most of the irrigation done by gravity flow.

Recent technological improvements in sprinkler irrigation systems have changed the relative costs of gravity flow and sprinkler application, which has led to a significant shift in emphasis. With total acres irrigated increasing by 3.7 million acres from 1970 to 1975 (from 41.6 to 45.3 million acres), gravity flow systems actually declined by 600,000 acres while an additional 4.3 million acres were sprinkler irrigated.[18]

Urban-related water problems are quite dissimilar in different parts of the country. In the higher rainfall areas of the East and Southeast, water supply problems stem more from inadequate storage capacity than from insufficient precipitation. In the Southwest and certain parts of the Great Plains demand for water exceeds local supplies, requiring the transfer of large amounts of water to population centers.

Except for water supply problems in the arid West, the most serious urban problem has been one of water pollution from disposal of wastes. Stream and lake pollution, both from household and industrial waste loads, has intensified the need for large investments in sewage treatment plants and industrial water recycling facilities. This is a problem common to all urban areas of the nation. Agricultural pollution of waterways has also become serious in many areas. The long life of residual herbicides and pesticides causes them to be present both in the soil and in water supplies, with uncertainty over their full ecological effects. Declines in water quality also result from siltation, increased salinity, and the eutrophication caused by leaching inorganic nitrate and phosphate fertilizers.

Energy Use in Agriculture. Energy of one form or another has played an increasingly important role through the long history of coaxing greater quantities of food from the earth. The succession of energy types from human power only, to animals, then inanimate sources, has served to reduce the energy cost component of the food we eat.

Fossil fuels have made possible the mechanical power improvements that have become so important a part of modern agriculture. Our heavy dependence on finite energy has been the cause of growing criticism. And the Arab oil embargo in 1973 made us even more aware of how much we rely on fossil energy. The sharp rise in energy costs, not only fuel energy, but fertilizers, pesticides, and other petroleum-based products as well, brought de-

[18]Ibid., p. 18.

mands for energy conservation. Research has since attempted to discover and identify uses and rates of use throughout the economy.

Table 11-5 summarizes estimates of use rates within the food system. Data that are both current and accurate are not yet as abundant as for many other segments of the economy. The studies from which this information was derived were, in themselves, incomplete estimates of separate components of the system. Such energy use information as has been made available is preembargo data, both for prices and use rates.

Increased energy prices, plus conscious efforts of firms and households to reduce their energy consumption, have undoubtedly had some effect. Gasoline provided farms with nearly 50 percent of their total energy in 1970, as compared to about 35 percent from diesel fuel. But nearly all new farm tractors bought now are diesel fueled which would alter the relative energy contributions of these two fuels. Likewise, home weatherstripping and insulation, the manufacturing of more energy-efficient home appliances, and the conversion of many industrial buildings and electrical power plants to coal heat would all contribute to changing fuel source proportions.

The food system components described in Table 11-5 include all activities involved in making food available to the consumer. The major divisions of the system included in the study are farms, all food processing, wholesale and retail firms and the transportation network, and all firms engaged in manufacturing inputs of all kinds for each of the sectors.

Table 11-5 Energy Use Estimates for the U.S. Food and Fiber System, 1970

Component of System	Petroleum Fuels	Natural and Propane Gas	Electricity	Other	Percentage Share of System Total
	--------percentage of own energy used--------				
Farm production	83	12	5	—	17
Food processing industries	11	48	30	11	34
Marketing and distribution	100	—	—	—	21
Input manufacturing	2	85	11	2	28
Percentage shares of system total	40	42	14	4	100

Source: "Energy Requirements in the U.S. Food System," *Agricultural Outlook,* Washington, D.C.: Economic Research Service, U.S. Department of Agriculture, AO-8, March 1976, pp. 18–21.

The food and fiber sector is estimated to use about 17 percent of total American energy use. Within the food and fiber sector, agricultural production uses about 17 percent, which amounts to about three percent of the United States' total. All other industry groupings use greater amounts of energy than do farms and ranches, with the highest user being the food processing industry.

Of the energy sources, gasoline, diesel, and fuel oils provide 40 percent of total energy used by the food and fiber system. A larger share, 42 percent, is derived from natural and propane gases, with the remaining 18 percent obtained from electricity, coal, and other minor fuels.

The report from which the data in the table were derived looked at all energy use from point-of-origin to delivery to the consumer, and thus did not take into account energy use in the home or out-of-the-home eating places. In-home and public eating places energy-use (including refrigerated storing) in food preparation has been estimated to require about six percent of total American energy use.[19] Comparing this energy use with agriculture's use, shows that it takes about twice as much to prepare our food to eat as it does to produce it.

Estimates have been developed that indicate energy costs in the food and fiber system contribute about eight percent to total food costs.[20] Thus out of each dollar's worth of food purchased by the consumer, eight cents goes to pay for the energy used. Other consumer goods have comparable energy costs, with the energy cost-share of final product values ranging from four to ten cents per dollar of product value.

Future energy price increases can be expected, and they will probably be substantial as supply shortages intensify. What will this do to the final price of food? If the eight percent estimate is reasonably close, a 25 percent increase in the price of energy will raise the energy cost component to 10 cents per dollar of final value.

Human and Other Resources. The human input in producing our supply of food and fiber is derived from farm families and other workers who provide the labor services to agriculture. Through most of the long history of mankind, increased food output has been closely linked to the number of people engaged in agricultural production. During much of this period, technology changed very little so that the labor/land/output porportions remained quite stable.

[19]*The Farm Index,* Economic Research Service, USDA, September 1977, pp. 8–11.
[20]Energy Requirements in the U.S. Food System," *Agricultural Outlook.* Washington, D.C.: Economic Research Service, USDA, AO-8, March 1976, p. 20.

In the more primitive societies, most if not all of agriculture's output must be used simply to support the human and animal power used to produce food. With no surplus output beyond resource support needs, economic progress leading to other consumer goods is inhibited. Only with the ability to produce in excess of one's own food needs can workers be released to produce better housing, medical services, education and other beneficial services. Over the past century, the technology of production improved so as to increase the amount of food a worker could produce.

The combination of labor and mechanical devices in agricultural production began with the invention and widespread adoption of such basic capital items as the moldboard plow, mechanical reaper, and the internal combustion engine during the 1800s. As such capital inputs became more generally available, the substitution of capital for labor intensified, with the productivity of labor being greatly enhanced in the process.

Purchased inputs and the technology represented have become increasingly important in agricultural production. Total horsepower use on United States farms is used as somewhat representative of capital in the form of mechanical power and other equipment (Table 11-6).

Total tractor horsepower used on farms and ranches increased by 45 percent between 1960 and 1975, while the number of tractors declined by about 10 percent. Offsetting the decline in numbers has

Table 11-6 Major Purchased Items and Their Contribution to Productivity, 1960–75

Year	Total Tractor Horsepower (million)	Tractor Horsepower per Worker	Fertilizer per Acre (lbs N-P-K)	Agricultural Chemicals per Acre (1960 = 100)	Labor Hours per Acre of Cropland[a]
1960	153	21.5	46	100	12.9
1965	176	31.4	74	154	10.2
1970	203	45.1	110	221	8.5
1971	206	46.8	112	240	8.5
1972	209	47.5	117	251	8.4
1973	212	49.3	112	261	8.3
1974	219	51.6	117	274	8.1
1975	222	51.8	105	253	7.9

Sources: Changes in Farm Production and Efficiency, Washington, D.C.: Economic Research Service, U.S. Department of Agriculture, Statistical Bulletin No. 561, September 1976; and *Agricultural Statistics (1975),* Washington, D.C.: U.S. Government Printing Office.

[a] Crop production labor only.

been an increase of more than 60 percent in horsepower per unit. Coupled with the changes in labor used, this has resulted in 2.4 times as much tractor horsepower available per worker to help labor produce our food and fiber.

The use of fertilizers (nitrogen, phosphate and potash) and agricultural chemicals have served to help increase yields on both a per acre and a per worker basis, further reducing the labor cost per unit of output. The combined effects of these and other such inputs has reduced the per-acre time requirements in crop production by almost 40 percent.

Table 11-7 indicates how the use of labor has declined in recent years. Just since 1950, we have seen the U.S. population increase by more than 40 percent, and that has been accompanied by higher per capita incomes and increased effective demand for agricultural products. At the same time, however, total labor use in agriculture declined by 53 percent.

Until the 1960s, more than three-fourths of all agricultural labor was provided by the farm family. By 1975, hired labor amounted to 30 percent of all labor used on U.S. farms and ranches.

Because of the seasonality of production, many farmers find it impossible to utilize their full labor force on a year around basis.

Table 11-7 The U.S. Farm Labor Resource

Year	Total Agricultural Labor	Family Labor	Hired Labor	Number of People Supported by One Farm Worker [a]
	---------thousands---------			
1950	9342	7252	2090	18
1955	8237	6341	1897	22
1960	7057	5172	1885	28
1965	5610	4128	1482	42
1970	4523	3348	1175	56
1971	4436	3275	1161	56
1972	4373	3227	1146	61
1973	4337	3169	1168	60
1974	4313	3111	1202	58
1975	4357	3033	1324	58

Sources: *Handbook of Agricultural Charts,* Economic Research Service, U.S. Department of Agriculture, Agricultural Handbook, No. 504, October 1976; and *Agricultural Statistics* (1955–75), U.S. Government Printing Office, Washington, D.C.

[a] Adjusted to account for net exports.

Migrant foreign nations and migratory workers have been utilized to meet such special needs.

The effect of the overall resource mix on the productivity of labor is demonstrated by the final series in the table which shows the number of people supported by each agricultural worker. In 1900, one farm worker was able to produce enough food and fiber for about six people. As farms have utilized more effective combinations of capital and labor, the number of people supported by an agricultural worker grew to 58 by 1975.

Figure 11-2 summarizes with indexes, the changes that have occurred in the productivity of the agricultural industry. We use 1960 as the base 100 for this diagram only for its value as a visual benchmark.

The overall resource commitment for producing our food and fiber has changed relatively little through the 15 years shown in the diagram. One would have to go back to 1941 to find a year when less, rather than more, resources have been used.

Output, however, has been a constantly increasing characteristic of the industry. Agricultural output in 1975 was 23 percent higher than was produced in 1960. And the further back in time we might wish to go in making comparisons, the greater becomes the percentage of increase. For instance, 1975 output was more than 50 percent

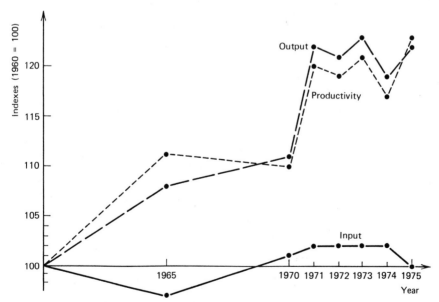

Figure 11-2. Index measures of resource uses and production.

greater than in 1950, 85 percent over that of 1940, and double that of 1936.

The line in the graph labeled "Productivity" is a measure of unit productivity, obtained by dividing the index of output by the corresponding input index. The result gives an estimate of output per unit of input for all agricultural resources together.

Summary

Natural resources are those resources provided by nature. They become valuable when the technology of their utilization and the demand for their products makes use feasible.

Some natural resources such as wind, the tides, and sunlight are available for use on a continuing or flow basis. Use of these resources need not diminish their future availability. Other resources, however, are present in a fixed (fund) quantity. Present use of such resources diminishes the physical amounts remaining for use in the future.

Whether land, petroleum, water or coal, the depleting supply of any resource will cause its price to increase, *cet. par.*, provided the market is permitted to function. With price increases that truly reflect economic conditions surrounding the use of a resource, a number of forces are set in motion: (1) the rate of depletion is reduced as marginal users are denied economic use of the resource; (2) the search for alternative sources of the same or similar services is intensified; (3) the economic supply expands as the increased price makes possible the use of lower quality sources of that resource; and (4) the higher resource price is reflected in the prices of certain consumer goods, causing consumers to restrict their purchases by shifting to alternative goods.

The largest use of land by far is agricultural, amounting to 55 percent of total United States land area. Is this a sufficient acreage to meet our future requirements? Land use trends through history would suggest the problem is much less serious than many would have us believe. We need as many acres as it takes to produce the food and fiber that we are willing and able to buy. As the supply of land for food and fiber declines (either relative to demand, or absolutely), food and fiber prices will rise. Increasing prices for food and fiber will be reflected back to land with the price of land also increasing. As the price of land increases, land conversions to other uses will be retarded or even reversed.

The relative prices of all resources used in agriculture are ever changing. Responses to these changes are implied by relative changes in the rates of use of land acres, water for irrigation, family and hired labor, energy in all its forms, and capital in the form of power, machines of all kinds, fertilizers and agricultural chemicals, etc. Resource substitution and the adoption of new technology have permitted an approximate doubling (in effect) of the economic supply of land since the mid-1930s. And this in spite of a decline in physical acres used for food and fiber production.

Chapter Highlights

1. Natural resources are all those resources provided by nature, including land, water, minerals, plants, animals, and humans themselves.
2. A natural resource has value only when an economic use has been discovered for it.
3. Fund resources are those whose quantities are finite, such as petroleum, oil, and minerals whose present use reduces the physical amount available in the future.
4. Flow resources are renewable, such as sunlight, wind, and flowing water, whose present use need not reduce their future supply.
5. Biological resources such as growing plants and animals exhibit characteristics of both fund and flow resources.
6. Proved reserves depend upon what we know about the existence of a resource, but the economically usable part of proved reserves depends upon the demand and supply of the resource.
7. The demand for a resource is derived from the demand for that resource's product, a derived demand.
8. The value of a resource is determined by the present value of its future net earnings.
9. The difference in value between present and future goods is determined by the rate at which we (each) discount those future values.
10. Individual rates of discount vary by the individual.
11. Resource conservation is an economic problem.
12. The total United States land area amounts to about 2.3 billion acres, with agriculture using approximately one-half of the total.
13. Cropland amounts to less than one-fourth of the total land area.
14. The consumption of water amounts to less than seven percent of the total water supply.
15. Water pollution problems result from both urban and agricultural uses of water and other resources.
16. Direct farm production uses less than three percent of all the energy used in America.
17. The agricultural marketing system uses more than three times as much energy as do the raw food and fiber producers.
18. More energy is used to prepare food for consumption than farmers and ranchers use to produce that food.
19. Energy costs make up eight percent of total food costs.

20. The increased use of capital inputs increases output of the other resources.
21. The use of labor in agriculture has declined dramatically, yet each laborer is able to support many more people than could be done earlier.
22. Output has increased greatly even though there has been no increase in overall inputs since the mid-1950s.

Review Questions

1. What are "natural" resources, and why do we value them?
2. What do we mean by the economic supply of land (or any natural resource) as compared with the physical supply?
3. Is the physical supply of a natural resource of any meaning to society?
4. Is economic growth incompatible with preserving the environment? Is it incompatible with conservation?
5. Why not just pass laws preventing the use of disappearing natural resources?
6. How much land should we reserve exclusively for agricultural use? Surely this is an economic question, so can that question be answered with anything but economic criteria?
7. "Since the supply of water is so limited, especially in the arid West, economic wisdom dictates that we reserve most of this resource for agricultural use." Analyze this problem carefully, taking into account the meaning of economic efficiency both for this resource and the economic well-being of all the members of society.
8. If banks (in a position of charging interest on borrowed money) aren't the true cause of interest, why should we have to use an interest rate in determining the present value of any resource?
9. What is $1000, to be received three years from today, worth to you? What could you sell that obligation for? Might these two values (the value to you versus the value to a buyer) be different?
10. American agriculture is frequently criticized as being "energy inefficient" because we use far more fossil energy to produce each unit of food and fiber than do foreign producers. Is this a valid efficiency criterion? If it isn't, what criteria should be used in judging the energy efficiency of U.S. agriculture?

Suggested Readings

1. Barlowe, Raleigh. *Land Resource Economics,* 2nd ed. Englewood Cliffs, N.J.: Prentice-Hall, Inc., Chapters 1, 2, 4, 8, and 10.
2. Brehm, Carl. *Introduction to Economics.* New York: Random House, Inc., Chapter 7.
3. Collins, Speir, "Reserves, Reserves, Reserves," *Petroleum Today.* Washington, D.C.: Petroleum Institute, 1976/two.
4. Cotner, M. L. "Land Use Policy and Agriculture: A National Perspective," Washington, D.C.: Economic Research Service, USDA, ERS-630, July 1976.
5. Cotner, M. L., M. D. Skold, and O. Krause. "Farmland: Will There be

Enough?" Washington, D.C.: Economic Research Service, USDA, ERS-584, May 1975.

6. "Farmland Resources for the Future," Washington, D.C.: Economic Research Service, USDA, Agricultural Information Bulletin No. 385, April 1975.

7. Gwartney, James D. *Microeconomics, Private and Public Choice.* New York: Academic Press, 1977, Chapters 12 and 13.

8. "Our Land and Water Resources," Washington, D.C.: Economic Research Service, USDA, Misc. Pub. No. 1290, May 1974.

9. Pavelis, George A. "Natural Resource Capital in American Agriculture," Washington, D.C.: Economic Research Service, USDA, Working Paper No. 37, September, 1977.

12

Courtesy of Doug Warren, Editor, Montana Agricultural Experiment Station, Bozeman.

AGRICULTURAL PRICE
AND INCOME POLICIES

AGRICULTURAL PRICE
AND INCOME POLICIES

Federal government price and income programs in agriculture have been in existence in one form or another since 1929. The programs have been changed, revised, and extended from time to time and continue to be important to most agricultural producers of grains, cotton, tobacco, peanuts, sheep and lambs, and sugar. Before we get into a discussion of agricultural policies, let us first look at the basis for the formulation of policy—the goals and values of people.

Hathaway has defined public policy as a specific type of group action designed to achieve certain aspirations held by members of society.[1] For any public policy to come into existence, national policy makers must have knowledge of the objectives of the group being represented. The policy must be consistent with many of the goals of society, the most basic of which is the "quality of life."

Quality of life includes such general goals as peace, security, freedom, and justice. We all know that peace is a world wide aspiration, but we also know that there have been very few periods in which confrontations have not been taking place. Peace has a high priority in this country; so much so that vast sums (30 percent of the federal budget) are spent on national defense in an attempt to deter foreign aggression.

When we speak of security, we include economic, political, and social stability. With the price level increasing recently at a six to eight percent annual rate, we have become concerned over the loss of economic security due to the decline in the purchasing power of the dollar. As far as political stability in the United States is concerned, we are fortunate that our governing system has stability built into it with the sharing of power between the executive, legislative, and judicial branches of government. Our great desire for personal security is evidenced in the fact that we have employed such policies as retirement programs, health insurance, unemployment insurance, social security, and medicare.

Freedom is basic to the United States' origin, but we must en-

---

[1]Dale E. Hathaway, *Government and Agriculture,* New York: Macmillan, 1963, p. 3.

force some restrictions in order that one person's freedom does not deny another person's rights. When we speak of justice, we must include not only the legal protection of life and property, but also economic and social justice as well. Women's rights and civil rights movements have been based to a large extent on securing economic (for example, the attaining of equal pay for equal work) and social justice (for example, the removal of discrimination because of race or sex).

Each of these goals of peace, security, freedom, and justice is based on society's values. Values are the principles that guide human action and are basic to our concepts of what is good or bad. Values are therefore a reflection of our cultural heritage. There can be, however, a conflict of values within an individual and more often within a group. Policy makers must consider tradeoffs between the attainment of one goal or another. As Heady has said, economists can suggest several different ways to solve U.S. farm problems, but any solution is dependent upon the resolution of conflicts in goals and values.[2]

Because of the many basic aspirations involved, no one policy will assure that all goals will be realized. One of the major tasks of policy formation is recognizing and weighing competing goals and values of individuals and groups in order to arrive at a policy which will provide the maximum quality of life to those people involved or affected.

Values of Farm People

Until recently, agricultural fundamentalism had an important impact on agricultural policy. These agrarian values are based on "laissez faire" economics, Jeffersonian Democracy, and the French physiocratic philosophy. These basic ideas were summarized by Paarlberg in what he called the Agricultural Creed. The creed's articles are:[3]

1. Farmers are good citizens and a high percentage of our population should be on farms.

2. Farming is not only a business, but a way of life.

3. Farming should be a family enterprise.

---

[2]Earl O. Heady, *Goals and Values in Agricultural Policy,* Center for Agricultural and Economic Development. Ames: Iowa State University Press, 1961, p. v–vi.
[3]Don Paarlberg, *American Farm Policy,* New York: John Wiley & Sons, 1964, p. 3.

4. The land should be owned by the person who tills it.

5. It is good to make two blades of grass grow where one grew before.

6. Anyone who wants to farm should be free to do so.

7. A farmer should be his/her own boss.

It is indeed true that a high proportion of farmers are good citizens, but it is also true that a high proportion of urban people are good citizens. One would be hard pressed to say that one group was better than the other and thus support the statement that a high percentage of our population should be on farms. In 1890, 65 percent of the population lived in rural areas as compared to 30 percent now. In 1920, about 30 percent of the population lived on farms as compared to the present four percent.

Farming has been a way of life, but it is being transformed into a business. Computerization of farm records, growth of the farm firm, and modern scientific advances have forced producers to take a more businesslike attitude toward farming. Farming in the United States is primarily a family enterprise and will continue to be in the foreseeable future. Farms have grown in size and complexity but technology has made it feasible for a producer and his family to remain a viable economic unit. The investment that producers have in the farm firm is much larger than for most businesses found in rural America. Modern agribusiness methods are a must for today's producers.

Most agricultural producers own their own farms, but it has been necessary for farm size to increase in order to maintain a competitive position. This has been done to a large extent through the purchasing of land on credit. Agriculture like any other business has found the wise use of credit to be a necessity. From 1900 to 1974, those producers who owned their farms free and clear of any mortgages increased from 56 percent to 61 percent. Over the same period, part-owners increased from 8 percent to 27 percent of all agricultural producers.

The implementation of article 5 of the agricultural creed has virtually eliminated the impact of much of this historic creed as a value basis in determining agricultural policy. Policymakers have been forced to determine agricultural policy on values outside of this agricultural creed. The scientific revolution in agriculture, coupled with the competitive structure and the physical nature of agriculture, has increased agricultural production much faster than the demand for agricultural products has increased. As a consequence, farm product prices have been declining relative to other prices in the economy, making agricultural policy decisions more important than ever to some agricultural producers.

Over the years, government policies have provided opportunities for people to farm. Since colonial times, the government has provided incentives to encourage land settlement throughout the United States. The major public land policy was the Homestead Act of 1862. Under this act, a settler could pay a small registration fee and then if the settler resided on and worked 160 acres of land for five years, the settler would gain title to the land; or the settler could reside on the land six months and pay $1.25 per acre and thus gain title. Between 1868 and 1879, 70 million acres of land were made available to farmers under this act.

At present, however, anyone desiring to farm has a limited opportunity to do so because of the capital requirements which are necessary to obtain an economic sized farm. It is almost essential to either inherit a family farm or have one's relations give the land or provide some substantial financial assistance. Stam has shown that the probability of a farm youth taking over an economic sized unit is only about one in twelve.[4]

Most producers who are financially sound are free to make production and marketing decisions, and thus are their own bosses. Most farmers who own their farms have maintained their managerial control even though they may have had to give up some managerial freedom because of credit requirements, vertical coordination, and governmental policies.

Property rights give producers the benefit of using their resources as they see fit. With population increasing, some discussion has been taking place as to the advisability of exclusive control over a resource. People are indirectly affected by property rights, and some feel that these rights should be amended to restrict the owner's control over the use of a resource so as to maintain its use in the public interest.

Even though some of these fundamental attitudes may have changed, they still influence the feelings with regard to agriculture. With this in mind, an update to the creed might include the following:

1. Farming should be a family business.

2. Country living has many virtues and it should be made available to urban residents (parks, green belts, etc.).

[4]Jerome M. Stam, "Farming Opportunities for Rural Farm Youth in the North Central Region," Economic Study Report No. 569–3, Department of Agricultural Economics, University of Minnesota, St. Paul, July 1969, p. 23.

3. Agriculture should provide adequate food and fiber at reasonable prices to producers and consumers.

4. Society should assist farm youth in providing farming and agribusiness opportunities.

5. A farmer should be his/her own boss.

6. The land should be controlled by the person who owns it.

7. Agriculture is vital to mankind and therefore should receive priority in national goals.

These articles will continue to provide the basis of our future agricultural legislation. Out of these articles one can derive policy goals that will form the basis of future policies.

A policy goal is defined as a desirable end being sought that is consistent with the values of the group proposing it.[5] To date, most farm policy has revolved around the concepts of the "family farm," "parity," and "equality of bargaining power."

Family Farms. Much discussion has taken place regarding the family farm. In most areas, the family farm is considered to be consistent with the values of freedom, political and social stability, and economic justice and will therefore influence agricultural policy for some time. In fact, many states have introduced legislation to restrict corporations from operating agricultural firms in order that the family farm might remain as the basic economic unit in agriculture. However, it is difficult to define a family farm. By a family farm some people mean a farm that is operated by one family and possibly some small amount of hired help. Others try to define a family farm in terms of size, such as acreage. Such size measurements are not very precise because one family may be able to operate only a few acres in a fruit, nut, nursery or vegetable farm, but thousands of acres in a wheat or cattle ranch.

Parity. Because of past problems of low incomes in agriculture, all major agricultural legislation has attempted to promote parity in some way. Some of the ways have been in terms of parity prices, parity incomes, or a fair return on factors of production used in agriculture. Parity price is the concept most discussed and presented in newspapers. Parity means equality of value. It means prices that will give a unit of an agricultural commodity the same purchasing power as that unit had in some previous period. So if a bushel of

[5]Dale E. Hathaway, op. cit., p. 61.

corn purchased a shirt during the base period, then parity means that one bushel of corn today should buy one shirt at current market prices. The historic base period for calculating parity for many commodities was August 1909 to July 1914. Full parity, therefore, would give agricultural commodities the same purchasing power as they had in the 1909–14 base period.

The definition of the parity concept, however, causes problems because it does not take into account changes in demand, supply and resource productivity over time. To allow for these changes and for product substitution, the calculation of parity price for wheat was modified in the Agricultural Act of 1948. This act changed the base period for calculating parity prices for individual farm products to the most recent 120-month moving average. An example of the modification of parity price for wheat is as follows.

A = average price of wheat for the last 120 months = \$2.58

B = average index of farm prices received for the last 120 months = 351

C = current index of the farm prices paid index = 687

Computation of parity price of wheat:

$$\frac{A}{B} \times 100 = \text{Adjusted Price}$$

$$\frac{\text{Adjusted Price} \times C}{100} = \$5.05$$

Although this formula may appear to be complicated, it is not. All this formula does is take the current price of wheat and divide it by the index (weighted average) of prices received by farmers in order to adjust for increases in inflation. This gives a "real" or adjusted price that takes out the changes in the value of the dollar, and also takes out the change in demand and supply for wheat relative to other farm commodities. This real price is then multiplied by the index of prices paid to inflate the price of wheat to reflect the increase in the costs of producing agricultural products.

Producers are now interested in other measures of parity since, at certain time periods, the formula just shown would not give them parity incomes. The new concept is one that is based on cost of production or a fair return on investment in land, labor, management, and capital. The measure then would be what these factors could earn in the nonfarm economy. This means that cost of production studies need to be conducted. One would have to impute the cost of labor, land, management, and capital and divide the sum of these costs by output to arrive at a cost per unit or parity price per unit. Since costs of production differ widely between farms and production regions for a particular crop, a sizable representative sample of firms on which to run cost studies would have to be selected. Even then the problems associated with imputing a value for land are severe.

Most of the problems associated with parity price are contained in the fair return concept. However, parity is consistent with the values of economic justice and social and economic stability, security, and freedom, and will continue to be a goal for a long time.

Equality of Bargaining Power. The central theme of the National Farmers Organization (NFO) formed in 1955 in Iowa is bargaining power for agriculture. The NFO feels that agricultural producers are being taken advantage of by the large processors, wholesalers, and retailers in the food and fiber system. The NFO states that "if producers want to price their products, they must go to the market place with equal or greater strength that those who buy their products." Thus, they are attempting to increase their muscle in the market place by forming a quasimonopoly organization that could hold products off the market for higher prices and use contracts to market agricultural products in an orderly manner (see Chapter 9).

While this method of increasing agriculture's bargaining power is used by the NFO, other farm organizations are using farmer owned and controlled cooperatives such as the National Farmers Union, National Grange, and American Farm Bureau Federation.

Bargaining power for agriculture has been with us since the 1920s and is consistent with farmer values of economic justice, economic stability, and security. This goal will also be around for some time to come.

Farm Problems

In general, farmers have not prospered as the rest of the economy has, primarily because the supply of agricultural products has been increasing faster than the demand for them. Agricultural production has been increasing at about two percent per year, while demand has been increasing at a slightly less rapid rate. Hence, agricultural prices and incomes have been realtively low. The major historical problem has been one of chronic overproduction, but other problems also exist. They include the variability of agricultural prices with changes in demand and supply and very low incomes for the producers who are marginal farmers.

Overcapacity. Many countries around the world have difficulties because they cannot adequately feed their people—this is not the problem in the United States. Rather, it is one of plenty, not scarcity. Excess production has not been especially large in American agriculture in absolute terms. It has been estimated at from 6 to 12 percent of total production, however its economic impact is large. This overproduction has caused price and income troubles for many agricultural products. We refer here to excess production in the aggregate, yet there have been lean and abundant years for individual products.

Tweeten estimates the price elasticity of demand at the farm level for domestic food to be −.25 in the short run and −.10 in the long run.[6] This means that a one percent increase in prices will decrease quantity demanded by .25 percent in the short run, and .10 percent in the long run. If we include foreign demand for U.S. products, this increases the price elasticities of demand to −.46 in a recent three to four-year period and to −1.11 in the long run.[7] Thus, agricultural prices should fluctuate greatly with small changes in agricultural output, with price fluctuations being lessened since the foreign market increases the price elasticity of demand.

Income elasticity of demand shows the relationship between food consumption and consumers' incomes. Tweeten estimates this to be .15 for all farm products; if consumer disposable income increases 1 percent, the demand for farm products will increase by only .15 percent.

Two major factors that affect food consumption are population and incomes. With the American population growing at 1.3 percent a year, and per capita real income at 2.5 percent, domestic demand for farm commodities should grow by a total of 1.68 percent per year [1.3 percent for population, plus (.15 × 2.5 =) .38 percent for income]. Thus, if farm output is increasing more than 1.68 percent per year, excess capacity will exist unless the export demand continues at the 1972–75 level, which is highly unlikely.

U.S. agricultural capacity to produce is immense. A recent report from the Economic Research Service, USDA, shows that American farmers have the potential to vastly increase their output of agricultural products by 1985 if prices are favorable, if there are no restrictions on land use, if inputs are adequate, and if growing conditions are normal (Table 12-1). Under these conditions, compared to 1973, the United States could increase feedgrain produc-

[6]Luther Tweeten, *Foundations of Farm Policy,* Lincoln, Neb.: University of Nebraska Press, 1970, p. 200.
[7]Ibid., p. 201.

Table 12-1 Actual and Potential Production of Selected
Crops, United States, 1969–85

Production	Average		Potential	
	1969–71	*1973*	*1980*	*1985*
Corn				
Harvested acres (mil)	58.7	61.5	73.7	75.5
Yield (bu/ac)	82.2	93.8	109.5	120.0
Production (bil bu)	4.8	5.8	8.1	9.1
Soybeans				
Harvested acres (mil)	42.1	56.2	64.1	65.7
Yield (bu/ac)	27.4	28.5	32.0	34.5
Production (bil bu)	1.2	1.6	2.1	2.3
Feedgrains				
Harvested acres (mil)	100.4	102.4	114.7	115.7
Yield (tons/ac)	1.81	2.05	2.47	2.72
Production (mil tons)	182	210	283	315
Wheat				
Harvested acres (mil)	46.1	53.7	62.3	62.3
Yield (bu/ac)	31.9	32.2	34.5	36.6
Production (bil bu)	1.5	1.7	2.2	2.3
Cotton				
Harvested acres (mil)	11.2	12.4	14.1	14.7
Yield (lbs/ac)	437	502	510	535
Production (mil bales)	10.2	12.9	15.0	16.4
Total acreage of crops harvested	292	318	345	350

Source: David W. Culver and Milton H. Ericksen, "American Agriculture, its Capacity to Produce," *The Farm Index,* Commodity Economics Division, USDA, Special Report, December 1973.

tion by 50 percent, soybean production by 44 percent, beef cow numbers by 44 percent, cotton by 27 percent, peanuts by 400 percent and rice by 200 percent.

Instability of Farm Prices.   One of the basic aims of government farm programs has been to reduce the year-to-year variation in farm prices and incomes. These programs included the granting of low interest loans to producers to build on-farm storage and the establishment of the Commodity Credit Corporation in 1933 to take delivery and sell agricultural products.

Farm prices are vulnerable to weather on the supply side, and to foreign demand on the demand side. The inelasticity of demand along with these other factors sharply reduces farm prices and incomes as production increases. As shown in Figure 12-1, a slight

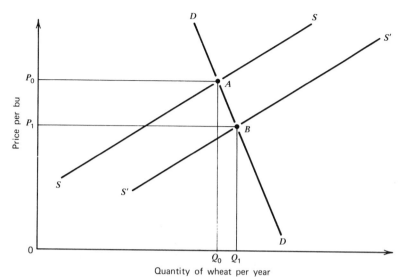

Figure 12-1. Price effect of a shift in wheat supply.

increase in production from Q_0 to Q_1 forces the price of wheat from P_0 to P_1. Also, total revenue drops from $0\text{-}P_0\text{-}A\text{-}Q_0$ to $0\text{-}P_1\text{-}B\text{-}Q_1$ because the percentage decline in price is greater than the percentage increase in production.

Changes (shifts) in demand as shown in Figure 12-2 can also cause large changes in farm prices. In this case, the demand curve shifts from DD to $D'D'$ so prices fall from P_0 to P_1 and total revenue falls from $0\text{-}P_0\text{-}A\text{-}S$ to $0\text{-}P_1\text{-}B\text{-}S$. These price changes result in income variations causing many family hardships, especially for the marginal producers.

Poverty.   In a study published in 1967, there were approximately 33.7 million people living in poverty.[8] In 1975, there were 26.0 million poor. Of these poor, 10.5 million lived in rural America. Thirty-two percent of the total population lived in rural areas, yet more than 40 percent of the nation's poor lived there. Only one in eight of poor rural families lived on farms. In that year, there were 1.3 million poor people who lived on farms comprising 14.7 percent of the total farm population.

Poverty is a realtive concept and difficult to define. Poverty for our purposes is defined as "a lack of access to respected positions and the lack of power to do anything about it; insecurity and un-

[8]*The People Left Behind,* A Report by the President's National Advisory Commission on Rural Poverty, Washington, D.C., September 1976, p. 3.

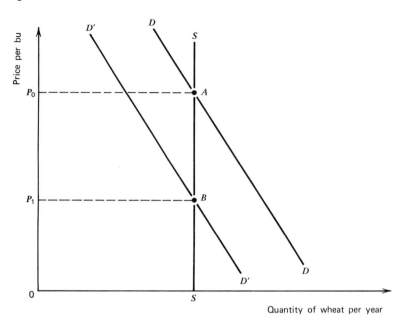

Figure 12-2. Price effect of a shift in wheat demand.

stable homes; and a wretched existence that tends to perpetuate itself from one generation to the next." The symptoms of poverty include low levels of formal education, high unemployment rates, high dependency rate on those of working age, and dilapidated housing. It means "an income level below that needed to provide the kind of living that our society considers a basic right."[9] The poverty income level changes with the above conditions. By 1978, the poverty level for an urban family of four was increased to $6200 per year.

Past U.S. agricultural programs have done little to help farm poverty. The reason for this is that government farm payments are based on production, and poor farms have little to sell. Thirty-nine percent or 1,083,000 farms have cash receipts of less than $2500 annually, and another 313,000 or 11 percent have sales less than $5000 annually. Subtracting production costs from such amounts received leaves little if any net agricultural income. The question then arises as to whether or not these farms have been able to supplement farm income with more adequate nonfarm income. Booth feels that in general there has been substantial substitution of non-

[9]W. W. McPherson, "An Economic Critique of the National Advisory Commission report on Rural Poverty," *American Journal of Agricultural Economics,* Vol. 50, No. 5, December 1968, p. 1363.

farm income for farm income, but there still remains some low income problems.[10]

In 1976, disposable income per capita for the farm population was 81 percent of nonfarm incomes, $4518 compared with nonfarm of $5552. The income from off-farm sources by those farms that had farm sales of less than $2500 was $15,630, and for those with farm sales between $2500 and $4999 it was $10,342. On the average, these farm families had farm and nonfarm incomes exceeding the poverty level, and enjoyed many benefits of life desired by most Americans, but these data tend to hide poverty problems that remain in agriculture.

History of Economic Thought Behind Farm Programs

Agricultural policy in the United States can be broken down into three basic types of programs. These are: (1) two-price plans; (2) land retirement programs; and (3) direct payment programs.

Two-Price Plans.   Two-price programs are designed to take advantage of the different elasticities of demand in the domestic and foreign markets so as to increase total revenue to agricultural producers. The relatively inelastic domestic demand and the relatively more elastic demand in the foreign market can be used to the producers' advantage. The price elasticity of demand in the foreign market is more elastic for most agricultural products because other countries' products are substitutes for many U.S. agricultural exports. The more substitutes there are for a product, the more elastic the demand curve becomes. As an illustration, consider the domestic and foreign demand for U.S. wheat. U.S. producers are usually the sole supplier to the domestic market partly because of import quotas restricting the amount of imports. The domestic demand for wheat is very inelastic (about $-.03$), which means that consumption does not vary much with price changes. In the foreign (or world) market, the United States competes for customers with Canada and Australia.

As shown in Figure 12-3, assume the United States has 1.5 billion bushels of wheat to sell. Now, by restricting domestic marketings to 500 million bushels, a $3.00 per bushel price is attained for a total domestic revenue of $1.5 billion. If the other one billion

[10]E. J. R. Booth, "The Economic Dimensions of Rural Poverty," *American Journal of Agricultural Economics,* Vol. 51, No. 2, May 1969.

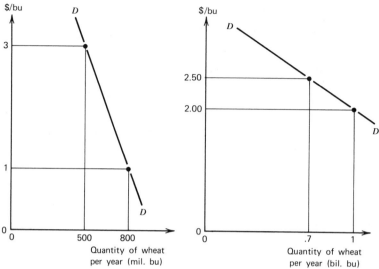

Figure 12-3. Economic effect of two-price plans.

bushels is sold at the foreign market price of $2.00 per bushel, total foreign revenue of $2 billion is attainable. Total revenue from both markets is $3.5 billion. If we were to market as much in the domestic market as possible (800 million bushels at a price of $1.00 per bushel), domestic revenue would be $800 million. Now if the remaining 700 million bushels is sold overseas, then foreign revenue is $1.75 billion, resulting in a total revenue of only $2.55 billion. This reduces total revenue by $950,000. Therefore, the two-price plans were enacted in an attempt to increase revenue to agricultural producers by restricting output sold in the domestic market that has an inelastic demand, and selling the balance in the foreign market that has a more elastic demand. In this illustration (disregarding costs of production and allocation costs between markets), total revenue is maximized when marginal revenue in the two markets is equalized.

These two-price plans were used by supporting the domestic prices of agricultural commodities above equilibrum prices and then merchandising the surplus output in foreign markets. This is shown in Figure 12-4. In a free market, given demand curve DD and supply curve SS, the equilibrium price and quantity produced and sold in the market would be P_0 and Q_0 respectively. If the support price is above equilibrium, say at P_1, then consumers will take quantity Q_1. Therefore a surplus (Q_1 to Q_2) remains which must be either stored or exported.

In the past, the Commodity Credit Corporation (CCC) has accumulated these surpluses through the use of nonrecourse loans. A nonrecourse loan is one where a loan is made to a producer par-

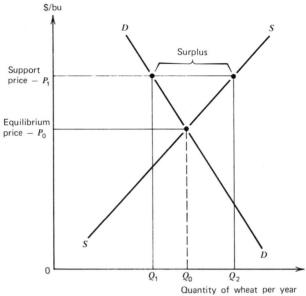

Figure 12-4. Economic effect of price supports above equilibrium.

ticipating in the program, with the borrower having the option of repaying the loan or turning over ownership of the commodity. If the market price rises above the loan rate (support price), the producer can sell the product on the open market and repay the loan plus interest. If the loan rate is above the open market price, the producer can relinquish the product to CCC in full payment of the loan. Therefore, during periods of excess production, CCC took delivery of large amounts of some agricultural commodities. CCC then had the responsibility of disposing of these surpluses in domestic aid programs and in foreign markets at prices in relation to the domestic loan rate as specified by Congress.

Two-price plans have been used extensively for many agricultural commodities. The government has used two-price plans since 1929, with the primary purpose of these programs being to increase the incomes of the agricultural producers.

Land Retirement. Land retirement has been used in conjunction with two-price programs to restrict production, and increase agricultural income. One of the most massive land retirement programs was the soil bank program established under the Agricultural Act of 1956. The act established an acreage reserve and a conservation reserve. The acreage reserve was a short-term land retirement program where producers were paid to divert part of their allotted acreage from current use. The conservation reserve was a long-term program to divert all or part of a producer's land from crop production to soil conserving uses.

The purpose of the land retirement was to reduce supply by limiting the land input. Remember, a part of the basic problem was that the supply curve was continuing to shift to the right, and a land retirement program attempted to reduce the amount by which the supply curve could shift, or even reverse it in the shorter run.

Figure 12-5 shows the open market equilibrium prices and quantities as P_0 and Q_0 given demand curve DD and supply curve SS. At a support price of P_1, consumers want only quantity Q_1 and producers supply quantity Q_2 so a surplus (Q_1 to Q_2) develops. In order to reduce this surplus, land retirement was used to take land out of production, shifting the supply curve from SS to $S'S'$. This movement of the supply curve reduces the surplus from (Q_1 to Q_2) to (Q_1 to Q_3). Payments to producers to restrict cropland use should reduce surpluses, and lower government storage costs.

In 1957, under the acreage reserve, 21.4 million acres were taken out of production. The conservation reserve program increased to a maximum of 28.7 million acres in 1960. The total acreage taken out of agricultural production under the conservation reserve and other acreage diversion programs reached a maximum of 65 million acres in 1962.

Direct Payment Programs. Direct payment programs were first proposed for agriculture in 1949, but not used until 1973. They were

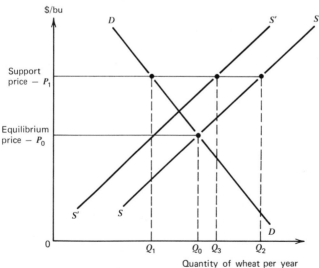

Figure 12-5. Economic effect of land retirement programs.

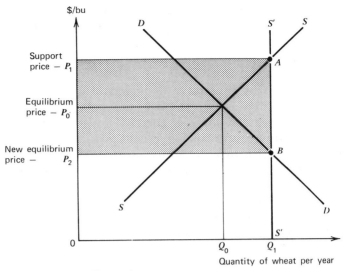

Figure 12-6. Economic effects of direct payment programs.

included in the Agriculture and Consumer Protection Act of 1973 for wheat, corn, cotton, and barley and in the Food and Agriculture Act of 1977.

Figure 12-6 illustrates the use of a direct payment program. It shows the equilibrium price and quantity as P_0 and Q_0 given DD and SS. If the support price is P_1, producers will supply quantity Q_1. Quantity Q_1 now represents the amount produced shown by $S'S'$. To get consumers to take quantity Q_1, the price in the market must drop to P_2 (where $S'S'$ and DD intersect). Thus under a direct payment program, the price would fall to the market clearing level of P_2. The U.S. Treasury would make up the difference between the support (or target) price P_1 and the free market price P_2. The supported income to producers would be the area 0-P_1-A-Q_1, consumers would pay an amount 0-P_2-B-Q_1, with the shaded area being the amount contributed by the U.S. Treasury. Thus, consumers have a large amount of the product at a low price, but tax revenues must be used to pay the amount represented by the shaded area.

Have Agricultural Programs Increased Agricultural Income?

While the three types of programs discussed above were intended to increase agricultural incomes, they have been unable to do so in the long-run. Income benefits are capitalized into land values, and therefore become production costs. Higher prices for agricultural commodities means that agricultural land is more productive, so people bid up its price because they want more land. In the long-run, benefits accrue to present landowners rather than later generations of producers.

Government programs have provided other benefits to farmers, however. Past federal farm programs have stabilized farm incomes and have reduced some of the risk and uncertainty in farming. Farm programs have also made it possible for some of the excess labor in agriculture to adjust to nonfarm employment. In addition, these programs have provided food stocks for national and international emergencies. More importantly, however, these programs have undoubtedly provided for a greater degree of political and social stability in the United States than would have existed without them. Agricultural producers have been more able to lead the life they desire, and made possible more stable and higher quality food supplies to urban dwellers at a lower real cost.

Alternative Programs

There are many alternative programs that could be employed to solve some of agriculture's problems. The alternative selected would depend on the criteria used to judge a program. For example, if the only criterion is to minimize treasury cost, a move to a free market would accomplish this objective, whereas a direct payment program would not do so. If economic efficiency is the criterion, a free market would be best, and a support program would be less desirable. Some of the most popular alternative programs are: (1) demand expansion; (2) free market; (3) land retirement; and (4) market quotas. These can be short-run programs. Long-run programs to move the labor resource from agriculture would include a national employment service, education, alternative skill training programs, and the relocation of industry to rural areas.[11]

Demand Expansion.   Increasing the domestic and foreign demand for products is often suggested as a method to increase farm prices and incomes. The United States carries on many demand increasing programs. These are the food stamp program, the school lunch program, and direct food distribution programs. In 1976, these programs cost some $6.5 billion. The food stamp program is of major assistance to low income people, as well as to agriculture. It

---

[11]Tweeten, op. cit., Chapter 11.

reduces the cost of food to low-income people and thus increases their consumption, expanding the market for agricultural commodities. In 1976, about 19 million people participated in this program. Those who participated bought food stamps for $3.4 billion that had a value of $8.7 billion in the grocery store. The government thereby increased the participants' purchasing power by $5.3 billion.

The food stamp program can be analyzed using indifference curve analysis, as in Figure 12-7. Budget constraint I shows what a consumer could purchase without food stamps. The budget constraint is tangent to indifference curve I_0. In equilibrium (at point A) this consumer would consume C_0 of other commodities and F_0 of food. Budget constraint II shows what happens when the price of food is subsidized. The subsidy has the same effect as decreasing the price of food, resulting in an increase in real income. Hence, the consumer is able to reach a new equilibrium at point B and a higher level of satisfaction and while food purchases increase to F_1, the consumer is able to increase the consumption of other commodities to C_1. Whether there is an increase in the consumption of other commodities depends on the consumers' tastes and preferences for food versus other commodities. This would be revealed in the slope of the indifference curves.

In foreign demand expansion, the United States has relied primarily on Public Law 480 (Food for Peace Program) to increase the demand for agricultural products. Under this program America

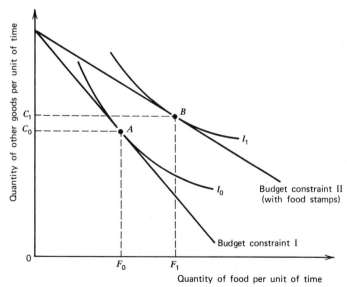

Figure 12-7. Effect on consumption of a food stamp plan.

sells commodities for foreign currency or long term credit, or sends products abroad for famine relief or barter. In 1975, the United States sent $1.2 billion worth of commodities overseas under this program. Also, the U.S. government spent $409 million in export subsidies in 1973 to move agricultural products abroad. Most of that total was used for wheat subsidies. These export subsidies were eliminated in 1975.

Economists feel that there has been some success in expanding the domestic demand for food. All income support programs help increase food demand since the income elasticity of demand for food is greater for low income groups. But this effort offers little long-run hope for solving agriculture's excess capacity problems. Food aid abroad could solve the capacity problem if the United States were willing to make the growing financial commitment that would be necessary to feed a larger portion of the world's population.

Free Market. Agriculture could return to a free market if the government decided to eliminate production controls and price supports on agricultural commodities. In the short run Tweeten estimates that for each one percent increase in farm output placed in the market, prices on the average would likely be depressed by two percent, gross cash receipts one percent, and net farm income almost three percent.[12] Therefore, if the excess capacity was from six to 12 percent in the 1955–66 period, and we use a conservative estimate of six percent, then farm products prices would drop 12 percent, cash receipts would fall six percent, and net farm income would be reduced by 18 percent. Producers would also lose their government support payments. The total loss in the short run would amount to a decrease in net farm income of 18 percent plus the forfeited government payments. This would have caused considerable hardship, unless the transition were to be buffered with a world shortage situation, such as the one that developed in 1972. After a four-year adjustment period, Heady and Tweeten estimate that farm prices, gross income and net income would recover to 90, 93, and 88 percent, respectively, of the level that existed before the release of five percent more commodities on the market.[13]

The major concern over returning to a free market is whether, because of its basic structure, agriculture can remain relatively stable, or whether it always will be feast-or-famine in terms of agricultural prices and incomes. Also producers are concerned that they may not have the political persuasion to get another farm bill passed.

[12]Luther Tweeten, op. cit., p. 325.
[13]Ibid., p. 325.

Land Retirement. Most proposals for land retirement are either "part-farm" or "whole-farm" retirement programs that divert farm land to soil conserving uses on a bid basis. Past programs to take agricultural land out of production on a part-farm basis have not been successful. The primary reason is that land is just one input in the production process. When the land input is restricted, producers tend to substitute other inputs such as capital equipment, agricultural chemicals and fertilizers. Consequently, rather than reduce output it may be increased. For this reason, many economists prefer long-term land retirement programs on a whole-farm basis. Although this type of program cures the above problem of substituting other inputs for land because all inputs are removed (land, equipment, labor, etc.), it does have other effects. One of these is the rural community problem. This problem develops because as producers rent their land to the government there is no need to purchase input items from the local feed, equipment, and other dealers. Many of these dealers will sell less of their goods and services causing financial difficulties that also spread to other businesses, and therefore may increase the migration of people from rural America. As expected, farm supply firms put pressure on Congress not to pass this type of legislation.

Market Quotas. Marketing quotas limit the amount of product a producer can sell or produce without penalty. Past marketing quota programs have been successful in reducing agricultural production, but this type of program has problems similar to the land retirement program in its effect on rural communities. This is especially true if marketing quotas are transferable. If farmers are allowed to sell their quotas, then these quotas will move to the most efficient farms. In most cases marginal land is concentrated and would affect the rural communities in those areas. If quotas are not transferable, then food prices would be higher than necessary largely as a result of fixing production into current production patterns.

This summary of some of the alternative farm programs that could be initiated is for perspective only. It should, however, give some idea of the advantages and disadvantages of each. Again, it is important to point out that different groups of people judge farm policy from different viewpoints. Farmers want a program that gives them maximum managerial freedom and the highest net income. Consumers want a plentiful and high quality food supply at a reasonable cost. The taxpayers want low government payments and low administrative burdens. Because basic conflicts of wants and values exist among these groups, any legislation must reflect a compromise among these conflicting forces—a compromise that changes as groups change their values or as political power shifts.

Common Agricultural Policy in the European Community

All developed countries protect their agricultural producers from the vagaries of the world market, and the European Community (EC) is no exception. The protection is both political and economic. It is political, both in that the EC is attempting to attain a high degree of self-sufficiency, and that government officials act in a manner conducive to reelection. It is economic in that they wish to maintain their farming culture.

Even though the EC was established in 1958, it was not until 1962 that the first Common Agricultural Policy (CAP) regulations were introduced. The first CAP regulations covered grain, poultry, pork, eggs, fruits, and vegetables. Regulations have been developed since that time for beef, milk, rice, fats and oils, sugar, tobacco, hops, seed, flax, silk, and fish. The three fundamental components of CAP are common pricing, community preference, and common financing.[14]

Common pricing in the EC can be explained using grains as an example. To promote intracommunity sales a target price is fixed in the major deficit consuming areas. For grains, the location used is Duisburg, Germany. Around this target price, small variations are permitted so that the open market forces can operate. These variations around the target prices are called "intervention prices." The government maintains the market floor by purchasing grain offered to them at the intervention price. A market ceiling price is maintained by the government through the selling of stocks. For example, assume an August 1 target price of $6.00 per bushel for wheat and intervention prices of $6.30 and $5.70. The "threshold price" would be the floor intervention price minus the costs of transportation from the port of entry to the major consuming areas. If this cost was 10 cents per bushel the threshold price would be $5.60 per bushel. This is the price of wheat at Rotterdam (the EC central grain market) plus transportation from there to Duisburg. This price is the minimum import price the EC could offer and maintain the intervention price in the major consuming areas. The difference between the import price (cost, insurance, and freight—CIF) and the threshold price is the variable levy that is used to protect the threshold price. This variable levy is a tax which varies with changes in the CIF import price or the target price of grains. In this way, the EC eliminates both price and quality competition from other grain exporting countries.

---

[14]John F. Hudson, "The Common Agricultural Policy of the European Community," Foreign Agricultural Service, USDA, FAS M-255, November 1973.

Community preference is accomplished through the use of variable levies and export subsidies. Because the variable levies provide a wall of protection for EC producers, imports can be restricted to any amount and quality desired. Since there are no production restrictions in the CAP, surpluses are produced and grains and dairy products are subsidized so that they can move into the world market. Also, subsidies are used on rice, olive oil, sugar, beef, pork, poultry, fruits and vegetables, and processed foods.

All countries in the EC are responsible for the financing of the CAP. The cost of agricultural support payments are met through the European Agricultural Guidance and Guarantee Fund that was established in 1962. The expenditures from this fund account for most of the EC budget. At present most of the revenue for agricultural support payments is coming from direct contributions from member states, custom duties, and levies on agricultural imports.

The Process of Policy Development

Anyone attempting to solve a problem systematically will tend to use the same method which we call the scientific method. This process can be broken down into at least six steps. These steps include: (1) recognizing and defining the problem; (2) outlining the issues; (3) developing alternative solutions; (4) choosing a policy solution; (5) putting the policy into effect; and (6) appraising its effectiveness.

Before one tries to solve a problem it is necessary to evaluate the facts so that everyone has the same feeling for the situation. The historical perspective gives the discussant some idea of what the problem is all about. A problem exists when people are troubled by a situation or when circumstances deviate from a norm or standard. These norms or standards may be viewed in terms of one's own values or goals. For example, a problem in the U.S. dairy industry is the large amount of dairy imports from the EC. These imports increase the supply of dairy products in the United States and reduce prices and incomes to U.S. dairy producers.

Once the problem is understood it is imperative to define what is involved in the controversy. This is called outlining the issues. Some of the issues in the dairy problem cited above are: (1) the EC is merchandising many of its products in the North Atlantic market; (2) they export these products by using export subsidies in order to compete; and (3) export subsidies violate the General Agreement on Tariffs and Trade.

In order for people to have a choice, more than one alternative solution must be developed and presented. Problems can be solved in many ways. The method selected will depend on the solution that fits the beliefs and values of the person or group adopting it.

Some alternative solutions to the dairy problem might be: (1) impose a tariff (tax) on EC dairy products so they will sell for the same price as U.S. dairy products; (2) put a quota limiting the quantity that can be imported so that the amount by which prices of dairy products decrease in the North Atlantic market is reduced; or (3) allow dairy imports into the United States, but subsidize domestic producers.

No solution is going to fit everyone's needs. Usually a compromise is reached after all groups involved have been consulted. The solution picked may be one solution or a combination of several. Policy solutions are adopted in the political process. This places a responsibility on interested individuals to express ideas to friends, special interest pressure groups, and elected officials. Pressure groups are people with common interests working together and thus presenting common aims with a stronger voice.

Once a solution to the problem is selected it must be put into effect or implemented. Normally, agricultural policy is directed to the Agricultural Stabilization and Conservation Service, USDA, for implementation. They perform the administrative tasks of interpreting the legislation and informing producers of specific conditions of the legislation.

Finally the policy must be appraised as to its effectiveness. Just as the world changes, so does the need to modify and adapt to new situations. What was needed yesterday may not be needed tomorrow. Therefore, policies must be reviewed periodically to insure that they meet the conditions for which the policy was intended.

Summary

Federal government programs in U.S. agriculture have been in effect since 1929. They have been used to support prices and incomes of farmers producing grain, cotton, tobacco, peanuts, sheep and lambs, and sugar.

The major policy goals of agriculture include the family farm, parity, and bargaining power for agriculture. Almost all agricultural legislation mentions these goals. These policy goals are consistent with farm values.

Overcapacity, price instability, and poverty are the primary agricultural problems. Agricultural policies have been enacted to deal with these problems. These policies have included programs that expanded demand for agricultural products, retired land from production, or reduced the amount of product that could be produced and sold under marketing quotas. The Food and Agriculture Act of 1977 is a policy that uses direct deficiency payments to producers with provisions for some acreage set-aside or land retirement program.

Agricultural programs have had only short–run impacts on increasing farm incomes. In the longer run, these income benefits are capitalized into land values. Thus, policy benefits in the long-run are captured by present landowners.

The process of policy development is a decision making process. The steps involved are: (1) recognizing and defining the problem; (2) outlining the issues; (3) developing alternative solutions; (4) choosing a policy solution; (5) putting the policy into effect; and (6) appraising its effectiveness.

Chapter Highlights

1. Government farm programs have been in existence since 1929.
2. Enactment of any public policy requires the resolution of conflicts in basic goals and values.
3. Agricultural fundamentalism has provided the impetus for much U.S. agricultural policy in the past.
4. Basic policy goals of agriculture are: (1) family farms; (2) parity; and (3) equality of bargaining power.
5. Agriculture has at least three farm problems: (1) overcapacity; (2) instability of farm prices; and (3) poverty.
6. The demand for many agriculture commodities is inelastic.
7. Historically, agricultural policy has revolved around three types of economic programs: (1) two-price plans; (2) land retirement programs; and (3) direct payment programs. All of these programs were enacted to increase farm incomes.
8. Farm programs have not increased farm income in the long-run because government support payments become capitalized into land values.
9. Benefits of past farm programs have included: (1) reducing the variability of farm income; (2) easing the out-migration of excess labor; and (3) providing food stocks for emergencies.
10. The U.S. has many programs to encourage domestic food consumption. The Food Stamp Program is the major program and 19 million Americans participate in it.
11. The primary program to increase foreign demand for U.S. agricultural commodities is Public Law 480 that was passed in 1954.
12. There is an infinite number of possible ways to solve our farm problems. Conflicts in goals and values keep us from adopting an effective long-run solution.

13. All countries of the world have some sort of farm programs to protect their farmers from very low prices and incomes.
14. The European Community's agricultural policy is a variable levy system designed to support domestic farm prices and control imports of farm products.
15. The scientific method is useful in finding a solution to any problem.
16. Agricultural policies may need to change from time to time in order to meet the cyclical nature of agricultural production.

Review Questions

1. What are values? Do the values of farm people influence agricultural policy?
2. Is the agricultural creed relevant today? What changes would you make in the creed in order to update it?
3. Define parity. Is parity price a useful device for measuring the "well being" of farmers and ranchers?
4. What are three of American agriculture's major problems? How have we attempted to solve these problems?
5. What is a two-price plan? Does this type of program take advantage of different elasticities of demand in the domestic and foreign market so as to increase total revenue to agricultural producers? Explain.
6. Explain a direct payments program. Does the price elasticity of demand for the commodity affect the amount paid by consumers and the government?
7. Have agricultural programs increased farm income? What has happened to land values? Discuss.
8. What is the Common Agricultural Policy? How does it differ from a direct payments type of program?
9. Explain the steps in the policy development process.

Suggested Readings

1. *Food and Agricultural Policy.* Washington, D.C.: American Enterprise Institute for Public Policy Research, 1977.
2. Halcrow, Harold G. *Food Policy for America.* New York: McGraw-Hill Book Company, 1977, Chapters 5, 8, and 11.
3. Hathaway, Dale E. *Government and Agriculture: Public Policy in a Democratic Society.* New York: The Macmillan Company, 1963, Chapters 1, 2, and 3.
4. Schickele, Rainer. *Agricultural Policy: Farm Programs and National Welfare.* Lincoln, Neb.: University of Nebraska Press, 1954, Chapters 1, 2, 3, 4, and 5.
5. Shepherd, Geoffrey S. *Farm Policy: New Directions.* Ames, Iowa: The Iowa State University Press, 1964, Chapters 7, 8, 9, 10, 11, 12, and 13.
6. Tweeten, Luther. *Foundations of Farm Policy.* Lincoln, Neb.: University of Nebraska Press, 1970, Chapters 3, 6, 10, and 11.

13

COMPARATIVE
AGRICULTURAL
SYSTEMS

COMPARATIVE AGRICULTURAL SYSTEMS

The term "economic system" encompasses all methods by which resources are allocated and goods and services are distributed. From country to country the systems differ, primarily on the basis of social and political considerations. In some countries the system is capitalism, in  others it is socialism, while in still others it is a mixture of capitalism and socialism.

Major Types of Economic Systems

Types of economic systems in their pure forms do not exist, but it is still worthwhile to study the characteristics of each. Such study makes it easier to compare and analyze existing economic systems.

Capitalism. The economic system labeled capitalism is a self regulating system with a government which is uninvolved in economic decisions. Capitalism is dependent on market forces to determine prices, to allocate resources, and to distribute income.

The factors of production are privately owned and controlled, causing decentralized decision-making. Each owner makes production decisions motivated by a desire to realize a profit. Production is begun or terminated by individual choice. The profits earned or losses incurred are a direct result of right or wrong business decisions.

Individual freedom of choice prevails in making consumption and occupational decisions under a system of capitalism. The consumer attempts to maximize satisfaction, given money income. A resource owner attempts to maximize income from the sale of services or resources controlled.

Under capitalism, free market prices are the sole guides to individuals and firms in making production, exchange, and consumption decisions; and competition is stressed in all types of economic activities.

State Socialism.   The basis of socialism as an economic system is collective ownership of all productive resources with state-directed decision-making. Industries are owned by society as a whole. Control of all property is held by the state for the mutual benefit of the people. This necessitates centralized decision-making by government planners and limits individual economic incentives.

State socialism involves the complete planning of all economic effort, with resources allocated according to these plans. The state also establishes and administers all prices. Direct economic competition is therefore eliminated, and the state alone initiates new business activity.

Mixed Economic Systems.   Most economies of the world would be termed mixed, a combination of the characteristics of both capitalism and socialism. For example, the United States is generally considered capitalistic, yet the U.S. government guides production in many industries, and government regulations exist in nearly all sectors of the economy. Government subsidies and grants are used to provide incentives and disincentives to produce specific goods and services. In total, however, the American system is relatively capitalistic and public enterprises are held to a minimum.

Elements of capitalism are also found in socialistic systems. In Great Britain, a highly socialistic economy, most large scale enterprises are nationalized. The state owns much of the coal, public transportation, and steel industries. On the other hand, private property does exist and many small businesses have been left to individual control.

Even in centrally planned economies such as the Soviet Union and Poland, some elements of capitalism exist. On the collective farms, each family is allowed a small private plot on which to raise crops and livestock. These products may be used for private consumption or sold at a local market. In Poland, much of the land is divided into small farms that are privately owned and cultivated.

The general economic system existing in a country dictates the type of agricultural system to be found. However, agriculture is difficult to plan and control. The agriculture industry does not lend itself to centralized control and planning as well as many manufacturing processes. Those countries with socialistic agricultural systems have come to realize that agricultural campaigns often go awry due to weather, disease, and distance from the planning headquarters.

Command Agricultural Systems.   No economy or agricultural system in the world is completely planned, but the Soviet economy is one of the oldest economies that is highly command-oriented and should provide some insight into how agriculture is organized in other parts of the world. What follows is a general overview of Soviet agriculture and planning organizations. Keep in mind that all the details of the Soviet system are not known and there are often rapid changes.

Agricultural production is fairly well limited to European Russia, the Volga, and Siberia. Because of the geographical location of the Soviet Union, one would expect problems in agriculture resulting from the severity of climatic conditions and poor agricultural soils. More than two thirds of the land area sown to grains in Russia is located in areas with insufficient precipitation. Only one percent of the arable land in the USSR lies in areas with annual precipitation of 28 inches or more, and 40 percent receives only 16 inches.[1] Severe droughts occur about every third year. Also, because most of the USSR agricultural land is north of the 49th parallel, there are short growing seasons and short frost-free periods. Because of these conditions, Russia has always had difficulty feeding itself.

Throughout the history of the USSR, there has been relatively little success in agriculture and many remedies and reforms have been implemented. The most dramatic reforms were those based on proposals by Marx and Lenin. They stated that large scale agriculture was necessary to increase the productivity of the agricultural sector and to provide the food necessary in their plans for urbanization and industrialization. Therefore, based on the Decree on Land of 1917 under which the right of private property was abolished, millions of peasant farm families were united into various collective organizations to form large-scale operations. In 1928 prior to collectivization, the average sown cropland per household was only five hectares. In 1969, the average collective farm had 3000 hectares under crops, and the average "state farm" had 6700 hectares under crops.[2]

Collectivization was begun on an entirely voluntary basis. However, when in 1929 the grain shortage was acute and the collective and state farms still represented only a minor part of agricultural production, Stalin instigated a plan of forced collectivization. The forced collectivization of agriculture took a heavy toll in terms of human life and livestock. The mass collectivization was in part a method by which to control the independent nature of the peasants as well as a way to channel agricultural efforts to meet national goals.

---

[1] Fletcher Pope, Jr., Valentine Zabijaka, and William Ragsdale. "Agriculture in the United States and the Soviet Union," Foreign Agricultural Economic Report, No. 92, ERS, USDA, October 1973.

[2] V. V. Matskevich, "Socio-Economic Changes and the Socialist System of Agriculture in the USSR," *Agriculture of the Soviet Union,* Moscow: MIR Publishers, 1970, p. 20.

Table 13-1 Number and Size of Collective Farms USSR, 1940–76

Year	Number	Average Size (Acres)
1940	236,945	3,531
1950	123,747	7,564
1960	44,944	15,928
1970	33,561	15,073
1976	28,600	16,100

Source: Economic Research Service, USDA, "Agricultural Statistics of Eastern Europe and the Soviet Union," ERS-Foreign 349, June 1973; and Foreign Agricultural Economic Report No. 92, January 1977.

Stalin's concession to the peasants was to allow each farm family to cultivate a private plot of land, ranging in size from one-half to one and one-half acres, depending on the productivity of the soil.

Collective Farms. Collective farms are large-scale farms organized by the Soviet State to bring households together in an attempt to apply modern agricultural technology and, thereby, increase agricultural output. All land in the USSR is state-owned and managed under a central state plan. The number of collective farms or *kolkhozes* decreased from 236,945 in 1940 to 28,600 in 1976, but the average size of these farms grew from 3531 acres to 16,100 acres over the same period, as can be noted in Table 13-1. A mass merger was instituted by Nikita Krushchev, pressuring the kolkhoz farms to merge into "supersized" farms which was expected to increase efficiency. In six months during 1950, the number of collectives fell from 252,000 to less than 124,000. In 1954, state farms started absorbing collective farms. This was especially apparent where agriculture remained weak after World War II, and heavy state investment was needed to increase productivity. Collective farms now occupy about one-half of the total cropland sown in Russia.

Rules by which collective farms operate were adopted in 1935 and revised in 1969. These rules express the rights of individuals on these farms and outline how the farm will be managed. The farm's day-to-day activities are guided by a Chairman elected from the general membership.[3] In large collective farms, where general

[3]These formally elected managers are actually selected and removed at will by Communist authorities. Lazar Volin, "Agricultural Policy of the Soviet Union," *The Soviet Economy: A Book of Readings,* Morris Bornstein and Darrell R. Rusfeld eds., Homewood, Ill.: Richard D. Irwin, Inc., 1962, p. 261.

membership meetings cannot be held, delegates are selected from each brigade (a 40- to 60-man work-unit) and production subdivision. These delegates elect the board of the collective farm that is responsible for production, organization, financial, cultural, service and educational activities of the farm. Specialists are appointed by the board to organize and fulfill the production and financial plans of that branch of farm production.

All citizens who have reached the age of 16 may work in the common enterprise on collective farms, with payment based on the quality and quantity of work done. They are also eligible to use a farmyard plot for subsidiary farming, erect a dwelling and farm buildings, and use collective pastures and transport facilities in a manner established by the farm.

Every collective farm family may have: a cow with a calf up to one year of age; one calf up to two years old; one sow with litter up to three months old or two pigs for fattening; up to 10 sheep and goats; beehives; poultry; and rabbits. These farmyard plots are significant in providing the Russian food supply. Although these small plots account for only about three percent of the sown acreage, they are responsible for a large portion of the farm's total output. For example, these plots in 1971 produced 37 percent of the vegetables, 63 percent of the potatoes, 35 percent of the meat, 35 percent of the milk, 50 percent of the eggs, and 20 percent of the wool.

The output from this small private sector is important as a family food source. Output over and above what is needed by the family is sold directly to consumers in so-called *kolkhoz markets* in the cities. Farmers can rent space at these markets and may sell their products at open market prices. They may not, however, sell their products through middlemen. For several years during the Stalin era, income to the members of the collectives from the kolkhoz market exceeded that from sales to the state.[4]

These household allotments have been under considerable scrutiny since the mid-1930s. Their position is deeply rooted in Russian rural society and it will probably be many years before they are discarded, if at all. In spite of the fact that these small plots are the last vestiges of rural capitalism, they are too important in the total agricultural picture to be eliminated.

State Farms.   State farms are operated like factory enterprises and labor is paid a wage. Collective farms, on the other hand, pay wages for certain jobs, but compensation is usually a share in the residual income after all production costs have been met and expenditures for investment have been made.

[4]Ibid., p. 261.

Table 13-2 Number and Size of
State Farms, USSR, 1940-76

Year	Number	Size (Acres)
1940	4,159	30,146
1950	4,988	36,818
1960	7,375	64,740
1970	14,994	51,397
1976	18,100	47,200

Source: Economic Research Service, USDA, "Agricultural Statistics of Eastern Europe and the Soviet Union," ERS-Foreign 349, June 1973; and Foreign Agricultural Economic Report No. 92, January 1977.

State farms were organized just after the Bolshevik Revolution in 1917. Over 573 million acres of land was taken from the large land owners. These large estates were not divided among the peasants, but were converted to nationalized state farms operated by the state. These farms were to demonstrate the advancements in agriculture to collective farms. They test new technologies, and their information is used by collective farms for increasing agricultural output.

Each state farm or *sovkoz* is operated by an appointed director who acts as a one-man management. The director is responsible for organizing production, and hiring and rewarding specialists and foremen who manage the farm's production subdivisions.

State farms are gigantic. The number of these farms doubled between 1960 and 1970. As shown in Table 13-2, the average size increased from about 37,000 acres in 1950 to nearly 65,000 in 1960, largely because of the development of new land in Soviet Asia. With the growth of urban populations in the European portion of the USSR, the average acreage of state farms has been declining as new state farms of smaller size have been established near cities and industrial centers. These new state farms specialize in vegetables, dairy, poultry, and livestock fattening to meet the needs of the nearby large urban populations.

Private plots are also farmed by state farm members in their spare time with the products being used for personal consumption, or sold in the open market.

Russian Agriculture in Change. Russia's problems in agriculture are related to a whole host of factors. Recent crop failures, while influenced by adverse weather, are intertwined with management dilemmas, poorly germinating seeds, shortages of insecticides and weedkillers, and the lack of repair parts for farm equipment.[5] Also, Russian leaders have found it difficult to plan and control the 28,000 collective farms that include more than 14 million households.

Currently, Soviet agriculture is being transformed in an attempt to allow for better control. This revolutionary change is taking place in the merging of collective farms into the state farm system. For many of the collective farmers, it means another movement further divorcing them from the farm life-style they once knew.

Transforming the collective farms into the state system is being accomplished through two means. Diversified collective farms are being divided and merged with state farms into specialized agricultural units. "Interfarm units" are also being established. Under the interfarm system, several collective farms are joined together to form large-scale specialized agricultural enterprises.

The interfarm complexes are operated by specialists, but are owned by the participating collective farms. The purpose of these complexes is to increase labor efficiency above the level now existing on collective farms. However, with respect to cost of production, the collectives have been doing relatively well. In fact for grain, potatoes, and milk, the collective farms' cost of production per metric ton have been substantially lower than that of the state farms.[6]

The specialized agricultural units and interfarm units are expected to continue to receive emphasis in the next five-year plan. Already there are approximately 5317 interfarm units. There are over 570 factory-type poultry and egg farms, 358 livestock units, 287 feedmills, and many artificial insemination centers.[7] Also, there are 550 machinery and repair stations to serve both collective and state farms.

Planning Soviet Agriculture. Agricultural production in the USSR is not as thoroughly planned as is industrial production, and total agricultural production really is not planned at all. What is planned is the amount of agricultural products which the state will purchase from the farms at specified prices. Once delivery quotas are met, farms can receive bonuses for additional output. Collective farms can also sell their excess products in the *kolkhoz* markets. "Private plot" agriculture is not centrally planned even though the private

[5]Alexander M. Derevany, "Soviet Agriculture at the Crossroads," *Ag World,* St. Paul, Minn., December 1975, p. 12.
[6]Ibid., p. 13.
[7]Alexander M. Derevany, "Soviet Agriculture at the Crossroads," Part II, *Ag World,* St. Paul, Minn., January 1976, p. 12.

plots produce about one-third of the total Russian agricultural output.

The Council of Ministers and the State Planning Commission (*Gosplan*) coordinate the planning of production, utilization, and export of agricultural commodities. The council of ministers is the cabinet of Russia headed by the premier. This is the policy-making body that includes 100 people who administer the entire economy. It makes decisions on the production of all commodities, investments, military production, consumer goods, foreign trade, construction, wages, and prices. *Gosplan* takes the general directives from the council of ministers and drafts a detailed economic plan. National acreage and production goals are broken down into goals for each of the 15 republics, and these are further refined by regions and districts. With these objectives in mind, the Soviet government prepares its five-year plans. The purpose of these plans is to set forth goals and priorities. With respect to agriculture, each five-year plan sets forth amounts of capital investment, fertilizer use, crop production, and land reclamation. These five-year plans stipulate the amounts that the state purchasing organization will purchase each year at a guaranteed stable price.

Proceeding from the *State Stable-Order Plan,* each farm draws up its own plan. This plan takes into consideration the farm's own resources, past production records, and national goals. In this process, compromise is necessary to arrive at production goals. These plans are also for five-year periods, but are divided into one-year components as well.

A difference between production goals and quotas should be noted. Production goals take resource requirements into consideration, and are basic to overall planning in the Soviet system. These goals set production targets for each farm, while farm quotas are the amounts that the farms must sell to the state purchasing organization. Since production goals are idealistic, quotas are always smaller quantities than the production goals.

Changes in Public Policy. Increasingly it is being recognized that the large grain imports by the Soviet Union in 1972–73 were due as much to a change in priorities as to a poor grain crop.[8] Consumer programs for the 1950s to the 1970s have brought visible improvements in the well-being of Soviet people.[9] During this period, the

---

[8]D. Gale Johnson, "Soviet Agricultural and World Trade in Farm Products," *Prospects for Agricultural Trade with the USSR,* ERS, USDA, 1974, p. 43.

[9]Gertrude E. Schroeder, "Soviet Economic Growth and Consumer Welfare: Retrospect and Prospect," *Prospects for Agricultural Trade with the USSR,* ERS, USDA, 1974, p. 4.

quality of diets improved considerably as did the quantity of food available. Despite these gains, the level of living is still behind that of many countries in Europe, and that of the United States. Soviet leaders are faced with an increasingly affluent and sophisticated population that wants more and better housing, personal automobiles, and more quality foods, especially meat.[10] In this effort, livestock product consumption is heavily subsidized to keep retail prices below production and marketing costs.

The Soviet Union has been increasing imports of livestock, poultry, meat, and breeding stock. Recently, Russia purchased 300 head of American cattle, 1000 head of Canadian cattle, and 100 Hereford bulls from the United Kingdom. These purchases of breeding stock were consistent with the ambitious goals the USSR had set for itself in its 1971–75 plan. Also, their new system of raising livestock in huge mechanized complexes shows the high priority placed on meat-production goals. Currently Russia has adopted a policy of moderate feed and meat imports with increased domestic feed production. This program could permit slow increases in per capita consumption of livestock products. Soviet livestock rations are deficient in digestible protein. Hence a large share of feed imports will consist of oilseeds or oilseed meal to improve the protein balance.

When comparing the 1971–75 plan with what actually occurred during that period, one can see that some goals were met while others were not. Production of grain, sunflower seeds, sugar beets, meat, and milk fell short of the planned amounts, while cotton and eggs exceeded projections.

The five-year plan to cover the years 1976–80 shows increases in all areas, over both the 1971–75 plan and the levels actually achieved during the 1971–75 period. However, the new five-year plan for Soviet agricultural development is more cautious on the whole, avoiding the extremely ambitious character of previous plans.[11]

Under the new plan there will be additional capital invested in agriculture, but the percentage increase will not be as great as in earlier plans. There is to be increased use of fertilizers and some increase in land reclamation. Much of the expected increase in crop production will be dependent upon these two factors. The plan will allocate 120 million tons of fertilizer annually by 1980, compared with 75 million tons used in 1975. Increased emphasis will be placed on fruit and vegetable production.

[10]Ibid., p. 6.
[11]David M. Schoonover, "Agricultural Trade Implications of the 1976–80 Soviet Economic Plan," Economic Research Service, USDA, 1976, p. 1.

A striking feature of the 1976–80 plan is the low-targeted growth of livestock product output.[12] In recent years personal incomes have been increasing, resulting in increased consumption of meat, milk, and eggs. Personal incomes are expected to continue to increase so there should be an increased demand for livestock products. It appears that the USSR will need to import livestock products to meet these expected increases in consumer demand.

The Soviet government has signed an agreement to import substantial amounts of grain from the United States during its 1976–80 plan. The knowledge that a source of grain was assured, allowed the planners to redirect some emphasis from grain production to other products.

Grain production is not being ignored in the 1976–80 plan. Under the new plan, production is to increase with much of the increase due to the application of additional amounts of fertilizer. To a lesser degree, a shift to higher yielding varieties of grains and more acreage planted are to account for the proposed increases over the 1971–1975 production.

Much of Russia's wheat production is used for feed. This amounted to 37 million metric tons for the 1970–71 crop year, and is estimated to have been 39 million metric tons in 1975–76. Anticipated feed use of wheat is about 40 percent of estimated wheat production.

Estimates show that the total feed deficit in the USSR in 1975–76 was around 19 million metric tons and may increase to 40 million metric tons by 1980.[13] These large feed deficits are placed primarily in the roughage area. In feed grains, the gap will be about one million tons for 1975 and will increase to possibly 16 million tons by 1980.[14]

The ministry of procurement has a program to increase mixed feed output to 100 million tons per year by 1990, because demand for mixed feed by collective and state farms is not currently being met. These enterprises are forced to use huge quantities of unprocessed grain from farms to fulfill livestock production plans. In some cases, farms are feeding milling quality wheat to livestock rather than selling it to the state.

Pressures on Soviet grain storage and drying facilities became particularly acute following 1973s all-time record grain crop, much

[12]David M. Schoonover, "Soviet Agriculture in the 1976–80 Plan," ERS, USDA, October 7, 1976, p. 7.

[13]David M. Schoonover, "The Soviet Feed-Livestock Economy: Prelimary Findings on Performance and Trade Implications," *Prospects for Agricultural Trade with the USSR*, ERS, USDA, 1974, p. 39.

[14]Ibid., p. 39.

of which was harvested under wet conditions. Some areas harvested wheat with moisture levels as high as 25 to 30 percent. As a result, it was necessary to store large quantities on the ground. The USSR is undertaking a massive construction program that includes grain storage, particularly elevators, new flour mills, and mixed feed plants.

As of October 1976, the Soviet Ministry of Procurement had storage capacity for only 140 million metric tons of grains and oilseeds, of which 40 million tons of capacity was in grain elevators.[15] State and collective farms have slightly over 100 million tons of additional storage capacity. The Ministry of Procurement plans to construct additional storage facilities with a 30 million ton capacity. Longer-range plans call for the building of new storage facilities with 140 million ton capacity by 1990.

Another major goal of agricultural planners is to increase mechanization. Currently, grains, potatoes, and sugar beets are all highly mechanized while for cotton, vegetables, and livestock, the degree of mechanization remains low. The USSR has about as many combines, but only about half as many tractors and trucks as the U.S. Their equipment seems to be much older, and maintenance is a problem because sufficient repair parts have been unavailable.

The production increases set forth under the 1976–80 plan in all areas will be dependent also on continued growth in the number and size of interfarm units. As mentioned earlier, the emphasis on interfarm units is an attempt for better control both in the setting of more realistic goals and priorities, and in achieving those goals.

USSR–USA Agricultural Comparisons

In recent years, agriculture has received relatively more attention in the Soviet Union. Agriculture represents 22 percent of the Soviet gross national product, and 3.5 percent of the United States gross national product. The amount of capital invested in Soviet agriculture is less than in the United States and the output produced is less.

American agricultural farms are, on the average, much smaller than Russian farms. There are 2.8 million farms in the United States, the average size of which is less than 400 acres. By comparison, in 1976 Soviet state farms averaged 47,200 acres; collective farms averaged 16,100 acres.

The administrative set-up for Soviet farms resembles that of

[15]Keith Severin, "Soviets Plan Expansion of Grain Storage Capacity," *Foreign Agriculture,* Foreign Agricultural Service, USDA, March 21, 1977, p. 8.

American corporations, with either appointed or elected managers. The Soviet state farm directors and collective farm chairmen, along with their cadre of specialists, make production management decisions. These decisions are made in accordance with the current five-year plan.

The Soviet labor force is half again as large as that of the United States. Agriculture employs 22 percent of this large labor force in the USSR, while in the United States, about four percent of the labor force is employed in agriculture.

The land area of the Soviet Union is about two and one-half times larger than that of the United States, but much of it is not suitable for agriculture. The Soviets have a cultivated land area that is 45 percent larger than the United States, but there is a greater drought susceptibility.[16] Lying 15° to 20° farther north, the USSR has a growing season and frost-free period similar to that of Canadian agriculture.

Soviet agricultural production has grown more rapidly than U.S. agricultural output in recent years: from 1966–76, farm output increased approximately 50 percent in the Soviet Union while increasing only 20 percent in the United States. However, in 1963, 1972, and 1975, Russian agricultural output dropped 12, 4, and 10 percent from the previous year, respectively, due primarily to adverse weather. Much of the Russian output growth has been due to its new lands program in which 70 million acres of land were developed for cropping in Siberia and Northern Kazakhstan.

Table 13-3 shows large increases in sown acreage in the Soviet Union between 1950 and 1976. The United States, on the other hand, has reduced total sown acreage in an attempt to cut its surpluses. These data also show that most of Russia's grain acreage is sown to foodgrains, wheat and rye, whereas in the United States most grain acreage is for feedgrains. Soybeans are the largest U.S. oil crop, compared with sunflower seeds in the USSR.

During the period from 1950 to 1976, Soviet livestock numbers increased and now are catching up to American levels. The low livestock numbers of 1950 are a reflection of the losses due to the forced collectivization in the 1930s, and the effects of World War II. As can be seen from Table 13-4, Russia produces more hogs, sheep, and goats than does the United States, but fewer cattle. Most of the cattle in the USSR are dual purpose, being raised for both milk and meat production. Russia has very few high grade beef cattle such as are raised in the United States for meat purposes. Most "beefsteak"

[16]Fletcher Pope, Jr., *Agriculture in the United States and the Soviet Union*, ERS, Foreign Agricultural Economic Report No. 92, Revised January 1977, p. 2.

Table 13-3 U.S.—USSR Distribution of Sown Acres

	1950		1976	
	U.S.	**USSR**	**U.S.**	**USSR**
	--------millions of acres--------			
Wheat	61.6	95.1	80.2	146.9
Rye	1.8	58.3	3.0	22.3
Corn	72.4	11.9	71.1	8.2
Oats	39.3	40.0	17.5	27.8
Barley	11.2	21.3	9.3	84.7
Potatoes	1.7	21.2	1.4	17.6
Vegetables	1.6	3.2	3.3	3.9
Tobacco	1.6	2.5	1.0	.5
Cotton	17.8	5.7	11.7	7.3
Forage crops	85.1	51.1	75.7	152.1
Fruit, berries, nuts	3.3	3.4	4.9	8.2
Sugar crops	1.3	3.2	2.2	9.3
Soybeans	13.8	0.0	50.3	0.0
Sunflower seeds	0.0	8.9	.7	10.8
Total crop acreage	336.4	364.9	332.9	528.4

Source: A Compendium of Papers, Joint Economic Committee, Congress of the United States, "Soviet Economic Prospects for the Seventies," 93rd Congress, 1st Session, June 27, 1973, *USSR Agricultural Situation,* Review of 1976 and Outlook for 1977, ERS, USDA, April 1977, and *Crop Production, 1976 Annual Summary,* Crop Reporting Board, SRS, USDA, 1977.

purchased in Russian restaurants is of poor quality. Also, while the Soviets produce more milk, the output per animal is less because of the breeds of animals used.

Levels of Technology. USSR technology lags far behind that of the United States. Soviet agriculture is typical of a developing nation's agriculture, that is, it is characterized by a high percentage of the labor force employed in farming, and by low levels of mechanization and mineral fertilizers used. This is a result of the low priority placed on agriculture over the years, and the inadequate agricultural background of most past Soviet leaders. Agriculture has received increasing attention as food problems have developed, but much more investment is needed to increase the productivity of agriculture.

Foreign Trade. Russia foreign trade has been increasing about 10 percent per year. Because of the Soviet need for Western technology

Table 13-4 Livestock Numbers

| | 1950 | | 1976 | |
	U.S.	USSR	U.S.	USSR
	----------millions of head----------			
Cattle	78	58	130	111
Cows	41	25	55	42
Hogs	59	22	50	58
Sheep and goats	32	94	15	147

Source: Economic Research Service, USDA.

and food, the increase in trade has been primarily with the West. The Soviet Union has been exporting crude oil and petroleum products, coal, coke, wood and wood products, cotton, metals, and diamonds to the West. Their imports from the West have included chemical equipment, automotive manufacturing equipment, steel and pipe, some consumer goods, and more recently, wheat and feedgrains.

The major events of 1972 were the proposed United States–Soviet Union trade agreement that was later rejected and the normalizing of relations with the Peoples' Republic of China. The American–USSR trade agreement called for a tripling of trade between 1973 and 1975. In 1972 the U.S. exported $547 million worth of goods to the USSR and imported $95 million.

United States agricultural trade with the Soviet Union before 1971–72 was relatively unimportant—United States exports to Russia consisted primarily of hides, skins, and almonds. However, with the easing of relationships, the removal of United States flag shipping requirements, and poor weather, Russia increased imports of feedgrains (corn), wheat, and soybeans. The value of United States agricultural exports to the USSR totaled $9 to $18 million between 1968–69 and 1970–71, increased to $157 million in 1971–72, and amounted to almost $2 billion in 1975–76 (Table 13-5). The USSR is also importing large amounts of wheat, corn, and raw sugar from countries other than the United States.

American imports from Russia are relatively insignificant. They amounted to $9 million in 1975–76. The primary imports are furs and skins, casein, and gelatin. Small amounts of mushrooms, essential oils, wine, and spices were also imported from the Soviet Union. The total agricultural exports of the USSR, as shown in Table 13-6, indicate that wheat and flour, barley, and cotton are their primary exports. Other exports include sunflower, vegetable oil, and groats.

Table 13-5 U.S. Agricultural Trade with the USSR,
1971-72—1975-76

Commodity	1971–72	1972–73	1973–74	1974–75	1975–76
	----------------million dollars----------------				
U.S. Exports to USSR:[a]					
Wheat	0.7	566.4	219.0	194.2	606.6
Coarse grains[b]	146.2	236.2	344.0	174.8	1,225.8
Corn	106.5	209.5	283.5	171.9	1,217.3
Other coarse grains	39.7	26.7	60.5	2.9	8.5
Soybeans	([c])	134.1	7.1	([c])	63.2
Cattle hides	6.5	8.3	3.2	8.1	1.8
Fruits, nuts, and berries	1.2	2.2	4.5	8.2	4.7
All others	2.4	7.2	7.0	24.4	27.0
Total	157.0	954.4	584.8	409.7	1,929.1
U.S. Imports from USSR:					
Furskins	2.7	3.6	3.4	3.5	4.9
Bristles	—	0.4	0.6	0.1	—
Gelatin	—	0.1	0.4	0.2	0.1
Casein and casein glue	—	—	0.4	2.5	1.6
All others	0.4	0.5	1.2	1.2	2.0
Total	3.1	4.6	6.0	7.5	8.6

Source: Economic Research Service, USDA.

Note: — means insignificant or none.

[a] Includes transshipments through Canada.
[b] Includes corn, rye, barley, oats, and sorghum.
[c] Less than $50,000.

USSR-US Grain Agreement. The governments of the USSR and the U.S. entered into a grain agreement in 1975. The purpose of the contract was to assure Russia a supply of grain and to indicate to U.S. producers the amount of grain the USSR would be purchasing. The agreement allows the USSR to purchase six million metric tons of wheat and corn in about equal proportions in each 12 month period between October 1, 1976 and September 30, 1981. The sales of U.S. grain would be from private commercial traders at prevailing market prices. The USSR may purchase an additional two million tons in any 12 month period unless the total grain supply in the U.S. falls below 225 million metric tons. Purchases of grain in excess of eight million tons per year can only be made after consultation with the U.S. government. This agreement covers only wheat and corn, permitting the USSR to purchase additional quantities of other U.S. grains such as barley, oats, and rice if needed.

Table 13-6 Principal Agricultural Exports, USSR, 1969–75

Commodities	1969	1970	1971	1972	1973	1974	1975
	------------------1000 metric tons------------------						
Grain:							
Total	7,205	5,698	8,640	4,560	4,853	7,030	3,578
Wheat	5,979	4,733	7,617	3,890	4,193	5,262	2,665
Barley	748	503	688	298	276	924	818
Corn	247	281	118	249	365	782	86
Rye	222	172	208	115	0	0	0
Oats	8	9	10	8	19	61	9
Flour	593	772	654	378	614	892	569
Groats	42	25	40	146	147	245	124
Pulses	422	65	150	55	47	58	50
Sugar, refined	1,081	1,079	1,002	50	43	95	53
Meat and meat products	98	55	35	60	75	56	44
Butter	74	73	24	16	18	18	20
Hides and skins[a]	3	2	1	1	([b])	([b])	([b])
Oilseed cake and meal	319	54	44	52	26	([c])	([c])
Sunflowerseed	345	143	84	74	73	63	61
Vegetable oils	696	372	408	423	371	513	416
Sunflower oil	656	351	379	394	342	481	388
Tea	13	10	11	12	12	14	17
Cotton, lint	452	516	547	652	728	739	800
Flax, tow	18	32	27	26	30	33	20
Starch	21	19	14	8	6	16	10

Source: Economic Research Service, USDA.

[a] Millions of hides and skins.
[b] Less than 500,000.
[c] Not reported.

The People's Republic of China

Another important command agricultural system is found in the People's Republic of China. Little is known about the agriculture of mainland China, but the normalizing of relations has made it possible to obtain some additional information about it.

In China, as in the Soviet Union, ownership of the land is held by the state on behalf of all the people. The land is divided into communes which may have as many as four- to five-thousand households.

The production team in each commune is the basic unit for agricultural production decisions, and for the distribution of farm income. A production team is composed of from 20- to 50- households. Production brigades made up of 8 to 12 production teams have the responsibility of farming a given land area and can requisition the inputs needed for production.

As in the Soviet Union, households are allocated private plots to farm. It has been estimated that five to seven percent of the arable land is allocated to these plots. Private plots are small gardens and provide only marginal additions to the general food supply.[17]

Agricultural plans or targets are formulated in the administrative structure. These administrative levels exist in the central government in Peking, in the provinces, in the counties, and in communes. Agricultural plans flow from the lower levels to higher levels, and vice versa.

Prices for state procurement are set by the government. Peasant markets do operate, however, that reflect "free" market prices. Even though production targets are set, the commune has considerable flexibility in adjusting the targeted delivery quotas. In 1973 about 30 percent of all grain produced was delivered to the state.[18]

Prices paid to farmers for foodgrains are the same throughout the country and these prices exceed the retail price. In fact, retail prices have been unchanged since 1950. Therefore, grain is heavily subsidized as procurement prices have doubled over this period.

A state monopoly, controlled by the ministry of foreign trade, handles all international transactions. China trades with about 100 countries, but its largest account is with Japan. American trade with China is very small but some experts believe that the United States has a potential to export chemicals, wheat, and fertilizers.[19] Basically, China is attempting to become self-sufficient in food production so that they will not have to rely on outside sources for much of their food supply.

Food production is increasing at a slightly more rapid rate than is population. Grain acreage has been increasing, multiple cropping is expanding, new varieties are being planted, and limited quantities of chemical fertilizers are applied to grain crops. In fact, grain production has been promoted at the expense of other crops. However, prices paid to farmers for grain are generally less than prices paid for other commercial crops. Subsidies are provided to communes for fertilizer, tractors, and fuels to encourage agricultural development.

---

[17]George E. Brandow, "Impressions of Chinese Agriculture: Viewing Flowers from Horseback in Winter," Department of Agricultural Economics and Rural Sociology, The Pennsylvania State University, A.E. 110, State University, Pa., March 1974, p. 11.
[18]Ibid., p. 8.
[19]U.S. Congress, Joint Economic Committee, "Economic Developments in Mainland China," 92nd Congress, 3rd Session, Washington, D.C., 1972.

Current agricultural plans emphasize capital investment in food production as well as in land and water management. Thus far, little progress has been made in these areas. Their plans also call for large production increases over the 1976 output. The size of the increases is a reflection of the unusually low production in 1976 due for the most part to adverse weather conditions. Two other factors also affected output, but to a lesser degree. The first was the death of national leaders causing a lack of direction as well as a possible shift

Table 13-7   Trade in Major Agricultural Commodities, People's Republic of China, 1971–76

Item	1971	1972	1973	1974	1975	1976[a]
	------------------------------1000 metric tons------------------------					
Total grain imports	3128	4642	7645	6790	3446	2140
From:						
Argentina	107	14	158[d]	735	172	—
Australia	33	—	768	1318	1352	900
Canada	2988	3687	2398	1772	1922	1100
United States[b]	—	941	4315	2759	—	—
Other	—	—	6	206	—	140[e]
Wheat imports	3021	4252	5987	5346	3339	2000
From:						
Argentina	—	—	—	145	65	—
Australia	33	—	768	1318	1352	900
Canada	2988	3687	2398	1772	1922	1100
United States[b]	—	565	2815	1905	—	—
Other	—	—	6	206	—	—
Corn imports	107	390	1626	1444	107	—
From:						
Argentina	107	14	126	590	107	—
United States[b]	—	376	1500	854	—	—
Rice exports	924	899	2142	1983	1440	1000
Soybean exports	460	370	310	340[a]	330[a]	200[a]
Soybean imports	—	2	255	619	36	25
Sugar imports[c]	464	749	736	411	235	N/A

Source: Economic Research Service, USDA.

Note: N/A means not available.
    — means none or negligible.

[a] Preliminary.
[b] Direct export plus transshipments through Canada.
[c] Raw value.
[d] Includes 32 thousand tons of sorghum.
[e] All rice.

in priorities. The second was the disruption caused by the several severe earthquakes which occurred during 1976.

U.S. agricultural trade with the Peoples' Republic of China resumed in late 1971 after 20 years of a trade embargo. In 1972, U.S. agricultural exports of grains and vegetable oil totaled $64 million. Our exports were needed to supplement domestic production and imports from other countries.

As shown in Table 13-7, China imported large amounts of wheat and corn in 1973 and 1974, with much of the wheat coming from Canada and Australia. In the years 1960–61 to 1964–65, China imported about four and one-half million tons of wheat compared to the eight million tons imported in 1973 and two million tons in 1976. In 1973, China signed long-term wheat agreements with Canada, Australia, and Argentina for grain to be delivered in the years from 1973 to 1977. However, China has not imported much grain from the U.S. since 1975, indicating the United States' role as a residual supplier of grain.

Summary

Most economies of the world are mixed. They have some characteristics of both capitalism and socialism. Capitalism is an unplanned, self-regulating system with no government involvement in private economic decisions. On the other hand, state socialism is an economic system with collective ownership of all productive resources with state-directed decision-making.

Soviet agriculture includes collective, state, and private plot farms. Collective and state farms are large compared to U.S. farms. The private plots are very small, but produce one-third of the total Russian agricultural output. Total agricultural production in Russia is not planned at all. What is planned is the amount of agricultural products which the state will buy from the farms at specific prices. When farms meet their delivery quotas, they can receive bonuses for additional output.

It appears that Russia is changing priorities. Consumer wants are receiving much more attention. Their increasingly affluent population desires better housing, personal automobiles, and a higher-quality diet.

Russian foreign trade has been increasing about 10 percent per year. They are exporting crude oil and petroleum products, coal, coke, wood, cotton, metals, and diamonds. Their imports include: chemical equipment; automotive manufacturing equipment; steel and pipe; consumer goods; and wheat and feedgrains.

U.S. agricultural trade opened with the Peoples' Republic of

China in 1971. China is importing grain and exporting rice and soybeans.

Chapter Highlights

1. The political philosophy of a nation determines the economic system within which agriculture operates.
2. The two general types of economic systems are capitalism and socialism.
3. The most prevalent system in the world is a mixture of capitalism and socialism.
4. The USSR and China are typical of socialistic or command economies.
5. Most of the agricultural output of the USSR and China comes from large scale communal farms.
6. Russia has three types of farms. These are collective, state, and private plot farms.
7. Private plot farms in the USSR account for only a small portion of total agricultural land, yet they produce one-third of the total agricultural output.
8. Increased attention is being given to agriculture in Russia because of their inability to meet domestic food desires.
9. Russia and China use five-year plans to provide production goals for agriculture.
10. Russia and China use quotas in planning the amounts of agricultural products their farms must deliver to the state.
11. Changes in priorities increasing food availability are as responsible as drought for the large increases in Soviet grain imports.
12. Russian planners are giving more attention to dietary improvements.
13. Increased output plus their grain imports have created new grain storage and processing requirements in the USSR.
14. Russian farms are very large by American standards.
15. Russian farms use much more labor per acre and are much less mechanized than American farms.
16. The performance of the Russian agricultural system is poor as compared with American agriculture.
17. The U.S. imports of Russian agricultural commodities are small, but our exports to them have grown to about $2 billion.
18. U.S. exports of wheat and corn to Russia are governed by the 1975 grain agreement.
19. The Peoples' Republic of China has patterned its agricultural industry similar to that of the USSR.
20. Current Chinese agricultural trade is with Canada, Australia, and Argentina.

Review Questions

1. What is the difference between capitalism and socialism? Do most countries have a pure economic system?

2. What is a collective farm? What is a state farm? How do collective and state farms in Russia differ from family farms in the United States?
3. Is Soviet agriculture planned? Describe the structure of their planning system.
4. Why is the Soviet Union importing American grain? Have their priorities changed?
5. The Soviet Union has been interested in increasing foreign trade with Western countries. What do they want? What do we get in exchange?
6. What are the provisions of the USSR–U.S. grain agreement? Is this grain agreement of any benefit to the United States?
7. Describe the structure of Chinese agriculture. Does it resemble the structure of agriculture in the USSR?
8. Why did the Peoples' Republic of China stop purchasing grain from the United States in 1975? Why did they sign long-term wheat agreements with Canada, Australia, and Argentina?

Suggested Readings

1. Bornstein, Morris and Daniel R. Fusfeld, eds. *The Soviet Economy: A Book of Readings,* 4th ed. Homewood, Ill.: Richard D. Irwin, Inc., 1974, Parts 1, 2, and 5.
2. Brandow, G. E. "Impressions of Chinese Agriculture: Viewing Flowers from Horseback in Winter," Department of Agricultural Economics and Rural Sociology, The Pennsylvania State University, A.E. 110, State University, Pa., March 1974.
3. Economic Research Service, USDA, "USSR Agricultural Stiuation," Foreign Agricultural Economic Report (annual), Washington, D.C.
4. International Conference of Agricultural Economists. *Agriculture of the Soviet Union.* Moscow: Mir Publishers, 1970.
5. Joint Economic Committee, Congress of the United States, "Soviet Economic Prospects for the Seventies," 93rd Congress, 1st Session, June 27, 1973.
6. McConnell, Campbell R. *Economics,* 4th ed. New York: McGraw-Hill Book Company, 1969, Chapter 44.
7. Nove, Alex. *The Soviet Economy.* New York: Frederick A. Praeger, Inc., 1965.

14

Courtesy of the Port of Seattle.

INTERNATIONAL
ECONOMICS

INTERNATIONAL ECONOMICS

International trade is the exchange of goods and services between countries. It occurs because a country is able to purchase goods abroad more cheaply than it can produce them at home. The result of trade is to increase a country's level of living.

Many people have difficulty in understanding international trade, but if we start from the premise that, in principle, international trade is no different than interregional trade (trade within a nation), its workings and value are more easily understood. There are some differences, of course, such as currencies, monetary systems, language, space, and national policies, but basically international and interregional trade are the same.

Within the United States, people take for granted trade between states or regions. For instance, trade with California for citrus products or with Michigan for automobiles is accepted. Most people recognize that a higher level of living is possible when each area specializes in producing those items in which it is relatively proficient and then exchanges some of its output for some of the output of other areas. For example, Montana exchanges wheat, barley, and beef calves for processed food from California and farm inputs from the Midwest.

On the other hand, when it comes to the international exchange of goods and services, many people fail to see any advantage to specialization and trade. However, because of differences in a country's resources, it is possible to produce products at different costs and prices which is crucial to trade and allows for increased levels of living for all participants.

Endowments of factors of production differ substantially from country to country and are significant in determining the types of economic activities in various areas of the world. The classical factors of production are land, capital, labor, and management. Since every country has varying amounts of these factors, each country has different advantages in producing products. Therefore, products requiring large amounts of labor in the production process should be produced in countries where labor is abundant, relative to other factors of production, and where wage rates are low, relative to the cost of other factors of production. One would expect that country to export labor intensive goods to other countries where labor is relatively scarce and wage rates are relatively high. This thesis holds true for other products that use substantial amounts of other factors of production as well.

Basis for Foreign Trade

The underlying proposition of foreign trade is that consumers benefit from the exchange of goods and services. Specialization increases the supply of goods and services available. To illustrate this point and to show that trade is beneficial, let's examine a simple example.

Assume a two-country world—the United States and the European Economic Community (EC)—and two commodities, wheat and wine. Also, assume that all factors of production are categorized under one input called labor, of which the total quantity is fixed.

	Output (Amount Produced)		
	Wheat (bu)		Wine (gal)
A U.S. day's labor will produce	20	or	5
A EC day's labor will produce	4	or	12

In this example it is obvious that America can produce wheat more cheaply than the EC because it gets a larger output with a day of labor service (20 bushels compared to 4). The EC can produce wine more cheaply since with the same amount of labor input they can produce 12 gallons of wine compared with 5 gallons for the United States. Therefore, one can say that the United States has an absolute advantage in the production of wheat and the EC has an absolute advantage in wine production.

If the United States and EC practice self-sufficiency, dividing their labor service in the production of both commodities equally, the United States could produce 10 bushels of wheat and 2.5 gallons of wine, while the EC could produce 2 bushels of wheat and 6 gallons of wine. The total world output would be 12 bushels of wheat and 8.5 gallons of wine. But if both countries specialize, they could produce 20 bushels of wheat and 12 gallons of wine, a gain of

8 bushels of grain and 3.5 gallons of wine. For these countries to benefit, they must trade.

It is easy to show that trade is beneficial if each country has an absolute advantage. What happens if one country has an absolute advantage in the production of all goods and services? Trade is still beneficial to both countries. Given the same assumptions as above, but with outputs changed as follows:

	Output *(Amount Produced)*		
	Wheat *(bu)*		*Wine* *(gal)*
A U.S. day's labor will produce	18	or	3
A EC day's labor will produce	2	or	1

From this example, one can see that the United States has an absolute advantage in the production of wheat (18:2 or 9:1) and in wine (3:1). The example also shows that even though America has an *absolute advantage* in the production of both commodities, it has a *relative* (or *comparative*) *advantage* in wheat (9:1) as compared to wine (3:1).

Assume that the United States specializes in wheat and the EC in wine. Before trade opens between the two areas, six bushels of wheat are worth a gallon of wine in the United States (18:3 or 6:1); in the EC, two bushels of wheat exchange for a gallon of wine. The domestic exchange ratio in the United States is 6:1, while in the EC it is 2:1. We know the United States will produce wheat; one bushel is worth 1/6 gallon of wine in the U.S. If the bushel of wheat was sold to the EC, it would procure ½ gallon of wine. Therefore, rather than getting ⅙ gallon of wine without trade, it is possible to get ½ gallon of wine with trade, and thus trade makes the U.S. consumers better off.

Since trade must be beneficial to both participants in order for it to occur, let's look at the situation from the viewpoint of the EC. With a gallon of wine, the EC can sell it domestically for two bushels of wheat, or, if they engage in trade with the United States, for six bushels of wheat. Therefore, they will produce wine. You can see that it pays the EC to specialize in wine production and America to specialize in wheat, and then trade, even though the United States has an absolute advantage in the production of both commodities.

It is *comparative advantage* that provides the basis for foreign trade. The law of comparative advantage states that "a country will

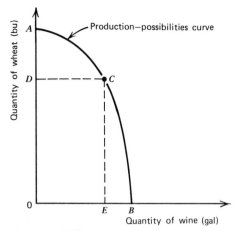

Figure 14-1. Production possibilities curve.

gain economically if it concentrates its efforts in those economic activities where it has the greatest relative advantage or the least relative disadvantage, and then trades with other countries."[1] In the foregoing example, the United States had its greatest relative advantage in the production of wheat and the EC had its least relative disadvantage in wine production.

Putting Trade Theory Together. Land, labor, capital, and management can be used to produce wheat or wine along what is called the "production-possibilities curve," which is shown in Figure 14-1.

If all resources are used to produce wheat, the United States could produce 0A bushels, whereas, if they produced only wine they could produce 0B gallons. It is also possible to produce some wheat and some wine at point C (or at any point along the curve AB). At this point, the United States can produce 0D bushels of wheat and 0E gallons of wine. It can be seen that the resources of the United States are better suited to producing wheat. The production-possibilities curve, however, only shows what is *possible* to produce, given the resource base and existing technology. How much is actually produced of each commodity also depends on the demand for these products. It is the demand and supply for commodities that determine their prices, and hence, comparative advantage. Before we analyze demand, however, let us look at the producer's position.

Maximizing Profits to Producers. Producers are in business to make a profit. If we assume a competitive industry, prices are fixed to the

[1]Walter Krause, *International Economics,* Boston: Houghton Mifflin Company, 1965, p. 11.

individual producers. The producer accepts the market price as given. If the market price of wheat is $2 per bushel and the price of wine is $8 per gallon, the relative prices may be represented in our diagram below, by isorevenue lines (Figure 14-2). These lines show the various combinations of wheat and wine which given the producer the same total revenue.

Isorevenue line I shows the various combinations of wheat and wine which will produce a revenue of $40. A revenue of $40 is possible by selling 20 bushels of wheat at $2 per bushel; or 5 gallons of wine at $8 per gallon; or 10 bushels of wheat at $2 per bushel *and* 2½ gallons of wine at $8 per gallon. Since market prices are fixed, isorevenue lines parallel and to the right of I, such as II, represent larger total revenues. Isorevenue line II represents a revenue of $80. Producers want to maximize their revenue for a given production possibilities curve and that point is shown at C where Isorevenue line III is tangent to the production-possibilities curve, producing 0D bushels of wheat and 0E gallons of wine.

Changes in the market price of commodities will cause changes in the amount of each product that will be produced. For example, in the previous illustration, the price of wine was $8 per gallon and the price of grain was $2 per bushel. If the market price of wine drops to $4 per gallon, the slope of the isorevenue line becomes flatter (Figure 14-3). A decrease in the price of wine would cause

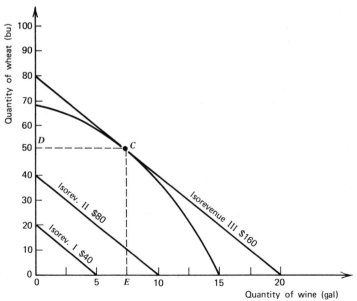

Figure 14-2. Isorevenue lines and production possibilities.

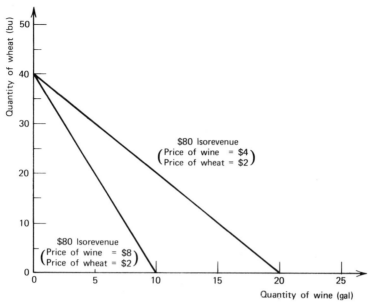

Figure 14-3. Isorevenue line showing a decrease in the price of wine.

producers to increase their production of wheat, the higher priced product, and reduce their production of wine as shown in Figure 14-4. In the initial equilibrium, firms were producing $0A$ bushels of grain and $0B$ gallons of wine. With the decrease in the price of wine, the isorevenue line becomes flatter (grain becomes relatively more profitable) so producers will increase their grain output from $0A$ to $0C$ and decrease their production of wine from $0B$ to $0D$.

Prices Determine Production and Consumption.   As producers attempt to maximize profits from their expenditures in the production process, consumers also attempt to maximize utility or satisfaction given the amount of money income that they earn from selling their labor services, or from rent from their owned resources. Economics represents consumer tastes and preferences by indifference curves which show the various combinations of goods or services that will yield equal satisfaction. An individual consumer has an entire indifference map, with indifference curves farther out from the origin showing higher levels of utility. Referring to Figure 14-5, I_0 may represents 50 units of utility, with I_1 representing 80 units of utility. The steepness or the flatness along the indifference curve indicates the preferences of consumers. Where the curve is steep, the consumer is willing to give up much grain for a unit of wine; and where

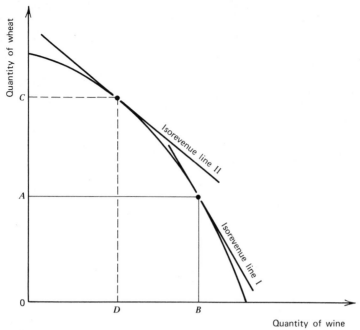

Figure 14-4. Change in equilibrium because of a change in the price of wine.

the curve is flat, the consumer is willing to give up only a small amount of grain for a unit of wine because the consumer has a lot of wine, and relatively little grain.

A consumer maximizes utility, given money income, in much the same way a producer maximizes profits. We represent the con-

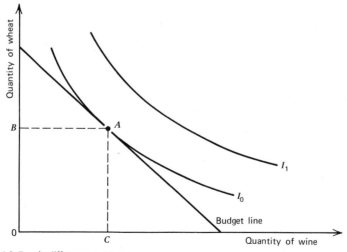

Figure 14-5. Indifference curves.

sumer's spending possibilities with a "budget line," in which the slope is determined by the market prices of the goods being bought (Figure 14-5). The budget line shows all the combinations of two goods the consumer may buy with the given money income.

Let's use the same pair of goods as above (wheat and wine) to demonstrate the principle of optimizing satisfactions. Our consumer may buy only wheat, only wine, or any combination of wheat or wine along the budget line. Given money income and market prices, the consumer tries to get to the highest indifference curve possible. Consumers are in equilibrium when the budget line is tangent to the highest indifference curve at point A. In equilibrium, the consumer is buying $0B$ of wheat and $0C$ of wine.

To arrive at a general equilibrium solution as to what will be produced and consumed, we must go from the individual to an indifference curve for a nation. This causes problems because the utility that people derive from consuming different amounts, or even the same amounts, of the same commodity varies from individual to individual. If we trade grain for wine, the wine drinkers are made better off, but the cereal lovers are made worse off. We simplify the exposition by assuming the tastes of a community can be described in the same way as the tastes of an individual.

Under these assumptions, a nation without trade is in equilibrium where the community indifference curve is tangent to the production-possibilities curve and the isorevenue line is tangent to

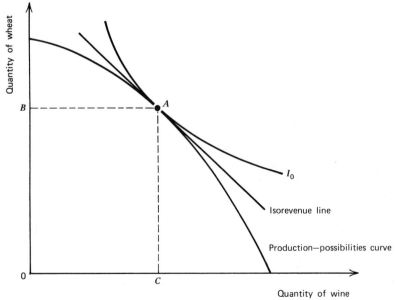

Figure 14-6. General equilibrium of a country without trade.

both, at point *A* in Figure 14-6. The nation is in equilibrium producing and consuming 0*B* bushels of wheat and 0*C* gallons of wine.

How Trade Makes Nations "Better-Off."   Now if we assume the United
States has a comparative advantage in wheat and the EC in wine, the
production possibilities will have the shape as in Figure 14-7. Before
trade, the isorevenue line (*BT*) will be steep in the United States
reflecting the high price of wine relative to grain since the United
States can produce a large amount of grain. The isorevenue line
(*BT'*) in the EC will be relatively flat reflecting the low price of wine
since wine is plentiful.

After trade, ignoring transportation and handling charges, the
prices of grain and wine should equalize in the two areas. Prices tend
to equalize because the United States will export grain and its price
will increase because available domestic supply has been reduced.
Supplies of grain have increased in the importing country and
therefore the price of grain should fall. Also, the EC will export wine
to the United States, which will increase its price in the EC and
decrease its price in the United States. The after trade isorevenue
lines are shown by *AT* and *AT'* which have the same slope. Because
market prices change after trade opens, the production of grains increases in the United States from 0*F* to 0*F'* and the production of
wine falls from 0*W* to 0*W'*. In the EC, the production of grain falls

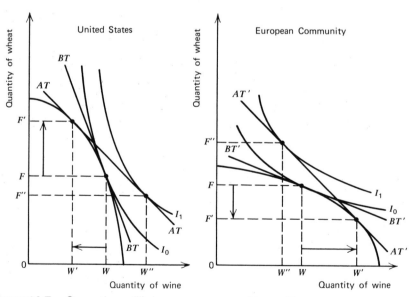

Figure 14-7. General equilibrium among countries with
trade.

from $0F$ to $0F'$ and the production of wine increases from $0W$ to $0W'$.

Consumers were in equilibrium before trade consuming all that was originally produced. Now that trade has taken place, consumers reach a higher indifference curve, I_1 rather than I_0 (Figure 14-7). Consumers in the United States are consuming $0F''$ of grain after trade and $0W''$ gallons of wine, while the EC is consuming $0F'''$ bushels of grain and $0W'''$ gallons of wine. After trade the United States produces $0F'$ and consumes only $0F''$ bushels of grain so it exports F' to F'' bushels of grain to the EC. The EC produces $0F'$ and consumes $0F'''$ bushels of grain. To do this it imports F' to F''' bushels of grain that equals the amount the United States exported. Thus, exports equal imports. The EC produces $0W'$ gallons of wine, but consumes only $0W'''$ gallons of wine and exports the difference (W' to W'') to the United States. The United States consumes $0W''$ gallons of wine but produces only $0W'$ and thus imports W' to W'' gallons from the EC.

The important concept is that international trade occurs because of differences in the prices of products in the two countries before trade. Consumers benefit by being able to consume more goods and services than the resources of a country could produce, allowing them to attain a higher level of satisfaction. It is important to remember that the goal of any production is to increase satisfaction (utility).

Many countries set up barriers to trade in order to "protect" a domestic industry, but which really negate the benefits of trade. Most barriers are detrimental to consumers but beneficial to special interest groups which use political pressure to maintain their market position. Because tariffs are determined by Congress, the tariff system in the United States reflects a variety of political interests.

What's Wrong With Trade Barriers?   The major purpose of a trade barrier is to reduce the volume of imports into a country. There are two general types which are used widely in the world. These are tariffs and import quotas. A tariff is a tax levied on a commodity when it crosses a national boundary. An import quota restricts the volume of imports by setting a maximum amount which can be imported.

In the early days, tariffs were imposed primarily as a source of revenue to finance federal government operations, but as mentioned, they are presently used to protect domestic industries from foreign competition. Two types of tariffs are used. One is an *ad valorem duty* and the second is a *specific duty*. The *ad valorem* tax is a fixed percentage of the value of the commodity. For example, poultry liver in the EC is taxed at 14 percent of its value. A specific duty is a tax which is a fixed sum of money per unit of commodity, such as $50 per imported motorcycle.

Import quotas have been employed in U.S. agricultural programs. For example, under these programs, the U.S. restricted the volume of wheat imported to 800,000 bushels. These limits were, of course, below what would be imported under free market conditions, or there would be no need to impose a quota. The United States uses quotas only to protect those agricultural industries which have been involved in domestic agricultural programs, and other countries use similar devices. Most underdeveloped countries use quotas on all products, but the only developed country where quotas are prevalent is Japan.

What is the Economic Effect of Tariffs and Quotas?

Most students feel that if a tariff is imposed by an importing country, this tax is passed on to consumers in the form of a price increase for the commodity. This is only partially true. Depending on the price elasticities of demand and supply for the commodity, part of the tax is paid by the consumers in the importing country in terms of higher prices and part is absorbed by the exporting country in terms of a lower world price.

As an example, let us assume that the United States puts a 10 cent per pound specific tariff on bananas from Central and South America as shown in Figure 14-8. This figure shows that at a price of $.20 per pound, U.S. consumers will purchase a million tons. Once the tariff is imposed, the price of bananas increases to 25 cents per pound because the supply curve shifts from SS to $S'S'$.[2] Given the demand curve for bananas, the increase in price forces consumers to consume a smaller quantity. They will switch to substitute products such as oranges or apples, while cutting consumption of bananas. This causes a reduction in the world demand and a reduction in the world price to $.15 per pound. In this case where the supply and demand elasticities are approximately equal, about 5 cents of the 10 cent tariff is passed on to consumers and 5 cents is passed back to banana producers in terms of a lower world price. Thus, the exporters are forced by the market system to pay part of the tax the United States imposed.

The distribution of the burden between importing and exporting countries is not the same in all cases because it depends on the

---

[2]The demand curve could have been shifted instead. The economic results are the same.

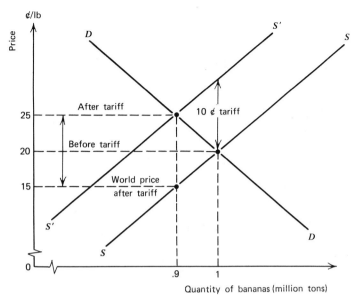

Figure 14-8. The economic impact of a tariff.

elasticities of supply and demand and the market power of the country imposing the tariff. In the example just mentioned, the world price fell because the United States consumes a large part of the bananas from Central and South America. If a small nation accounting for only a small share of world imports imposes a tariff, then only a slight reduction in consumption would result, and there would be only a small impact on the world price of the commodity.

The economic effects of an import quota are shown in Figure 14-9. In this illustration assume that all of this product is being supplied by foreign producers. The demand and supply[3] curves intersect at a price of P_0 and the equilibrium quantity taken of Q_0. If the quota is effective and sets an absolute limit on imports, the new supply curve (S') is vertical at that physical limit ($0Q$) and the price increases to P_1. Quotas restrict the amount of a commodity consumers can purchase and, thus, force consumers to pay a higher price. This action causes consumers to switch to less desirable substitute commodities, while domestic producers of substitute commodities expand their output under the quota protection, using resources drawn from more efficient industries.

Domestic Effects of a Tariff or Quota. To analyze the domestic effects of a tariff imposed by a country, let us make two assumptions. First,

[3]This supply curve (S_f) includes only foreign supplies.

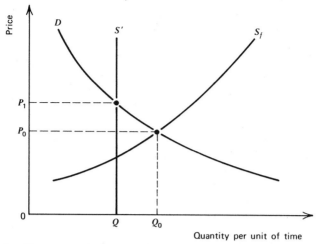

Figure 14-9. The economic impact of a quota.

assume the country is small so that it does not influence world prices by its actions; and second, assume this country can import all the products it wants at the prevailing world market price (Figure 14-10).

Before trade occurs, this country is producing quantity Q_0 at a market price of P_0 where its demand and domestic supply curves intersect. After free trade, the new supply curve is $S_d + S_f$ because at the world price this country can purchase all it wants. The demand curve and the "new" supply curve intersect at quantity Q_1 so consumers in this importing country increase their consumption under free trade from Q_0 to Q_1 and purchase this larger quantity at price P_1. At price P_1 domestic producers supply only $0Q_2$ of the market and foreign suppliers provide Q_2 to Q_1. Thus the benefits of free trade are obvious. The consumers get more of the product at lower prices through trade than they would get through domestic production.

Assume a tariff is imposed in the amount of T (or P_1 to P_2). This tax raises the free trade price by the amount of the tariff to $S_d + S_f + T$. Now the supply curve intersects the demand curve at P_2 so the price increases by the amount of the tariff. Consumers reduce consumption to Q_3 and domestic producers increase output to Q_4. This tariff reduces imports from (Q_2 to Q_1) to (Q_4 to Q_3).

Because of the tariff, the loss to consumers is area P_2BFP_1. Area P_1P_2AC is redistributed to producers. This increase in producer earnings is why you read about industries wanting tariff protection; American cattle producers want to keep out New Zealand and Australian beef, and most major manufacturing firms also wish to re-

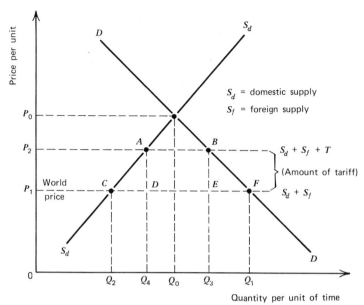

Figure 14-10. Domestic effects of tariffs or quotas.

strict foreign competition. This redistribution of income from consumers to producers is called the *redistribution effect* of the tariff.

Area *ADEB* is called the *revenue effect* of a tariff. This loss to the consumer goes to the government in the form of tax collections. Area *ADEB* is equal to the amount of tariff (P_1 to P_2) times the amount imported, which is quantity (Q_4 to Q_3).

Triangle *ACD* is called the *protective effect* of a tariff. It is the loss to the consumer due to the fact that producers must withdraw resources from other sectors of the economy to increase output from Q_2 to Q_4. Using these resources in this protected sector causes a reduction in productive efficiency and it is a real loss to the economy. The same is true for triangle *BEF*. This *consumption effect* is also a loss to the consumer that is a residual not accounted for by the other effects.

The *domestic effect* of a quota is the same as that given for a tariff if the quota is Q_4 to Q_3. Rather than having a revenue effect, area *ADEB* does not go to the government, but to the importing firm. This revenue is referred to as monopoly profit.

With respect to economic efficiency, quotas are much more harmful than tariffs in general. With tariffs, the domestic price can never exceed the world price by more than the tax. With a quota, on the other hand, any increase in domestic demand must cause the domestic price to rise because the amount of imports cannot be increased. Thus, there is no limit to the difference that can exist between the domestic and world price of that commodity.

Arguments for Protection. Many arguments are given as reasons why Congress should protect some special interest groups. These arguments run from national security, balance of payments, infant industry, to cheap foreign labor, and numerous other reasons. The most reasonable argument is the infant industry case that states that when a young industry starts business, it takes a few years to grow and develop its markets internationally and to exploit its economies of a scale so that it can be competitive. This argument has appeal, but the U.S. steel industry unsuccessfully tried this argument on Congress in the 1960s.

A Move Toward Freer Trade. The issue of tariffs in America has always been mixed with national politics and its economic aspects have been confused by the activities of pressure groups. From 1789 until the Hawley-Smoot Tariff of 1930, the U.S. tariffs were very protective. Since 1934, the United States has been attempting a program of orderly tariff reductions, except for the mixed mood of the country because of the balance of payments problems beginning in 1971.

Two main approaches have been used in the last 30 years to liberalize trade. One is the international approach under the General Agreement on Tariffs and Trade (GATT), and the second is a regional approach.[4] This latter approach is illustrated by organizations such as the EC where a number of countries agree to liberalize trade between themselves, but maintain common and uniform tariffs against others.

International Approach. GATT, an international organization, came into being in 1948. For the United States to participate in reciprocal tariff negotiations under GATT, enabling legislation must pass through Congress. In the past, the U.S. has participated in GATT negotiations under the authority of the Trade Agreements Act of 1934 and its extensions, the Trade Expansion Act of 1962 and the Trade Act of 1974.

GATT's membership presently includes 76 nations and these nations are responsible for about 80 percent of the world's trade. The basic purpose of GATT is to serve as a vehicle to handle multilateral tariff negotiations among its members by establishing rules, regulations, and principles to govern the conduct of trade. Its three

[4]Mordechai E. Kreinin, *International Economics: A Policy Approach,* 2nd ed. New York: Harcourt Brace Jovanovich, 1975, p. 307.

main features are: (1) provision for equal treatment among all parties (all countries receive unconditional most-favored-nation treatment which means that any concession one country grants to another it must also grant to all other GATT countries); (2) provision for eliminating quantity restrictions to trade except when a country is having balance of payments difficulties; and (3) provision for members to hold meetings to discuss and settle trade problems.

The United States has participated in two major GATT negotiations. In 1961 they participated in what was called the "Dillon Round" and, from 1962 to 1967, in what was called the "Kennedy Round."

Regional Approach.   Customs unions, common markets, and free trade areas are types of regional integration. A "custom union" is an economic and political organization between two or more countries abolishing trade restrictions among themselves and establishing a common and uniform tariff to outsiders. A "free trade area" is the same as a customs union except there is no common and uniform tariff imposed on those excluded from the union. Likewise, a "common market" is the same as a customs union, except that it includes the free mobility of factors of production.

Some of the customs unions which have been formed are located in Europe and Central and South America. The EC was established in 1959 and originally included West Germany, Italy, France, Belgium, the Netherlands, and Luxembourg. In 1973, it was expanded to include Great Britain, Ireland, and Denmark. There are 18 African countries now associated with the EC and several candidate nations in the Mediterranean area which receive preferential tariff treatment.

The European Free Trade Association (EFTA) contains the nations of Austria, Norway, Portugal, Sweden, and Switzerland, with Finland as an associate member. While the EC and EFTA are the organizations most people have heard of, there are also two such organizations in Central and South America. The Latin American Free Trade Association was formed in 1961 and includes Argentina, Bolivia, Brazil, Chile, Colombia, Ecuador, Mexico, Paraguay, Peru, Uruguay, and Venezuela. The other customs union is the Central American Common Market existing between the nations of Costa Rica, El Salvador, Guatemala, Honduras, and Nicaragua. These two organizations are merging into one union called the Latin American Common Market.

While regional integration reduces tariff barriers between those countries inside the organization, it does not necessarily provide economic benefits to these countries. The economic effects of integration on resource efficiency of the nations involved may be positive or negative.

The benefits of a regional organization are called *trade creation*. Trade creation is generated when the output of any given product shifts from a country, in which the cost to produce that item is high, to a participating country with lower production costs. The benefit to the consumers in the regional association is that they are now able to buy more imports at a lower price. *Trade diversion* may also occur within an association if a country changes its trade to purchase a particular good from a high-cost intraunion source rather than from a low-cost external source as before. To determine whether an economic union makes a country better off, one must determine whether trade creation offsets trade diversion. Each case must be investigated separately.

Agricultural Trade of the United States

Because of excess capacity in agriculture in the United States, the export market has been important for the agricultural sector. In the past, the export market has been a place to dump surplus production, but with the recent changes in the demand for agricultural commodities it appears that agribusiness firms will have an opportunity to sell more of their output in foreign markets. This is especially relevant if worldwide food shortages continue to exist, and production controls on U.S. agriculture are not needed to maintain farm income.

In 1976, agricultural exports amounted to 20 percent of all merchandise exports of the United States. In the last 10 years, the United States has made great strides in developing foreign markets for feedgrains in the EC and wheat and soybeans in Japan. The large fluctuations in the export demand for agricultural commodities make it difficult for American farmers to establish consistent production patterns. Since 1960, the value of U.S. agricultural exports increased from $5.9 billion to $23.0 billion. With the very inelastic demand and supply curves in the short-run for farm products at the farm level, large fluctuations in demand cause large changes in agricultural prices and income. When wheat exports fell between 1976 and 1977, prices received by farmers dropped 70 cents per bushel. This decrease in price was a direct result of the increase in wheat production in the United States that occurred in an attempt to meet expected export demand.

There has been much discussion about a strategic food reserve system to stabilize grain flows to the market and to reduce price instability. This is being considered by the United Nation's Food and Agricultural Organization. In addition, a strategic reserve is being considered by the U.S. Congress. These types of programs would establish an organization to purchase and store commodities for future consumption. The major problem with this type of arrangement concerns the guidelines established to determine when reserves are to be released. Reserves would probably be adjusted to dampen price fluctuations. Producers and consumers would disagree on the price level at which stocks should be placed on the market. Much debate over the issue of reserves will continue for years to come.

Exports. Table 14-1 shows U.S. agricultural exports from 1964 to 1976 by individual products. Feedgrains and wheat continue to be the largest components of exports over this period. Soybeans rank third and cotton fourth of the major agricultural exports. Cotton and tobacco, once very important, are still significant, but grains and preparations, oilseeds, animals, and animal products now dominate exports.

At present, 24 percent of U.S. farm cash receipts are derived from the export market. In terms of 1976 crop production, the United States exported about 55 percent of the wheat crop, 51 percent of the soybean crop, 27 percent of the corn crop, 31 percent of the grain sorghum crop, and about 27 percent of the rice crop (Figure 14-11).

Asia and Western Europe are the largest markets for U.S. agricultural exports (Table 14-2). Asia has been increasing its imports of rice, wheat, soybeans, and feedgrains. In 1973, Japan became our first three billion dollar agricultural customer, becoming the largest single importer of U.S. farm products. Also, it was the first year in which Asia took significantly more products than Western Europe. However, this situation reversed itself in 1976.

As seen by Table 14-2, trade with the Soviet Union and Eastern Europe has increased considerably after 1973. In 1976, Russia spent almost $1.5 billion and Eastern Europe $900 million, primarily on grains. One must remember, however, that the centrally planned economies have a great desire to maintain their self-sufficiency for reasons of national security and to insulate themselves from the problems of the capitalistic system.

Foreign trade in command economies is nationalized and conducted by state trading organizations. These countries conduct trade to import what they consider to be essential. Thus, exports are not considered to be an end in and of themselves, but a financial means to obtain foreign exchange with which to purchase imports.

Table 14-1 U.S. Agricultural Exports: Value by Commodity, Calendar Years 1964–76 (Millions of Dollars)

Commodity	1964	1966	1968	1970[a]	1972	1973	1974	1975	1976[b]
Animals and animal products:									
Dairy products[c]	211	114	131	127	150	60	76	148	142
Fats, oils, and greases	250	192	152	247	209	333	585	360	443
Hides and skins, excluding furskins	93	154	121	187	292	375	337	293	518
Meats and meat products	115	107	118	132	204	374	301	432	617
Poultry products[d]	74	67	57	56	90	120	138	158	262
Other	84	75	82	101	170	323	339	302	398
Total animals and animal products	827	709	661	850	1,115	1,585	1,776	1,693	2,380
Cotton, excluding linters	682	432	459	372	503	928	1,335	991	1,049
Fruits and preparations	277	314	275	334	429	535	596	699	770
Grains and preparations:									
Feed grains, excluding products	854	1,331	923	1,064	1,522	3,539	4,646	5,239	5,978
Rice, milled	206	230	348	314	388	431	754	614	475
Wheat and flour	1,532	1,534	1,100	1,111	1,452	4,154	4,589	5,293	4,041
Other	75	97	97	107	122	357	322	474	381
Total grains and preparations	2,667	3,192	2,468	2,596	3,484	8,481	10,311	11,620	10,875

Oilseeds and products:									
Cottonseed and soybean oils	210	154	107	244	241	237	695	466	368
Soybeans	567	767	810	1,228	1,508	2,762	3,537	2,865	3,315
Protein meal	145	227	262	358	434	985	999	672	899
Other	86	93	101	91	225	324	478	449	488
Total oilseeds and products	1,008	1,241	1,280	1,921	2,408	4,308	5,709	4,452	5,070
Tobacco, unmanufactured	413	482	524	517	672	714	886	877	939
Vegetables and preparations	169	188	182	206	257	373	473	504	674
Other	305	323	379	463	533	755	913	1,058	1,238
Total Exports	6,348	6,881	6,228	7,259	9,401	17,680	21,999	21,893	22,995

Source: Foreign Agricultural Trade of the United States, Economic Research Service, USDA, February 1977.

[a] Beginning January 1970 export values include small amounts of commodities formerly classified as nonagricultural.
[b] Preliminary.
[c] Includes some additional commodities starting in 1971.
[d] Includes live poultry starting in 1971.

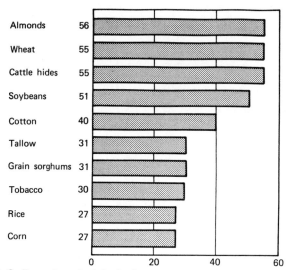

(*Source:* U. S. Department of Agriculture,
Economic Research Service for year ending June 30.)

Figure 14-11. Ten leading U.S. agricultural exports, as percentages of farm production, 1976.

When the Soviet Union has a crop failure, they occasionally tighten their belts. Recently they have, instead, come into the market, as they did in 1972 when they purchased 400 million bushels of wheat from the U.S., popularly called the "Russian Grain Deal." Also, the Peoples' Republic of China imported about 6.2 million tons of grain in 1972–73 including 5.4 million tons of wheat and 800,000 tons of corn. In 1976–77 China was expected to import 3.7 million tons of grain, mostly wheat. China usually signs long-term wheat import agreements with Canada and Australia. China's method of payment has been from her rice exports.

Imports. The United States increased its agricultural imports in 1976 (Table 14-3). Imports rose 18 percent over 1975 to $11 billion. The major imports were coffee, meat and meat products, and sugar. Most of the U.S. import trade has been with Brazil.

Agricultural Trade Balance

Although the trade balance is not always an important figure, you will find it in many publications and its meaning should be under-stood. The balance of trade is the value of exports (goods) minus value of imports (goods). If this figure is positive, it is said a country has a "favorable balance of trade"; if this figure is negative (imports

Table 14-2   U.S. Agricultural Exports by Regions,
Calendar Years 1973–76 (Millions of Dollars)

Region[a]	1973	1974	1975	1976[b]	Change[c] (%)
Western Europe	5,605	7,029	7,155	7,882	+ 10
Enlarged EC	4,526	5,504	5,564	6,422	+ 15
Other Western Europe	1,079	1,525	1,591	1,459	− 8
Eastern Europe and USSR[d]	1,498	927	1,752	2,414	+ 38
USSR	920	300	1,133	1,487	+ 31
Eastern Europe	577	627	619	927	+ 50
Asia	6,509	8,357	7,622	7,582	− 1
West Asia	521	1,262	1,160	883	−24
South Asia	564	835	1,293	1,040	−20
Southeast Asia, excluding Japan & PRC	1,851	2,128	2,008	2,096	+ 4
Japan	2,998	3,479	3,082	3,563	+16
Peoples' Republic of China (PRC)	575	653	80	[e]	—
Latin America	1,692	2,565	2,279	1,942	− 15
Canada, excluding transshipments	1,034	1,282	1,305	1,497	+ 15
Canadian transshipments	677	552	503	381	− 24
Africa	583	1,138	1,157	1,179	+ 2
North Africa	307	713	768	706	− 8
Other Africa	276	425	388	473	+ 22
Oceania	83	149	110	119	+ 8
Total[f]	17,680	21,999	21,884	22,995	+ 5

Source: Foreign Agricultural Trade of the United States, Economic Research Service, USDA, February 1977.

[a] Not adjusted for transshipments.
[b] Preliminary.
[c] Value change from 1975 to 1976 computed from unrounded data.
[d] Includes Yugoslavia.
[e] Less than $500,000.
[f] Totals may not add due to rounding.

greater than exports), a country is said to have an "unfavorable balance of trade." This unfortunate terminology came from the Mercantilist period (approximately 1500 to 1750). During this era, countries thought it was desirable to have an export trade surplus in order to accumulate gold and other precious metals which they thought were measures of wealth. It was Adam Smith who pointed out in his *Wealth of Nations* in 1776 that goods rather than gold are the true wealth of a nation. Smith demonstrated that through division of labor, specialization, and free trade, benefits in terms of

Table 14-3 U.S. Agricultural Imports: Value by Commodity, Calendar Years 1964–76 (Millions of Dollars)

Commodity	1964	1966	1968	1970	1972	1973	1974	1975	1976[a]
Complementary[b]									
Bananas, fresh	127	179	182	188	186	193	201	224	282
Cocoa beans	131	122	136	201	151	212	316	324	358
Coffee, green	1,197	1,067	1,140	1,160	1,182	1,570	1,504	1,562	2,633
Drugs, crude	18	25	27	25	31	29	62	79	121
Essential oils	23	29	34	32	40	52	94	41	66
Fibers, unmanufactured	35	25	21	19	19	20	44	28	25
Rubber, crude, excluding allied gums	201	177	188	231	190	340	507	353	512
Silk, raw	22	23	18	7	5	6	5	5	6
Spices	35	44	42	55	59	72	96	90	96
Tea, crude	60	57	61	53	63	70	79	88	95
Wool, carpet	90	72	48	31	43	48	13	14	21
Other complementary	47	44	89	159	214	255	314	285	490
Total complementary products	1,986	1,864	1,986	2,161	2,183	2,867	3,235	3,093	4,705
Supplementary[c]									
Animals and animal products:									
Cattle, dutiable	42	97	91	111	152	193	107	77	157
Dairy products	62	118	101	125	168	330	363	215	269
Hides and skins	71	83	71	110	117	163	146	77	88
Meats and meat products, excluding poultry	411	598	744	1,010	1,219	1,669	1,337	1,130	1,423
Wool, apparel	115	157	110	59	25	37	10	28	63
Other animals and animal products	82	106	105	146	150	175	227	289	318
Total animals and products	783	1,159	1,222	1,561	1,831	2,567	2,190	1,816	2,318

Cotton, raw, excluding linters	21	18	12	6	12	6	17	14	30
Fruits and preparations	101	101	149	146	182	219	239	247	279
Grains and preparations	46	41	49	70	97	113	176	173	164
Nuts, edible, and preparations	72	81	110	100	116	149	167	154	177
Oilseeds and products:									
Coconut oil	47	60	64	77	63	94	235	200	182
Copra	43	42	62	38	26	45	14	0	0
Olive oil, edible	18	15	20	20	26	32	40	38	38
Other oilseeds and products	47	68	74	67	98	142	310	343	301
Sugar and molasses:									
Sugar, cane, or beet	458	502	641	725	832	925	2,256	1,872	1,148
Molasses, inedible	34	31	42	43	54	97	122	86	111
Tobacco, unmanufactured	110	127	142	139	150	169	200	245	294
Vegetables and preparations	133	181	220	298	364	426	408	376	455
Wines and malt beverages:									
Wines	62	77	100	145	210	289	257	259	315
Malt beverages	23	23	26	32	35	49	68	94	139
Other supplementary vegetable products	98	101	104	141	188	230	282	318	336
Total supplementary products	2,096	2,627	3,037	3,608	4,284	5,552	6,981	6,235	6,287
Total Agricultural Imports[d]	4,082	4,491	5,024	5,770	6,467	8,419	10,216	9,328	10,992

Source: Foreign Agricultural Trade of the United States, Economic Research Service, USDA, February 1977.

[a] Preliminary.

[b] Complementary agricultural import products consists of all products that are not commercially produced in the United States.

[c] Supplementary agricultural import products consists of all products similar to agricultural commodities produced commercially in the United States, together with all other agricultural products interchangeable to any significant extent with such U.S. commodities.

[d] Totals may not add due to rounding.

increased output are possible and the gains are divided among nations through international trade. However, Smith did not argue for an import balance either. He realized that exports must equal imports in the long run.

In most years throughout our history, we have been running a positive balance of trade. Since World War II, it has been around $5 billion. A negative balance of trade occurred in 1971, 1972, 1974 and 1976.

The balance of trade surplus in agricultural commodities ran about $1 to $2 billion a year until 1972. In 1972, the balance of trade was positive by almost $3 billion and it jumped to over $11 billion in 1976. In fact, in 1976, the agricultural surplus helped offset a $19 billion deficit in the nonagricultural trade balance for the United States to end 1976 with a negative trade balance close to $8 billion.

Summary

International trade is the exchange of goods and services between countries. People recognize that through trade, a higher level of utility is reached when one specializes in those products where one is superior and then exchanges some of this output for products of another.

The basis for foreign trade is the law of comparative advantage. This principle states that a country will gain economically if it concentrates its efforts where it has the greatest relative advantage or the least relative disadvantage and then trades with other countries.

The major international trade barriers are tariffs and import quotas. The sole purpose of these barriers is to reduce the volume of imports, thus reducing foreign competition. As a consequence, domestic consumers pay a higher price for the product and are forced to purchase less, *cet. par.*

Two approaches have been used in recent years to move the world toward freer trade. One is the international approach under GATT and the second is the formation of customs unions called the regional approach.

Customs unions have been formed in Europe and Central and South America. They include the European Free Trade Association, the European Community, the Latin American Free Trade Association, and the Central American Common Market.

International trade is very important to U.S. agriculture. We export large amounts of feedgrains, wheat, soybeans, and cotton. Our primary agricultural imports are coffee, meat, and sugar.

Chapter Highlights

1. International trade is the exchange of goods and services between countries.
2. A country engages in international trade because it increases that nation's level of living.
3. Specialization and trade are made possible by a nation's comparative (relative) advantage.
4. International trade permits a nation to consume beyond its production possibilities.
5. Tariffs and quotas are trade barriers that reduce the gains from trade.
6. Special interest groups favor trade barriers because of their redistribution effects.
7. International and regional associations can be effective in eliminating trade barriers.
8. U.S. agricultural commodity exports totaled $23 billion in 1976, 20 percent of all U.S. exports.
9. Exports of agricultural commodities constitute 24 percent of U.S. farm cash receipts.
10. Major export commodities are wheat, soybeans, corn, grain sorghum, and rice.
11. Our best agricultural customers are Japan and Western Europe.
12. U.S. agricultural imports were $11 billion in 1976, nine percent of all U.S. imports.
13. Major import commodities are coffee, meat and meat products, and sugar.
14. Agriculture provided a trade surplus of more than $11 billion in 1976.

Review Questions

1. Explain comparative advantage. In what commodities do we have a comparative advantage? Can America have a comparative advantage in the production of every commodity?
2. Show graphically the gains to a country from being involved in international trade. (Assume a two-country and two-commodity world.)
3. Utilizing a demand-supply diagram, show and explain the economic effects of tariffs and quotas.
4. What are the two major approaches that are being used to liberalize international trade?
5. What is meant by the terms "trade creation" and "trade diversion?" How are these concepts used to determine whether or not a regional organization would make a country "better off"?
6. Why are export markets important to U.S. agriculture? What impact do these markets have on agricultural prices?
7. What countries are the primary importers of U.S. agricultural products? Has the make up of these countries changed much over time?
8. What agricultural products are we exporting and importing? Why do we export and import some of the same commodities?

9. How is the balance of trade computed? What does a "favorable" balance of trade mean?

Suggested Readings

1. *Food and Agricultural Policy.* Washington, D. C.: American Enterprise Institute for Public Policy Research, 1977, Part 3.
2. Caves, Richard E., and Ronald W. Jones. *World Trade and Payments: An Introduction,* 2nd ed. Boston: Little, Brown and Company, 1977, Chapters 1, 11, 12, 13, and 14.
3. Ingram, James C. *International Economic Problems,* 3rd ed. Santa Barbara, Calif.: John Wiley and Sons, Inc., 1978.
4. Kindleberger, Charles P. and Peter H. Lindert. *International Economics,* 6th ed. Homewood, Ill.: Richard D. Irwin, Inc., 1978, Chapters 2 and 3.
5. Snider, Delbert A. *Introduction to International Economics,* 6th ed. Homewood, Ill.: Richard D. Irwin, Inc., 1975, Chapters 13, 14, and 15.
6. Wexler, Imanuel. *Fundamentals of International Economics.* New York: Random House, 1968, Chapters 13, 16, and 17.

15

MAN AND HIS FOOD
SUPPLY

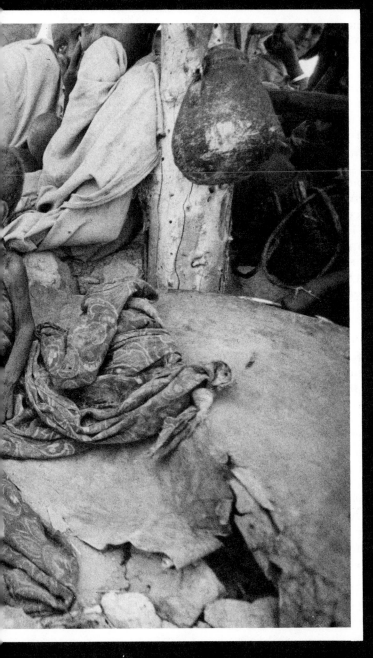

MAN AND HIS FOOD
SUPPLY

One of the basic needs of human life is, of course, food. Since the beginning of time, man's activities and very existence have been governed by a quest for food. Only relatively recently have developed countries been able to provide adequate food supplies for their populations. Many less developed countries still suffer from constant shortages and from frequent famines caused by drought and other natural disasters.

Current estimates of the situation in the world today indicate that 460 million people either do not consume enough calories per day, and are considered undernourished, or are not able to consume the nutrients needed for an adequate diet and are therefore malnourished (Table 15-1). Of these undernourished and malnourished people, about one-half are children who are chronically hungry, or actually starving. These figures include only those people who suffer from food shortages; they do not include those persons who have the required foods available, but are malnourished because of a lack of education in regard to basic nutritional needs.

World Diets. Each of us consumes different kinds of foods. Individual tastes and preferences are such that some people like steak, others like chicken, and still others like fruits and vegetables. In the United States we take the availability of food for granted. It is plentiful and cheap. In many other countries, however, food supplies are not plentiful, nor do they have the range of fresh and processed products that are offered in our supermarkets; the choice of products is much more limited. Their marketing systems are underdeveloped, many of which cannot respond to consumer desires. They lack the legal, transportation network, and pricing mechanisms to form an effective market system. The world's food supplies are not canned ham, frozen vegetables, nor cake mixes, as we know them. Available products for most of the world's people are commodities that are purchased in raw form with the family unit transforming these commodities into usable foods.

Table 15-1 Estimated Number of People with Insufficient
Protein/Energy Supply by Regions, 1970

Region	Population (Billion)	% Below Lower Limit[a]	Number Below Lower Limit[a] (Million)
Developed regions	1.07	3	28
Developing regions (excluding Asian centrally planned economies)	1.75	25	434
Latin America	0.28	13	36
Far East	1.02	30	301
Near East	0.17	18	30
Africa	0.28	25	67
World (excluding Asian centrally planned economies)	2.83	16	462

Source: United Nations World Food Conference, *The World Food Problem: Proposals for International Action,* August 1974.

[a] The lower limit used for assessing the incidence of food deficiency is the maintenance cost of energy that was set at 1.5 times the basal metabolic rate. The basal metabolic rate is a measure of the rate at which body substance is oxidized to support the continued maintenance of life.

The world's daily diet is composed primarily of cereal products. These foodgrains are wheat, rice, corn (maize), and sorghum, accounting for 52 percent of the caloric intake per day. Wheat is an important food in North and South America, Europe, parts of Asia and the Middle East; rice is the major foodgrain in Asia; whereas maize is a significant food in Africa and Latin America.

Meat and animal products make up 14 percent of the world's daily diet per capita in terms of calories. Consumption of meat is highest in the developed countries. Milk is widely used throughout the world.

Roots and tubers account for eight percent of the world diet; fats and oils nine percent; sugar for nine percent; pulses (dry beans and peas), nuts, and oilseeds for five percent; and fruits and vegetables for three percent.

When we speak of the world's food, we are talking basically about cereals, primarily wheat and rice and to a lesser extent maize, barley, and sorghum.

World Population Increases.   Estimates show that there are more than four billion people in the world today. Censuses of population were

Table 15-2 Estimated World
Population and the Number of Years
It Takes to Double the Population

Date	Estimated World Population	Doubling Time
8000 B.C.	5 million	
1650 A.D.	500 million	1500 years
1850 A.D.	1 billion	200 years
1930 A.D.	2 billion	80 years
1975 A.D.	4 billion	45 years

Source: Paul R. Ehrlich and Anne H. Ehrlich,
Population Resources, Environment, 2nd ed.,
San Francisco, Calif.: W. H. Freeman and
Co., 1972, p. 6.

not kept before the 1800s, but scientists have attempted to estimate populations based on interpretations of archeological evidence.[1] It is estimated that around 8000 B.C. there were only five million people. During the period from 8000 B.C. to 1600 A.D., the population doubled approximately six times. In other words, it took on the average, 1500 years for the population to double during this period. Between 1600 and 1850, it doubled again. Population then doubled again by 1930 and again by 1975. Thus, as one can see (Table 15-2), population has been increasing at an ever increasing rate.

The world population is expected to increase 21 percent between 1975 and 1985, reaching a total of about 4.8 billion people by 1985 (Table 15-3). It has been estimated that by the year 2000 there will be between six and seven billion people on this planet. In 1975, the less developed countries accounted for 71 percent of world population, and by the year 2000 they will account for 78 percent (Table 15-4). Those countries with the greatest food problems are also expected to have the greatest increases in populations. Africa's population is projected to increase 103 percent between 1975 and 2000, Asia's population by 61 percent, and Latin America's 91 percent. Smaller increases are anticipated in Europe, North America, and the USSR.

World Food Needs

Since population and income are both factors determining food consumption, one must take account of these variables in order to

[1]Paul R. Ehrlich, and Anne H. Ehrlich, *Population, Resources, Environment,* 2nd ed. San Francisco, Calif.: W. H. Freeman and Co., 1972, p. 6.

Table 15-3 World Population Estimates and
Projections to Year 2000 for Regions and Countries

	Populations (Millions)			
Area	1970	1975	1985	2000
World	3610	3967	4816	6253
Europe	459	473	500	540
Western Europe	148	152	160	171
Eastern Europe	103	106	113	122
USSR	243	255	282	315
North America	226	237	262	296
United States	205	214	236	264
Canada	21	23	27	32
Oceania	19	21	26	35
Australia/New Zealand	15	17	20	25
Asia	2027	2256	2789	3636
Japan	104	111	122	133
China	772	839	973	1148
India	543	613	783	1059
Indonesia	119	136	175	238
Latin America	283	324	426	620
Mexico	50	59	83	132
Brazil	95	110	145	212
Africa	352	401	531	813

Source: United Nations, May 1975, Median Projections.

Table 15-4 Percentage of Total World Population by
Selected Countries and Regions, 1975–2000

	Percentage of World Population		
Region	1975	1985	2000
Asia	57	58	58
China	21	20	18
India	15	16	17
Africa	10	11	13
Latin America	8	9	10
All Underdeveloped World	71	74	78
Europe	12	10	9
USSR	6	6	5
North America	6	5	5
Oceania	1	1	1
All Developed World	29	26	22

Source: United Nations, 1975.

Table 15-5 Extrapolated Growth Rates of Food
Production and Population, 1969–71 to 1985

	Food Production (% per yr)	Population
Developed countries	2.8	0.9
Market economies	2.4	0.9
USSR and Eastern Europe	3.5	0.9
Developing countries	2.6	2.4
Developing market economy countries	2.6	2.7
Africa	2.5	2.9
Far East	2.4	2.6
Latin America	2.9	3.1
Near East	3.1	2.9
Asian centrally planned countries	2.6	1.6
World	2.7	2.0

Source: United Nations World Food Conference, *The World Food Problem, Proposals for International Action,* August 1974.

make projections of world food demand. Between 1970 and 1985, world food demand is expected to grow at a rate of 2.4 percent per year. About two percent of this increase will be caused by the increase in population and about 0.4 percent from the rising purchasing power of consumers.[2] In the poorest countries, food demand may grow at 2.4 percent for population and one percent per year for income.[3]

World food production over this same period is expected to increase at 2.7 percent per year, Table 15-5. In the developing market economies, food supplies are estimated to increase at 2.6 percent per year. Thus many African, Far Eastern, and Latin American countries will have continual problems in producing enough food domestically to feed their populations. The specific countries that may have food problems are Algeria, Bangladesh, Barbados, Chad, Chile, Columbia, Cuba, Dahomey, Dominican Republic, Haiti, Indonesia, Iraq, Jordon, Kenya, Lesotho, Liberia, Mali, Mauritius, Morocco, Nepal, Nigeria, Paraguay, Rivanda, Somalia, Syrian Arab Republic, Trinidad and Tobago, Tunisia, Uganda, Uruguay, Yemen Arab Republic, Yemen Democratic Republic, and Zaire. These diet-deficient areas are shown graphically in Figure 15-1, nearly all falling within 30° of the equator.

[2]United Nations World Food Conference, *The World Food Problem, Proposals for International Action,* August 1974, p. 79.
[3]Ibid., p. 79.

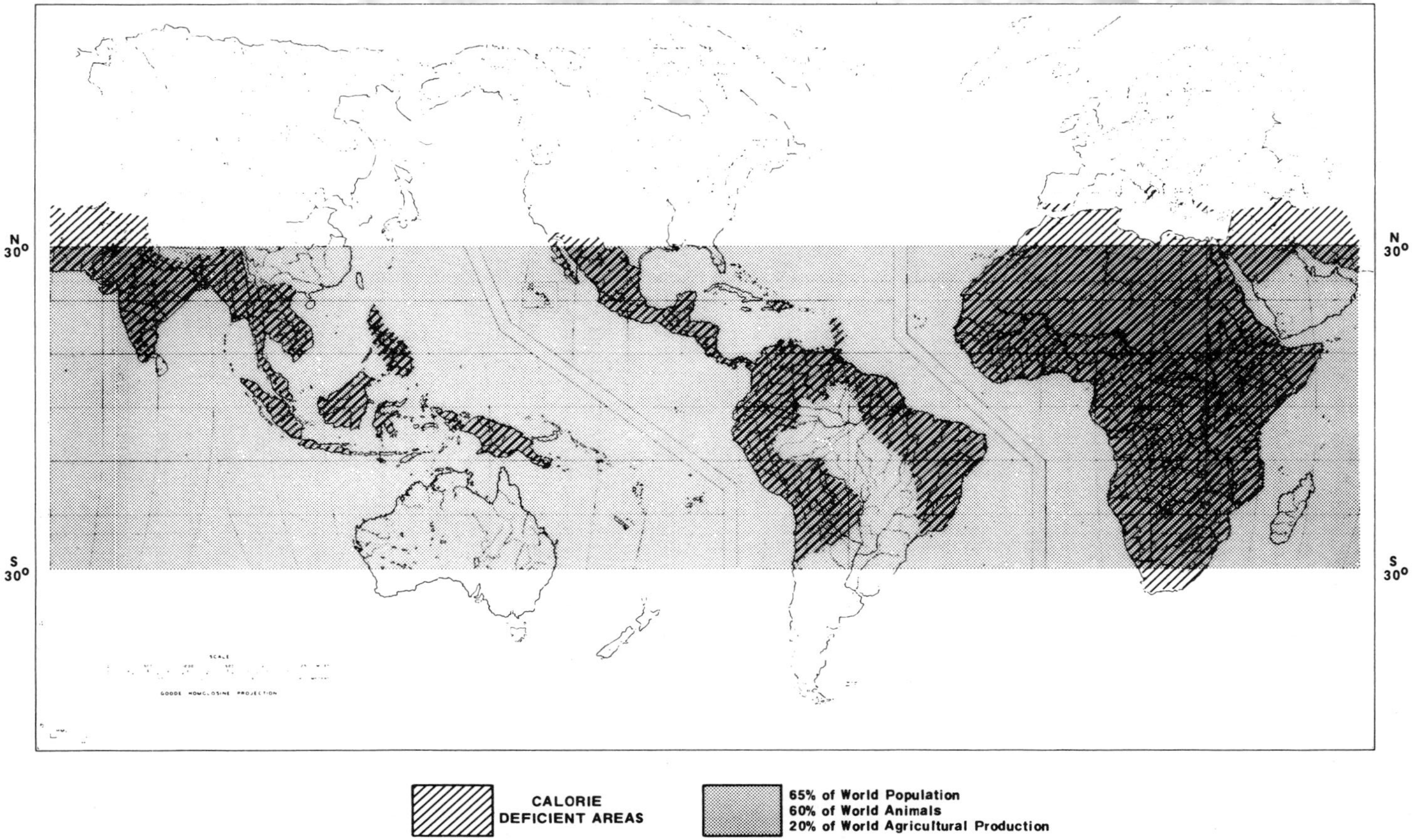

CALORIE
DEFICIENT AREAS

65% of World Population
60% of World Animals
20% of World Agricultural Production

(*Source:* Harold O. Carter et al., *A Hungry World: The Challenge of Agriculture,* University of California, Davis, July
1974, p. 193.)

Figure 15-1. Geographical distribution of world food problem, 1985.

These projections show the food gap between separate estimates of demand and supply indicators. In reality, effective demand must equal effective supply at some equilibrium price and output of food. At this equilibrium, it still is possible to have either plenty or shortages of food.

This economic meaning is not to be confused with the discussions of nutritional needs. The calculations of biological necessities to meet a specific reference individual, has nothing to do with whether or not food will be produced or a consumer has enough purchasing power to make wants effective in the market place. Estimates such as these are useful in calculating quantities of needed food aid. But we must realize that there is a big difference between needing something and being able to purchase it; the food hunger problem is directly related to purchasing power. It is the poor people of the world who suffer from food shortages, not the rich (even in the poorest of countries).

The world food problem is one of an energy intake deficiency. Food energy and protein recommendations made in 1973 by the World Health Organization and the Food and Agricultural Organization, indicate it is likely that if energy requirements are sufficient, the diet would also be sufficient in protein. More food intake alone, even from cereals and pulses, will normally be adequate to meet both energy and protein needs. An exception to this, however, is for young children who have a limited ability to consume more food.

The amount of additional food that is needed to close the food gap, so that all people have a nutritionally adequate diet, is impossible to calculate with the data available. The energy requirements determined for 1961 and 1969–71 do give a clue to the amount of deficiency. As seen by Table 15-6, the total world food situation improved significantly in all regions of the world. All developed countries in 1970 had adequate energy and protein supplies. They were actually 23 percent above requirements. The developing countries did meet protein requirements, but energy needs were five percent below requirements. Africa needed an additional 140 calories per person per day, the Far East needed 133, and the Asian centrally planned economies needed 89 more in 1970. If we assume that 460 million people need from 200 to 500 more calories per person per day, that would amount to from 10 to 24 million tons of cereals per year. At $100 per ton, the cost would range from about $1 billion to more than $2 billion. This, however, assumes sufficient knowledge of where these people are, and a distribution system that can deliver food to those in need. Hence, the amount of food needed to close the food gap actually would probably be two or three times this amount. Even so, the cost is relatively insignificant, so one

Table 15-6 Average Energy and Protein Supply, by Region[a]

	Energy Supply		Protein Supply		Energy as a Percentage of Requirement	
	1961	1969–71	1961	1969–71	1961	1969–71
	(cal per capita)		(gm per capita)			
Developed Market Economies	2950	3090	87.5	95.1	115	121
Western Europe	3020	3130	89.3	93.7	118	123
North America	3110	3320	92.3	105.2	118	126
Oceania	3210	3260	92.7	108.1	121	123
Other Developed Market Economies	2420	2550	73.3	79.1	102	108
Eastern Europe & USSR	2990	3260	85.8	99.3	116	127
Total Developed Countries	2960	3150	87.0	96.4	116	123
Developing Market Economies	2130	2210	55.0	56.0	93	97
Africa	2120	2190	55.7	58.4	91	94
Far East	2050	2080	51.3	50.7	92	94
Latin America	2410	2530	63.7	65.0	100	105
Near East	2200	2500	62.3	69.3	89	102
Asian Centrally Planned Economies	2020	2359	54.7	60.4	86	92
Total Developing Countries	2100	2316	54.9	57.4	91	95
WORLD	2380	2480	65.2	69.0	100	104

Source: United Nations World Food Conference, *The World Food Problem, Proposals for International Action*, August 1974, p. 58.

[a]The figures relate to the protein and energy content of the food available at the retail level, after allowing for storage and marketing losses and waste.

might wonder why more effort is not spent in solving the problem. Maybe this is your chance to help improve the world's food situation!

World Food Crises of 1972–75. Food crises occur every year in one part of the world or another. Agricultural production is affected by variable weather patterns, insects, diseases, and natural disasters such as floods, earthquakes, and tornadoes. These relatively small disasters are handled by food aid programs.

In 1972 world grain production fell by 33 million tons, the largest drop in 20 years. This was caused by grain crop failures in the USSR and in the rice producing areas of Asia. World stocks were drawn upon which stripped America and Canada of the large stocks that were on hand. Then in 1974, North American stocks were not restored because of a poor corn crop. These short supplies drove grain prices far above their pre-1972 levels.

In addition, the energy crisis and the unstable world monetary system aggravated conditions. The energy crisis made it difficult for many farmers in underdeveloped countries to purchase oil and gasoline in order to farm. Also the devaluation of the dollar made American grain cheaper than it would have been in the world market, leaving less grain available for food aid. These latter two factors were not large but did make a bad situation worse.

The 1972–75 experience has shown that the world is ill equipped to handle food shortages and their resultant price impacts. It is evident that some sort of arrangement is needed to coordinate world product flows and reserves in a way to cope with both surpluses and shortages.

Dependence on North American and Australian cereals has been increasing for some time. Asia, Africa, and Latin America import mainly food grains, whereas Western and Eastern Europe, Japan, and the USSR need feedstuffs (Table 15-7). The United States alone has about 40 percent of the international trade in wheat, 60 percent of the coarse grain market and 30 percent of the rice market. Because of the large percentage of the world market the United States has for food, some people suggested during the food shortage that the U.S. use its "Agri-power" to force and keep farm prices up. Cartel-type arrangements probably would not work in the longer-run because of the increased production world wide that would result from the higher prices. In the long-run, U.S. agriculture can produce much more than we can generally sell for domestic and export purposes.

Improvements Made Since the 1974 World Food Conference. Because of the widespread food shortages, a global World Food Conference

Table 15-7 Net Exports (+) and Imports (−) in All Cereals, by Region (in Millions of Metric Tons)

	Year								
Region	*1934–38*	*1960–63*	*1969–72*	*1972–73*	*1973–74*	*1974–75*	*1975–76*	*1976–77*	*1977–78*
North America	+ 5	+43	+55	+91[a]	+86[a]	+78[a]	+90[a]	+93[a]	+87[a]
Latin America	+ 9	+ 1	+ 3	0	− 1	− 3	0	+ 6	+ 4
Western Europe	−23	−26	−22	−18	−22	−19	−18	−33	−23
Eastern Europe (including the USSR)	+ 4	0	− 3	−27	−10	− 9	−33	−20	−14
Africa and Middle East	+ 1	− 4	− 9	− 9	−11	−15	−14	−13	−15
Asia	+ 2	−16	−28	−35	−40	−40	−36	−38	−41
Oceania (Australia and New Zealand)	+ 3	+ 7	+11	+ 6	+ 9	+11	+12	+12	+13

Source: World Agricultural Situation, Economic Research Service, USDA, December 1975 and July 1977.

Note: Minor imbalances in a given period are due to rounding or variations in reporting methods used by certain countries.

[a]The United States accounted for the following portions of these totals (in millions of metric tons): 1972–73, 71.9 metric tons; 1973–74, 72.9; 1974–75, 65.2; 1975–76, 82.6; 1976–77, 76.6; and 1977–78, 71.0.

was held in Rome, Italy in November of 1974. From this conference has come new international institutional improvements that should be helpful in organizing a global perspective on farm and food policies. The major organization formed to carry out the resolutions of the World Food Conference was the *World Food Council* established in February 1975 (Figure 15-2). This council has 36 member countries made up of food-deficit, food-exporting and food-importing countries. It is the council's function to provide an integrated and coordinated approach to world food problems and make recommendations to other United Nations agencies.

Another organization established in 1977 is the International

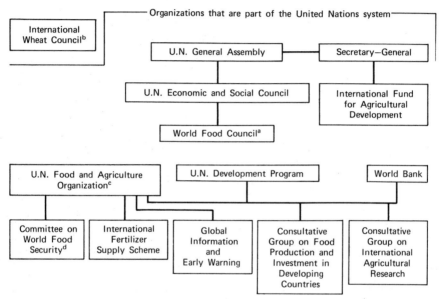

Figure 15-2. Major intergovernmental bodies in the food field.

(*Source:* Martin M. McLaughlin, "World Food Insecurity: Has Anything Happened Since Rome?" Overseas Development Council, No. 27, 1975.)

aMembers of the World Food Council are: Argentina; Australia; Bangladesh; Canada; Chad; Colombia; Cuba; Egypt; France; Gabon; Germany (Fed. Rep. of); Guatemala; Guinea; Hungary; India; Indonesia; Iran; Iraq; Italy; Japan; Kenya; Libyan Arab Republic; Mali; Mexico; Pakistan; Romania; Sri Lanka; Sweden; Togo; Trinidad and Tobago; Union of Soviet Socialist Republics; United Kingdom of Great Britain and Northern Ireland; United States of America; Venezuela; Yugoslavia; and Zambia.

bThis loosely organized but important London-based consultative mechanism—which is outside the U.N. system of organizations and, therefore, without official responsibility for implementing the recommendations of the World Food Council—now involves some sixty countries, including the USSR. It is the body within which international wheat agreements have been negotiated since the late 1940s.

Fund for Agricultural Development. The purpose of this fund is to provide additional funds to increase food production in developing countries. Initial pledges of $1 billion have been made.

Other organizations under the Food and Agriculture Organization are: the (1) global information and early warning systems; (2) international fertilizer system scheme; and (3) committee on world food security. These institutions are a movement in the proper direction, but it will take much more effort and willpower to solve the hunger problem.

The United States has been the most active of all countries in providing food aid and attempting to increase food production in the developing countries. In fact, before the 1972 food crisis it provided almost all of the world's food aid.

Even though food production is not a problem in the world, the distribution of food is concentrated in the hands of a few developed countries. Some food-deficit countries can afford to pay for imports. These include the industrialized countries such as Japan, the USSR, most European countries, and the OPEC countries that can pay for food with their oil earnings. However, there are many less-developed countries that are unable to pay for their food imports. Therefore, it is the policy of the World Food Council to attempt to increase food production in these countries and decrease their reliance on the few major grain exporters.

Historical Food Production. Total world food production has been increasing as much in less-developed countries as in developed countries (Table 15-8). Since 1961–65, the food production index in both areas of the world increased 34 percent. However, on a per capita basis, food production increased 21 percent in the developed countries, but only eight percent in the less developed countries. This means that because of larger populations their per capita food supply was only slightly larger than in the 1961–65 period. And during the 1972–75 food crisis, per capita food production in the less developed countries fell from an index of 106 in 1970 to 101 in 1972.

Increasing the World's Food Supplies

There are two primary ways of increasing agricultural production. Yields per unit of land can be increased or the land area under production can be expanded. Other important factors are the weather and an agricultural policy that provides incentives to producers.

Table 15-8 Indexes of World Food Production[a]
(1961-65 = 100)

Calendar Year	World		Developed Countries		Developing Countries	
	Total	per Capita	Total	per Capita	Total	per Capita
1954	77	91	77	86	77	86
1955	80	92	81	90	78	95
1956	84	96	85	93	82	97
1957	85	96	86	93	83	96
1958	90	99	91	97	87	98
1959	91	98	92	97	89	98
1960	94	100	96	100	92	99
1961	95	99	95	97	94	99
1962	98	100	98	99	97	100
1963	100	100	99	99	100	100
1964	103	101	103	102	104	102
1965	104	100	104	102	104	99
1966	109	103	111	107	106	98
1967	114	106	115	110	111	101
1968	118	107	119	113	115	102
1969	118	105	117	110	121	104
1970	121	106	119	111	126	106
1971	127	113	126	117	126	105
1972	126	110	125	115	125	101
1973	133	115	133	121	133	103
1974	132	113	131	118	131	103
1975	134	113	129	115	129	107
1976	139	115	134	119	134	108

Source: Economic Research Service, *The World Food Situation and Prospects to 1985,* Foreign Agricultural Report No. 98, U.S. Government Printing Office, Washington, D.C., 1974, p. 1.

[a] World excluding communist Asia.

Crop Yields. There is a wide disparity in yields between the developed and the less-developed countries. For example, the 1975 yield of wheat per hectare in Pakistan was 1.2 metric tons, less than one-third that of West Germany's 4.4 tons per hectare.[4] For corn, Indian production was .9 tons, only one-sixth the U.S. yield of 5.4 metric tons per hectare. These high yields in the developed countries come essentially from improved seeds, fertilizers, plant protection, irrigation water, and a sound financial system. Applying these

[4] One hectare equals 2.47 acres.

agricultural input packages continues to offer opportunities to increase yields in developing countries.

The introduction of high-yielding varieties (HYV) of wheat and rice to Asia has been called the "green revolution." Planting these short stalked, nitrogen responsive, and photoperiod insensitive plants has doubled and even tripled yields per hectare over traditional plant varieties. By 1972–73 about 17 million hectares of HYV wheat were planted in Asia and North Africa, and about 16 million hectares of HYV rice. Also about 500,000 hectares of HYV rice was planted in Latin America.[5] To date the green revolution is small, covering 35 percent of the wheat area of Asia and 30 percent of the rice area. Additional emphasis on improved plants and the agricultural inputs complementary to them should show large dividends in future years.

Land Area. As one looks at a map of the earth's surface, large areas of water, polar ice, and mountains are evident. The report of the President's Scientific Advisory Committee estimated that the land surface is only about 25 percent of the total global area. This amounts to about three times as much land as is actually harvested in a year. Africa and South America have the largest areas of potentially arable land (Table 15-9). Probably three billion acres could be developed for cultivation. Presently Africa is farming roughly 20 percent of its potentially arable land, and South America 10 percent. The United States, Canada, Australia, and New Zealand have more than a billion acres of land that could be farmed. There appears to be substantially less land left to farm in Asia, Europe, and the USSR. In Asia there is little land remaining to be cultivated without water development.

The world is using 44 percent of its 7.88 billion acres of arable land. Of this arable land, only 850 million acres is irrigated. If HYV are to be grown in Asia, it will be necessary to increase water projects. The Food and Agriculture Organization estimates land development costs in Asia at $400 per hectare, and to develop irrigated land at $1500 per hectare. The cost of bringing in 222 million acres of additional cultivated land into production between 1974 and 1985, is estimated at $90 billion. These estimates should give some idea that it is not yet economically feasible to develop much additional land.

For the short term, it might make more economic sense to increase yields per unit of land. Land will only be developed when it

---

[5]Economic Research Service, *The World Food Situation and Prospects to 1985,* Foreign Agricultural Economic Report No. 98, U.S. Government Printing Office, Washington, D.C., 1974, p. 67.

Table 15-9 Land Area of the World (Billions of Acres)

Continent	Total	Potentially Arable	% of Total	Cultivated	% of Total
Africa	7.46	1.81	24	0.39	5
Asia	6.76	1.55	23	1.28	19
Australia and New Zealand	2.03	.38	19	.04	2
Europe	1.18	.43	36	.38	32
North America	5.21	1.15	22	.59	11
South America	4.33	1.68	39	.19	4
USSR	5.52	.88	16	.56	10
Total	32.49	7.88	24	3.43	11

Source: President's Science Advisory Committee, *The World Food Problem*, Vol. II, U.S. Government Printing Office, Washington, D.C., 1967, p. 434.

becomes economical to do so, at least in the capitalist countries. Command economies may appear able to disregard their costs and returns, but it is only because they can disguise the consequences of uneconomic development.

Through 1985, the land area sown to crops will expand rather slowly, as it has since 1950 (Table 15-10). The current projections show an increase of only 149 million hectares between 1970 and 1985. If one hectare of land area will feed about 2.5 people, this land could feed an additional 372 million people, whereas the increase in population over this same period is expected to be 1.2 billion people. Hence, simply increasing the land area used for crops will not alone solve the food problem.

Table 15-10 Arable and Potentially Arable Land by Region (Millions of Hectares)

Area	(1) 1950	(2) 1960	(3) 1970	(4) 1985	(5) Potentially Arable
World	1418	1426	1461	1610	3190
Europe	150	153	145	137	174
USSR	225	221	233	252	356
NSC America[a]	313	329	355	400	1106
North America	224	226	236	252	—
Latin America	89	103	119	148	—
Oceania	24	28	47	95	154
Asia	463	456	467	484	628
Africa	243	239	214	242	733

(Columns (1)–(4) are grouped under "Arable Land.")

Source: H. O. Carter, et al., *A Hungry World: The Challenge to Agriculture*, Davis, Calif.: University of California, July 1974, p. 72.

[a]North, South, and Central America.

World Food, 1985

The United States Department of Agriculture has projected world demand, production, and trade in grains to 1985, given two different sets of conditions (Table 15-11). Alternative I, assumes a return to a pre-1972 world where there is only moderate growth in world import demand, and U.S. exports are at low levels. Under this

Table 15-11 World Output with Average Projections for Wheat, Coarse Grains,[a] and Rice (Millions of Metric Tons)

				1985 Alternatives	
Country/Region	1961–71	1973–75	1975	I	II
United States					
Production	208.7	229.1	248.0	290.5	346.4
Consumption	169.0	158.2	154.7	213.8	234.6
Net exports	39.8	74.1	84.1	76.7	111.8
Other Developed Countries					
Production	190.5	210.1	206.7	269.0	268.7
Consumption	205.5	220.7	221.9	277.3	287.6
Net imports	9.4	10.8	7.2	8.4	18.7
Other Major Exporters[b]					
Production	86.0	96.3	99.5	133.4	143.7
Consumption	52.1	50.1	55.7	74.0	76.3
Net exports	34.7	46.1	42.9	59.7	67.4
Centrally Planned					
Imports	17.3	30.7	40.5	20.8	26.1
Exports	10.6	9.5	6.3	1.4	4.3
Net imports	6.7	21.2	34.2	19.4	21.8
Less Developed Countries[c]					
Production	288.8	308.5	320.9	432.1	443.6
Consumption	302.2	341.6	352.0	481.0	511.6
Exports	8.0	12.4	16.2	24.8	27.4
Imports	30.2	46.8	47.0	73.7	95.4
Net imports	22.2	34.4	30.8	48.9	68.0
World[d]					
Production	693.3	753.7	782.6	991.5	1058.7
Consumption	682.5	729.9	741.6	972.1	1033.7
Exports	74.7	114.7	130.8	143.0	189.0

Source: Economic Research Service, USDA, "World Economic Conditions in Relation to Agricultural Trade," June 1976, p. 34.

[a] Coarse grains include corn, barley rye, oats, sorghum, and millet.
[b] Includes Canada, Oceania, Argentina, South Africa, and Thailand.
[c] Includes Argentina and Thailand.
[d] World totals include Centrally Planned for trade but not for production or consumption.

assumption, the world's agricultural capacity would increase faster than consumption so that major exporting countries would probably adopt policies to restrict grain production. The European Community, Eastern Europe, and the USSR would approach self-sufficiency in grains. Under Alternative II, the scenario includes high U.S. exports and a large increase in demand for coarse grains and protein meals for animal feed.

In the first situation, world grain production (excluding the centrally planned countries) increases at an annual rate of 2.4 percent between 1970 and 1985. Developed countries would expand grain at a rate of 2.3 percent and developing countries at a rate of 2.7 percent. In the second situation, both regions of the world would increase food production at 2.9 percent per year. The productive capacity of the major grain producing countries would be sufficient to meet any foreseeable increase in import demand levels to 1985.

Under the first alternative, grain import demand is projected at 77 million tons, however, export supply would be 137 million tons. An even larger margin of supply over demand is projected under Alternative II. The reason for this margin is that U.S. production is responsive to world import demand, and adjustments in feed use in livestock are possible. Animal feeding is a very flexible grain user. Between 1972 and 1974, because of the unfavorable beef to grain price ratio in the United States, feedgrains fed to livestock declined 63 million tons.[6] Thus, during periods of high grain prices, economic adjustments are possible in the livestock industry that greatly increase cereal availability for human consumption. Also, livestock is a food stock that can be slaughtered for meat. It is true they consume more energy than they produce, but many of the calories for livestock are derived from forage and feed grains that are not used for human consumption.

World Crops and Livestock

The major grains for food are wheat, the coarse grains, and rice. Recent years' world output of these grains, and the leading producing areas are summarized in Table 15-12.

Wheat. Worldwide wheat production for the 1977–78 crop year was estimated at 403 million metric tons.[7] This was below the 1976–77 record crop of 414 million tons.

[6]Henry B. Arthur and Gail L. Cramer, "Brighter Forecast for the World's Food Supply," *Harvard Business Review*, May–June 1976.

[7]One metric ton equals 1000 kilograms, which amounts to 2204.62 pounds (or 36.74 bushels of 60 pound wheat).

Table 15-12 World Production of Wheat, Coarse Grains, and Rice (Millions of Metric Tons)

Crop and Producing Areas	Year				
	1973–74	*1974–75*	*1975–76*	*1976–77*	*1977–78*
Wheat					
Canada	16.2	13.3	17.1	23.5	16.8
Australia	12.0	11.4	12.0	11.8	13.0
Argentina	6.6	6.0	8.6	11.2	7.0
West Europe	50.8	56.7	48.5	50.9	52.4
USSR	109.8	83.8	66.2	96.9	105.0
East Europe	31.5	34.0	28.4	34.7	33.6
India	24.7	21.8	24.1	28.3	27.0
Others	73.8	80.5	87.1	97.9	92.9
Total non-U.S.	325.2	307.5	292.1	355.2	347.8
United States	46.4	48.9	58.1	58.4	55.1
World total	371.6	356.4	350.1	413.6	402.9
Coarse Grains					
Canada	20.4	17.4	20.0	21.2	20.1
Australia	4.7	4.5	5.6	5.3	6.1
Argentina	17.9	13.8	12.4	17.3	16.6
South Africa	11.9	9.7	7.7	10.1	9.6
Thailand	2.5	2.7	3.3	3.0	3.7
Brazil	16.9	16.9	18.5	19.6	20.6
West Europe	84.1	85.1	81.5	72.8	84.6
USSR	101.0	99.7	65.8	115.0	95.0
East Europe	55.7	57.3	59.6	58.9	60.0
Others	158.8	162.9	175.1	175.1	173.1
Total non-U.S.	473.9	469.0	449.5	498.3	489.4
United States	186.6	150.5	184.9	193.1	194.9
World total	660.5	620.4	634.5	691.4	684.3
Rice					
Bangladesh	17.6	17.1	18.9	18.9	
Burma	8.6	8.6	9.2	9.3	
India	66.1	59.4	74.3	65.3	
Indonesia	21.5	22.5	22.6	22.7	
Japan	15.2	15.4	16.5	14.7	
Republic of Korea	5.8	6.2	6.5	7.2	
Pakistan	3.7	3.5	3.9	3.7	
PRC	112.9	120.0	119.0	118.0	
Thailand	14.3	14.5	15.2	15.2	
Subtotal	265.8	267.0	286.0	275.1	

continued

Table 15-12 *continued*

| | Year | | | | |
Crop and Producing Areas	*1973–74*	*1974–75*	*1975–76*	*1976–77*	*1977–78*
EC-9	1.1	1.1	1.0	0.9	
Australia	0.4	0.4	0.4	0.5	
Argentina	0.3	0.4	0.3	0.3	
Brazil	6.5	7.0	8.5	7.2	
All others	46.0	49.0	51.4	52.3	
Total non-U.S.	320.1	324.9	347.7	336.4	
United States	4.2	5.1	5.8	5.3	
World total	324.3	330.0	353.5	341.7	

Source: Foreign Agricultural Service, USDA, *Foreign Agricultural Circular,* Washington, D.C., 1977.

The world's major wheat producers are the USSR, the United States, the Peoples' Republic of China, India, France, Canada, and Australia. Russia produces 26 percent of the world's supply, and the United States produces about 14 percent. Major exporters of wheat are the U.S., Canada, and Australia. China, Eastern and Western Europe, USSR, and Japan are large wheat importers. Wheat is a staple foodgrain in almost all developed countries.

Coarse Grains. Coarse grains include corn, barley, oats, rye, millet, and sorghum. A near-record crop was produced in 1977–78. Important producers are the U.S., Russia, and the People's Republic of China. The U.S. is the largest producer, growing 28 percent of the world's harvest. In the U.S., we normally think of coarse grains as feedgrains for livestock, but these grains are foodgrains as well for many countries in Africa, Asia, Latin America, and the Middle East. The leading exporters of coarse grains are the United States, Argentina, Canada, and Australia. Western Europe and Japan import most of the coarse grains for livestock feed. Coarse grains, like wheat, are grown primarily in temperate climatic zones.

Rice. Rice is the major food crop in the world and is consumed mainly in countries of the Far East. The world rice crop totaled 342 million metric tons in 1976–77. Of this total, Asian countries produced 80 percent and the Peoples' Republic of China alone accounts for 34 percent. Asia imports about seven million tons of rice. And, a surprising statistic for many, the United States is the world's major rice exporter, shipping about two million tons a year.

Livestock.   The cattle industry is concentrated in Europe and North and South America. In 1977, the U.S. had an inventory of 123 million head (Table 15-13). Brazil, the European Community, and Argentina accounted for another 231 million head. Beef is a significant food in the American diet. The United States produced about 12 million metric tons of beef and imported about 900,000 tons or roughly eight percent of production. Each American consumer eats about 55 kilograms (121 pounds) of beef and veal per year. Major beef importing countries are the U.S., the European Community,

Table 15-13 Numbers of Livestock in Specified Countries (Millions of Head)

Type of Livestock and Producing Areas	1975	1976	1977
Cattle and Buffalo			
United States	131.8	128.0	122.9
USSR	109.1	111.0	110.3
Brazil	94.0	95.0	96.0
European .community	79.2	77.4	76.9
Argentina	59.6	59.0	58.4
Australia	32.8	33.4	32.0
World[a]	724.5	722.5	715.5
Hogs			
United States	55.1	49.6	55.1
USSR	72.3	57.9	63.0
EC-9	69.7	68.1	70.2
Brazil	43.5	45.0	47.0
World[a]	385.7	364.4	379.3
Sheep			
USSR	145.3	141.4	139.7
Australia	151.7	148.6	136.0
New Zealand	55.3	55.3	55.9
European community	44.4	43.9	44.1
World[a]	697.3	686.6	668.7

Source: Foreign Agricultural Service, USDA, *Foreign Agriculture Circular,* U.S. Government Printing Office, Washington, D.C., June 1977.

[a]Selected countries total only.

the USSR, and Japan. Australia, New Zealand, and Argentina are the leading beef exporters.

Pork is a popular meat in Western and Eastern Europe. Pork consumption per capita is higher in those regions than is beef. Major hog producers are the European Community, the USSR, the United States, and Brazil.

Mutton and lamb are produced primarily in the USSR, Australia, New Zealand, and the European community. The leading exporters of sheep and lambs are New Zealand and Australia. Per capita consumption of mutton and lamb is 22 kilograms per year in Australia, 17 in New Zealand, and 13 in Greece. Russian consumption averages only four kilograms per capita.

Food From the Sea

Aquatic products are an important source of food in Japan, Norway, Spain, Iceland, Portugal, and Southeastern Asia. In the early 1970s, the world's oceans and other bodies of water provided about 70 million metric tons of fish. Less than 45 million tons of this amount was used for human food, the balance being used mainly in the manufacture of animal feeds. Fish and fish products consumed by humans were just 2.6 percent of total food by weight, only one percent of all food calories, and two percent of our protein from all food sources.[8]

To suggest the seas as a food source that can solve the world's hunger problem is little more than wishful thinking. With present management and technology, the long-run potential fish harvest has been estimated to be somewhere in the range of 100 to 150 million metric tons. But even tripling or quadrupling fish harvested for food would still leave this as a minor source of calories and protein for the world's people.

The Malthusian Dilemma[9]

The Reverend Thomas R. Malthus, writing in 1798, gained fame for what he called "the principle of population." The basic significance of his proposition was that the food supply can only be expected to

[8]Harold O. Carter, et al., *A Hungry World: The Challenge to Agriculture,* Davis, Calif.: University of California, July 1974, p. 176.
[9]Henry B. Arthur, and Gail L. Cramer, "Brighter Forecast for the World's Food Supply," *Harvard Business Review,* May–June 1976.

expand arithmetically, while population will tend to expand geometrically, until starvation or some equally fatal deterrent intervenes.

It may be fairly pronounced, therefore, that considering the present average state of the earth, the means of subsistence, under circumstances the most favourable to human industry, could not possibly be made to increase faster than in an arithmetical ratio.[10]

The arithmetic nature of food expansion rested primarily upon the economic premise of diminishing returns on a fixed supply of land as more and more labor is applied to it. The geometric expansion of population, meanwhile could not be maintained in the longer run because it would rapidly encounter the arithmetic food barrier. Thus, hunger and other population checks (most of them related to hunger and poverty) would keep the unhappy balance. The logically pessimistic conclusion derives from the fundamental premises on food production and population, earning for Malthus the label of "gloomy dean."

The fact of the matter is that in the century and three-quarters since Malthus wrote his treatise, both food supplies and population have persistently followed not the arithmetic expectation of the theory, but a pronounced geometric pattern. Hunger, never absent in this imperfect world, has been relatively less widespread and less acute in the past few decades than in any half-century of the world's history. (We say this for perspective, not as cause to celebrate a "victory" over the hunger problem.)

With the world's population estimated at about one-quarter billion at the time of Christ's birth, growth has been very slow, with occasional sharp declines from severe famines and epidemics. Rapid growth as we know it today is only a recent phenomenon. A sketch of the population data from Table 15-2 for the years beginning with 1650, as in Figure 15-3, presents a striking picture of what Malthus meant by a geometric population growth potential.

But what about production? With some (relatively) minor variations, can it have been anything other than the same trend line as for population? Obviously, it can't have been less than that for population or there would have been an excess of people over the food needed for their support. Thus food production must also have exhibited a very similar geometric progression.

A variety of circumstances have (so far) prevented the predicted

[10]Thomas R. Malthus, *The Principle of Population*, 1878 edition. London: Reeves and Turner, 196 Strand, pp. 5–6.

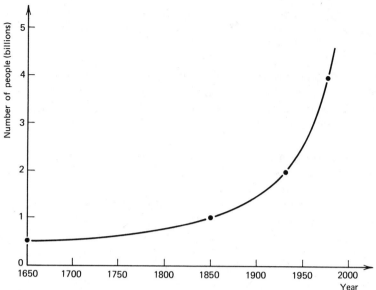

Figure 15-3. World population estimates, selected years.

catastrophe: (1) For the first hundred years or so following Malthus' prediction, the opening of new lands provided the world with greater quantities of food; (2) beginning in the 1920s mechanization in important food production areas increased yields, releasing many millions of acres formerly used to provide feed and forage for draft animals; and (3) the application of science to agriculture over the past 30 years or more (commerical fertilizers, pesticides, genetics, etc.) sharply increased the output of many important foods.

Does this all mean that Malthus was right at least on the population side of his principle? In one sense, yes. The laws of nature provide the *potential* for abundant human propagation, as it does for almost all natural species. Moreover, there is no doubt that food requirements of the world are so massive, and the machinery for producing and delivering these requirements is so complex, that we cannot complacently assume that adequate supplies will be forthcoming as needed. The dilemma is there, even if events for more than a century and a half have not provided the expected outcomes. The best information we have seems to call for a reappraisal, however. The two horns of the dilemma may not be as terrifying as was feared, either independently or together.

Births are undoubtedly becoming more discretionary, both in terms of technology and in cultural acceptance, despite the drags of ignorance and tradition. In many of the developing countries, as well as in the USSR, Japan, some East European countries, the

United States, and Canada, birth rates are declining. Estimated world population figures show that the global total birth rate has fallen, especially in the past ten years.

The continuing growth of population results mostly from longer life spans due to medical technology and better diets. This factor of population increase still has a distance to go in many countries, but it is a one-time shift, not a continuing growth factor; its effect tapers off as age-spans approach a (present) biological limit.

We have seen that the food side of the dilemma has in fact been able to attain a geometric growth pattern in the past 150 years—not of course matching the biologically *potential* population expansion, but none-the-less geometric in rate, and very impressive in actual volume. The assumed ceiling with which Malthus dealt—the result of limited and unexpandable land resources—has been breached by revolutionary changes in technology and in the use of capital to produce dramatic increases in per-acre yields. The world's available food has actually outrun population growth so that *in the aggregate* the world has been eating better (per capita) than at any time in history.

This is not the place to predict how far into the future we can expect the situation to continue. Unlike many others, however, we see no indication of the exhaustion of the kind of unforeseeable ingenuity that has found answers in the past. New developments, however, are no guarantee that the rate of expansion of the food supply will match what may be needed by the world's people.

In other words, the dilemma persists, if only in the sense of the ominous potential on either side. To date we seem *not* to have pressed against the food barrier as Malthus contemplated and we are even a little ahead of the game on a global basis.

Such a statement as this is no comfort at all to the millions who are ill-fed and poverty stricken in many parts of the world. But it does seem most clear that theirs is not a problem of food alone.

The World Food Council's Agenda

Before the World Food Council are many recommendations to improve the world food situation. Some of the major proposals are:

1. That food-deficit countries initiate specific studies to determine the amount of investment and food policy requirements to increase their food production at a rate of four percent per year.

2. That all food surplus countries continue to refrain from domestic production controls until a world food reserve system can be established.

3. That food aid donors attempt to achieve a minimum yearly target of 10 million tons of cereals given for food assistance.

4. That increased emphasis be given to nutrition improvement in developing countries.

5. That a 500,000 ton emergency food reserve be established.

These proposals are a beginning, but much more needs to be done. The United States is building up large stocks of food, and will not participate in a world food security (reserve) program that determines its domestic agricultural policies. The United States, however, is willing to maintain a food stock that will handle emergency international food needs. United States food reserves will continue to be a result of domestic price support programs.

The United States will also contribute its agricultural knowledge to help increase foreign food production. Title XII of the U.S. Foreign Assistance Act called "The Famine Prevention and Freedom from Hunger Act" provides the enabling legislation. This law was passed in 1975 as a means of extending U.S. research, teaching, and extension activities to assist farmers in the developing nations. The basic approach is to promote the role of U.S. agricultural colleges and universities in solving the critical food and agricultural problems of the world. In order to supervise this legislation, Congress established a National Board for International Food and Agricultural Development.

There is hope of feeding our hungry world better, but voluntary population control is a must. It does not make sense to increase the quantity of life if it diminishes the quality of life. If world population were to grow at two percent per year to the year 2100 we would have 47 billion people on this planet. While it may be possible to feed this many people a subsistence cereal diet, our way of life, as we know it today, could not exist. The sheer numbers would put a tremendous strain on all aspects of our environment. In order to avoid future food problems, we must spend as much time and effort on population education and planning as on food supplies. More recent estimates indicate that population may level off in the next century at around 12–16 billion people.[11] This in itself however will cause enough of a challenge for world agriculturists.

Summary

Excepting the Asian command economies, there are at least 460 million people suffering from hunger who do not have the income

---

[11]L. R. Brown, *By Bread Alone,* New York: Praeger Publishers, 1974, p. 191.

nor means to purchase enough food. These people live in Asia, Latin America, and Africa. The size of the food gap is around 10 to 24 million tons of cereals per year.

The world food crises of 1972–75 were caused by crop failures, a decrease in world stocks, the energy crisis, and an unstable monetary system. These factors came together at about the same time. It was apparent that the world was not prepared to handle the food shortages and the resultant price increases.

Since the World Food Conference several new international institutions have been formed to handle food problems. These include the World Food Council, the International Fund for Agricultural Development, and a committee system under the Food and Agricultural Organization.

Recently, food production has been increasing as rapidly in the developing countries as in developed countries. However, if the food supply is going to continue to keep pace with population growth rates, much more emphasis must be placed on increasing yields per hectare in the food-deficit countries. At present, both food supplies and population are following a pronounced geometric growth pattern. In total, world agriculture should be able to meet the food needs of the world's population, but the distribution of food is inadequate to meet the needs of those without the means to purchase it.

Chapter Highlights

1. There are at least 460 million people in the world suffering from hunger. This estimate includes 200 million children.
2. World population will increase to more than 6 billion people by the year 2000. The developing countries have about 70 percent of the world's population. By the year 2000 they will have 78 percent of the world's population.
3. The cereals comprise 52 percent of the caloric intake per day of the average individual on earth. Foodgrains are primarily wheat and rice, although corn, barley, and sorghum are important foods in many developing nations.
4. Between 1970 and 1985 population will grow around 2.0 percent per year and food production will increase at 2.7 percent per year.
5. There is enough food available worldwide to feed all people. However, many people in Asia, Latin America, and Africa do not have the income to purchase it.
6. The primary food problem is that most of the hungry people are not getting enough calories. It is likely that most of these people would attain adequate supplies of protein if they ate enough staples to meet energy requirements.
7. It would take from 10 to 24 million tons of cereals to close the food gap. This amount of food would probably cost $1 to $2.5 billion per year.
8. The 1972–75 world food crisis occurred because of crop failures in various

parts of the world, a draw-down in North American food stocks, and the devaluation of the dollar.

9. Institutional improvements made since the world food crisis include the formation of: (1) the World Food Council; (2) the International Fund for Agricultural Development; and (3) the three new committees under the Food and Agriculture Organization.

10. Per capita food production has increased 19 percent from the 1961–65 average production in the developed nations, but only eight percent in the developing countries.

11. World dependence on North American and Australian cereals has increased greatly since 1969–72.

12. Both the U.S. Department of Agriculture and the United Nations project adequate world food supplies to the year 2000.

13. Animals are flexible grain users. Livestock derives much of its feed from forage and feedgrains.

14. Many of the developing nations associated with the OPEC can afford to pay for their food imports.

15. It has been U.S. policy to help food-deficit nations increase their food supplies rather than rely on food aid. Increased food supplies are likely to come from increased yields per unit of land and expanded acreage.

16. Food from the sea will not add much to the world's energy or protein supply in the foreseeable future.

17. The World Food Council is attempting to increase food output in developing countries at a rate of four percent per year. They also are working on a world food security system.

18. The U.S. provides most of the world's food aid, but in addition the United States is trying to use the land grant college concept to increase food production in developing countries.

19. Malthus stated that food supply could only be expected to expand arithmetically while population would expand geometrically.

20. Both food supplies and population have followed a pronounced geometric growth pattern over the past 150 years.

21. World population may stabilize at around 12–16 billion people during the next century.

Review Questions

1. What is the world food problem? Is it one of protein, calories, food production, or income distribution?

2. World population has been increasing at a very rapid rate. What factors influence the rate of population growth? Do you think the rate of population growth will decrease in the years ahead? Why?

3. What is the difference between effective demand and nutritional needs for food?

4. The food crises of 1972–75 were very severe. Why did they occur? How can we prevent future food crises?

5. During the food crises, some people were arguing that Americans should reduce their meat intake so that more grain would be available for the hungry world. If Americans cut their meat consumption, would that grain saved as a result be shipped to the hungry in the developing countries? Discuss.
6. A number of new institutions have been formed in order to improve the information flow about world food problems. Why are they needed? Will these institutions be able to handle the next large food crises?
7. Aquatic products are an important source of food. Can the world's food problems be solved by developing only this source of food?
8. Malthus thought that the food supply could be expected to expand arithmetically while population would tend to expand geometrically. Was he right or wrong? Why was he right or wrong?
9. What efforts are being made to increase food production in the developing countries? What impact will these efforts have on the export market for U.S. products?

Suggested Readings

1. Carter, Harold O., et al. *A Hungry World: The Challenge to Agriculture.* Davis, Calif.: University of California, July 1974.
2. Dolan, Edwin G. *Basic Economics.* Hinsdale, Ill.: The Dryden Press, 1977, Chapters 34 and 35.
3. Economic Research Service. *The World Food Situation and Prospects to 1985.* Foreign Agricultural Economic Report No. 98. Washington, D.C.: U.S. Government Printing Office, 1974.
4. Ehrlich, Paul R. and Anne H. Ehrlich. *Population, Resources, Environment,* 2nd ed. San Francisco, Calif.: W. H. Freeman and Company, 1972, Chapters 2 and 3.
5. Johnson, D. Gale, "World Food Problems and U.S. Agriculture," *Lectures in Agricultural Economics,* Economic Research Service, USDA, Washington, D.C., June 1977.
6. *Proceedings: The World Food Conference of 1976, June 27–July 1.* Ames, Iowa: The Iowa State University Press, 1977.
7. Reynolds, Lloyd G. *Economics,* 4th ed. Homewood, Ill.: Richard D. Irwin, Inc., 1973, Chapter 36.

16

Courtesy of Doug Warren, Editor, Montana Agricultural Experiment Station, Bozeman.

RURAL DEVELOPMENT

RURAL DEVELOPMENT

R ural development may be defined as making rural America a better place in which to live and work.[1] Emphasis is directed to the well being of people rather than on economic growth itself. Development of rural areas may or may not be associated with an increase in real per capita incomes. Many studies of rural development concentrate on how to attract industry to an area to improve living standards. But this is only one part of rural development. Other concerns of rural development are poverty problems, population distribution, rural housing, public services, and employment opportunities. All of these are included in the meaning of the term "quality of life."

The quality of life in rural communities is directly influenced by local agricultural producers; and the well being of agricultural producers is affected by their rural communities. Rural communities are the service and shopping centers for agricultural producers. This is where producers buy most of their farm supplies, market their products, handle their finances, and purchase their food, clothing, cars, education, services, recreation, and entertainment. Rural communities depend on agricultural producers to provide them with employment and a desirable place to live. Most farm people feel that the quality of life in rural America should be comparable to life in the rest of the country. Farm families are concerned, as they should be, about the quantity, quality, and costs of the public and private goods they purchase.

Renewed Interest in Rural Development

Historically, rural development was restricted to improving conditions on farms and in economically depressed areas. Today the emphasis on rural development is to provide greater equity for all rural people in incomes, housing, health care, and other goods and services. Public policy is being used to disperse population and alter

[1]"Community Improvement—The Rural Component," Report of the Young Executives Committee, USDA, June 1973.

economic growth patterns. Many believe that by decentralizing people and industry it will increase economic efficiency, improve their social well being and improve communications in the political process.

The crisis of the large cities in handling their social problems has had a large impact on renewing interest in rural development.[2] Major U.S. cities are plagued with clogged transportation facilities, air, water, and noise pollution, housing and building decay, and high crime rates. At present, about three-fourths of the population lives on about two percent of the land area.[3] When people are packed into such environments, it brings out the worst in human behavior. This type of dehumanization is unnatural, unhealthy, and is the cause of many social problems. It has been estimated that it would take $100 billion over a 10-year period to rebuild and remodel our major cities.[4]

In the past, the migration patterns of people have been from farm and rural areas to cities, putting pressure on already heavily populated centers. City problems, and the imbalance in population distribution, provide support for the belief that many of the social and economic difficulties were caused by "big cities being too darn big."[5] Thus, current policy is attempting to reduce the migration from the countryside, and possibly even to reverse the trend.

National Population Distribution

The population of the United States has increased from near four million in 1790 to about 216 million in 1977. Before World War I, immigration was a significant factor in population growth. A more important factor in population growth recently has been the reduction in the death rate.

Regional population patterns have been influenced by early settlements, westward migration and urbanization. In 1790, most of the population lived along the Atlantic coast, with just three percent of the population living in the interior part of the country. By 1975, the East Coast population comprised less than 40 percent of the total. Between 1800 and 1900, there was a large movement of people westward to settle farmland.

[2]"Potential for Economic Growth in Montana—The Pros and Cons," Bozeman, Mont.: Montana State University, p. 119.
[3]"A New Life for the Country," The Report of the President's Task Force on Rural Development, March 1970, p. 2.
[4]Ibid., p. 2.
[5]Op. cit., "Potential for Economic Growth in Montana—The Pros and Cons," p. 119.

About this time the pace of industrial development began to increase. Industries located along the Atlantic and Pacific coasts, the Gulf of Mexico and the Great Lakes, where water transportation was available. This started the rural to urban migration pattern that was to dominate regional population trends from about 1900 to 1950.

In 1790, only five percent of the population lived in communities of more than 2500 people. The United States was considered primarily rural until 1920 when the census showed just under 50 percent of the population in rural communities. By 1975, about 75 percent of the U.S. population was living in cities of more than 2500 people, and 58 percent of the population lived in urban areas with a population of over 50,000. The declining sectors of agriculture, mining, railroading, fishing, and forestry were major reasons for the rural to urban migration. The substitution of capital for labor in these industries has induced outmigration. Also, people were moving to population centers, seeking higher incomes, and away from poverty.

Decline and Growth of Rural Areas and Communities

Increases in population and changes in its distribution have provided substantial benefits to our level of living, but many undesirable secondary effects of migration patterns have emerged. We find rural areas having: large amounts of poverty; a smaller percentage of the rural population graduating from high school and college; fewer medical and dental personnel; evidence of substandard housing and lower quality public services such as police and fire protection and sewage disposal; less air transportation; and fewer recreational and cultural opportunities.

Even with lower quality services many people desire a place to live with a lower density of population. A Gallup poll in 1966 showed that 47 percent of the residents living on farms and ranches preferred to remain on farms, 29 percent preferred a small town of less than 2500, 18 percent preferred the suburbs, and only six percent preferred the city. For persons residing in cities of less than 2500, 23 percent indicated farm, 69 percent small towns, eight percent suburbs, and none indicated a preference for the city. For individuals in cities with a population between 2500 and 50,000 the survey showed 10 percent preferred farms, 62 percent small towns, 23 percent suburbs and five percent preferred city life. Residents of the largest cities, those over 50,000, preferred the larger cities and suburbs. Six percent of these people preferred the farm or ranch, 23 percent small towns, 35 percent suburbs and 36 percent liked cities of over 50,000 population.[6] Other more recent opinion polls show similar results. There are many people in concentrated populated areas that would prefer rural living.

A study was conducted by the Economic Research Service, U.S. Department of Agriculture of the characteristics of areas in the United States with noncommuting populations.[7] The study excluded those counties with 25,000 or more urban population, those with 10,000 or more nonfarm wage and salary jobs, or with 10 percent or more of all workers commuting to work in urban employment centers. The remaining counties were considered isolated or noncommuting areas.

In 1970, the United States had 1718 counties that were isolated from urban centers. Those counties included 24 million people, 12 percent of the total population, and are located primarily in the North Central states and in the South. Although total population increased 13 percent between 1960 and 1970, these isolated counties lost one percent of their population. Outmigration has been heaviest in the Great Plains states, an area with a high rate of outmigration by its young people, and a high proportion of residents over 65 years of age.

There are 10,289 towns near large urban areas. About 2800 of these towns had fewer than 500 people (Table 16-1). Between 1960 and 1970, more than one-third of these smaller towns experienced a decrease in population. There were more than 7500 towns in isolated counties, and nearly one-half of them had a population under 500 residents. Over one-half of the smallest-sized towns lost population between 1960 and 1970, the only grouping in which more towns lost population than gained. Although many rural areas were declining in population, only the very small are losing their social and economic vitality.

Even though nonmetropolitan areas had a net loss of three million people between 1960 and 1970 the trend has reversed itself between 1970 and 1975.[8] During this period, nonmetropolitan areas had a net increase in population of 1.8 million people, a growth of 6.6 percent against the metropolitan area increase of only 4.1 percent. This has significantly reversed a trend since World War II

[6]R. P. Devine, "Citizens' Attitudes Toward Their Cities," in *Micro-City,* Edward Henry, ed., Collegeville, Minn.: St. John's University Center for the Study of Local Government, 1970, p. 42.
[7]Economic Research Service, USDA, "Characteristics of U.S. Rural Areas with Noncommuting Population," Committee Report for the Committee on Agriculture and Forestry, U.S. Senate, 92nd Congress, 2nd Session, June 30, 1972.
[8]"Rural development Progress," Fourth Annual Report of the Secretary of Agriculture to the Congress, USDA, January 1977, p. 18.

Table 16-1 Growth or Decline in Population of Towns, by Size, Among Urban Commuter and Isolated Counties, U.S. 1960–1970

County Designation and Town Size [a]	Number of Towns	Towns Declining in Size %	Percentage of Towns Growing More Than 15%
Urban Commuter Places	10,289	29.3	39.6
10,000 or more population	1,473	29.6	38.6
2,500 to 9,999	2,069	25.7	44.0
1,000 to 2,499	2,149	25.4	42.4
500 to 999	1,829	28.3	36.7
Under 500	2,769	35.2	37.1
Isolated Counties	7,537	51.5	19.5
10,000 or more population	175	42.9	20.0
2,500 to 9,999	963	38.7	22.9
1,000 to 2,499	1,339	42.7	20.0
500 to 999	1,398	47.9	19.7
Under 500	3,662	59.9	18.3

Source: Economic Research Service, USDA, "Characteristics of the U.S., Rural Areas with Non-commuting Population," Committee Report for the Committee on Agriculture and Forestry, U.S. Senate, 92nd Congress, 2nd Session, June 30, 1972.

[a] Town size as of 1960.

when rapid urban growth and decline in many rural and farm communities was experienced. It appears that the growth in rural areas is in the open country and smaller villages rather than in the larger rural towns. Retirement homes are a partial explanation for this rural growth rate.

Problems in Rural Communities

Income and Employment. The average income of all families in the United States was $15,546 in 1975.[9] Average nonfarm family income was $15,640, and family farm income was only $13,251. This income differential also exists between average family incomes in metropolitan and nonmetropolitan areas. Average metropolitan income per family was $16,685 and average nonmetropolitan income was $13,214 in 1975. The regional variation in family income is large. In the South, average income per family in 1975 was $2000 less than in other regions of the United States.

[9] Bureau of Census, U.S. Department of Commerce, *Consumer Income*, Series P-60, No. 103, September 1976, p. 9.

Table 16-2 Residence of Persons of Low Income States,
U.S., 1959–75

	Number Below Low-Income Level				
Persons	1959	1967	1969	1972	1975
	----------------------Millions----------------------				
Total	38.8	27.8	24.3	24.5	25.9
Nonfarm	N/A	25.1	22.3	23.1	24.6
Farm	N/A	2.7	2.0	1.4	1.3
Metropolitan Areas	17.0	13.8	12.3	14.5	15.3
Nonmetropolitan Areas	21.8	14.0	12.0	10.0	10.5

Source: Bureau of Census, U.S. Department of Commerce, *Consumer Income,* Series P-60,
No. 103, September 1976, p. 43.

In 1975 the Bureau of the Census reported almost 26 million
Americans with incomes below the poverty line of $5500 for a non-
farm family of four (Table 16-2). These persons accounted for
about 12 percent of the U.S. population. The number of low income
persons has declined by 33 percent since 1959. In recent years,
however, the number of people below the poverty line has been
rising because of high rates of inflation and higher unemployment
rates.

Nonmetropolitan areas had 32 percent of the population in the
United States, but 41 percent of the poverty. Farms had four percent of the U.S. population and five percent of the poverty in 1975.
More than one in every six people in rural America had incomes
below the poverty level. This condition affected over 2.2 million
rural families. Low income farm persons dropped from 2.7 million
in 1967 to 1.3 million in 1975, a decline of 52 percent.

Regionally the South has the highest proportion of low income
residents, but poverty is widespread and is evident nationwide. The
rural areas have fewer absolute numbers of poor, but the poor represent a higher proportion of the total rural population than the
poor of the cities represent of the total urban population.

Housing. The number and quality of housing units have improved
since 1950. In 1975, the Census of Housing showed 72.5 million
occupied housing units in the United States. This is a 14 percent
increase over the 63.4 million units available in 1970, and nearly 70
percent over 1950. Much of the large increase is attributable to
various federal and state programs to help people obtain adequate
housing.

Thirty-two percent or about 23 million housing units are in

rural areas. Only 1.9 million of these units are substandard. A unit is classified as a substandard unit if it is dilapidated or lacks inside plumbing. The inside plumbing must include one or more of these facilities: hot water, a private flush toilet, and a private bathtub or shower.[10] The percentage of substandard housing in rural areas has dropped from 59 percent in 1950 to 8 percent in 1975. This shows how effective insured or guaranteed loans have been through Farmers Home Administration and the Federal Housing Administration. During the 1950s and 1960s, federal housing assistance to rural residents was provided by the Federal Housing Administration and the Veterans Administration. Currently the Farmers Home Administration is assisting with home financing in towns of under 20,000 population located outside metropolitan areas.

Government Expenditures.   Rural Americans do not share proportionately in federal government programs according to the President's Rural Development message of January 1977.[11] The federal government funded 275 programs having an impact on rural development, with funding obligations totalling $267 billion in fiscal year 1975. These programs can be categorized into programs for human resource development, community and industrial development, housing, agriculture and natural resources, and defense and space (Table 16-3). Nonmetropolitan counties received only one-fourth of the federal outlays. On a per capita basis rural areas received $1148 compared with $1305 in urban counties. Sparsely populated rural counties, however, received the largest amount on a per capita basis in 1975.

Federal expenditures per capita for human resource development programs such as social security, health care, education, and employment training were about the same in metropolitan as nonmetropolitan counties. Urban areas were granted $650 per capita compared with $647 per capita in rural areas. Totally rural counties received $690 per capita.

Housing loans showed a large differential between metropolitan and nonmetropolitan counties. Federal housing loans were $85 per capita in urban areas and $50 in all rural nonmetropolitan counties.

Per capita federal outlays for community and industrial development were higher in nonmetropolitan areas in 1975. It was

---

[10]Ronald Bird, and Ronald Kampe, "Twenty-Five Years of Housing Progress in Rural America," Agricultural Economic Report No. 373, Economic Research Service, USDA, June 1977.
[11]*Rural Development,* Message from the President of the United States, 95th Congress, 1st Session, House Document No. 95-51, U.S. Government Printing Office, Washington, D.C., January 19, 1977.

Table 16-3 Distribution of Federal Outlays for Five
Program Areas, Metropolitan and Nonmetropolitan
Counties, Fiscal Year 1975

Program Type and Allocation	Total	Metropolitan Counties	Nonmetropolitan Counties		
			Urbanized	Less Urbanized	Totally Rural
Human Resources (bil. $)	$137.2	$99.5	$14.3	$18.7	$4.9
Percent of total	100	72.5	10.4	13.6	3.6
Dollars per capita	$649	$650	$624	$661	$690
Housing (bil. $)	$15.9	$13.0	$1.3	$1.3	$0.3
Percent of total	100	81.6	7.9	8.3	2.2
Dollars per capita	$75	$85	$55	$47	$49
Community and Industrial Development (bil. $)	$26.9	$17.5	$3.0	$4.7	$1.7
Percent of total	100	65.1	11.1	17.6	6.2
Dollars per capita	$127	$114	$131	$166	$239
Agriculture and Natural Resources (bil. $)	$6.4	$1.8	$1.0	$2.6	$1.1
Percent of total	100	28.2	14.9	40.2	16.7
Dollars per capita	$30	$12	$44	$92	$155
Defense and Space (bil. $)	$80.3	$68.0	$9.3	$2.5	$0.5
Percent of total	100	84.7	11.6	3.1	0.6
Dollars per capita	$380	$445	$406	$88	$70
TOTAL (bil. $)	$266.7	$199.8	$28.3	$29.6	$8.5
Percent of total	100	74.9	10.6	11.1	3.2
Dollars per capita	$1,262	$1,305	$1,236	$1,046	$1,202

Source: Compiled from Tables 1, 2, and 3, *Rural Development,* Message from the President of the United States, 95th Congress, 1st Session, House Document No. 95–51, U.S. Government Printing Office, Washington, D.C., January, 1977.

Note: Individual items do not add to totals because of rounding.

$114 per capita in metropolitan areas and $161 per capita in nonmetropolitan counties. Federal outlays per capita were highest in totally rural areas. All development loans favored rural counties as do programs in agriculture and natural resources.

National defense and space outlays are weighted heavily toward metropolitan areas. Per capita defense expenditures were $445 per capita as compared to $210 per capita in rural America.

Over the last decade there has been a substantial increase in federal expenditures in rural areas. The pressure for more evenly balanced urban-rural growth has caused government decision makers to direct greater per capita allocations to rural areas.

Education. The United States devotes huge amounts of resources toward educating its citizens, and a great many employable individuals forego substantial earnings while taking advantage of the educational opportunities available to them. Both society and the individuals incurring those costs must have decided that an education is worth its cost.

In looking at the value of an education we will separate the noneconomic from the economic rewards of an education. Directing our attention to the latter does not imply that noneconomic rewards are unimportant. Both are somehow considered when a person weighs the pros and cons of an education.

Two elements in the economic returns from an education can be identified: the "investment" and "consumption" components.[12] The investment component regards the process of education as an investment in an individual's increased productivity that yields increased future earnings. Educational investments in improving the knowledge and productivity of people is an investment in "human capital." It involves committing present costs for expected future returns, and can thus be analyzed in the same manner as investments in physical capital. The consumption component includes both the immediate and longer run satisfactions (utility) that the individual derives from an education. Consumption benefits accrue primarily to the student, but there frequently are satisfactions to his or her family as well.

The amount spent on a student's education is determined by the estimated benefits associated with that student's increased productivity and satisfactions, and the cost requirement of those gains. In economic terms the student will spend an amount on education that equates private marginal benefits to private marginal costs, both in terms of their present values.

When goods are bought and sold in a perfectly competitive market, an equilibrium is determined by the intersection of the demand and supply curves. At that intersection point the last unit consumers buy yields a benefit equal to the cost of producing that unit. Its benefits and costs at the margin are equal, and net benefits to society are maximized.

---

[12]T. W. Schultz, *The Economic Value of an Education,* New York: Columbia University Press, 1963, p. 5.

But there are special requirements that must be met in this equilibrium. If there are other benefits or costs beyond those involved in the transaction, the equilibrium cannot be a social optimum.

You will buy a steak dinner by equating your own private marginal benefits and marginal costs; no other costs or benefits are imposed on others by your decision. Suppose, however, that you are buying plants and flowers to beautify your home's appearance. If others also derive pleasure from this, total benefits exceed your private marginal costs. Or, you may optimize the use of your stereo by listening to a rock concert at 1:00 A.M. (at high volume, of course). If this prevents people in the apartment next door from sleeping, a disutility (cost) has been incurred. Such benefits or costs to others, being external to your cost and returns equation, mean that a social optimum is not achieved with your private optimizing. In the landscaping example, too little of the product is bought; in the latter, too much has been purchased.

An interesting aspect of education is that society derives benefits in addition to the individual's benefits. These added benefits to the larger society (they could also be costs) are called "externalities" or "spillover effects." They have important repercussions on economic decisions. If education is to be socially efficient and equitable it requires that the cost burden of an education also be shared. This is one of the major arguments for public funding of education.

Educational expenditures must be extended beyond the point where private marginal costs (*PMC*) equal private marginal benefits (*PMB*). In this case the socially efficient expenditure on education is where the private marginal costs plus external marginal costs equal private marginal benefits plus external marginal benefits. To illustrate, let's assume a student is considering the amount of education to purchase as shown in Figure 16-1. The student would equate private marginal benefits and private marginal costs and purchase quantity *A*. This student could not take into account the added benefits to society of his or her education. Hence, usually by public funding of education, and regulations or graduation requirements, the student equates private marginal costs (in this example we assume no external marginal costs) with private marginal benefits plus the public marginal benefits. A larger quantity of education is therefore consumed. Quantity *B* is purchased rather than *A*; from society's viewpoint, quantity *B* is optimal.

Educational achievement has increased rapidly between 1950 and 1975. In 1950, the median years of schooling (50 percent above and 50 percent below this number) completed by persons 25 years old and over was 9.3 years. By 1975, the median education level had

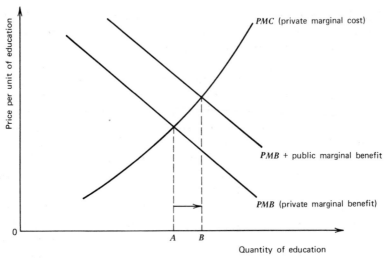

Figure 16-1. The economic effect of externalities in education.

increased to 12.3 years. Metropolitan residents completed 12.3 years in 1975, nonmetropolitan 12.1 years and farm residents 12.0 years of schooling.

These figures tend to mask some of the differences between urban and rural residents. Many researchers have found that regardless of the measurement system used, rural students "consistently rank lower" than their urban counterpart.[13] A Missouri study measuring educational quality found that the average score on the Ohio State University psychological test for the smallest rural schools (0–199 students) was 43.6 compared to large urban schools (1000 or more students) with a score of 56.5. The average for all urban schools was 15 percent higher than for all rural schools.[14]

The President's National Advisory Commission on rural poverty contends that the extent to which rural people have been denied equality of educational opportunity is evident not only in the output of the educational system, but also in the resources that go into the system.[15] The commission felt that upgrading rural schools would increase educational opportunities for rural poor, but would not solve the problems of economically deprived students.

While rural youth are getting a better education than their par-

[13]Op. cit., "Rural Development Progress," p. 32.
[14]Jerry G. West, and Donald D. Osburn, "Quality of Schooling in Rural Areas," *Southern Journal of Agricultural Economics,* July 1972, p. 86.
[15]Report by the President's National Advisory Commission on Rural Poverty, *The People Left Behind,* Washington, D.C.: U.S. Government Printing Office, September 1967, p. 41.

ents had, they continue to lag behind urban students, but the gap may be narrowing. A Montana study shows that on basic skills (as measured by the Stanford achievement test) at the senior level in high school, no significant differences exist in mean test scores based on size of the school.[16] At the sophomore level, however, the larger urban high school students scored better on these achievement tests than students from the smaller rural schools. It is necessary to realize that these achievement tests evaluate basic skills only and do not include the enrichment programs of the larger high schools.

In Chapter 11 we discussed how the present value of any resource is determined. That same concept is appropriate in appraising the economic value of an education, and the rate of return on that investment.

The rate of return on investment or "payoff from schooling" has been relatively high. Although the studies were completed some years ago, their conclusions still should be valid. These studies show a rate of return on primary education of 10 to 20 percent, on secondary education of 15 to 30 percent, and on post-secondary education of 10 to 20 percent.

A comparison by areas (rural versus urban) shows that the educational payoff is higher for rural white males than urban males. What this comparison says is that public educational efforts have been less intensive in rural than in urban areas. All is not well in rural education. There are 500,000 rural adults who have not been to school at all and two million rural adults that are functionally illiterate.[17] Also, there are at least five percent of all rural school-aged children that are not enrolled in school.[18]

Community Services

Wherever one might look in rural America, change has been the order of the day, much of it with undesirable results. Agricultural firms have been forced to adjust the kinds and quantities of resources used, and to adopt new technologies, in order to remain competitive. In the process, farm numbers have fallen from a high of near 6.8 million in 1935 to 2.8 million by the mid-1970s. During

---

[16]John W. Kimble, Gail L. Cramer, and Verne W. House, "Basic Quality of Secondary Education in Rural Montana," Agricultural Experiment Station Bulletin 685, Bozeman Mont.: Montana State University, April 1976.

[17]Op. cit., "Rural Development Progress," p. 32.

[18]Ibid., cited from Marion W. Edelman, Marylee Allen, Cindy Brown, Ann Rosewater, et al. *Children Out of School in America,* Cambridge, Mass.: Children's Defense Fund, 1974, p. 37.

the same 40-year period, farm population declined to 8.3 million from its high of 32.2 million people.

Declines in farm numbers and farm population became most rapid in the 1945–65 period. Over those 20 years the number of farms declined by 130,000 per year. Farm population dropped in that same period by an average of 600,000 each year. The ten years from 1965 to 1975 saw a considerable slowing in their rates of decline, however. Farm numbers declined by about 60,000 per year, less than one-half the previous rate, while the 410,000 per year decline in the number of farm people was about one-third less than the previous rate.

For rural communities, organized to serve the needs of more than 32 million people, a loss of nearly 75 percent of their potential customers has had a serious impact. The most severely affected communities are to be found in the Great Plains and the Mountain states. Communities in other areas of the United States are much less concentrated, with scattered pockets of hard-hit areas. Other regions such as Appalachia, face problems that stem more from urban origins than from the loss of farm people. Yet other central communities have been more fortunate. Located near growing urban centers, farm losses have been more than offset by people establishing homes farther and farther out in the rural area. This has caused other urban-related problems, but the effect of depopulation is not one of them.

Farm mechanization and the corresponding need to increase acreages is only one important factor in changing rural communities. With improved transportation and related conveniences, it became easier for rural community residents to obtain necessary supplies and services in the larger towns and cities, to the detriment of their own community's service center.

In choosing between daily travel to elementary or high school for their children, some opted for a second residence in the town of the preferred school. Local health care facilities have suffered both patronage and personnel losses in the same way and for the same reasons.

Most if not all public and private services are greatly influenced by population density of the serviced area. Not only do local stores of all kinds suffer from a declining population, but problems of inventory maintenance and upkeep of facilities cause the cost of goods sold to increase sharply.

On a per capita basis roads and transportation, schools and libraries, hospital and health care facilities, farm electrification and telephone services, newspapers, radio and television, and police and fire protection among other public and private services all are provided at much higher cost in sparsely populated areas. Either the scale of each of these is reduced to the size that can serve the local market's needs, or the geographic area served must be expanded, both of which have a direct bearing on the quantity, quality, and delivery costs of these services. Thus, there can be no parity of costs for the more isolated rural areas in comparison to their urban counterpart.

Concern over rural-urban disparities in obtaining services begs the question of what can be done to avoid or alleviate these problems. Questions need to be directed at what forms of community reorganization might lead to improved quality of services and reduce their costs. Rural areas have an institutional structure that is more appropriate to heavily populated areas. But their problem is one of trying to devise institutions that might overcome distance-related problems and escape the high "social cost of space."[19]

The village, town, or city holds a position of dispenser of goods and services to its outlying trade area. The size of that area depends upon how well those functions are performed, and upon local-patron loyalty to and identification with that service center.

How large must a town be to offer the variety of services a community requires at reasonable costs? We may conceive of "units" of services in the same way as we recognize units of resources, or units of products produced. We then may consider the average total costs per unit of those services in the same manner as with physically produced goods.

The efficiency of providing public services depends upon the economies of scale in production, population density of the area served (thus, the demand for services), and the costs of organization and delivery of those services. Estimates of approximate populations required to provide the most cost-efficient high school, school administration, fire protection, police protection, and hospital services are shown in Table 16-4.

The Local School Problem.   As can be seen, a substantial population base is needed to be able to provide these services at least cost. Because they have a smaller population, rural areas typically must bear higher costs for these services and also receive lower quality services. A good example of this is the problem of the small rural school.

Most rural schools are too small to exhibit any degree of cost

---

[19]Social cost of space is a term first used by A. H. Anderson, "Social Cost of Space," *Journal of Farm Economics,* Vol. XXXII, August 1950, pp. 411–30. The costs of public and private goods and services were there related to greater delivery distances in sparsely settled rural areas.

Table 16-4 Scale Economies in Public Services

Service	Result
High Schools	ATC is U-Shaped, with a minimum at about 1700 pupils
School Administration	ATC is U-Shaped, with a minimum at about 44,000 pupils
Fire Protection	ATC is U-Shaped, with a minimum at about 110,000 population
Police Protection	ATC is about horizontal
Hospitals	ATC is declining to about 800 beds

Source: Condensed from W. Hirsch, *The Economics of State and Local Government,* New York: McGraw-Hill, 1970, p. 183.

Note: ATC = average total cost.

effectiveness in providing building space, educational equipment aids, and faculty. Faced with low enrollments and sharply rising costs, rural school districts early bore the brunt of having to "do something" in both low population density and depopulating areas.

To demonstrate community size requirements, let's use the high school information from the table above. If we estimate the size of an average rural family as four people, only about one-fourth of the children under 18 will be of high school age. Thus it would take a community of more than 25,000 population to minimize the cost of high school educational services. Few of the nation's rural counties have that large a population. (The data in Table 16-1 show that more than 90 percent of all the towns in those counties identified as "urban commuter" and "isolated" have populations of less than 10,000.)

School district consolidation is one approach toward reducing the costs of educating rural youth. Less than 30 percent of the more than 67,000 school districts that existed in 1952 remain today. At the small end of the scale, the push to consolidate has been of both administrative and citizen reaction in origin. The state threatens or denies accreditation because of unacceptably low program quality, and taxpayers find that minimum quality entails unbearably high costs. Transportation costs (bus ownership and operation costs, and driver wages) become an important component of school costs, a cost per student that varies inversely with population density. Another cost not included in cost tallies, but a real cost nevertheless, is the time spent riding to and from school. For many students, this amounts to more than two hours per day, and they find it difficult to use this time productively.

Although average total cost for high schools is minimized at about 1700 students (Table 16-4), the more dramatic cost reductions are to be had in combining the smaller schools.[20] But an inadequate school often is the rural area's sole community "identity," with its athletic programs (especially football and basketball) being the focus of that attachment. Important as such a unifying institution might be, the price of maintaining a small school in the local community for this purpose is high. And the young bear this cost in their restricted educational opportunities.

Hospitals and Health Care.[21]   Because of their low population density, rural residents also face cost and quality problems in obtaining health care services locally. Increasingly specialized professional skills, new medical knowledge and technology, and greater consumer expectations all have served to raise both the capacity and fixed costs of health care facilities. The costs of providing health care may be indicated by the following equation:

$$\text{Average total patient cost} = \frac{\text{Total fixed cost of the minimally acceptable facility}}{\text{Number of patients treated}} + \frac{\text{Total variable cost of the minimally acceptable facility}}{\text{Number of patients treated}} + \text{Average travel cost for patient}$$

To assign numerical values in the above equation, a minimally acceptable facility must first be determined. The minimum variety and quality of services, the minimum amount of equipment, the greatest distance, and the maximum number of patients per physician that are locally acceptable all have a bearing on the facility and the level of its costs at any point in time. This becomes the standard of acceptability—a social norm—which is very much influenced by comparable facilities available to urban residents.

The components of cost for such a facility change through time, as society's expectations change, and as advances are made in the body of medical knowledge and in the sophistication of medical equipment.

Once the minimally acceptable facility has been specified, the amount of fixed (or overhead) costs may be determined. Total fixed

[20]The degree of cost saving through consolidation is indicated by some Montana data relating costs per student and size of school. Small rural high schools (those with less than 50 students) had an ATC per student that was more than three times greater than larger urban schools with more than 1000 enrolled: From the Biennial Report of the Montana State Department of Public Instruction, Helena, Mont.

[21]More completely discussed in R. J. McConnen, "Communities and Their Impact on Rural Life in the Years Ahead," Great Plains Agricultural Publication No. 44, Bozeman, Mont., 1972.

costs are all those annual costs incurred in providing the facility itself. These costs remain the same no matter how many patients are treated (including such cost items as property taxes, depreciation and maintenance, utilities, and salaries for the minimal staff). These costs are unaffected by the intensity with which the facility may be used, being the same whether five or 500 patients are treated there.

Those costs which we call variable change as patient numbers increase or decrease. Some of these costs, such as medicines and medical supplies used, vary directly with the volume of use, while others such as office salaries do not vary directly with the patient load.

Travel costs are those costs incurred by the patient in getting to and from the health care facility. These costs include transportation plus other expenditures for meals, lodging, and the opportunity cost of the time that it takes to obtain the needed treatment.

Figure 16-2 compares the average cost per patient in two different periods, 1968 and 1978. The average costs are shown for each year at various rates of use of the facility.

Assume that the facility treated 100 patients in 1968 with an average total cost per patient of $100. Under this assumption, the facility treated only one-half the number of patients that it could have handled. Average total costs would have been somewhat higher than if the facility had been used to its capacity.

Over the 10-year period, certain factors have changed that af-

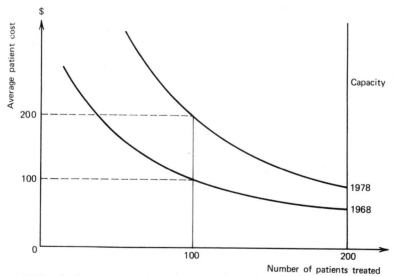

Figure 16-2. Patient treatment costs, and the effects of time and utilization rate.

fect patient costs. Inflation shows up in increased fees and salaries, equipment costs, taxes, medicines and other supplies, insurance, and other operating costs.

During this period, society's interpretation of a minimally acceptable facility also changed. With new developments in the field of medicine came increased expectations regarding the quality as well as quantity of medical treatment provided by the facility. The adoption of higher-cost diagnostic equipment and other new medical technology have greatly increased the unit's fixed costs. These cost changes are indicated by the shape and location of the average cost curve for 1978.

Historically, these changes have served to increase the ratio of fixed to variable costs. As fixed costs have increased relative to other costs, the average total cost curve will exhibit a steeper slope than it had in the earlier period. What was acceptable in 1968 was below the acceptable level for 1978. As a result, the average cost curve of providing a minimally acceptable health facility increased.

The cost increase is much greater at the less intensive use rates and approximates the experience of sparsely populated rural areas which have attempted to provide modern health care facilities locally. With 100 patients also treated in 1978, costs were increased to $200 per patient, which is much higher than for the earlier period. It is higher also than the comparable cost per patient had the facility been used to its capacity.

Schools and health care are but two examples indicating how the very attribute of extra space, so strongly desired by some people, also causes large costs to those residents. The social cost of space is further magnified by the fact that rural incomes are lower than urban incomes. Rural residents cannot afford to pay as much for services as the city dweller must pay, yet comparable services frequently cost much more in rural areas. Thus the rural resident often is forced to do without a particular service or to accept less, both in quantity and quality.

Alternative Solutions.[22]   Differences between rural and urban social expectations have been reduced, making rural people less willing to accept second rate services. Modern communication systems have made Americans much more aware of the factors affecting the quality of life. And transportation improvements have made it easier for rural people to make greater use of services available in the larger communities. It thus becomes a question of a rural community's ability to compete effectively for local residents' service needs by

[22]Ibid.

using properly organized services. The alternative is to permit a sometimes distant urbanized area to do the job that might have been done at home, and possibly even more economically.

As mentioned earlier, the increasingly higher costs of presently structured institutional services are part of the problem. Appropriately structured to serve more populous areas, both cost and quality of services suffer in low population density areas. They cannot offer the variety of services expected of them at a cost sufficiently low to attract local users to those services, and the seeds of community decline have been planted. Since institutions themselves are part of the cause of rural area decline, their reorganization ought therefore to hold promise of favorable results.

One possible approach would make use of electronic technology. Computer terminals could be located in rural stores which would link them to a central warehouse capable of serving a large number of rural areas. The selection of items available to those rural stores would be much larger and more varied than any of them could provide individually. Such an operation would greatly reduce local storage needs, reduce inventory investment costs, cut insurance costs, and be able to take advantage of bulk buying.

Another approach would establish agricultural shopping centers in rural areas. These centers would provide one-stop shopping for rural residents at lower costs than the separately housed enterprises ordinarily found in rural towns. Some rural towns have already made changes from separate-building businesses to the shopping center concept.

A number of rural areas have adopted an encouraging approach in the health care field. They have organized multicounty regional medical centers which link local area service units as outlying branches of the main center. Scheduled travel to the center by medical professionals provides the needed specialty services, leaving outpatient treatment to local doctors and nurses. Such use of modern communications facilities permits a high degree of coordinated service between an isolated community and the highly trained specialist who must locate in a more densely populated area. More importantly, highly specialized services are thereby made available to rural areas whose costs would be prohibitively high if they were to attempt to provide them locally.

A fourth proposal concerns education facilities for rural youth. Through modern technology, such as two-way television, instruction can be transported long distances. Now there is a choice: transport students to achieve the desired class size, or carry televised instruction to the students. Cost savings can thus be achieved even while improving instructional quality.

These examples do not exhaust the possibilities open to rural areas. Many other potential cost savings can be attained in both public and private services. Part of the reason for the declining population in many rural areas is the disparity of services (both cost and quality) between rural and urban areas. Many rural communities must, somehow, overcome local cost and quality problems so as to prevent further deterioration.

The answer may lie in adopting new institutions, or the use of new cost-reducing technologies, or a combination of both. Improvements in rural government services might be achieved in a number of ways, one being the outright consolidation of two or more counties. This has been politically unattractive in the past, however, because it would result in one or more of those counties losing their identity. That problem can be avoided by a regional approach in which the participating counties each provide different specialized services for the other counties in the group while continuing to maintain their separate identity.

In other instances some of the more sparsely settled counties have contracted with adjoining counties for snow removal, road repair and maintenance, and similar services requiring investment in heavy equipment. The per capita burden for those services is thereby reduced.

Within county boundaries similar services by county and city offices may be combined to effect savings to local taxpayers. Sheriff and police departments have been consolidated in a number of rural areas with favorable results.

Whether it be the consolidation of schools or other governmental units, the competition between counties, towns, or county and town must first be overcome. Barring that, savings still might be realized through some form of interunit agreement that shares costs and services.

The Rural Development Act of 1972

While other rural development legislation passed by Congress has had effects on rural areas, none has had the force or commitment of the Rural Development Act of 1972. This act contains six titles:

Title one makes provisions for business and industrial loans, community facility loans, and industrial development grants. These programs are administered by the Farmers Home Administration.

Title two of the act provides for cost-sharing in watershed protection and flood prevention programs.

Title three authorizes technical assistance to, and cost-sharing arrangements with, public agencies and organizations in order to provide rural community water supplies, control and abatement of agriculturally related pollution, disposal of solid wastes in rural areas, and water storage in rural areas for fire protection.

Under *Title four*, the Secretary of Agriculture is authorized to provide financial and technical assistance to equip local areas to prevent and control wild fires in rural areas.

Title five, because of the low income problem in agriculture, funds research programs that emphasize new approaches to the management of small farms.

Title six is a miscellaneous part of the act directing federal organizations to give priority to rural areas in locating new government offices and facilities. Also included in this section is authorization for the government to pay part of the cost of agricultural conservation programs and related pollution abatement and control programs on 10-year contracts.

The most important section of the act on rural development is title one which is designed to attract business to rural areas. Hopefully, this will promote development in rural communities and improve living conditions.

While most rural development programs under the Farmers Home Administration are small at the present time, they will receive increased emphasis in future years. Appropriations for 1974 rural business and industrial loans were only $200 million, or about $4 million per state. These loans were to be used by public, private or cooperative organizations to improve the economic and environmental atmosphere in rural communities. Business and industry loans are available in communities of up to 50,000 population. At present levels of business and industry funding, this program was expected to create about 20,000 jobs per year nationally, less than seven percent of the number needed to stop rural migration and to increase labor participation in rural regions.

Community facility loans are made to communities with population of 10,000 or less. In 1974, $50 million was available to public bodies and nonprofit associations. One million dollars per state is very inadequate to finance such things as fire facilities, ambulance service, or industrial parks.

Many grants are also available for environmental concerns, but these are also small and inadequate. Much more effort must be directed at rural America if it is to provide the quality of life offered in urban areas. Earl Heady of Iowa State University has said that "no land grant university has put rural development as the major item on its agenda of affairs presented to the state."

Rural Development Efforts by the Eisenhower and Kennedy Administrations

Low income problems of small farmers were given specific attention in the Rural Development Program of 1955. The major objectives of this program were to increase employment opportunities in rural areas, to raise the income level of rural people, and to use local committees to determine and guide developmental plans. This program was administered by the USDA through the Cooperative Extension Service.

The Congress provided $2 million to operate the program. By 1960, it was estimated that 210 countries participated in the program and that 18,000 new jobs had been created. However, it did not touch the "hard core underemployment-poverty problem in rural areas."[23]

The Kennedy Administration renamed the Rural Development Program, the Area Redevelopment Act of 1961. The objective of the act was to provide continued employment in areas of unemployment or underemployment. About $100 million was allocated for depressed rural areas.

The Department of Commerce administered the Area Redevelopment Act. An office of rural areas development was established in the U.S. Department of Agriculture to handle the rural portion of the act. This program was larger than the 1955 program and it worked with 853 rural counties. Between 1961 and 1966 the rural areas development program promoted 20,000 projects ranging from community facilities to industrial parks, but again it was not a large enough program to solve the rural development problem.[24] The Area Redevelopment Act authorized only $394 million. Only $10 million was authorized to assist unemployed workers or small farmers, while they were training to improve their skills. Also, only $4.5 million was available to finance retraining programs. Most of these funds went to industrial and commercial projects and grants and loans to communities for public facilities such as water and sewage systems.

Although city people may glamorize rural America for its nice, easy, clean, quiet life, rural people frequently are unhappy with their situation. America's rural areas require greater funding in the

[23]Willard W. Cochrane, *City Man's Guide to the Farm Problem*, St. Paul, Minn.: University of Minnesota Press, 1965, p. 202.
[24]Ibid.

solutions of their problems before satisfactory progress can be made.

Summary

Rural development is concerned with the quality of life in rural communities. Rural communities affect agricultural producers because they are the service centers for agricultural producers. Rural communities in return depend upon farmers and ranchers for employment and a place to live.

Rural areas have large amounts of poverty, a smaller percentage of high school and college graduates, fewer medical personnel, lower quality public services, and fewer cultural opportunities. These rural-urban disparities need attention and ways must be found to help alleviate these problems.

Chapter Highlights

1. Rural development emphasizes the improvement of rural life.
2. Agricultural producers influence, and in turn are influenced by, the quality of rural communities.
3. Recent interest in rural development has been heightened by social and economic problems of the city.
4. Outmigration from farms and ranches became most rapid after 1945.
5. This population redistribution has contributed to rural area problems.
6. Since 1970, there has been a renewed interest in rural living.
7. Average rural family incomes are lower than urban family incomes.
8. Farm-dwellers comprised four percent of the American population in 1975, but five percent of its poverty.
9. More than one in six rural people have incomes below the poverty line.
10. The quality of rural housing has improved considerably since 1950.
11. Government expenditures per capita are increasing in rural areas, yet are below urban counterparts.
12. Education is important in rural America in order to improve opportunities for rural youth.
13. Education can be viewed as an investment in human capital in the same manner as investments in nonhuman capital.
14. The externalities of an education justify public support of education.
15. Because of the distance factor, low population density in rural areas creates serious cost and quality problems for community services.
16. Some form of institutional reorganization would appear to hold promise for improved rural services at reasonable costs.
17. There are economies of scale in public services, thus a substantial population base is required to provide these services at least cost.

18. Increased government funding for rural development projects has been made since 1972, but it remains inadequate.

Review Questions

1. What is rural development? Is it primarily concerned with economic growth? Discuss.
2. Why is there a renewed interest in rural development? What impact will this interest have on farmers and ranchers?
3. What factors are important in explaining the recent increase in population in nonmetropolitan areas?
4. Explain the concept of poverty. Why do nonmetropolitan areas have a larger proportion of people in poverty?
5. What are externalities? Write down some examples, and discuss the problems they cause.
6. Why does it cost more per unit to provide public services in rural areas?
7. What alternative forms of community reorganization might lead to improved quality of services and reduce their costs?
8. Do economies of scale exist in public services? Explain with an example.

Suggested Readings

1. Barkley, Paul W. and David W. Seckler. *Economic Growth and Environmental Decay.* New York: Harcourt Brace Jovanovich, Inc., 1972, Chapters 4 and 8.
2. Hirsch, Werner Z. *The Economics of State and Local Government.* New York: McGraw-Hill Book Company, 1970, Chapter 7.
3. Mansfield, Edwin. *Economics: Principles, Problems, Decisions.* New York: W. W. Norton and Company, Inc., 1974, Chapters 18 and 28.
4. Reynolds, Lloyd G., George D. Green and Darrell R. Lewis, eds. *Current Issues of Economic Policy.* Homewood, Ill.: Richard D. Irwin, Inc., 1973, Readings 29 and 33.
5. Summers, Gene F., Sharon Evans, Frank Clemente, E. M. Beck, and Jon Minkoff. *Industrial Invasion of Nonmetropolitan America.* New York: Praeger Publishers, 1976, Chapters 4 and 5.
6. Tweeten, Luther, *Foundations of Farm Policy,* Lincoln, Neb.: University of Nebraska Press, 1970, Chapters 12, 13, and 14.

A List of Reference Books for The Beginning Student (you can locate these in your campus library)

1. Barkley, Paul W. *Economics: The Way We Choose.* New York: Harcourt Brace Jovanovich, Inc., 1977, 652 pp.
2. Barlowe, Raleigh. *Land Resource Economics,* 2nd ed. Englewood Cliffs, N.J.: Prentice-Hall, Inc., 1978, 616 pp.
3. Bishop, C. E. and W. D. Toussaint. *Introduction to Agricultural Economic Analysis.* New York: John Wiley and Sons, Inc., 1958, 258 pp.
4. Bradford, Lawrence A., and Glenn L. Johnson. *Farm Management Analysis.* New York: John Wiley & Sons, Inc., 1953, 438 pp.
5. Brown, Lester R., and Erik P. Eckholm. *By Bread Alone.* New York: Praeger Publishers, 1974, 272 pp.
6. Buse, Rueben C. and Daniel W. Bromley. *Applied Economics: Resource Allocation in Rural America.* Ames, Iowa: Iowa State University Press, 1975, 623 pp.
7. Castle, Emery N., Manning H. Becker and Frederick J. Smith, *Farm Business Management: The Decision Making Process.* New York: The Macmillan Company, 1972, 340 pp.
8. Dahl, Dale C. and Jerome W. Hammond. *Market and Price Analysis: The Agricultural Industries.* New York: McGraw-Hill Book Company, 1977, 323 pp.
9. Goodwin, John W. *Agricultural Economics.* Reston, Va.: Reston Publishing Company, 1977, 372 pp.
10. Gwartney, James D. *Microeconomics, Private and Public Choice.* New York: Academic Press, 1977, 389 pp.
11. Halcrow, Harold G. *Food Policy for America.* New York: McGraw-Hill Book Company, 1977, 564 pp.
12. Heyne, Paul T. *The Economic Way of Thinking.* Chicago: Science Research Associates, Inc., 1973, 289 pp.
13. Heyne, Paul and Thomas Johnson. *Toward Economic Understanding.* Chicago: Science Research Associates, Inc., 1976, 816 pp.
14. Hopkin, John A., Peter J. Barry, and C. B. Baker. *Financial Management in Agriculture.* Danville, Ill.: The Interstate Printers and Publishers, Inc., 1973, 459 pp.
15. Ingram, James C. *International Economic Problems,* 3rd ed. New York: John Wiley and Sons, Inc., 1978, 174 pp.
16. Kohls, Richard L. and W. David Downey. *Marketing of Agricultural Products,* 4th ed. New York: The Macmillan Company, 1972, 432 pp.
17. Leftwich, Richard H. *The Price System and Resource Allocation,* 6th ed. Hinsdale, Ill.: The Dryden Press, 1976, 442 pp.

18. Peterson, Willis L. *Principles of Economics: Micro,* 3rd ed. Homewood, Ill.: Richard D. Irwin, Inc., 1977, 441 pp.
19. Roy, Ewell P., Floyd L. Corty and Gene D. Sullivan. *Economics: Applications to Agriculture and Agribusiness,* Danville, Ill.: The Interstate Printers and Publishers, Inc., 1971, 455 pp.
20. Samuelson, Paul A. *Economics,* 8th ed. New York: McGraw-Hill Book Company, 1970, 868 pp.
21. Shepherd, Geoffrey S., *Agricultural Price Analysis,* 5th ed. Ames, Iowa: Iowa State University Press, 1966, 328 pp.
22. Shepherd, Geoffrey S., Gene A. Futrell and J. Robert Strain. *Marketing Farm Products—Economic Analysis.* Ames, Iowa: Iowa State University Press, 1976, 485 pp.
23. Sjo, John. *Economics for Agriculturalists: A Beginning Text in Agricultural Economics.* Columbus, Ohio: Grid, Inc., 1976, 232 pp.
24. Snodgrass, Milton M. and L. T. Wallace. *Agriculture, Economics, and Resource Management.* Englewood Cliffs, N.J.: Prentice-Hall, Inc., 1975, 521 pp.
25. Tomek, William G. and Kenneth L. Robinson. *Agricultural Product Prices.* Ithaca, N.Y.: Cornell University Press, 1972, 376 pp.
26. Tweeten, Luther. *Foundations of Farm Policy.* Lincoln, Neb.: University of Nebraska Press, 1970, 537 pp.
27. Wilcox, Walter W., Willard W. Cochrane, and Robert W. Herdt. *Economics of American Agriculture,* 3rd ed. Englewood Cliffs, N.J.: Prentice-Hall, Inc., 1974, 504 pp.

Basic Sources of Agricultural Statistics
(you can locate these in your campus library).

Economics, Statistics, and Cooperatives Service, USDA, *Agricultural Finance Outlook,* Washington, DC.

Economics, Statistics, and Cooperatives Service, USDA, *Agricultural Outlook,* published Monthly, except January, United States Government Printing Office, Washington, DC.

Economics, Statistics, and Cooperatives Service, USDA, *Cotton and Wool Situation,* Washington, DC.

Economics, Statistics, and Cooperatives Service, USDA, *Demand and Price Situation,* Washington, DC.

Economics, Statistics, and Cooperatives Service, USDA, *Farm Income Situation,* published in February and July, Washington, DC.

Economics, Statistics, and Cooperatives Service, USDA, *Farm Real Estate Market Developments,* Washington, DC.

Economics, Statistics, and Cooperatives Service, USDA, *Fats and Oils Situation,* Washington, DC.

Economics, Statistics, and Cooperatives Service, USDA, *Feed Situation,* Washington, DC.

Economics, Statistics, and Cooperatives Service, USDA, *Fertilizer Situation,* Washington, DC.

Economics, Statistics, and Cooperatives Service, USDA, *Foreign Agricultural Trade of the United States,* Washington, DC.

Economics, Statistics, and Cooperatives Service, USDA, *Fruit Situation,* Washington, DC.

Economics, Statistics, and Cooperatives Service, USDA, *Livestock and Meat Situation,* published in February, March, May, August, October, and November, Washington, DC.

Economics, Statistics, and Cooperatives Service, USDA, *National Food Situation,* Washington, DC.

Economics, Statistics, and Cooperatives Service, USDA, *Poultry and Egg Situation,* Washington, DC.

Economics, Statistics, and Cooperatives Service, USDA, *Price Spreads for Farm Foods,* Washington, DC.

Economics, Statistics, and Cooperatives Service, USDA, *Rice Situation,* Washington, DC.

Economics, Statistics, and Cooperatives Service, USDA, *State Farm Income Statistics,* Washington, DC.

Economics, Statistics, and Cooperatives Service, USDA, *Sugar and Sweetener Situation,* Washington, DC.

Economics, Statistics, and Cooperatives Service, USDA, *The Farm Index,* published monthly, Washington, DC.

Economics, Statistics, and Cooperatives Service, USDA, *Tobacco Situation,* Washington, DC.

Economics, Statistics, and Cooperatives Service, USDA, *Vegetable Situation,* Washington, DC.

Economics, Statistics, and Cooperatives Service, USDA, *Wheat Situation,* published in February, May, August, and November, Washington, DC.

Economics, Statistics, and Cooperatives Service, USDA, *World Agricultural Situation,* Washington, DC.

Foreign Agricultural Service, USDA, *Foreign Agriculture,* Washington, DC.

Foreign Agricultural Service, USDA, *Foreign Agriculture Circular—Grains,* Washington, DC.

Foreign Agricultural Service, USDA, *Foreign Agriculture Circular—Livestock and Meat,* Washington, DC.

Foreign Agricultural Service, USDA, *World Agricultural Production and Trade,* Statistical Report, Washington, DC.

Economics, Statistics, and Cooperatives Service, USDA, *Agricultural Prices,* Washington, DC.

Economics, Statistics, and Cooperatives Service, USDA, *Agricultural Situation,* Washington, DC.

Economics, Statistics, and Cooperatives Service, USDA, *Cattle,* Washington, DC.

Economics, Statistics, and Cooperatives Service, USDA, *Cattle on Feed,* Washington, DC.

Economics, Statistics, and Cooperatives Service, USDA, *Crop Production,* Washington, DC.

Economics, Statistics, and Cooperatives Service, USDA, *Lamb Crop and Wool,* Washington, DC.

Economics, Statistics, and Cooperatives Service, USDA, *Livestock Slaughter,* Washington, DC.

Economics, Statistics, and Cooperatives Service, USDA, *Meat Animals: Production, Disposition, and Income,* Washington, DC.

Economics, Statistics, and Cooperatives Service, USDA, *Milk Production,* Washington, DC.

Economics, Statistics, and Cooperatives Service, USDA, *Quarterly Grain Stocks,* Washington, DC.

Economics, Statistics, and Cooperatives Service, USDA, *Seed Crops,* Annual publication, Washington, DC.

USDA, *Agricultural Statistics,* Annual volume, United States Government Printing Office, Washington, DC.

GLOSSARY

Agribusiness—involves the manufacture and distribution of farm supplies; production operations on the farm; and the storage, processing, and distribution of farm commodities and items made from them.

Agricultural economics—an applied social science dealing with how mankind uses technical knowledge and scarce productive resources to produce food and fiber and to distribute them for consumption to society over time.

Arbitrage—the simultaneous purchase and sale of a commodity in two different markets to take advantage of differences in the prices of that commodity in the markets.

Assets—items of money value owned by a business, including land, buildings, tractors, combines, etc.

Balance of trade—the value of merchandise exports minus the value of merchandise imports.

Basis—the difference between a futures price and the cash price of a commodity at a particular time.

Budget line—shows all possible combination of goods that a consumer can buy with a given money income.

Capitalism—a type of economic organization in which private individuals or groups own and manage all resources.

Ceteris paribus (*cet. par.*)—holding some variables constant, while letting specific variables change.

Change in demand—a shift in the entire demand schedule.

Change in quantity demanded—a movement along a given demand curve in response to a price change.

Change in quantity supplied—a movement along a given supply curve in response to a price change.

Change in supply—a shift in the entire supply schedule.

Collective farm—typically, a farm in the USSR, owned by the government, but operated by a number of families, which share in the farm-derived revenue.

Comparative advantage—a situation in which a nation, relatively superior at producing some goods, gains by trading for goods that another nation is relatively more proficient at producing.

Cross price elasticity—the responsiveness of the quantity demanded of one commodity to a one percent change in the price of another commodity, *cet. par.*

Demand curve—shows the quantities of a good that a consumer will buy at different prices for that good, everything else unchanged.

Derived demand—is used to specify demand schedules for resources that are used in producing final products. The demand for land depends upon the intensity of our demand for its products.

Economic rent—return in excess of opportunity cost.

Economic supply—the part of the physical supply of resources that is used to satisfy human wants.

Embargo—a complete prohibition against the imports or exports of a commodity.

Entrepreneurship—organizing resources to produce and market goods and services.

European Community (EC-9)—a group of countries which have reduced or abolished tarrifs among themselves and established a common and uniform tariff to outsiders. The EC includes nine countries: West Germany, France, Italy, Belgium, the Netherlands, Luxembourg, Great Britain, Denmark, and Ireland.

European Free Trade Association (EFTA)—a group of countries which have reduced or abolished tariffs among themselves, but have not established a common tariff to outsiders. The EFTA includes five countries: Sweden, Norway, Switzerland, Austria, and Portugal.

Exports—products and services sold to foreign countries.

Farm (1974 census of agriculture)—any establishment which, during the census year, had or normally would have had agricultural product sales of $1,000 or more.

Fiscal policy—the use of government policy to achieve specific economic goals by manipulating expenditures or the tax rate.

Fixed costs—those costs incurred for resources which do not change as output is increased or decreased.

Flow resources—resources whose available quantities are constantly being replenished. E.g., using the wind's power or the heat energy from the sun, does not reduce the supply of these resources to others.

Fund or stock resources—resources whose quantities are fixed in their natural state. Coal, oil, and iron ore are examples of these nonrenewable resources.

Futures contracts—standardized contracts for future delivery of commodities that are traded on organized exchanges.

Gosplan—the central planning organization of the Soviet Union.

Hectare—a metric measure of land area (one Hectare equals 2.4710 acres).

Import quota—a maximum limit on the quantity of a commodity that can be imported.

Imports—goods and services purchased from foreign countries.

Indifference curve—shows all the combinations of goods that yield an individual the same amount of satisfaction or utility.

Income elasticity—the responsiveness of quantity purchased to a one percent change in income, *cet. par.*

Insurance hedging or hedging—establishing an equal but opposite position in the futures market from the one taken in the cash market.

Interest rate—the price of borrowed money.

Isocost line—shows the various combinations of resources that can be purchased with a given dollar outlay.

Isoquant—shows the different combinations of inputs that can produce a given amount of output or product.

Isorevenue line—shows all the combinations of products sold that will bring in the same total revenue.

Kolkhozes—collective farms in the USSR.

Law of diminishing marginal utility—as an individual consumes additional units of a specific good, holding everything else constant, the amount of satisfaction from each additional unit of that good decreases.

Law of diminishing returns—as successive amounts of a variable input are combined with a fixed input, the total product will increase, reach a maximum, and eventually decline.

Liabilities—items of money value owned by a business representing creditor's claims against assets.

Long position—purchases of futures contracts not offset by sales.

Long-run—a time period so long that all factors of production can be varied.

Marginal cost—the change in total cost when output is changed by one unit.

Marginal factor cost (MFC)—the amount added to total cost when one more unit of the variable input is used in production.

Marginal physical product (MPP)—the amount added to total physical product when another unit of the variable input is used in production.

Marginal value product (MVP)—the amount added to total value product when another unit of the variable input is used.

Marginal revenue—the amount added to total revenue when an additional unit of output is produced and sold.

Market—consists of buyers and sellers with facilities to communicate with each other.

Market demand curve—a horizontal summation of individual demand curves for a product.

Market equilibrium—that point where the market demand curve intersects the market supply curve. The market clearing price where quantity demanded equals quantity supplied.

Market orders and agreements—government authorized programs that producers can use to determine the terms and conditions under which a commodity can be marketed.

Market power—a firm's ability to influence product prices either on the buying or selling side of the market.

Market supply curve—a horizontal summation of individual supply curves of a product.

Marketing—business activities that direct the flow of goods and services from producer to consumers.

Marketing margin—the difference between the price that consumers pay for the final product and the price received by producers for the raw product.

Metric ton—a metric measure of weight (one metric ton equals 2204.622 pounds).

Monetary policy—manipulation of the money supply and the interest rate to achieve specific economic goals.

Monopoly—single seller in an industry.

Monopsony—single buyer in an industry.

Natural resource—a factor of production provided by nature. Examples are land, water, minerals, wind, tides, etc.

Net worth—the excess of assets over liabilities representing the owner's residual claim to assets.

Opportunity cost—the value of other opportunities given up in order to produce or consume any good.

Parity—that price which gives a unit of agricultural commodity the same purchasing power as it had in a specified base period.

Poverty line—the income level required for a family of a specific size and type to be classified as not being in need of the basics of life.

Price ceiling—a government decreed maximum price for a commodity or service.

Price elasticity of demand—the percentage change in quantity demanded due to a one percent change in price, *cet. par.*

Price elasticity of supply—the percentage change in quantity supplied due to a one percent change in price, *cet. par.*

Price floor—a government decreed minimum price for a commodity.

Price-searcher—a seller in an imperfectly competitive market structure. A seller that has market power and can determine the price or quantity sold.

Price support—a government determined price that is above the equilibrium price.

Price-taker—a seller in a purely competitive market. A seller without market power.

Production-possibilities curve—shows all combinations of products that can be produced with a given set of resources.

Profit—a surplus over all opportunity costs.

Pure competition—a market organization of many firms in an industry, a homogeneous product, and the freedom of firms to enter or leave the industry. No firm in this type of industry can influence the market price of its product by the amounts they buy or sell.

Pure monopoly—a market organization of one firm in an industry. Competition in the product market is absent.

Rediscount (or discount) rate—the rate of interest charged by the federal reserve bank on loans to member banks.

Resources—inputs with which goods and services are produced.

Rural development—making rural America a better place in which to live and work.

Short position—sales of futures contracts not offset by purchases.

Short-run—a time period where one or more of the factors of production are fixed.

Socialism—a type of economic organization in which the government owns all resources and directs all economic activity.

Speculation—the purchase or sale of title to goods or financial obligations in the expectation of favorable price movements.

Supply curve—the amount of a good or service a producer is willing to offer for sale at different prices, holding everything else constant.

Tariff—a tax on imported goods.

Utility—the satisfaction an individual gets from consuming goods and services.

Variable costs—those costs which increase or decrease as varying amounts of the resources are used.

INDEX